W9-BMA-535

101 WAYS TO PROMOTE YOUR WEB SITE

Fourth Edition

Other Titles of Interest From Maximum Press

Marketing With E-Mail, Third Edition: Kinnard, 1-885068-68-9

Business-to-Business Internet Marketing, Fourth Edition: Silverstein, 1-885068-72-7

Marketing on the Internet, Sixth Edition: Zimmerman, 1-885068-80-8

101 Internet Businesses You Can Start From Home: Sweeney, 1-885068-59-X

The e-Business Formula for Success: Sweeney, 1-885068-60-3

Internet Marketing for Information Technology Companies, Second Edition: Silverstein, 1-885068-67-0

Internet Marketing for Less Than $500/Year, Second Edition: Yudkin, 1-885068-69-7

The Business Guide to Selling Through Internet Auctions: Hix, 1-885068-73-5

Internet Marketing for Your Tourism Business: Sweeney, 1-885068-47-6

Exploring IBM e-Business Software: Young, 1-885068-58-1

Exploring IBM Technology, Products & Services, Fifth Edition: Hoskins, 1-885068-82-4

Exploring IBM @server pSeries, Eleventh Edition: Hoskins, Bluethman, 1-885068-81-6

Exploring IBM @server iSeries, Eleventh Edition: Hoskins, Dimmick, 1-885068-92-1

Exploring IBM @server xSeries, Twelfth Edition: Hoskins, Wilson, Winkel, 1-885068-83-2

Exploring IBM @server zSeries, Eighth Edition: Hoskins, Frank, 1-885068-91-3

Building Intranets With Lotus Notes and Domino 5.0, Third Edition: Krantz, 1-885068-41-7

Exploring IBM Network Stations: Ho, Lloyd, & Heracleous, 1-885068-32-8

For more information, visit our Web site at *www.maxpress.com*
or e-mail us at *moreinfo@maxpress.com*

101 WAYS TO PROMOTE YOUR WEB SITE

Fourth Edition

Filled with Proven Internet Marketing Tips, Tools, Techniques, and Resources to Increase Your Web Site Traffic

Susan Sweeney

MAXIMUM PRESS
605 Silverthorn Road
Gulf Breeze, FL 32561
(850) 934-0819
www.maxpress.com

Publisher: Jim Hoskins

Manager of Finance/Administration: Joyce Reedy

Production Manager: ReNae Grant

Cover Designer: Lauren Smith Designs

Compositor: PageCrafters Inc.

Copyeditor: Ellen Faulk

Proofreader: Jacquie Wallace

Indexer: Susan Olason

Printer: P.A. Hutchison

This publication is designed to provide accurate and authoritative information in regard to the subject matter covered. It is sold with the understanding that the publisher is not engaged in rendering professional services. If legal, accounting, medical, psychological, or any other expert assistance is required, the services of a competent professional person should be sought. ADAPTED FROM A DECLARATION OF PRINCIPLES OF A JOINT COMMITTEE OF THE AMERICAN BAR ASSOCIATION AND PUBLISHERS.
Copyright 2003 by Maximum Press.

All rights reserved. Published simultaneously in Canada.

Reproduction or translation of any part of this work beyond that permitted by Section 107 or 108 of the 1976 United States Copyright Act without the permission of the copyright owner is unlawful. Requests for permission or further information should be addressed to the Permissions Department, Maximum Press.

Recognizing the importance of preserving what has been written, it is a policy of Maximum Press to have books of enduring value published in the United States printed on acid-free paper, and we exert our best efforts to that end.

Library of Congress Cataloging-in-Publication Data

Sweeney, Susan, 1956-
  101 ways to promote your web site : filled with proven internet
marketing tips, tools, techniques, and resources to increase your web
site traffic / Susan Sweeney.— 4th ed.
      p. cm.
Published simultaneously in Canada.
Includes index.
  ISBN 1-885068-90-5 (pbk. : alk. paper)
  1. Internet marketing. 2. Web sites—Marketing. I. Title: One
hundred one ways to promote your web site. II. Title: One hundred and
one ways to promote your web site. III. Title.
  HF5415.1265 .S93 2002
  658.8'4—dc21
                                    2002009159

Acknowledgments

Many, many, many thanks to my right hand Tammi Henderson... to be Tammi Hayne in very short order. We've got quite a tag team. Thanks for all the extra hours to meet our deadline. Now let's get that online digital course finished. ;-)

Thanks to Jim Hoskins and Joyce Reedy at Maximum Press. This is our eighth book together. It's always a pleasure to work with you. One of these days we're going to have to meet face to face!

Many, many thanks to ReNae Grant of PageCrafters, who is absolutely wonderful to work with. ReNae manages the process of taking my files through the copy editing, typesetting, and printing process and making sure we have a great-looking finished product.

The Internet is a fascinating and vast, publicly accessible resource from which we can learn a great deal. I'd like to thank all those people who share their information so freely on the Net with sites like WilsonWeb *(www.wilsonweb.com)* by Dr. Ralph Wilson and newsletters like The Internet Home Business Marketing Newsletter by Robert Smith, Jayde Search Smart, Chronicles, Internet Gazette, I-Search by Detlev Johnson, and I-Sales by John Audette.

Special thanks to my absolutely wonderful husband Miles who makes all things possible. I wouldn't be able to do what I do if not for you. Also thanks to our three amazing children—Kaitlyn, Kara, and Andrew—for their love, encouragement, and support. Love you more than the last number!

Special thanks to my mom and dad, Olga and Leonard Dooley, for always being there and for instilling in me the confidence to know that I can do anything I set my mind to. It's amazing what can be done when you "know you can."

Disclaimer

The purchase of computer software or hardware is an important and costly business decision. While the author and publisher of this book have made reasonable efforts to ensure the accuracy and timeliness of the information contained herein, the author and publisher assume no liability with respect to loss or damage caused or alleged to be caused by reliance on any information contained herein and disclaim any and all warranties, expressed or implied, as to the accuracy or reliability of said information.

This book is not intended to replace the manufacturer's product documentation or personnel in determining the specifications and capabilities of the products mentioned in this book. The manufacturer's product documentation should always be consulted, as the specifications and capabilities of computer hardware and software products are subject to frequent modification. The reader is solely responsible for the choice of computer hardware and software. All configurations and applications of computer hardware and software should be reviewed with the manufacturer's representatives prior to choosing or using any computer hardware and software.

Trademarks

The words contained in this text which are believed to be trademarked, service marked, or otherwise to hold proprietary rights have been designated as such by use of initial capitalization. No attempt has been made to designate as trademarked or service marked any personal computer words or terms in which proprietary rights might exist. Inclusion, exclusion, or definition of a word or term is not intended to affect, or to express judgment upon, the validity of legal status of any proprietary right which may be claimed for a specific word or term.

Table of Contents

Chapter 4:
Spreading the Word with Viral Marketing   **60**

Chapter 5:
Permission Marketing   **75**

Chapter 6:
Designing Your Site to Be Search Engine Friendly   **85**

Chapter 7:
Search Engine and Directory Submissions   111

Chapter 8:
Utilizing Signature Files to Increase Web Site Traffic 144

Chapter 9:
The E-mail Advantage   154

Chapter 10:
Autoresponders   176

Chapter 11:
Effective Promotional Use of Newsgroups   183

Chapter 12:
Effective Promotion through
Publicly Accessible Mailing Lists   201

Chapter 13:
Establishing Your Private Mailing List   213

Chapter 17:
Maximizing Promotion with Meta-Indexes   282

Chapter 18:
Winning Awards, Cool Sites, and More   294

Chapter 19:
Productive Online Advertising   304

Chapter 20:
The Cybermall Advantage

331

Chapter 21:
Maximizing Media Relations   347

Chapter 22:
Increasing Traffic through Online Publications   369

Chapter 23:
Web Rings as a Promotion Tool   384

Chapter 24:
Webcasting and Rich Media   394

Chapter 28:
Web Metrics   **437**

Introduction

Over the past few years there has been literally a tidal wave of companies building Web sites. This phenomenal boom in Web site creation and online traffic has intensified the battle for the consumer's time and attention. A secondary component or required follow-on to Web site design involves developing comprehensive online marketing strategies to capture online market share. The need for information and advice on developing Internet marketing strategies is tremendous.

Building a Web site, however, is just the first step. Driving business to your site takes knowledge, planning, time, and effort. If you are intent on maintaining a competitive advantage, then you need to build the traffic to your site by implementing an effective Internet marketing strategy.

Whether you are an experienced marketing professional or are just dreaming of starting your own Internet business, you will benefit from the information contained in this timely book. *101 Ways to Promote Your Web Site* offers comprehensive, hands-on, step-by-step advice for building Web site traffic using hundreds of proven tips, tools, and techniques to achieve optimal results. You will find out how to:

- Make your site unique

- Attract new visitors and keep them coming back

- Prepare and submit to hundreds of search engines and directories to be listed in the top search results

- Maximize your Web site promotion using meta-indexes

- Pull traffic to your site by implementing a personalized, targeted e-mail campaign

- Develop an effective banner ad campaign to draw the right customers to your site

- Use newsgroups and mailing lists to communicate with your target market and build your reputation

- Hype your company in the media for increased exposure through interactive press releases

- Increase company and brand awareness with webcasting and rich media

- Use one of the most effective Internet marketing tools—*links*

- Find and use free promotion tools available on the Internet

- Develop your own affiliate or associate program

- Use permission and viral marketing effectively

You will be provided with a wealth of information on how to use specific promotion, marketing, and advertising strategies to increase the traffic to your site. Entrepreneurs, corporate marketing managers, small-business owners, and consultants will be given a proven method to turn their commercial Web site into an online success.

Your "Members Only" Web Site

The Internet world changes every day. That's why there is a companion Web site associated with this book. On this site you will find updates to the book and other Web site promotion resources of interest. However, you have to be a member of the "101 Ways Insiders Club" to gain access to this site.

When you purchased this book, you automatically became a member (in fact, that's the only way to join), so you now have full privileges. To get into the "Members Only" section of the companion Web site, go to the Maximum Press Web site located at *http://www. maxpress.com* and follow the links to the "101 Ways" area. From there you will see a link to the "101 Ways Insiders Club" section. When you try to enter, you will be asked for a user ID and password. Type in the following:

- For your user ID, enter: 101ways4e

- For your password, enter: tendon

You will then be granted full access to the "Members Only" area. Visit the site often and enjoy the updates and resources with our compliments—and thanks again for buying the book. We ask that you not share the user ID and password for this site with anyone else.

Susan Sweeney's Internet Marketing Mail List

You are also invited to join Susan Sweeney's Internet Marketing Biweekly Internet Marketing Tips, Tools, Techniques, and Resources Newsletter at *http://www.susansweeney.com*.

1

Planning Your Web Site

With millions of Web sites competing for viewers, how do you get the results you're looking for? When asked if they are marketing on the Internet, many people say, "Yes, we have a Web site." However, having a Web site and marketing on the Internet are very different things. Yes, usually you need a Web site to market on the Internet. However, a Web site is simply a collection of documents, images, and other electronic files that are publicly accessible across the Internet. Your site should be designed to meet your online objectives and should be developed with your target market in mind. Meanwhile, Internet marketing encompasses all the steps you take to reach your target market online, attract visitors to your Web site, encourage them to buy your products or services, and make them want to come back for more.

Having a Web site is great, but it is meaningless if nobody knows about it. Likewise, having a brilliantly designed product brochure does you little good if it sits in your sales manager's desk drawer. It is the goal of this book to help you take your Web site out of the desk drawer, into the spotlight, and into the hands of your target market. You will learn how to formulate an Internet marketing strategy and match it with your objectives, your product or service, and your target market. This chapter provides you with an overview of this book and introduces the importance of:

- Defining your online objectives

- Defining your target market and developing your Web site and online marketing strategy with them in mind

- Developing the Internet marketing strategy that is appropriate for your product or service

The Fundamentals—Objectives, Target Markets, and Products and Services

Things have changed dramatically over the past several years in terms of Web site design and development methodology. Back in the olden days—a couple years ago—it was quite acceptable and the norm for an organization to pack up all their brochures, ads, direct-mail pieces, news releases, and other marketing materials in a box, drop it off at the Web developer, and after a short conversation ask when they might expect their Web site to be "done." By going through this process, organizations ended up with "brochureware." Brochureware is no longer acceptable on the Web if you want to be successful. Sites that are successful today are ones that are designed around the:

- Objectives of the organization

- Needs, wants, and expectations of the target markets

- Products and services that are being offered

Everything related to Internet marketing revolves around these three things—objectives, target markets, and products and services. It is critically important to define these things appropriately and discuss them with your Web developer. It is *your* responsibility to define these things, not your Web developer's. You know, or should know, what your objectives are more clearly than your Web developer. If you don't articulate these objectives and discuss them with your Web developer, it is impossible for him or her to build a site to achieve your objectives!

You know your target market better than your Web developer. You know what your buyers want, what they base their buying decision on, and what their expectations are better than your Web developer. You need to provide this information so that your Web developer can build a Web site that meets the needs and expectations of your target market.

Let's spend the remainder of the chapter on these fundamentals—objectives, target markets, and products and services—so you can be better prepared for the planning process for your Web site.

Common Objectives

Before you even start to create your Web site, you must clearly define your online objectives. What is the purpose of your site? Brainstorm with all parts of your organization from the front-line clerks, to marketing and sales personnel, to customer support, to order fulfillment and administration. Generate a list of primary and secondary objectives. Every element of your site should relate back to your objectives. When you decide to update, add, or change any elements on your Web site, examine how these changes relate to the primary and secondary objectives you have identified. If there is not a clear match between your objectives and your intended changes, you might want to reconsider the changes. It's amazing how many Web sites have been developed without adequate planning or tie-in with the corporate objectives.

Some of the most common primary objectives include:

- Advertising your product or service

- Selling your product or service

- Providing customer service and product support

- Providing product or corporate information

- Creating and establishing company identity or brand awareness

Advertising Your Products or Services Online

The objective of some sites is simply to advertise but not directly sell an event, product, or service. A prime example of this is a movie studio that develops a Web site to promote a "soon-to-be-released" movie. The objective is to create awareness or a "buzz" about the movie, generate interest in the film, and, ultimately, have a large number of people attend the movie when it is released. This type of site might include multimedia clips of the movie, pictures and stories of the actors in the movie, viral marketing ("Tell a friend about this movie") elements to encourage word-of-mouth marketing, an intriguing story about the film, press releases for entertainment writers, and other elements to help them achieve their objective with their target market in mind.

Selling Your Products or Services Online

Selling products or services online is a common objective. The Internet provides a broad geographic reach and a huge demographic reach. Often businesses combine the objectives of advertising their products or services with trying to sell them through their Web site. This works well because visitors are not only given information about your products and services, but they are given the option of easily ordering and purchasing online. The easier you make it for people to make a purchase from your company, the more likely they will be to buy. You will have to provide detailed information on your products and services, your return policies, guarantees and warranties, and shipping options. If you are planning to sell directly from the site, you will also need to address security issues.

Providing Online Customer Service or Support

You may decide that the main reason for your business to have an online presence is to provide more comprehensive customer service and support. A great benefit of a Web site is that you can provide customer assistance 24 hours a day, 7 days a week, 365 days a year. If your company develops software, it would be a good idea to include downloadable upgrades as well as an FAQ (Frequently Asked Questions) section where you can provide solutions to common problems. By providing an easy way for your customers to solve their problems, you will increase customer loyalty. You will also increase the likelihood that they will return to your company when they need to improve their system. You should include the appropriate contact information if customers have more complicated problems to be solved and need to talk to a human.

Providing Product or Corporate Information

Some organizations simply wish to provide information on their products or services to a particular target market. Others may want to provide corporate information to potential investors. Information-driven Web sites tend to be text-oriented, with graphics used only to accentuate the points being made and to provide visual examples. These types of sites usually have an FAQ section where they provide useful and pertinent information on their company, products, or services. If the organization courts the media, it might include a Media Center, which could include all its press releases, a corporate backgrounder, information on key company officials, articles that have been written about the company, and a gallery of relevant pictures that the media can use, as well as a direct link to the company's media person.

Creating and Establishing Company Identity or Brand Awareness

Another objective might be to create and establish company identity or brand awareness. To "brand" your product, a memorable name and an eye-appealing product logo are necessities. Also, the graphics developed for your Web site must be top-notch and reflect the colors associated with the product logo. A catchy slogan will further promote brand identity. The same branding techniques are also applicable to establishing corporate identity. If building and reinforcing corporate and brand identity are important to you, your Web site must have a consistent look and feel. Likewise, all offline promotional campaigns and materials must be consistent with your online presence.

Based on the success of companies such as America Online, Yahoo!, Netscape Communications, Amazon.com, and eBay, it is apparent that branding a company or product on the Web can occur swiftly. It is amazing how quickly these relative newcomers to the business world have achieved megabrand status. Although they all had significant financial resources, each company used a combination of online and offline advertising to meet their objectives. Their Web sites reflect the branding idea. Each of their sites features a prominent logo, consistent imagery, and a consistent color scheme. Check out the sites of these upstarts that have become big online players if branding is your goal. There is a lot we can learn from them.

Other Primary Objectives

Brainstorm with all the stakeholders in your organization to come up with other primary objectives for your organization. This process is critical to the organization's online success. Everything else revolves around your objectives—the elements included on your site and the Internet marketing techniques you use. If you were building a new office, you would want to include the input of all people working in your office to ensure that their needs were taken into consideration and the office was designed appropriately. The same is true when building a Web site—everyone must be included in the brainstorming session.

As much time should be spent in the planning stage as in the construction phase. By going through this process, you will be able to develop the best "blueprint" for your proposed Web site.

Other Things to Consider Up Front

Although setting your primary objectives is vital, it is just as important to identify your secondary objectives. By setting appropriate secondary objectives, you will be more prepared to achieve all your online goals. Many companies identify only primary objectives for their Web site and completely neglect secondary objectives that will help them to succeed online. Following are some common secondary objectives for online businesses to consider:

- The site should be designed to be search engine friendly.

- The site should be designed to encourage repeat traffic.

- The site should encourage visitors to recommend it to others.

- The site should include elements to leverage its sales force.

- The site should be designed to encourage visitors to give permission to send them e-mail on a regular basis to build an online community.

- The site should be designed to encourage customer loyalty.

- The site should encourage visitors to stay a while and visit many areas of the site.

Designing Your Site to Be Search Engine Friendly

Creating a site that is search engine friendly should be an objective of every company that wants to do business on the Internet. Search engines are the most common way for Internet surfers to search for something on the Net. In fact, 85 percent of all people who use the Internet use search engines as their primary way to look for information. By using keywords relating to your company in appropriate places on your site, you can improve how search engines rank you. You want these chosen keywords in the "keyword meta-tags" as well as in each page's "description meta-tag." Some of the other places where you want to have these keywords are your domain name if possible, your page titles and page text, your Alt tags for graphics, and your page headers. Recently, many search engines have begun to put emphasis on the number of links to a site to determine its ranking. This means that the more Web sites you can get to link to your site, the higher your site will be shown in search engine results. (See Chapter 6 for more information on designing your site for the search engines.)

Including Repeat Traffic Generators on Your Site

Every Web site should be designed to entice its site visitors to return again and again. No matter if the primary objective of your Web site is to sell your products and services or to create brand awareness, generating repeat traffic to your Web site will help you achieve these goals. Generating repeat traffic to your site is a key element of your online success and can be accomplished in numerous ways. Using contests and competitions, as well as games, advice columns, and many more techniques, will increase your Web traffic. Chapter 3 describes many of these repeat traffic generators in much more detail.

Getting Visitors to Recommend Your Site

The best exposure your Web site can get is to be recommended by a friend or "unbiased" third party. It is critical that you try to have elements of your Web site recommended as often as possible; therefore, you should have a way for people to easily tell someone about your site and its contents. The best way to encourage people to recommend your site is to include viral marketing techniques such as a "Tell a Friend" button on your site. You may want to include some variations on this as well. Under articles or press releases, you can have an "E-mail this article to a friend" to try to have people refer their friends and associates to your site. Virtual postcards are also a good way to get people to send more people to your Web site. There are many ways to encourage viral marketing. These are discussed in detail in Chapter 4.

Leveraging Your Sales Force

If your objectives include trying to sell your products, you may want to leverage your sales force by making use of an affiliate or associate program. Affiliate programs once again use the advantage of having your site recommended to create traffic to your site. The difference is that an affiliate program is more formal than just having your site recommended by site visitors. Most affiliate programs involve having a contractual agreement, having specific links placed on the affiliate's site to yours, and having software to track where your traffic is coming from so that you can compute and send referral fees to your affiliates as they are earned. The contract will usually state the compensation you will pay to your affiliates for the sales they produce. This is one more way to have other people working to build traffic to your Web site. (See Chapter 16 for details on affiliate or associate programs.)

Using Permission Marketing

You always want your company to be seen as upholding the highest ethical standards, so it is important not to send out unsolicited e-mail, or "spam," promoting your company or its products. This is why it's important to develop a mailing list of people who have given you permission to send them messages, including company news and promotions. When you're developing your Web site, an objective should be to get as many visitors to your site as possible to give you their e-mail address and ask to be included in your mailings. You can do this by having numerous ways for your visitors to sign up to receive newsletters, notices of changes to your Web site, coupons, or new giveaways. Chapter 3 has many examples of ways to encourage visitors to request to be added to your e-mail list.

Creating Loyalty among Visitors

The way to create loyalty among visitors is to provide them with some incentives for joining your online community and provide them with proof that you really appreciate their business. You can do this by having a "Members-only" section of your Web site that has special offers for them as well as discounts or freebies. When people sign up to join your "Members-only" section, you can ask for their permission and their e-mail address to send them e-mails regarding company or product promotions and news. People like to do business with people who appreciate their business. We are seeing a real growth in loyalty programs online.

Including "Stickiness" Elements

To get your visitors to visit your site often and have them visit a number of pages every time they visit, you need to provide interesting , interactive, and relevant content. You want to have your site visitors feel as if they are part of your online community and to want to make your site one of the sites they visit every day. You create "stickiness" by including many elements that keep your visitors' attention. Your site could have an advice column for people to read that changes daily, descriptions of your many products, a discussion forum with constantly changing interesting conversations relative to your products, a news section that is updated daily, as well as a weekly contest they can enter. The combination of these elements would create stickiness for the visitors on your site. You want your site to be a resource that people go back to often and not a one-time event.

A Final Word on Objectives

Setting your Web site's objectives before you begin building your site is essential so that you can convey to your Web master what you want your Web site to achieve. You will obviously want to create a number of different objectives for your site, but many of the objectives you set will work together to make your Web site complete.

Whatever your objectives may be, you must carefully consider how best to incorporate elements in your Web site and your Internet marketing strategy to help you achieve them. Successful marketing on the Web is not a simple undertaking. Before you begin to brainstorm over the objectives of your Web site, be certain you have read and studied all the information that is pertinent to the market you are attempting to enter. Read everything you can get your hands on, and examine the findings of industry experts.

The Web site objectives will form a critical element in your Web site design and development, as you will see in the next chapter on Web site design and development methodology.

Target Markets

It is important to define every one of your target markets. Your Web site is designed for them! For each and every one of your target markets, you need to determine:

- Their needs

- Their wants

- Their expectations

For each and every one of your target markets, you should also try to determine an appropriate "WOW" factor. What could you provide for them on your Web site that would WOW them? Your objective should be to exceed the target market's expectations.

Your main target market may be your potential customer, but other target markets might include existing customers, the media, those who influence the buying decision for your potential customers, associates, or affiliates.

When you look at—really look at—potential customers and existing customers, you realize that their needs from your Web site are probably different. Someone who is an existing customer knows your company. Your products, your business practices, and the like are not a priority for them on your site. A potential customer needs these things before giving you their first order. "Customer" is such a huge target market, it needs to be broken down into segments. Every business is different. If you were a hotel, for example, your customer target market might be broken down further into:

- Business travelers

- Vacation travelers

- Family travelers

- Meeting planners

- Handicapped travelers

- Tour operators

- Groups

You get the idea. You need to segment your customer target market and then, for each segment, you need to do an analysis of needs, wants, and expectations. If the media is part of your target market, make sure you plan to have a media center; or if you want to reach potential investors, make sure you have an investor relations page.

If you intend to market children's products, your Web site will be colorful and the text will be simple and easy to understand in keeping with what appeals to your target market. Chances are, fun-looking graphics will be used extensively on your site to draw children further into it (see Figure 1.1). If you market financial services, your Web site will require a more professional approach. The graphics will convey a clean appearance, and the text will be informative and written in a business-like fashion (see Figure 1.2). As this example demonstrates, the content

Figure 1.1.   Web sites designed to appeal to children include fun, colorful images.

and tone of your site must be tailored to your target market. After all, this is the best way to attract the attention of the people who are interested in purchasing your product or service.

Another aspect of the design of your Web site to consider with regard to your target market is their propensity to utilize the latest technologies and the configuration they are likely to be using. An online business that markets custom-made, streaming multimedia presentations would expect its clientele to be technically inclined. These clients are more likely to have the latest software, advanced Web browser technologies, and faster machines.

On the other hand, clients of a vendor who sells gardening supplies online might be less likely to have fully embraced the latest technologies. Most people looking for these products will be connecting from home rather than from their workplace. They may have a slow dialup connection to the Internet, slower machines, and outdated software.

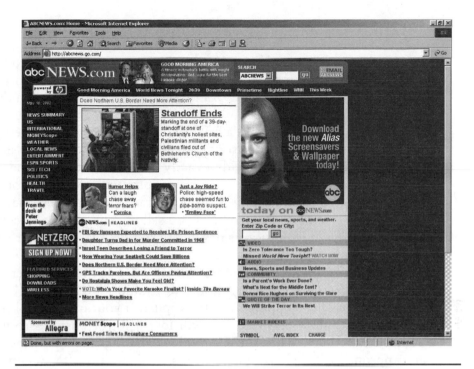

Figure 1.2. A business-oriented site incorporates informative text and clean, magazine style layout.

They might still be using the Web browser that was originally installed on their system, simply because they are uncomfortable downloading the latest version of the browser, are unaware of the more recent version, or are uninterested in downloading a large file. If your target market includes this demographic, you will have to be careful with your use of Java, Flash, and large graphic files.

What does this mean for developing and designing your Web site? Well, streaming multimedia developers could design their Web sites with more graphics and dynamic multimedia effects because their clients expect to be impressed when they visit the developer's site. If gardening supplies vendors designed their sites similarly, many of their clients could be alienated because the site would be too slow to load. They might take their business elsewhere. The gardening supplies vendor's site will require a more basic design: less concentration on large graphics and multimedia effects and more focus on presenting information.

Products and Services

It is important to define the products and services you want to promote online. Sometimes the products and services you offer offline in your physical store are the same as in your online store, but quite often there are differences.

Business owners who have a bricks-and-mortar location sometimes assume that their online storefront is an extension of their offline storefront and that they will provide exactly the same products and services online as offline. In some cases, fewer products are offered online than in the physical store. This is often the case if you are test-marketing, but also if some of the products you sell in your physical location are not appropriate for online sales due to competitive pricing or shipping logistics.

In other cases, your online store will offer more products or services than the bricks-and-mortar location. For example, your offline bookstore may not offer shipping or giftwrapping. If your online bookstore does not offer these services, you will lose a lot of business to your online competition. When a site's product offerings include items that are appropriate for gift giving, it is essential to also offer wrapping, customized cards, shipping to multiple addresses, and shipping options. The consumer is king and is very demanding. You have to meet and beat your consumers' expectations online to garner market share. People shopping for gifts online are looking for convenience, and the site that provides the greatest convenience and the greatest products at the greatest prices will be the winner.

Web sites and Internet marketing strategies will differ depending on the product or service you are selling. A company that markets toys will have to develop a fun and interactive Web site that is attractive to children. The Web site will then have to give children a way to tell their friends about the site as well as a reason to return to the site. The toy company might wish to offer an electronic postcard service whereby children can send a colorful and musical message to their friends and tell them about the site.

Another idea would be to provide a "wish list" service. Children could make a list of the toys they want, and this list would be sent to the parents via e-mail. The parents could then make more-targeted purchasing decisions and may become loyal to the toy company's site. Likewise, some toy companies offer reminder services that send an e-mail message to visitors who have registered and completed the appropriate questionnaire to remind them of a child's birthday and to offer suggestions for gift ideas. Once again, this promotes sales and repeat traffic and increases customer loyalty.

In another example, a software development company may want to provide downloadable demo versions of its software products and allow people to review its products for a specified period of time before they must make a purchasing decision. When consumers decide to buy the software, a robust e-commerce system will need to be in place to handle the orders.

A travel agency's Web site might include features such as an opt-in mailing list to send people information on weekly vacation specials or a page on the site detailing the latest specials. They might also want to include downloadable or streaming video tours of vacation resorts to entice visitors to buy resort vacation packages. Another idea would be to have a system in place to help customers book vacations, rent cars, and check for available flights. The travel agency might also want to store customer profiles so that they can track where particular customers like to sit on the plane, the type of hotel room they usually book, and their credit card information, to make bookings more efficient for the customer and the agency.

If you are marketing a service online, it is difficult to visually depict what your service is all about. Visitors to your site need some reassurance that the service you are selling them is legitimate and valuable. Therefore, you might wish to include a page on your site that lists testimonials from well-known customers. This will give prospective customers more confidence about purchasing your service.

The Fundamentals

Once you have clearly defined your online objectives, your target markets, and the products/services you want to promote online, you are ready to move on to the next phase of planning your Web site. It is critically important that you take this phase seriously, as it is the foundation for everything else related to your online presence.

Using Competitor Sites to Your Advantage

One of your Web site's objectives will always be to meet and beat the competition in terms of search engine rankings and Web site content. In order to do so, you have to understand exactly what it is your competition is doing. Take the time to research competitors and compare them on an element-by-element basis.

There are a number of ways you can identify your competition online. You probably have some marketing materials from your competition's Web site that you can review. You can also find your competition by conducting searches with the appropriate keywords, seeing which competing Web sites rank highly in the major search engines and directories. Similarly, there are many other resources online you can use to research your competition, including the Yellow Pages (*http://www. yellowpages.com, http://www.canada411.com*), Hoovers Online (*http:// www.hoovers.com*), and Business.com (*http://www.business.com*), as well as industry-specific Web portals and directories.

Once you have gathered a list of competing Web sites, you can analyze them element by element to determine which Web elements your competitors include on their sites and how their sites compare to one another. Other components you should analyze include the visual appeal of your competitors' sites, content, ease of navigation, search engine friendliness, interactivity, and Web site "stickiness," or what they do to keep people on their site. This information will provide you with details on what you need to incorporate into your site to "meet and beat" the competition.

You have to realize that your online competition is different from your offline competition. Online you are competing with all organizations that have an online presence and sell the same products and services you do. When doing your competitive analysis online, you want to select the "best of breed"—those fantastic Web sites of organizations selling the same products/services you do no matter where they are physically located.

When we do competitive analysis for clients, we reverse-engineer or dissect the competing Web site from a number of different perspectives. Generally you will choose five or six of the absolute best competing Web sites. Then you will start to build a database using Excel or a table in Word.

Start with the first competing Web site and from your review start to add database elements to the first column. You will note any types of content, target markets defined, repeat traffic techniques used, viral marketing techniques used, search engine friendliness features used (you'll get these in Chapter 6), download time for different types of Internet connections, cross-platform compatibility, cross-browser compatibility, innovative elements, etc. When you have dissected the first competing Web site and have noted appropriate database elements for comparative purposes, you'll move on to the second competing Web site. You go through the same process, but adding only different or new elements to what you already have in your database. Continue building the first column of your database by continuing through all the sites you wish to include in your competitive analysis.

The next step is to develop a column for each of the sites you want to include in the competitive analysis. Add two more columns—one for your existing Web site to see how your site stacks against the competition and the second for future planning purposes.

One next step is to go back and compare each site against the criteria for column 1, noting appropriate comments. For content information you will want to note whether the particular site has the specific content and how well it was presented. For download speeds you will note specific minute and seconds for each type of connection. Tools to help you with this element can be found at:

- BizLand Download Time Checker: *http://www.bizland.com/product/downloadChecker.html*

- Calculate Download Times: *http://www.sercomm.net/download.htm*

For each repeat traffic generator, you may choose to include details or just Yes/No. You will continue with this process until you have completed the database, including your own existing site.

By this time you have a really good feel for the users' experience when they visit your competitors' sites. Now you are ready to do your planning. In the last column you will review each of the elements in the first column, and where appropriate, you will complete the last column by categorizing each of the elements as one of the following:

- Need to have, essential, critical element, can't live without

- Nice to have if it doesn't cost too much

- Don't need, don't want at any price

Now you have done your competitive analysis. Having completed your identification of your objectives, target markets, products and services, and your competitive analysis, you are ready to develop your storyboard or architectural plan or blueprint for your site.

Storyboarding Your Web Site

Next you are ready to visualize and plan your Web site—integrate your objectives, your target market information, the findings of the competitive analysis, and your own ideas as well as those of others. This is done through the process of storyboarding. The storyboard is the foundation of your Web site. It should show you, on paper, the first draft of the content and layout of your site. It gives you the chance to review the layout and make changes before development begins.

A Web site storyboard can be thought of much like a hierarchical organizational chart in a business. In a typical business structure, the executives sit on top, followed by their subordinates, and so on. Figures 1.3 and 1.4 are examples of two modified sections of a storyboard layout developed by our office for a client prior to building a Web site. Think of your Web site storyboard like this: You begin with your main page or home page at the top. Under the main page you have your central navigation bar. Each of the navigation options should be available on each page, regardless of where the user is on your site. Within each of the sections listed on your main navigation bar, you're going to have subsections, and so on.

The storyboard can be done with a software program, with sheets of paper, or with any other mechanism you choose to use. Quite often when we are starting out we'll start with yellow sticky notes on a wall. Very

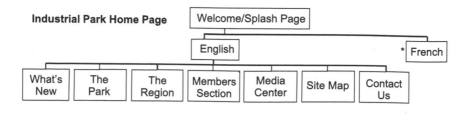

Figure 1.3. A sample layout of a home page and the main site components.

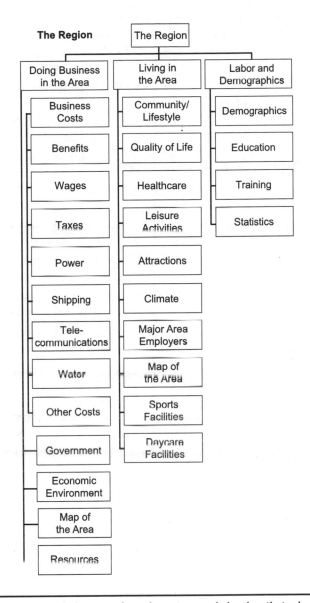

Figure 1.4. A sample layout of a subsection and the details included within.

low tech, but it works! It is very easy to get a visual of the navigation structure and easy to fill in the content pages (one per sticky note) in the appropriate places. It is also very easy to edit—simply move a sticky from one section to another or add another sticky note for a new page.

Once your first draft is done, you need to go back and review the proposed Web site against each and every one of your objectives, each and every one of your target markets (needs, wants, expectations, WOW factor), and each and every one of your products and services. You need to review the proposed Web site from the competitive analysis viewpoint. Have you included all the must-haves and left an opportunity for the elements that fit into the would-be-nice category? Will the proposed Web site beat the competition? Review the proposed site with the stakeholders and a few in your target market. Get feedback and tweak the "blueprint" until you've got it right. It is easy (and cheap) at this stage to add new content and change the layout.

When developing your storyboard, remember to keep the layout of your site simple and logical in flow, as this is how it will be laid out for users once the site is completed. Do not move forward with the Web development process until you have finalized the layout of the storyboard, ensuring that it is easy for your target audience to use and that it provides all the elements you need to achieve your objectives. Review your storyboard to ensure that all of the target markets have been addressed. If you want to address the media, be sure to include a Media Center. If you want to attract potential investors, be sure to include a comprehensive Investor Relations section. Give consideration to viral and permission marketing elements that can be included on your site and where they can be included. We discuss these elements in depth in later chapters.

Once you have the completed and approved storyboard, it becomes the blueprint for construction of your site. You are now ready to move on to the actual construction. The next chapter discusses some of the content and design elements of your site.

Internet Resources for Chapter 1

Creating a Link Storyboard for Your Site
http://www.prowebsitemanagement.com/articles/linkstoryboard.html
Some helpful ideas to use when brainstorming about your storyboard, as well as some tools to assist you in its creation.

Designing Your Web Site from a Storyboard
http://www.grokdotcom.com/storyboard.htm
An article on Web site creation based on storyboards.

Five Steps to Defining Your Target Market
http://linz1.net/biz/Library/111700.html
A step-by-step plan to help you define your target market.

SmartDraw
http://www.smartdraw.com
A software program that will assist you in creating your storyboard. A free demo is provided so you can try before you buy.

Target Market Analyst
http://www.virtualtechnocrats.com/selfhelp/businessebook/marketing/targetmarket.html
A handy checklist to help you define your target market.

2

Your Site—From Storyboarding to Programming

Your storyboard is the blueprint for your site, but there are many steps to take before you can start construction. In Web development, the majority of the time should be spent in the planning. In this chapter we cover:

- Detailed planning of your site before a line of code is ever written

- Content guidelines

- Text guidelines

- Color guidelines

- Navigation guidelines

- Graphics guidelines

- Visual guidelines

- Other guidelines

Detailed Web Site Planning

In the previous chapter you learned how to develop your storyboard. The storyboard is your blueprint for the site, but now you need to think about construction. For each page of your site, you need to develop the content—the text and the graphics.

Generally you will develop the first draft of the text for each page. You know your target market best—you know what makes them buy, you know what they want. The next step is to have this text reviewed and edited by an online copywriter. Online copywriters usually have a background in advertising, where they learn to get the message across in as few words as possible. They know how to grab the reader's attention. Internet users don't want to read pages and pages; they want to get what they're looking for quickly. The text will be short and to the point.

Once the online copywriter has done his magic, you will review and approve. You want to make sure that only the form, but not the substance, has been changed.

The next step is to have the content reviewed and edited by an Internet marketer—someone who has expertise in search engines and their ranking criteria as well as repeat traffic generators and viral and permission marketing. The Internet marketer will review and edit the text and graphics, again making sure that the keywords are used in the appropriate places for high search engine ranking. There is a real science to this: The keyword assigned to a particular page should be used appropriately in the page title, the text throughout the page, the meta-tags for keyword and description, the headers, the Alt tags, and the comments tags.

The Internet marketer will usually develop the content for these tags, titles, and headers at this point. Sometimes the Internet marketing is part of your Web developer's team and sometimes it is a separate outsourced activity. You'll learn more about designing your site to be search engine friendly in Chapter 6.

The Internet marketer will also ensure that you have used the right repeat traffic generators (see Chapter 3), appropriate permission marketing techniques (see Chapter 5), and appropriate viral marketing techniques (see Chapter 4). Again, you will review and approve the changes to make sure your message is still presented appropriately for your target market.

The next step is graphic design. Sometimes the graphic designer is part of your Web development team and sometimes this activity is outsourced. The graphic designer develops the "look and feel" for your site—the navigation bar, the background, and the separator bars. The graphic designer knows that your online and offline corporate ID should be consistent. Again, you review and approve the graphic design.

Once all this has been done and has been approved, your site is ready to be programmed.

Content Notes

Make your contact information readily available. Consider including contact information on every page. This includes your address, phone and fax numbers, and especially your e-mail address. Make it easy for people to get in touch with you.

Avoid "Under Construction" pages on your site; they are of no value to the visitor. When you have information, post it. Until then, don't mention it.

Security information. Explain to your customers when transactions or exchanges of information on your Web site are secure. This is important if your site will be accepting credit card orders.

Privacy policy. Tell people how their personal information (i.e., their name, e-mail address, etc.) will and will not be used. This will make visitors more comfortable submitting inquiries to your site or joining your mail list.

Minimize use of background sounds and autoplay sounds. Some people surf the Web from their office at work and wish to discretely go from one site to the next. Background sounds and sounds that load automatically can compromise their discreteness. Give your visitors the option of listening to a sound, but do not force it upon them. If you do, you could lose visitors forever.

Text Notes

The tone of your text and the design of your graphics will convey your intended image. When determining the text content of your site, be mindful of the fact that your own biases may preclude you from placing information on your site that is second nature to you but important data for your visitors. Review all text content on your site to ensure that you have not omitted anything crucial.

Also, keep text brief. Almost 80 percent of Web users scan text online as opposed to actually reading it. Therefore, make your key points quickly and succinctly, and use lots of bulleted lists, headers, and horizontal rules to create visual "breaks" in the content. This will keep visitors interested enough to read the information on your site. If they are faced with huge blocks of text, most visitors will be overwhelmed by the quantity of the information and be too intimidated to read your message. Write for scannability.

Don't set your text size too small, as this is too hard to read. But don't set it too large, as this looks like you are shouting. Also, avoid using ALL CAPS, WHICH ALSO COMES ACROSS AS SHOUTING.

Color Notes

Keep your online and offline image consistent. Be consistent with your use of logos, corporate colors, and other marketing collateral associated with your company.

Choose your background and font colors carefully. Using backgrounds that are too busy will obscure your text and will not provide a pleasant viewing experience for your visitors. Only some colors will show up properly on certain backgrounds. A light background with dark text is easiest on the eyes.

White text displays best on black backgrounds, and black text is most readable on white backgrounds. Of course, you can use other color schemes, but choose your scheme carefully, as mentioned. There is nothing worse than a Web site that is unreadable. Also, be mindful that some people might wish to print pages from your site. If you incorporate a lot of your text into the actual graphics on your site, the text might be difficult to read when printed. Also, graphic-intensive sites load more slowly. If you have to incorporate text content into your graphics, be sure that it is sensible to do so.

Use the default colors for links whenever possible. Blue text usually indicates an unvisited link. Purple, maroon, or darker blue usually represents a link you have visited, and red is the color of an active link. It should not be difficult for visitors to identify your links. If you decide not to use the default colors, your links should be emphasized in a consistent manner through font size, font style, or underlines.

Navigation Notes

Ease of navigation is very important to your site. Provide a navigation bar at a consistent location on every page that links to all of the major pages of your site. Make it easy to get from one page to any other. Search engines can index any page from your site, so your home page might not be the first page visitors come to. Never have dead-ends where viewers scroll down a page or two of information only to find that they must scroll all the way back up to the top to move on (because you have no links at the bottom of the page). A consistent-looking and well-positioned navigation bar with functioning links is the key to efficient site navigation.

Your visitors should be able to get anywhere they want to go on your site in three clicks or fewer. Develop an effective navigation bar as previously described. For very large sites (i.e., sites consisting of eight to ten major sections), it is a good idea to include a site map that users can access from any page in your site. Site maps, as shown in Figures 2.1 and 2.2, are usually text-based lists that name all of the site's pages and their content. Site maps make it easy for users to access the information they are looking for without causing them much frustration. Include a link from your main navigation bar to the site map for the easiest possible reference.

An additional feature you may wish to include is an internal search tool. This allows users to enter their query and have all relevant matches returned, based on their query. This is a particularly useful feature if you sell many products directly on your Web site or if your site contains many pages of content. It allows the user to quickly search for the desired item or information using the product's name or a relevant keyword. Intel operates multiple sites and offers many products and services. To help users locate the information they're looking for, they have integrated a useful search tool. Keep the design of your site consistent. Font types, headers, footers, navigational bars, buttons, bullets, colors, and so on, should be consistent throughout the site to maintain a polished, professional look.

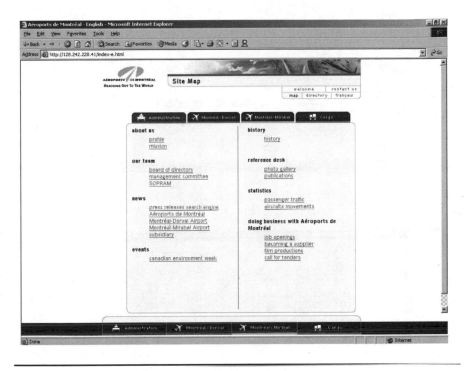

Figure 2.1. Montreal International Airport's site map.

Graphics Notes

Graphics that are too time-consuming to download may cause visitors to leave your site before they get a chance to see it. The combined size of the text and graphics on any Web page should not exceed 50K.

Some people turn graphics off in their browsers to save time, so you should provide all of your information in text as well as graphics. Use descriptive **Alt attributes** in your image tags. The Alt text will load in place of the images when the graphic does not display for any reason. Visitors who choose not to browse with graphics turned on will have an easier time navigating your site. Also, Alt text is spidered and indexed by a lot of the major search engines. Using keywords in your Alt text in your image tags will improve your ranking in search engines and will provide a description of the images in the event that they are not loaded. If

Alt attributes
Descriptive text associated with respective images on a Web site.

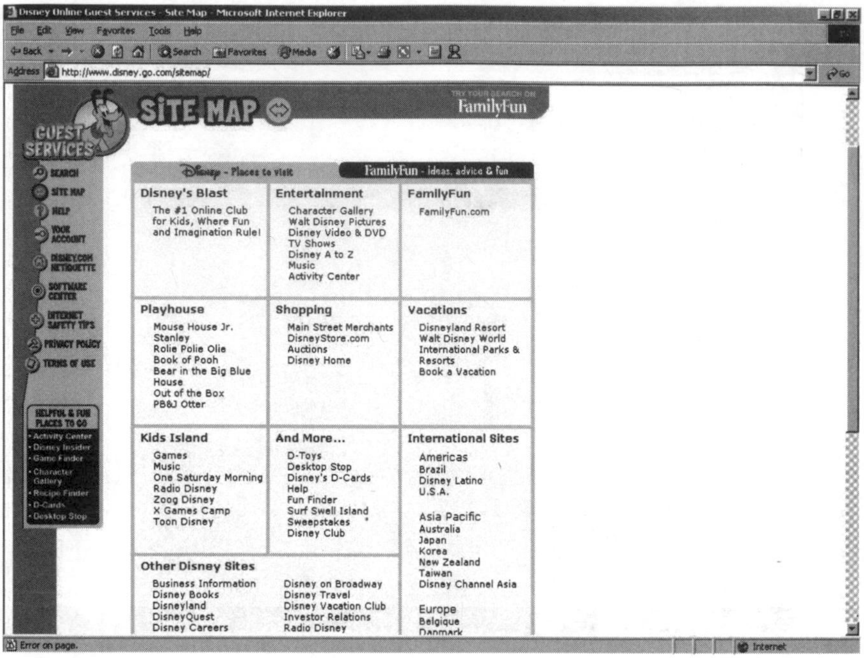

Figure 2.2. Disney's site map.

you use any large files for graphics, audio, or video, warn your visitors by providing some text stating the size of the files.

Use thumbnail graphics where applicable. When you have a page with a lot of large images (i.e., an online photo collection), create small "thumbnail" versions of each image and give visitors the option of clicking through to the larger versions. This is far superior to making your visitors wait for a series of large images to load.

You should be careful with your use of image maps as well. Image maps are large graphics with clickable "hot spots." Image maps typically are used for navigation and usually have text embedded in the graphic. Search engines cannot read text embedded in a graphic, so from the standpoint of search engine friendliness, if you use image maps always ensure that you provide your appropriate text and Alt tags for the search engine.

Very often, when a large graphic is used for an image map, visitors must wait for the entire image to load before it is apparent where they must click to begin navigating a site. Instead of using a large image map, break the image into smaller images so that visitors will receive faster feedback from your site without having to wait for a huge graphic to load. Also, always provide an alternate text link navigation system to assist people who surf with their graphics turned off.

Visual Notes

Check your site using different browsers. What viewers see when your site is downloaded depends on what browser they are using. Different browsers will display the same Web site differently. Before you post your site online, check your site with the most popular browsers:

- Netscape Navigator 7.x

- Netscape Navigator 6.x

- Netscape Navigator 4.x

- Microsoft Internet Explorer 6.x

- Microsoft Internet Explorer 5.x

- Microsoft Internet Explorer 4.x

- America Online 7.x

- America Online 6.x

Also make sure that you review your site on a Mac and a PC. Design for various screen widths. Try to accommodate visitors regardless of the screen resolution they use. Some Web users still run their systems at 640 pixels wide by 480 pixels high, so keep this in mind when designing your site.

Your Web site should steer clear of scrolling-marquee text. Scrolling marquees are difficult to read and are not compatible with all browsers. Simply post text directly on your pages if you have something important to say.

her Notes

Home page
The main page
of a Web site.

Your **home page** should be 50K or less and should be displayed on no more than one or two screens. Studies have shown that visitors will rarely wait beyond 15 seconds to download a site. Test the download time of your site using different connection speeds to ensure that it is reasonable for all users.

Also avoid dead links. These are links that don't go anywhere and the viewer usually receives a "404—File not Found" error message from the Web server after clicking on a dead link. Verify periodically that all your links are still active.

Internet Resources for Chapter 2

I have included a few resources for you to check out regarding designing your Web site. For additional resources on a variety of topics, I recommend you visit the Resources section of my Web site at *http://www.susansweeney.com/resources.html*. There you will find additional tips, tools, techniques, and resources.

REVIEW YOUR SITE
NetMechanic
http://www.netmechanic.com
A number of tools to improve your site's mechanics, including HTML code validation and GIF optimization.

Northern Webs
http://www.northernwebs.com/set
Northern Webs' Engine Tutorial is one of the most recognized leaders in exposing the nuances of the various search engines and explaining what makes them tick. See if your site can stand the test of their exclusive Meta-Medic!

Smith Family.com Webmaster's Tools
http://www.smithfam.com/tools.html
This site includes interactive tools for Web masters and site designers. Use these tools to submit and promote your Web site or to find prob-

lems. They have included site offerings such as utilities site tune-ups, link checking, meta-writing, site submission, and search tools.

REFERENCES

CNET Builder.com
http://www.builder.com
An outstanding resource and how-to site for all things related to Web site design.

Color Matters
http://www.colormatters.com/entercolormatters.html
Explores the use of color and the effects color combinations have on your design.

Design Basics
http://www.efuse.com/Design/index.html
Covers Web site navigation, graphics, content, and much more.

Eyewire
http://www.eyewire.com/tips/design
A great list of articles on Web design.

Web Developers Virtual Library (WDVL)
http://www.stars.com
A comprehensive illustrated encyclopedia of Web technology, the WDVL is for Web masters and Internet developers. It's a well-organized goldmine of tutorials, demos, and links to great resources.

Web Monkey
http://hotwired.lycos.com/webmonkey
The Web developer's resource.

Whatis.com
http://www.whatis.com
Whatis.com is "definition" paradise. It defines any computer-related word you ever wondered about.

The World Wide Web Consortium
http://www.w3c.org

"The World Wide Web Consortium (W3C) develops interoperable technologies (specifications, guidelines, software, and tools) to lead the Web to its full potential as a forum for information, commerce, communication, and collective understanding"—description quoted from site.

GRAPHICS

gif.com
http://www.gif.com
An extensive resource for Web graphic design.

Graphics 101
http://builder.cnet.com/webbuilding/0-3883-8-4892140-1.html
A series of tutorials covering Web graphics: preparing images for the Web, color depth, transparencies, techniques, and more.

3

Web Site Elements That Keep 'Em Coming Back

There are many little things that will spice up your Web site to "keep 'em coming back." Learn the tips, tools, and techniques to get visitors to return to your site again and again. In this chapter, we cover:

- Attractive Web site content

- How to have your own What's New page, Tip of the Day, and Awards page

- Hosting online seminars

- Ensuring that you are bookmarked

- Cartoons, contests, jokes, and trivia

- Calendar of events and reminder services

- Interesting bulletin boards

- Online chat sessions, workshops, and discussion groups

- Special guests or celebrity appearances

- Giveaways, awards, and surveys

- Offline tactics for promotion

Encourage Repeat Visits

Just as you would want customers to visit your place of business frequently, so too in cyberspace do you want customers and potential customers to visit often. The more often people visit your site, the more likely they are to purchase something. You want to ensure that the techniques you use to get repeat traffic are appropriate for your target market. For example, if you were having a contest on your site targeted toward children, you would not want to give away a breadmaker as the prize. That would be okay, however, if your target market is families or homemakers. You want to offer something of interest to the market you are targeting. If your target is business professionals, then something like a Palm Pilot that they could use in their everyday business would be appropriate. If your target market is skiers, then a weekend in Vail might be appropriate. You should always remember your objectives when doing any form of online marketing, because you don't want to do something inappropriate that might drive your target audience away from your site.

Use a What's New Page for Repeat Visits

A What's New page can mean different things to different sites. For some, this page updates users with the summaries of the most recent features and additions to a particular site, as in Figure 3.1. Your What's New page should be accessible from your home page so that when people visit your site they will not have to search through your entire site to find out what is new. If visitors repeatedly find interesting additions in the What's New section, in whatever context you use it, they will come back to your site on a regular basis to check out what's new. Without

Figure 3.1. You can use a What's New page to tell users about updates to your site and about what's going on in your company.

this, they may visit and search through your site and find that nothing was new and they just wasted 20 minutes looking for anything new. Here, too, you can leverage this repeat-traffic generator with permission marketing by asking if visitors would like to be notified via e-mail when you've added something to the What's New section. It's all about getting their permission to send them e-mail and therefore include them in your community.

For other sites, What's New may cover What's New in their industry or What's New in their product line. Whatever it is, you should always make sure that it is of interest to your target market. Again, you can ask your visitors if they would like to be notified when updates are made to your Web site. This once again gives you permission to e-mail them and present them with new information that will make them want to come back to your site again.

Free Stuff—Everyone Loves It

Giving items away for free is a great way to increase traffic—everybody likes a freebie. If you give something different away each week, you are sure to have a steady stream of repeat traffic. When you have freebies or giveaways on your site, your pages can also be listed and linked from the many sites on the Internet that list places where people can receive free stuff. To find these listings of free stuff, simply go to a search engine and do a search on "Free Stuff Index" or "Free Stuff Links." You will be amazed at how many people are giving things away online.

You don't have to give something away to everyone. You could simply have a drawing every week. You could then ask entrants if they would like you to notify them of the winner, which again gives you permission to e-mail them. An example of a site that has a monthly drawing is Lobster Direct (*http://www.lobsterdirect.com*). Lobster Direct is a site that ships live Nova Scotia lobsters anywhere in North America the next day via an overnight delivery service. They have a drawing for a lobster dinner for four every month (see Figure 3.2). So, every month many people enter this drawing for their chance to win the free lobster. When the drawing is done, Lobster Direct e-mails everyone to inform them of the winner, at the same time taking the opportunity to remind them of the monthly specials. This certainly can't hurt sales.

If you want to bring only people from your target market to your site, then don't give away mainstream things like screen savers, shareware games, utilities, and so on. Try to give away something that only people interested in your industry would want. If you don't care what traffic comes your way, and any traffic is good traffic, then give away useful things that everybody needs. Try to have your logo and URL displayed on the item. For example, a neat screen saver can be made that displays your logo and URL. When this is made available as a download, there are no handling or shipping charges associated with it. If your freebie is something that has your URL on it and is something that is generally kept around a computer, it reminds and encourages people to visit your site. A mousepad with your URL would be a good example.

You should change your freebie often and tell people from your site how often you do this. Something like "We change our free offer every single week! Keep checking back" or "Click here to be notified by e-mail when we update" will work well.

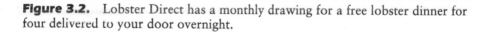

Figure 3.2. Lobster Direct has a monthly drawing for a free lobster dinner for four delivered to your door overnight.

Freebies provide ideal viral marketing opportunities as well. Have a "Tell a friend about this" button near the freebie so site visitors can quickly and easily tell their friends.

Give a Taste of Your Product with Sample Giveaways

Use a traditional marketing approach and give away free samples of your product from your Web site. After giving away the samples, follow up with an e-mail. Ask the people who received a sample what they thought of it, if they had any problems, and if they have any questions. Direct the samplers back to your Web site for more information and discounts on purchasing the regular version of the product. If you have a number of products, you might consider alternating your free samples. Ask if visitors would like to be notified by e-mail when you change your free sample. This gives you permission to e-mail the visitors on a regular basis to remind them about the sample. You also get to update them with new information regarding your Web site, your products, or your company. This will entice them to visit your site again. Make sure you include your signature file in your e-mail message.

Free samples also provide a great viral marketing opportunity.

Resisting a Deal with Coupons and Discounts Is Hard

Offer coupons and discount vouchers that can be printed from your site. You can change the coupon daily or weekly to encourage repeat visits. People will come back to your site again and again if they know they will find good deals there. This is a great strategy to use in conjunction with a free sample giveaway. If people liked the sample, give them a coupon to purchase the regular version at a discount. If they like the regular version, they may purchase it again at full price or recommend the product to a friend. You can also ask people if they would like to be notified by e-mail when you update the coupons on your Web site. This once again gives you the opportunity to present them with new information about your business. Offering coupons is a great idea if you have a physical location as well as a Web site. These can be your loss leader to get customers to come into your store.

You can develop a coupon banner ad that links to your site, where the coupon can be printed. The banner ads should be placed on sites frequented by your target market. You can trade coupons with noncompeting sites that target the same market that you do. Your coupon on their site links to your site, and their coupon on your site links to their site.

By offering coupons from your Web site, you also cut down your overhead cost because people are printing the coupons on their own printers, thus not using your paper. Remember that you should have terms and conditions on the coupons that are available for printing. For example, you should have an expiration date. Someone could print a coupon, then visit your store in a year and try to use it. You should try to have the expiration date close to the release of the coupon. This will entice the visitor to use the coupon more quickly and then come back for more coupons.

Today we are seeing an increase in the number of coupon-related sites that are appearing on the Internet. CoolSavings.com *(http://www. coolsavings.com)* is an online coupon network where businesses can advertise and place coupons for their products and services, as seen in Figure 3.3. The site has been operating since 1997 and provides the service to businesses in the United States only. Sites like this are a good way to promote your business, for they receive a high amount of traffic. CoolSavings.com has been a household name since it launched its national advertising campaign during 1999. If you offer coupons from your site, it would benefit you to be listed on these types of sites. If you are not aiming for a national appeal, you should search to find out if there are coupon networks in the geographic location that you are targeting (see

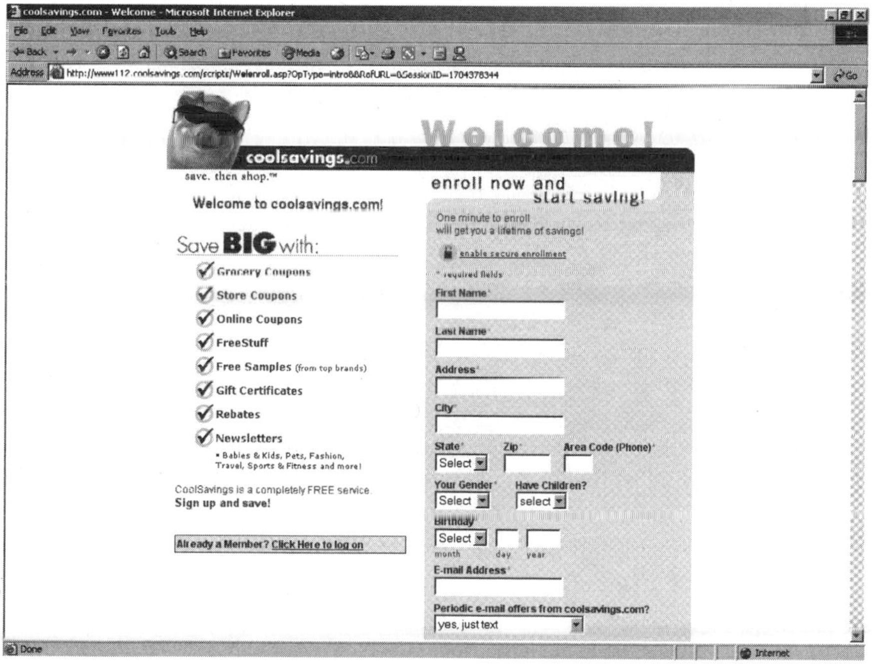

Figure 3.3. CoolSavings.com offers coupons from businesses to people all over the USA.

Figure 3.4). Other coupon sites are listed in the Internet Resources section at the end of this chapter. There are meta-indexes to sites with coupons or discounts from which you can be linked for greater exposure.

Coupons provide ideal viral marketing opportunities—for example, "Send this coupon to a friend."

Specials and Promotions

Everyone likes to get a deal. You might consider having a special promotions section on your Web site. You'll want to change your promotion fairly frequently and let your site visitors know: "We change our specials every week. Bookmark our site and keep checking back!"

You might employ permission marketing here as well: "We change our specials every week. Click here if you'd like to be notified when we

Figure 3.4. The Coupon Network targets people in the province of Nova Scotia by offering coupons for that geographic region.

update" or "Click here to receive our e-specials weekly." If you send e-specials via e-mail, make sure you give them a reason to visit your site and provide the appropriate hypertext links in the e-mail.

Make it easy to have your site visitors tell their friends about your specials. Have a "Tell a friend about this special" button appropriately placed on the page with your special promotions. You can leverage the viral marketing with an incentive: "Tell three friends about our special and be included in a drawing for [something appropriate for your target market]."

A Calendar of Events Keeps Visitors Informed

A comprehensive, current calendar of events related to your company or your industry will encourage repeat visits. A sample calendar is shown in Figure 3.5. Your calendar should always be kept up-to-date and be of value to your readers. A calendar of events for a band might show their scheduled appearances. A calendar of events of what is going on in your business community is very appropriate for a Chamber of Commerce or Board of Trade site. This will encourage a lot of repeat traffic as long as it is current and complete. Calendars of events are also appropriate on community sites, because residents access these calendars often in order to stay current with what is going on. Again, you can ask people if they'd like to be notified via e-mail when you update your calendar of events.

If you have a great calendar of events, you can encourage others to use it by providing a link to it from their Web site. This offer works well in that you are providing them with great content that is kept current and they are providing you with traffic.

Luring Customers with Contests and Competitions

Contests and competitions are great traffic builders. According to Jupiter Communications, a New York-based market research firm, online contests are among the fastest-growing online activities. They report that 49 percent of all American Internet users have entered online contests.

Some sites hold regular contests on a weekly or monthly basis to generate repeat visitors. Holding contests is also a great way to find out about your target market by requesting information on the entry form.

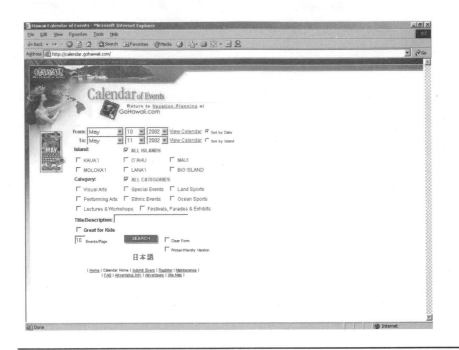

Figure 3.5.   You can use a Calendar of Events to keep your audience informed of what's coming up in the future.

What type of contest you hold depends upon your Internet marketing objectives. If you want to attract as many people as possible to your site regardless of who they are, then offer items such as money, trips, cars, computers, and so on, as in Figures 3.6 and 3.7. If you would like to attract potential customers from your target market, then give away something that relates to your products and industry.

You could simply request that people fill out an electronic ballot including their name, address, phone number, and e-mail address to enter the contest. If you want to find out something about the people entering, ask them to answer a question about your products. If the prize is one of your products, consider asking entrants to write a short note outlining why they would like to have the product you are giving away. You can award the winner(s) with the product and follow up with the other entrants. These people may be in a position to buy your products, and you will have gained some valuable knowledge from the notes submitted.

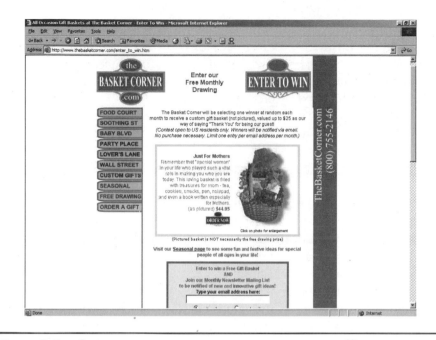

Figure 3.6. Contests are a great way to encourage repeat traffic.

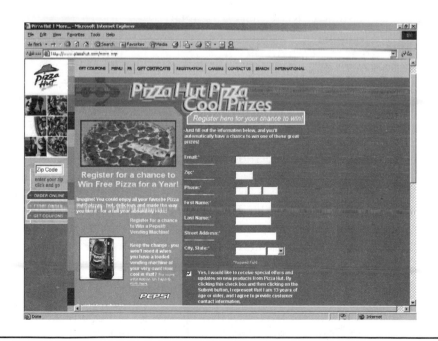

Figure 3.7. Pizza Hut offers visitors a chance to win free pizza for a year.

If your product is appropriate for a prize that would be of interest to many different types of people, you might consider finding contest sites that would be willing to offer your product as the prize on their site. This will generate brand awareness for your product. You could have the site show a picture of your product with a link to your site. The contest site should be more than happy to do this because you are offering to give something for free that adds value to that site.

You can turn a contest into a competition. If your Web site relates to cooking or baking, ask entrants to submit their best recipe using your food product. People will visit your site to see the winning recipes, and you may get some ideas for future marketing efforts. Other competitions may include things like best photo with product X, best short story about product X, best drawing of product X, and so on. This creates better brand awareness and reinforces sales of your product. The closer the contest relates to your product, the better. Instead of offering just one prize, offer a number of smaller prizes as well. This makes the odds look better and people feel they have a better chance of winning.

You might have contestants answer three questions relating to your product or service on the entry form. Of course, to find the answers to the questions, the visitor has to visit a number of pages on your site, and the three questions are marketing related.

You can have the contest one where you get information about your target market. Perhaps they have to rank what influences their buying decision. The information requested could also provide you with demographic or psychographic information.

Allow site visitors one contest entry per day—you're happy to have visitors return to your site often. You might consider changing the information around the entry form on a regular basis. Provide links to other repeat-traffic generators like your coupons or your e-specials.

Whatever type of contest you determine will best meet your marketing objectives, be sure you encourage permission marketing ("Click here to be notified when we have a new contest") and viral marketing ("Tell a friend about this great contest"). Leverage, leverage, leverage: "Tell five friends and receive an extra ballot for yourself."

Make your contest conditional: "Sign up to receive our weekly e-specials and be included in our drawing for [something of interest to your target market]."

Before you go ahead with holding any kind of contest, check out all of the legal issues. There may be restrictions that you don't know about (e.g., you may be required to purchase a legal permit to hold lotteries).

You should also remember to ask the entrants the e-mail address at which they would like to be notified of the winner. This, again, grants you permission to e-mail them to tell them who the winner was, and also to inform them of the specials that you may have at your site that month.

You will want to promote your contest through public and private mail list postings, newsgroup postings, your e-mail signature file, press releases, and links from contest sites. Some popular contest sites you might want to be listed from include:

- Contest Guide (*http://www.contestguide.com*)

- Contest Hound (*http://www.contesthound.com*)

- About Contests (*http://contests.about.com*)

- Red Hot Sweeps Sites (*http://www.redhotsweeps.com*)

- Contests and Sweepstakes Directory (*http://www.sweepstakes-contests.com*)

- Winning Ways Online Sweeps (*http://www.onlinesweeps.com*)

Using Employment Opportunities to Increase Visitors

People involved in a job search or interested in new job opportunities will revisit your site occasionally to see your list of available positions. See Figure 3.8 for a sample employment page.

Creating Useful Links from Your Site

Provide visitors with links to other sites similar to yours or a meta-index of links that would be of interest to your target market (see Figure 3.9). Do not put outbound links on your home page. Place them down a level or two after the visitors have seen all the information you want them to see before you provide the links away from your site. Links can be incorporated in two ways. The first is where clicking the link loads

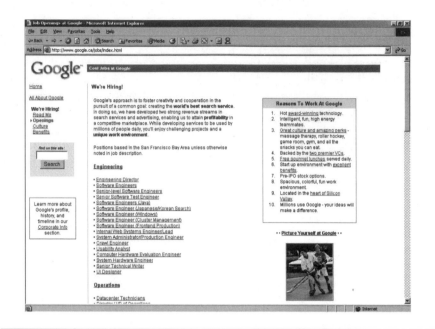

Figure 3.8. Google provides information on employment opportunities from its Web site.

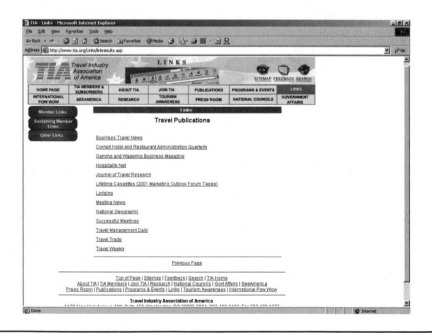

Figure 3.9. The Travel Industry Association of America provides useful links for travel industry professionals from its site.

the new page in the same browser window. (It replaces the content of your page with the content of the "linked page.") The second and more preferred method is to have the link open a new browser window. (Your page stays where it is and the content from the "linked page" opens up in the new browser window.) This is preferred because once visitors are finished with the new page, they can close the new browser window and your page is still there in the "old" browser window. Try exchanging links with others so you receive a link from their site to your site. As long as the links are of value to your visitors, people will come back to see if you have found any new and interesting sites for them to visit.

You might consider asking if visitors would be interested in being notified when you update your list of links or just make updates to your site in general. By offering this, if they choose to do so, you have the opportunity to send people an e-mail message and remind them about your site while presenting them with new information about what might be going on with your site.

Investing in Online Chat Sessions

Chat rooms are very popular and, to some, even addictive. If you have a chat forum on your site, make sure that the topic relates to your business and that participants are likely to be your target market. To encourage repeat visitors, you could change the topic from day to day or week to week. You could also have celebrity appearances in your chat sessions. These sessions should be regularly scheduled, and the upcoming events should be posted on your site so that your visitors will know what is going on when, and will not miss the session if it is of importance to them. They could be on Sunday from 3 to 5 p.m., or on Tuesday from 7 to 9 p.m. Also remember to have the information in your signature file and do some postings through your appropriate mail lists and newsgroups to promote the event.

You should try to post the topics of the discussions at least a week in advance so that your visitors will remember to come for the entire session if they are interested in the topic. You would be surprised how many people would schedule time so that they could chat with someone special or knowledgeable in an area that interests them. You might also think of asking your visitors if they would be interested in being notified of upcoming chat sessions or celebrities who may be visiting your site to chat. This again gives you the opportunity to e-mail people, at their request, and present them with information that will entice them to visit your site again. You can also ask your community whom they'd like to see as a guest or what topics they would like to have discussed.

Providing a Tip of the Day to Encourage Repeat Visits

Have a section that offers cool tips that relate to your business, your products or services, or your target market, as in Figure 3.10. These tips can be from one sentence to one paragraph long. If visitors find your advice helpful, they will return repeatedly to see what interesting piece of information you have displayed that day. Ask your visitors if they would be interested in receiving the tip via e-mail or if they would like notification when the tip has been updated so they could then visit your Web site. Encourage people to send the tip to a friend. You can also

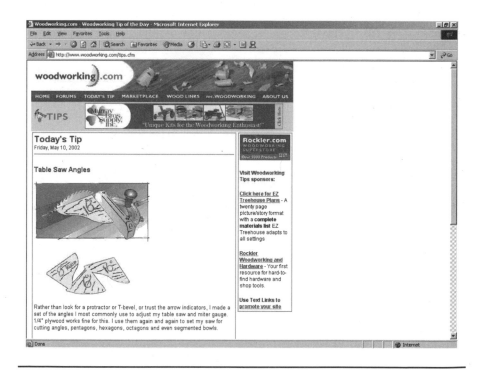

Figure 3.10. Tips of the Day can encourage repeat visitors.

encourage others to use your tip on their Web site as long as they provide a link back to your site as the source.

Ensuring That Your Site Gets Bookmarked

Encourage visitors to add you to their bookmark list. At appropriate parts of your site, display the call to action "Bookmark me now!" (see Figure 3.11). A call to action is often effective. Make sure the title of the page that has the "Bookmark me now!" clearly identifies your site and its contents in an enticing way, because the title is what will appear in the bookmark file as a description. Whenever I see "Bookmark this site now!" I always consider it. Sometimes I do and sometimes I don't, but I always consider it. Often, when the call to action is not presented, I

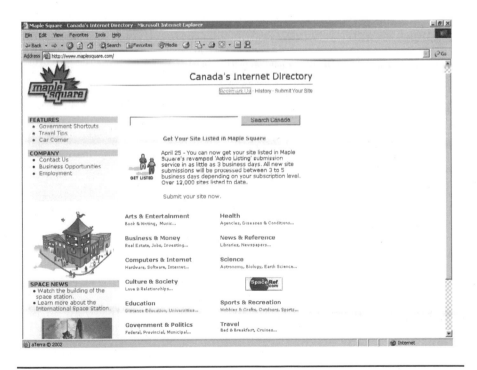

Figure 3.11. When you see a "Bookmark this site now!" or "Bookmark Us!" call to action, nine times out of ten you will at least consider it.

don't think about it and don't bookmark it. Then, days later when I want to go back there, I wish I had remembered to bookmark.

World Interaction with Bulletin Boards

It can be very satisfying to see people join in from all over the world just to interact with each other about a topic that relates to your Web site, as shown in Figure 3.12. Beware, you will have to keep an eye on the messages and may even have to play referee occasionally.

Inviting Visitors to Contribute with Surveys

Performing surveys is a way to increase the traffic to your site. For people to want to fill out the survey and see the results, the survey topic must be interesting. To encourage input, the survey results might be available to participants only. Your survey could be on a topic concerning current events or something pertaining to your industry. The more controversial or debatable the topic of the survey, the more people will visit to contribute or see the results. If you want to draw a very targeted audience, pick a topic that would be interesting to that market alone.

In performing these surveys, you are building repeat traffic and you are gathering valuable information on your market. If you hold an interesting survey every week or every month, then you will be sure to retain a loyal audience of repeat visitors. If your surveys are newsworthy, then you can send out press releases to publicize the results and gain publicity for your site.

Your surveys should be short and to the point. Let people know why you are asking them to do the survey and when the deadline is. Make your questions clear and concise. The responses should be Yes/No or multiple choice. When reporting the results, don't just put them on your Web page; post the results to newsgroups and mailing lists that would be interested. Don't forget to add your sig.file. If you are holding weekly or monthly surveys, let people know via your sig.file what the next survey topic will be and that there is more information on your Web site.

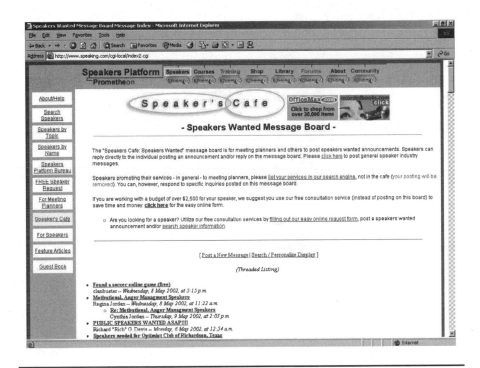

Figure 3.12. The Speaker Café is a great bulletin board where people can request information about professional speakers for conferences and trade shows.

Again, you should ask people if they'd like to be notified of survey results, either via e-mail or by prior notification as to when the results will be posted on the site so they will be able to visit your site and find out. You might also ask if they'd like to be notified when you are conducting a new survey.

Encourage Repeat Visits with Your "Site of the Day"

Having your own "Site of the Day" (see Figure 3.13) or "Site of the Week" (see Figure 3.14) listing will mean a lot of work, searching the Internet for a cool site to add or looking through all the submissions. However, if your picks are interesting to your audience, you may find that avid Internet users come back every day to see what great new site

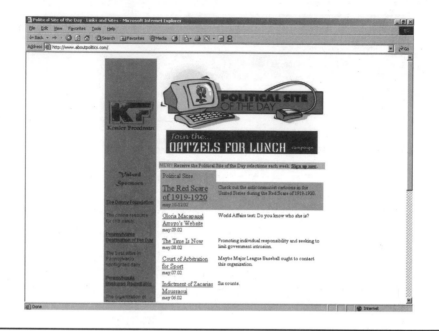

Figure 3.13. The Political Site of the Day focuses on different politically related Web sites and offers an e-mail notification service to inform its visitors of the new Site of the Day.

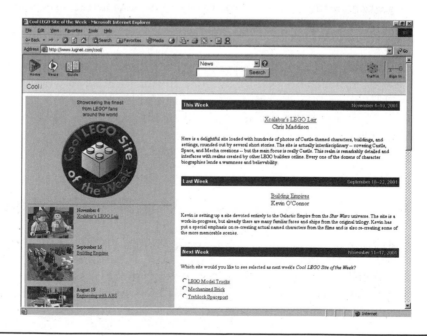

Figure 3.14. Cool Lego Site of the Week showcases Lego fans around the world and their works of art.

is listed. Remember that this must be updated on schedule; displaying a week-old Site of the Day will reflect poorly on your site and your company. For more information, see Chapter 18 about hosting your own award site.

Keep Them Happy with Cartoons

Displaying relevant cartoons keeps your site dynamic and fun. You do not necessarily have to create all of the content and features yourself. If you update this weekly, ask if visitors would like to be notified via e-mail when you update your Web site. A good example of a site that uses cartoons is the Myke Ashley-Cooper Cartoons4Fun site (*http://www.cartoons4fun.com/c4f.shtml*), which continuously provides humor to its viewers (see Figure 3.15). Cartoons provide a great viral marketing opportunity.

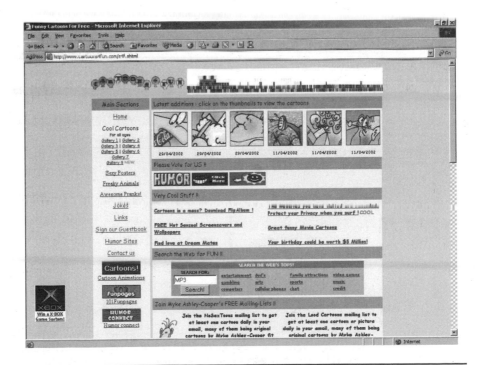

Figure 3.15. The Cartoons4fun site offers amusing cartoons.

Benefiting from Humor with Jokes and Trivia

"Laughter is the best medicine" and could prove to be a popular feature of your Web page (see Figure 3.16). People enjoy trivia, or a "Thought of the Day" (see Figure 3.17), and there are many sources for you to draw from. Be sure to update regularly. Again, this gives you the opportunity to ask if your visitors would like to be notified when you update this section of your Web site and offers a viral marketing opportunity as well.

Who Doesn't Love Games?

More and more sites are featuring fun activities and games. (A sample game site is shown in Figure 3.18.) Just about anything goes here. You can host anything from a Star Wars trivia contest to having guests play an interactive game with other visitors. Allow visitors an easy way to "Tell a friend" about your game.

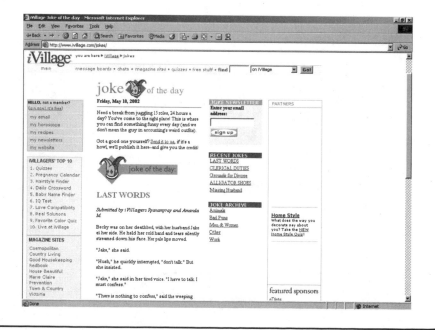

Figure 3.16. iVillage.com has a Joke of the Day that you can view online or can sign up to receive in your e-mail box in the form of a newsletter.

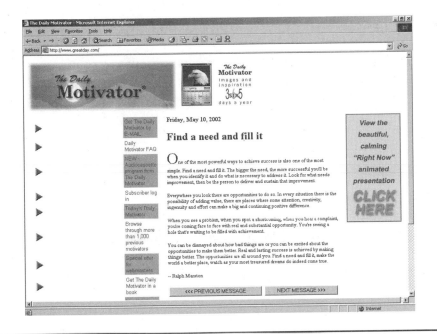

Figure 3.17. The Daily Motivator (*http://www.greatday.com*) allows you to sign up to receive your daily motivation via e-mail and also encourages others to put the Daily Motivator on their sites.

Figure 3.18. Sony Online has many games for its users to enjoy.

Keep Customers in Touch with Update Reminders

Ask visitors to your site if they would like to be notified when there are updates or content changes to your pages. This is similar to a mailing list except that you write to the "list" only when changes have been made. This is effective when you have a newsletter or a frequently visited calendar of events on your site.

Special Events Reminder Services

People can sign up to be reminded of something via e-mail on specified dates (see Figure 3.19). This feature was originally thought of by a florist to remind people about important dates. You can remind people about any number of things relating to your business. If you own a site

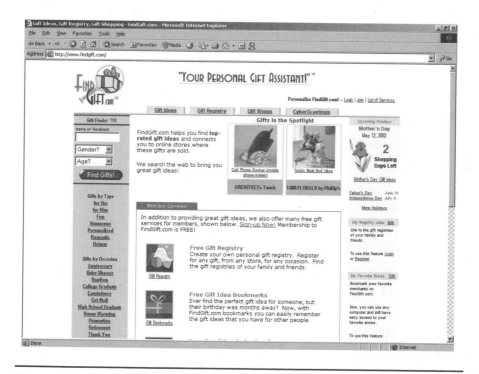

Figure 3.19. FindGift.com has a reminder service where you can register to receive e-mail reminders for special dates.

that sells fishing and hunting gear, you could get people to sign up to be reminded when certain fishing or hunting seasons start. You should try to develop a reminder service that relates to something that you sell from your site. In your reminder you can include suggestions about what fishing fly works best at this time of the year.

Reminder services are becoming very popular with e-commerce sites. Their services are very much appreciated by busy people who are not good with remembering dates. This has saved me on more than one occasion and made it very easy to purchase from the site that provided the reminder. I have five nieces and nephews across the country. I have registered their birthdays with a site that also asked for some details about the reminder—things like what the date is, the relationship that I have with the person, their ages, things they enjoy, and how far ahead of time I want to be notified. Like clockwork, ten days prior to Kyle's birthday, I got this e-mail: "Susan, your nephew Kyle's birthday is in 10 days. He will be 12 years old. Kyle likes Gameboy video games. We happen to have several that may be appropriate as a gift for Kyle. Click here for more details."

I am then able to choose the gift that I want to purchase, the paper I want it wrapped with, and the text that I want on the card that will be attached to the gift. Then I simply provide the address I want it sent to and give them my credit card number, and they send it off. Everyone is happy, especially me.

Adding Image with Advice Columns

Some Web sites are incorporating advice columns, as in Figure 3.20. People will return again and again to read the e-mails asking for advice and to see the responses that are given. This also helps perpetuate an image of your company as an expert in your given field.

Internet Resources for Chapter 3

I have included a few resources for you to check out regarding repeat-traffic generators. For additional resources on a variety of topics, I recommend you visit the Resources section of my Web site at *http://*

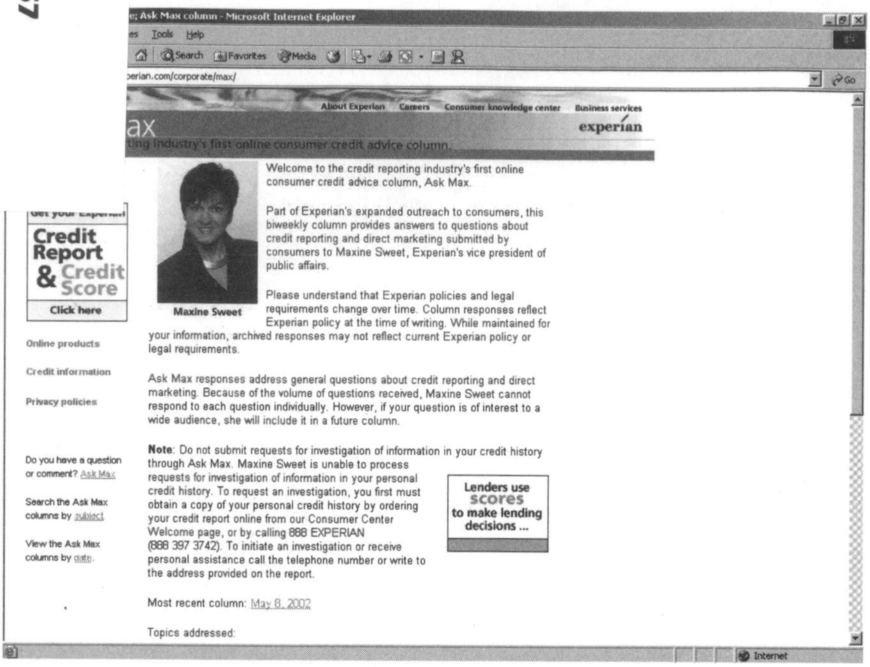

Figure 3.20. A column that gives consumer credit advice is at *http://www. experian.com*.

www.susansweeney.com/resources.html. There you will find additional tips, tools, techniques, and resources.

Bring 'em Back for More
http://www.lunareclipse.net/bringemback.htm
You shouldn't just work to get visitors to your site; you should work to keep them coming back time and time again. This site gives you some tips on how to do just that.

Driving Traffic Back
http://ezine-tips.com/articles/strategy/20001031.shtml
An article on how you can use e-zines to create repeat traffic.

More Hits for Your WWW Site
http://www.adze.com/zine/morehits.html
Instruction on how to get people to keep coming back to your site.

6 Things You Can Do to Increase Your Repeat Traffic Today
http://www.wizardzone.com/content/reptraf.htm
Some great ideas for encouraging repeat visitors.

Stimulate Repeat Traffic with Bookmarks
http://wilsonweb.com/wmta/bookmark.htm
An article about using bookmarks to increase the likelihood of repeat traffic.

10 Secrets of the Web Masters
http://www.i-strategies.com/10secret.html
A guide to Web design and strategy to attract visitors and make them return.

4

Spreading the Word
with Viral Marketing

Have you ever visited a Web site and found an article, a coupon, a special, or something else that impressed you so much that you immediately sent an e-mail to your friends about it? If you have, you've already been bitten by the viral marketing bug! Viral marketing, which is often referred to as "word of mouse" marketing, is a low-cost, highly effective way to market your product or service using the Internet. Just like a flu virus in humans, viral marketing replicates and propagates itself online. Viral marketing enables you to capitalize on referrals from an unbiased third party—the consumer! The power that peers and reference groups have over the purchasing decision is phenomenal. Similar to how a positive testimonial from a reliable source can add credibility to a product or service, the opinions of friends, business associates, and family can also help influence a consumer's purchasing decision. By implementing various viral marketing techniques on your Web site, you are provided with a dynamite opportunity to leverage the opinions of the consumers' reference groups. In this chapter, we will cover:

- How you can use viral marketing to increase traffic

- – Word-of-mouth viral marketing

- – Pass-it-on viral marketing

- – Tell a Friend scripts

- • Various ways to leverage your viral m

- • Incentives to encourage viral marketir

Capitalizing on Viral Marketing Opportunities

Viral marketing can be one of your most powerful online marketing techniques. Viral marketing is using the power of associations to spread the word. Viral marketing is still evolving, but today we see three common forms being used:

1. Word of mouth such as "Tell a friend," "Send this coupon to a friend," or "Recommend this to a friend"

2. Pass-it-on, where we receive an e-book, cool tool, or funny video and then forward to friends

3. Product- or service-based where a free tool is used online and that tool includes an embedded marketing message, like Hotmail

Word of Mouth

You can use viral marketing techniques in a number of different ways throughout your Web site. By placing a "Tell a friend about this product" or "Share this page with a friend" button on your site, you enable users to quickly and easily spread the word about your site and your products. Visitors can click on the button, provide appropriate information in the "To" and "From" fields (including name and e-mail address of both the recipient and the sender), and a brief message. Although the message is personalized, your business can include addi-

information about the product, including features, benefits, the ice, and a link directly to the page where the recipient can purchase the item. Since the message is personalized from a friend, the recipient will be more apt to visit the site to find out more about the product than he or she would be if the e-mail came from a traditional corporate e-mail campaign.

Amazon.com (see Figure 4.1) is a prime example of a company that has implemented viral marketing features throughout the site. When visitors browse through Amazon.com's 3 million-plus product listings, they are always presented with the opportunity to "Tell a friend about this product." Providing this feature leverages the effectiveness of the Amazon.com Web site and ultimately results in increased sales for the company.

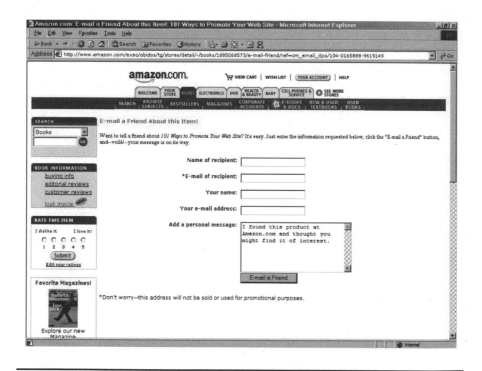

Figure 4.1. Amazon.com leverages the opinions of its customers by incorporating a "Tell a friend about this product" option for all of the products on the Web site.

In addition to the aforementioned techniques, there are many different ways that you can implement viral marketing techniques on your Web site. If you have a newsletter on your site, you can add a "Tell a friend about this newsletter" button on the site. You can also incorporate a message in the body of your e-mail newsletter encouraging readers to forward a copy to friends they think would benefit from the information included in the newsletter. You should also include information in the message on how to subscribe to the newsletter. The recipients will then be able to send a copy of the newsletter to their friends, who will in turn be presented with the opportunity to subscribe and regularly receive the newsletter (see Figure 4.2). The opportunities for viral marketing are endless.

A good word-of-mouth viral marketing strategy enables a visitor to your site or a recipient of your e-mail to share your site or e-mail content with others with just one click of a button or link. The design

Figure 4.2. Including a "Tell a friend" button on your newsletter can encourage readers to forward a copy to their friends.

and placement of that link or button is critical to the success of the campaign.

First of all, you should look to every repeat-traffic generator you have on your site for viral marketing opportunities. Repeat-traffic generators like coupons, newsletters, e-specials, and contests all provide ideal opportunities for "Tell a friend" or "Send a copy to a friend." Once you have determined the viral marketing techniques you are going to use, you will want to make it easy for the site visitor or e-mail recipient to spread the word.

To be effective, you have to make it obvious what you want your visitors to do. Use a call to action to get them to do it. A button with "Send this coupon to a friend" or "Tell a friend about this e-special" works well. Don't assume that people will take the time to open their e-mail program and send an e-mail to a friend about your e-special or coupon or will include the URL to the page on your Web site just because you have a great offer—it doesn't happen! You have to make it easy.

Here are some tips to make your word-of-mouth campaign effective:

- Have a fantastic button or graphic that grabs their attention.

- Provide a call to action telling the visitors what you want them to do.

- Place the button in the appropriate place away from clutter.

- Have the button link to an easy-to-use "Tell a friend" script.
  The "Tell a friend" script accepts the name and e-mail address(es) of the friend(s) and the name and e-mail address of your site visitor that is sending the message to a friend. You need to provide a section for a message. You might provide clickable options for this such as "Thought this might be of interest" or "Knew you'd be interested in this."

- Give clear instructions on how to participate; make it simple, intuitive, and easy.

- Offer an incentive to encourage them to do what you want them to do: "Tell a friend and be included in a drawing for [something of interest to the target market]."

- Leverage, leverage, leverage: "Tell five friends and be included in a drawing for [something of interest to the target market]."

- Avoid using attachments in the message you want spread. This will avoid any potential technical problems with the attachments being opened as well as allaying any fears related to viruses.

- Have your privacy policy posted. If the user is going to pass along a friend's e-mail address, she wants to be assured that you will not abuse the contact information.

The viral marketing will only be successful if the content is good enough or valuable enough to be passed along.

Pass-It-On Viral Marketing

When we find a great resource, a funny video, or a cool game, we usually forward it to our colleagues or friends that we know would be interested in it. This old "they tell two friends and they in turn tell two friends" formula works very effectively online to enable you (with the right content) to reach a tremendous number of your target market.

For this type of viral marketing to be successful, you have to start with great content that recipients will want to share with others. It can take many forms:

- E-books

- Small utility programs

- Fun videos

- Digital games

- Checklists

- A sound bite or **audiozine**

- Articles

The pass-it-on viral marketing methodology works best using small files that can easily be spread around.

E-Books

E-books are very big these days. If you have great content that clearly shows your depth of knowledge on a particular topic, an e-book can do wonders to create great exposure for you, your site, and your products/services. Ensure that you have clear references to you and links to your Web site that provide a reason for people to click-thru. You might provide additional resources on your site or encourage people to visit for copies of other e-books you have developed. Then market, market, market that e-book. Encourage e-zine and newsletter providers to send a copy to their subscribers, and promote through your sig.file, in newsgroups, and in publicly accessible mail lists.

You can provide a shareware or freeware program that would be of interest to your target market. Of course, you will want to ensure that you again appropriately reference your site throughout the program and give them a reason to visit.

Small Utility Programs

You can offer small utility programs for your target market which include your logo. For example if you own a speaker bureau you could offer a small program that helps speakers organize their speaking engagement dates. If you are a car dealer you could offer a small program that reminds car owners of safety inspections, license renewals and scheduled tune ups. If you are a real estate agent you could offer a program that allows the user to calculate amortization on a mortgage. Think of your target market and what might be handy and helpful for them.

Fun Videos

Nothing seems to spread faster on the Web than funny video clips. We've all seen the enraged employee attacking his computer and the bear taking salmon from the fisherman. Sometimes these video clips are cartoons, seen one slide at a time with embedded audio, and other times they seem to be full-scale productions.

Digital Games

If your organization can develop a digital game or you have access to the rights to use a game, incorporate your logo and link back to your Web site within the game. A good game will spread very quickly.

Checklists

If you have a checklist that others might find useful, why not include links to your site in it and then provide it to your target market for use? For example, you might have a great checklist for making your site search engine friendly, or if you are a travel agent you might provide a handy checklist for travel planning. Think about your target market and what they might find useful. Always remember to encourage them to pass it on through viral marketing.

Sound Byte or Audiozine

New technology can send sound bytes. As long as the sound byte is relevant, pertinent, and of value to your target market or people in the industry you serve, people will pass it on.

> **Audiozine**
> A magazine in audio format.

Articles

Writing articles that can be distributed as content for newsletters or e-zines is another form of viral marketing. These articles can also be distributed to be used as Web site content as well. Just make sure that you have clearly stated that others are free to use your article as long as they include it in its entirety verbatim *and* include the Source box. The article should contain links to your site. The Source box should include information on you, your company, and your Web site.

You should track your viral marketing rate of infection. You want to know what is working and how fast it is working. You can always include a graphic in the article or e-book or digital game that is accessed from your site. Then you can use your Web traffic analysis to find information on the effectiveness of your pass-it-on viral marketing campaigns.

Product- or Service-Based Viral Marketing

Two of the most prominent service-based viral marketing campaigns are Hotmail and Blue Mountain.

The Hotmail Example

MSN.com (*http://www.msn.com*) has capitalized on viral marketing to the fullest extent with its Hotmail service. Hotmail is a free e-mail service that is provided by MSN.com and is used by millions of people around the world. Why is a free e-mail account a viral marketing technique? Because whenever a message is sent from a Hotmail account, a tagline is automatically inserted into the body of the e-mail message that tells the user about Hotmail's e-mail service. The message reads as follows:

> *Join the world's largest e-mail service with MSN Hotmail*
> *http://www.hotmail.com.*

This small message results in hundreds of new e-mail accounts being opened daily on the Hotmail Web site. Although Hotmail doesn't provide any commercial services (i.e., they don't sell anything), this viral marketing technique creates mass exposure for the MSN.com Web site. Visitors typically log in to their Hotmail account on the MSN.com Web site, which creates exposure for the other product and service offerings available on MSN.com (see Figure 4.3).

Blue Mountain—Taking Viral Marketing to the Next Level

Blue Mountain (see Figure 4.4), the site that is synonymous with electronic greeting cards or e-cards, is a business that is truly taking viral marketing to the next level. Initially Blue Mountain received thousands of visitors daily who all sent free electronic greeting cards to friends all over the world. Today Blue Mountain still offers this service to the public, although a nominal annual fee is now charged, and it also provides a wide range of gift-purchasing opportunities as well. The following step-by-step guide illustrates how Blue Mountain is attempting to capitalize on its viral marketing strategy.

Initially when you visit the Blue Mountain Web site, you are presented with an array of different options such as e-cards, gifts, paper greeting cards, and downloadable screensavers. When you decide to send a friend an electronic greeting card and finally select a greeting

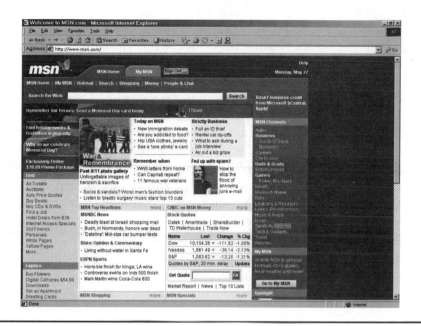

Figure 4.3. Thousands of people access their Hotmail account through the MSN.com Web site every day, thus creating exposure for MSN.com's other product and service offerings.

Figure 4.4. Blue Mountain has one of the largest collections of electronic greeting cards on the Internet.

card from the thousands of cards available on the site, you are asked to fill out the contact information for the individual who will be receiving the card. This process is illustrated in Figure 4.5.

In an attempt to capitalize on the traffic their electronic greeting card service brings, Blue Mountain asks visitors if they would be interested in attaching a gift to this message (as can be seen in Figure 4.6). Blue Mountain has partnered with various online retailers to offer a wide variety of gift products including flowers, chocolates, gift certificates, paper greeting cards, and prepaid calling cards. At the visitor's expense, he or she can easily attach a gift to the electronic greeting card. When recipients receive an electronic greeting card, they are also notified of the gift that they will be receiving via traditional mail. It is at this point that Blue Mountain continues to leverage its viral marketing strategy. The following message appears at the bottom of all Blue Mountain cards that arrive in a recipient's e-mail box:

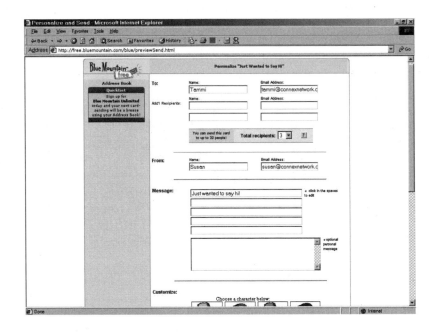

Figure 4.5. Visitors can send electronic greeting cards to multiple recipients on the Blue Mountain site.

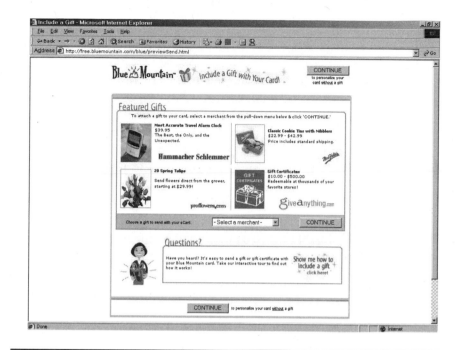

Figure 4.6. Visitors can then purchase and attach real gifts to their electronic greeting card, which are sent to that individual via traditional mail.

What's new on Blue Mountain? See our latest eCards!

http://www.bluemountain.com/new

By including this message, Blue Mountain encourages the recipient to visit the Blue Mountain Web site to reply to the sender with another electronic greeting card. Blue Mountain doesn't miss an opportunity! When a card recipient views the e-card, he or she is provided with a "Reply with an eNote card!" call to action and also a "Send this card to someone else" call to action. This again provides Blue Mountain with the opportunity to sell the individual gift products attached to any e-card that is sent. Through viral marketing, Blue Mountain is able to spread the word about its business quickly and in a cost-efficient manner.

Virtual Postcards

Today a large number of businesses, especially those that are tourism-oriented, are increasing traffic to their sites by offering virtual postcards on their Web site, which enables them to capitalize on viral marketing opportunities. Visitors can send virtual postcards to their family and friends. The postcard should not actually be sent as an attachment, but rather, an e-mail notice is sent saying that a postcard is waiting for them at a particular Web address. By clicking on the Web address, the recipient is sent to the Web site to view the personalized postcard.

An example of this would be Carlson Wagonlit Travel (*http://www.carlsonwagonlit.ca*), a site that gives visitors the opportunity to send their friends colorful postcards via e-mail from different locations around the world (see Figure 4.7). When you send a postcard to your friend, he or she receives an e-mail containing a link to the page where the post-

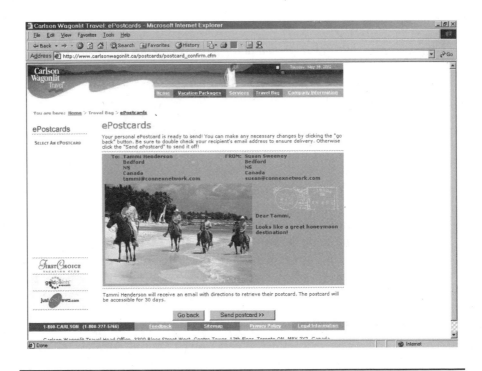

Figure 4.7. Carlson Wagonlit Travel (*http://www.carlsonwagonlit.ca*) offers free virtual postcards to generate exposure for its Web site.

card can be viewed. When your friend clicks thro
card, there is also a Carlson Wagonlit Travel log
sections of the Web site. Offering electronic postc:
generate repeat visitors to your site and to spread
site through the use of viral marketing.

Internet Resources for Chapter 4

I have included a few resources for you to check out regarding viral marketing. For additional resources on a variety of topics, I recommend that you visit the Resources section of my Web site at *http://www. susansweeney.com/resources.html*. There you will find additional tips, tools, techniques, and resources.

Recommend-It.com
http://www.recommend-it.com
A network that helps you drive traffic to your Web site through referrals; it offers incentives for visitors to tell a friend and affiliate opportunities for site owners.

Refer-A-Buddy.com
http://refer-a-buddy.com
A tool that allows you to incorporate a tell-a-friend script into your Web site. A year's subscription to the service is U.S.$15.

Tips for Optimizing Viral Marketing Campaigns
http://www.clickz.com/em_mkt/opt/article.php/837511
A great article on viral marketing and some tips to follow to create an effective campaign.

Various Tell-a-Friend Scripts
http://www.freecode.com/projects/tellafriendscript1/?topic=219,223
http://www.letemknow.com
http://send-a-link.com
http://wwwtoolz.com/scripts/descriptions.asp?a=3

Viral Marketing Case Studies
http://www.viralmarketer.com/vmcases.html

This extensive list of viral marketing case studies provides an in-depth look at many successful online businesses that are leveraging viral marketing opportunities on their Web site.

Viral Marketing Tips
http://www.emage-emarketing.com/viral-marketing.htm
Dr. Ralph Wilson provides some valuable information and tips on how to leverage viral marketing on your Web site in this dynamite article on viral marketing.

5

Permission Marketing

Permission marketing is an important aspect of Internet marketing. When you put forth the additional effort in proactively asking your target market to do something, you will receive a much better response than if you just sit back and "hope they do it." Similarly, if you ask people for their permission to send them materials on a specific topic, and they accept, you do not risk intruding on their privacy. Companies that force content on individuals through the Net hold little credibility in the eyes of their target market—and bad news spreads fast. When you play your cards right, permission marketing can be a valuable asset to any marketing campaign. In this chapter we discuss permission marketing and its uses to provide you with a greater understanding of this topic.

Permission Marketing Explained

Permission boils down to asking your target market and Web site visitors for the authority to perform a specific action—for their permission to do, or send them, something. Many businesses and advertisers compete for the attention of their target market on a daily basis, but it is very difficult to break through all of the advertising clutter. The key to permission marketing is to get your target market to willingly volunteer to participate in the process. In order to do this, whatever it is you are proposing must be of value to your target market—you have to make it clear to the user by answering the question "What's in it for me?" If your target market sees no benefit in participating, then they will not participate—it's that simple.

Chapter 3 discusses many ways to encourage repeat visits to your Web site. Almost every repeat-traffic generator provides an opportunity for permission marketing. Examples would include:

- "We change our coupons every week! Click here to join our mail list to be notified as soon as we update."

- "Click here to join our mail list and receive our bi-weekly Internet marketing tips, tools, techniques, and resources newsletter."

- "We have new specials on a regular basis. Click here to be notified by e-mail when we post our new specials."

- "We have a new contest every three weeks. Keep checking back or Click here if you'd like to be notified by e-mail every time we begin a new contest."

- "We constantly update our Calendar of Events. Keep checking back or Click here if you'd like to be notified by e-mail every time we update."

What makes permission marketing so effective? Permission marketing is not intrusive. Your target market volunteered to receive the information you're sending because it is of interest to them, and as a result they expect to receive it. This significantly increases the likelihood of your target market's viewing the material that has been sent to them and their being receptive of it. When implemented correctly, permission marketing can be a valuable asset in acquiring new customers and maintaining relationships with existing ones. We discuss some of the ways in which you can use permission marketing to increase your online marketing success in the next section.

Uses of Permission Marketing

Permission marketing techniques can be integrated with many Internet marketing tools, including newsletters, surveys, contests, and so on. Chapter 3 covers many repeat traffic and customer loyalty-building tools that you can use on your Web site. Permission marketing is an excellent way to enhance the use of those tools—a few of which are covered in depth in this chapter.

Newsletters are one of the most popular resources for permission marketing. You can ask visitors if they would like to receive notification of new products, updates to your site, relevant tips, advice, industry news, and so on—whatever might be of interest to your target market. People who sign up to receive your newsletter do so because they have a clear interest in what it is you have to say. In your newsletter you can integrate strategic promotional opportunities to encourage users to come back to your site or to take some other course of action. If your newsletter is about recent happenings in your business or new product updates, encourage users to "click here" to see the updates and then, when they do, transport them to your Web site. A newsletter keeps you in front of your target market and constantly reminds them of your presence. Permission marketing opens the door for communication with your target market; this is an important step in building a long-lasting and profitable relationship with them.

Warranty registrations offer you an opportunity to capitalize on permission marketing. On the warranty registration card or online registration form for your product, you can include a section encouraging the consumer to sign up to receive additional information on your products and services. Many software vendors integrate the warranty or user registration process into their software and allow the user to submit it via the Internet once complete. On the registration form, the software vendor will usually ask consumers if they would like to be notified of upgrades to their product or if they would like to receive additional information on new products being released. The consumer would then click "yes" to receive additional information or "no" to not receive any additional information. Users usually will click "yes" because they want to be notified when updates become available. Along with the information they requested, you can include relevant promotional opportunities. The simple act of posing the question increases your chances of capturing your consumers because you have put the idea into their head—something that may not even have crossed their mind beforehand.

Contests and sweepstakes represent another ideal opportunity to put permission marketing to work. In this case, the contest is the primary motivator to encourage people to sign up. The e-mail notification sent out to notify each contestant of the winner can also include promotional material and can encourage people to visit your Web site. In order for people to sign up for your contest, it must be of significant interest to them.

Say, for instance, that you are an online electronics retailer. When consumers visit your site, they could immediately be presented with the opportunity to enter a daily contest to win electronic-related merchandise such as a Rio MP3 Player. There is a direct correlation with the prize being given, the target market, and the purpose of the site, and as a result of the strategic fit, you will likely receive many entrants into the contests.

Once users enter the contest, they should be sent an e-mail confirmation stating that the entry was received. Also include in the e-mail a viral marketing call to action to tell others about the contest as well as a call to action for the user to visit the site and shop around. Referring back to the contest window, directly under the e-mail address entry field should be the option for the visitor to sign up to receive details on the latest hot deals at your site. This is an excellent example of how to combine contests, newsletters, and permission marketing and maximize the opportunity. Not only is the target market encouraged to enter the contest, but they are also encouraged to sign up for the hot deals newsletter while their interest is piqued.

Privacy Concerns

When used correctly, permission marketing can be a very rewarding and cost-effective means of promotion; however, if you make ill use of this technique, you can do more harm than good. In order to avoid this pitfall, remember that you should never send your target market anything that they did not ask to receive, and you should never use their personal information for anything other than what they were told they were signing up for.

If you send your target market information they did not ask for, they will consider it spam. If you use their personal information for anything other than what your visitors expect, you could find yourself in bad public light as well as in significant legal trouble. Misuse of permission marketing also damages your relationship with your target market because you have violated their trust. This can also lead to bad publicity as the target market will be very likely to turn around and tell many of their friends and associates about their bad experience with your company, ultimately resulting in lost business for you.

Companies that are successful in their permission marketing endeavors tend to leverage their campaign by prominently displaying their privacy and security policies. People like to know how their personal information will be handled and are very reluctant to hand over their details to a company or organization that does not explain how their information will be used. Privacy and security policies help in building trust and confidence with your target market. These days, people are inundated with junk e-mail and are reluctant at the best of times to provide their e-mail address. You will miss out on a lot of permission marketing opportunities if you don't prominently display and clearly state your privacy policy.

Personalization

When asking permission to communicate with your target market, you want to make it easy. Don't have visitors complete a long form on which they have to provide all kinds of information. At this point, less is better. Have a simple form on which they provide their e-mail address and their first name. You want the first name so that you can personalize your communication. Most mail list software programs these days allow you to easily personalize the text in the body of the message you are sending and also the text in the subject line. You will want to use a software program that manages all the permissions— the unsubscribes as well as the subscribes. See Chapter 13 on private mail list marketing for details.

Sell the Benefits

When you are asking permission to communicate with someone on an ongoing basis, you need to sell the benefits. People are inundated with junk e-mail and need to be "sold" on why they should subscribe to or join your communication list. "Join our weekly newsletter" just doesn't cut it. "Join our weekly newsletter to receive our Internet-only specials, coupons, and tips from our pro" will get you more subscribers. You have to know your target market well and know what would be enticing enough to get that permission (see Figure 5.1).

Data Mining

Data mining is sorting through data to identify patterns and establish relationships. Over time, you may want to ask a question or two in an

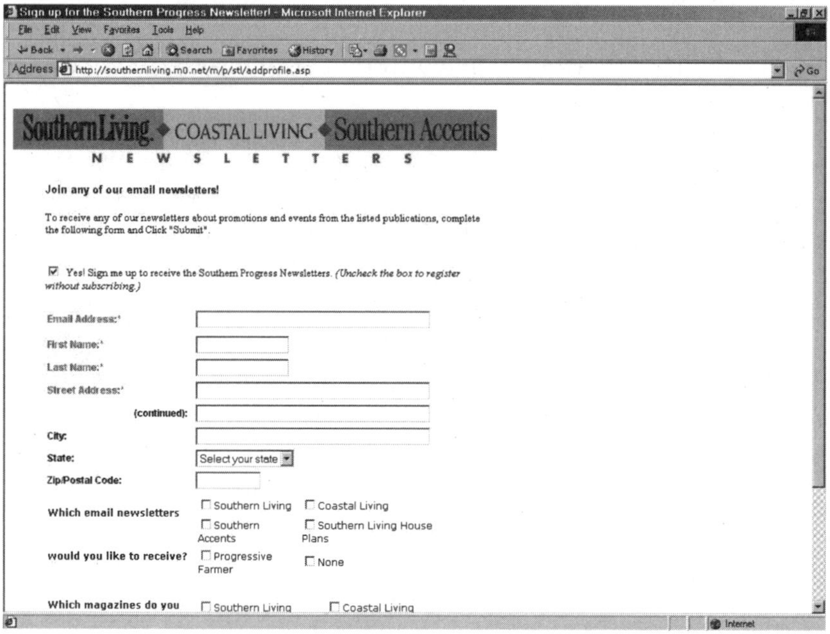

Figure 5.1.   Southern Progress allows you to sign up for their various newsletters about promotions and events.

appropriate manner to learn more about your subscribers so that you can target your communication with them a little better (see Figure 5.2).

Cooperative Permission Marketing

Cooperative marketing is starting to take hold on the Internet. Look for opportunities to form an alliance with other sites that are trying to reach the same target market you are, and then see how you can do some win–win marketing. For example, if you have a monthly newsletter, you can allow subscribers to sign up to receive alliance partners' newsletters at the same time they sign up to receive yours. In return, your alliance partners do the same. The same can be done for many repeat-traffic generators like coupons, e-specials, e-zines, etc. Get innovative.

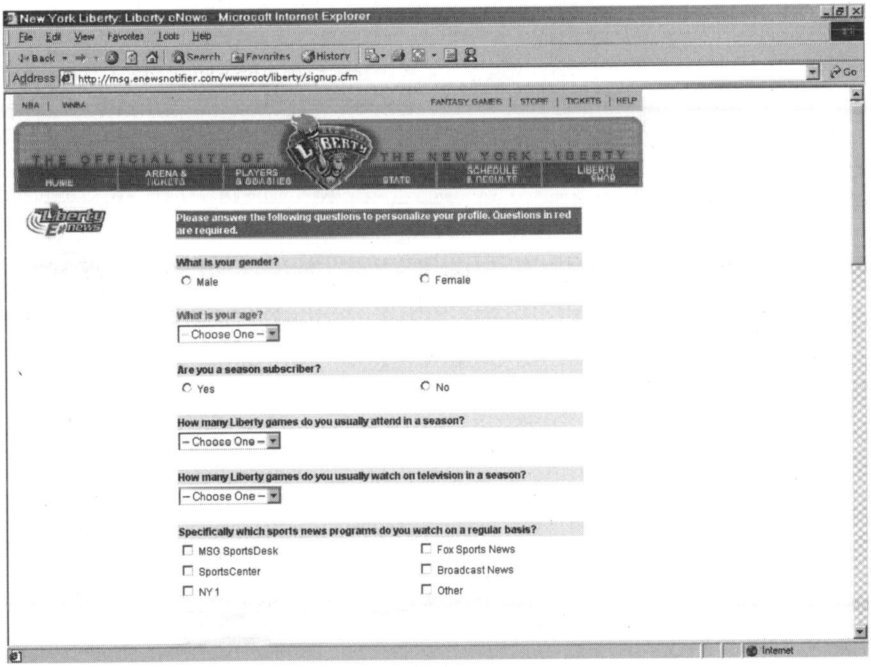

Figure 5.2. The New York Liberty basketball team's Web site asks subscribers questions so they can learn more about their target market.

Incentive Based Permission Marketing

To increase the response to any permission marketing opportunity, you might consider offering an incentive: "Sign up to receive our Internet-only e-specials and be included in a drawing for [something of interest to your target market]."

You can also offer a free gift to new e-members or subscribers. It could be a sample of one of your products or an e-book on a topic of interest to your target market.

A Closing Comment on Permission Marketing

Permission marketing adds leverage to online marketing campaigns. Once you are in front of your target market, you want to take every opportunity to stay there and continue to communicate with them time and time again. Permission marketing helps you achieve this, but it is a game of give and take. You give them a reason to give you permission to send them e-mail; they provide you with the permission and their personal information; you provide them with valuable content. There is a trade-off and the cycle continues. Over time, you will gain more knowledge about your target market, which will empower you to provide them with a better overall experience in dealing with your company through more-targeted promotions and better fulfillment of customer needs.

Why should you use permission marketing? To summarize, permission marketing can return a much higher response rate over intrusive advertising; it can increase sales, build your brand, and help develop relationships with your target market; and it is cost-effective.

Internet Resources for Chapter 5

I have included a few resources for you to check out regarding permission marketing. For additional resources on a variety of topics, I recommend that you visit the Resources section of my Web site at *http://www.susansweeney.com/resources.html*. There you will find additional tips, tools, techniques, and resources.

Canadian Marketing Association
http://www.the-cma.org
The Canadian Marketing Association represents information-based marketers—those who reach consumers through media such as the Internet, television, telephone, radio, and addressed advertising mail. CMA provides a voice for responsible marketers and has earned a reputation for leadership in the area of self-regulation with respect to consumer protection, privacy, electronic commerce, and marketing to children.

ClickZ: Permission Marketing
http://www.clickz.com/mkt/permis_mkt/index.php
You should look at ClickZ's section on permission marketing, updated weekly by Nick Usborne.

DM Review: Customer Relationship Report: Interruption versus Permission Marketing
http://www.dmreview.com/master.cfm?NavID=55&EdID=2812
An interesting article on the benefits of permission marketing.

ENewsNotifier
http://www.relevantmarketingtechnologies.com
This is a powerful permission marketing solution that allows you to set up and maintain your permission marketing campaign. Worth checking out. Some of its users include *Esquire* magazine, the Dallas Symphony, and the New York Knicks.

MessageMedia: Ten Rules for Permission-Based E-mail Marketing
http://www.messagemedia.com/rc/ten_guides.shtml
MessageMedia primarily delivers e-mail marketing, online customer intelligence, and online customer care services. This is an article from the resource center on its site pertaining to the guidelines companies should follow when developing permission-based e-mail marketing campaigns.

Permission Marketing
http://www.fastcompany.com/online/14/permission.html
This is an interesting article on permission marketing by FastCompany.com's editor, William Taylor.

Seth Godin's Web Site

http://www.sethgodin.com/sg/index.html

Seth Godin is author of four books that have been bestsellers around the world and have changed the way people think about marketing, change, and work. His book *Permission Marketing* was an Amazon.com Top 100 bestseller for a year and a *Fortune* Best Business Book, and it spent four months on the *Business Week* bestseller list. It also appeared on the *New York Times* business book bestseller list. Check out his site for lots of info on permission marketing.

The Direct Marketing Association

http://www.the-dma.org

This is the Web site of The Direct Marketing Association, the leading direct-marketing organization.

6

Designing Your Site to Be Search Engine Friendly

When Internet users are looking for a particular product, service, subject, or information pertaining to an area of interest to them, how do they do it? The most common search tool used is the search engine. Because search engines can bring significant volumes of traffic to your site, you must understand how the major search engines work and how the design of your site can influence the indexing of your site by the search engines. When people conduct Internet searches, they rarely go beyond the first few pages of results. If you want to be noticed, you will need to appear in the top 20 search results. But before you submit to the search engines, you have to be sure your site has been designed to be search engine friendly. In this chapter, we cover:

- The methodology to make your site search engine friendly

- The key elements of Web site design to accommodate search engines

- Using your competition and industry leaders as guidance

- The all-important content

- The importance of keywords in all aspects of your Web site

- Meta-tags and how to optimize them for search engine placement

Methodology to Make Your Site Search Engine Friendly

To make your site search engine friendly, you have to:

- Decide which search engines are critical for your success

- Learn as much as you can about their ranking criteria and the weighting given to each criterion in their algorithm

Then you must:

- Determine the keywords that your target market is using in the search engines to find what you have to offer

- Assign those keywords to specific pages throughout your site, and then

- Populate the pages with the assigned keywords in the appropriate places given the ranking criteria for your targeted search engines

The remainder of this chapter walks you step by step through this process.

Understanding Search Engines

BOTS
Programs used by search engines to search the Internet for pages to index.

Search engines use programs or intelligent agents, called **bots,** to actually search the Internet for pages, which they index using specific parameters as they read the content. The agent will read the information on every page of your site and will then follow the links. For example, AltaVista's spider continually crawls the Web looking for sites to index and, of course, indexes sites upon their submission. Inktomi also uses a spider; however, a user cannot search

Inktomi's information directly. Instead, the user will submit its site to other search engines and directories that use Inktomi's search engine technology. Inktomi is very important in the search engine community, so be sure your site is easily accessible to its spider. Spiders are described in more detail later in this chapter. A detailed discussion on submissions to search engines and directories can be found in Chapter 7.

Registering with search engines is fairly simple. In most cases, you simply submit your URL or Internet address on their submission form. Even if your URL is not registered with search engines, a number of the major search engines will eventually find you since their bots are continually roaming the Internet looking for new sites to index. There are millions of sites out there, so I suggest that you be proactive and register your site to ensure a speedier listing. Once you are registered, some of the bots will periodically visit your site looking for changes and updates.

A common problem faced by Internet marketers is how to influence search engines to index their site appropriately and how to ensure that their site appears when people use relevant search criteria. Many of the interesting and creative sites on the Internet are impossible to find because they are not indexed with the major search engines. The majority (85 percent) of Internet users employ search engines or directories to find what they are looking for on the Web. They do this by typing in a keyword or phrase that represents what they are looking for. The following sections explore how to make your Web site more search engine friendly.

Many search engines and directories either partner with or license the use of another search engine's or directory's search technology. If you submit your site to a search engine that uses Inktomi's index, then the design of your site influences how you're indexed in all search engines that rely on Inktomi for their search results. In a similar fashion, you will find other search engine and directory data intermixed or included in some form with another search engine's or directory's data.

When designing your site, you must always keep the search engines in mind. Something as simple as a drop-down menu on your site can cause problems with the search engines and the indexing of your site if implemented incorrectly. You want to do everything you can to ensure that your site is designed to meet the needs of your target audience while remaining completely search engine friendly. Search engines can produce a significant amount of traffic to your site if you can manage to be placed in the top search results.

Decide Which Search Engines Are Important

To start this process, you want to decide which search engines you are going to be concerned about when taking the necessary steps to rank high in their search results. You are going to limit your selection to those search engines that are not "pay to play." (Ranking high in the pay-to-play search engines is discussed in the next chapter.) You will want to select a number of the most popular search engines for your concentration. You will also limit the number to 8 to 12 search engines. You can find the most popular search engines by doing your research online through sites like Search Engine Watch (*http://www. searchenginewatch.com*) or Search Engine Showdown (*http://www. searchengineshowdown.com*). You can keep up with what's happening in the search engines by joining one of the discussion lists on the topic. I recommend I-Search (*http://www.adventive.com*), published and moderated by Detlev Johnson, a leading search engine expert.

Learn the Search Engine Ranking Criteria

Each search engine has its own unique ranking criteria and its own unique algorithm or formula giving different weighting to each criterion in the formula. For the search engines that you have decided to focus on, you have to learn as much as you can about their ranking criteria and relative weighting.

The search engines are all fighting for market share. The more market share a search engine has, the more valuable the company is. To gain market share, a search engine has to provide better results than its competition. It is for this reason that the search engines are changing and improving their formulas on an ongoing basis. You have to keep up with changes in these formulas; tweak your site accordingly and resubmit when necessary.

The search engines use different databases for their search results. They have different algorithms or formulas for their ranking. They have different weighting for the various elements within their formula. They change their formulas over time, and they change their ranking over time. Sound complicated?

At the time this book was written, AltaVista used the following databases:

- LookSmart

- Open Directory

AltaVista's formula looked for keywords in:

- The page title

- The first line of text

- Keyword meta-tag

- Description meta-tag

- Comments tag

- Header

Other elements in its formula included:

- Link popularity

- Link relevancy

Excite used the LookSmart database, and its ranking formula looked for keywords in the page title and throughout the text on the page.

Google used the Open Directory database. Its ranking formula looked for the keywords in the visible text (not in the meta-tags) and gave a very heavy weighting to the link popularity, with extra points for quality of links and relevancy of text around the links.

HotBot used the following databases:

- Open Directory

- Direct Hit

- Inktomi

HotBot's ranking formula looked for keywords in:

- The page title

- The keyword meta-tag

- The description meta-tag

- Text on the page

See Appendix C for some information on specific search engine ranking criteria.

There are a number of common places that the search engines look for keywords:

- Domain names

- Page titles

- Page text

- Keyword meta-tags

- Description meta-tags

- Comments tags

- Alt tags

- Headers

More and more of the search engines are giving heavy weighting to link popularity—the number of links to your site from other sites on the Internet. The search engines are getting very sophisticated in the weighting of link popularity, with some search engines giving extra points for link relevancy—how high the site with the link to your site would rank for the same keyword. Other points are awarded based on the keywords around the link. For strategies on generating significant links to your site, see Chapter 15.

Keywords Are Critical

Keywords are an important aspect of every Web page because the search engines use keywords in determining your site's ranking, and these are the words people are most likely to use when they're searching for your site. Selecting the right combination of keywords for each page on your site is critical to your success. When creating your keyword list, don't use just nouns. Think of descriptive words that may be associated with benefits of your products or services. For example, if your site offers information on weight loss, then some of your keywords may be "weight," "weight loss," "diet," "exercise," "nutrition," and so on. You can also add some keywords that describe advantages a person may receive from visiting your site, such as "thin," "slim," "healthy," "in shape," and so forth.

When determining what your keywords will be, always keep the customers or your target visitors in mind. Try to think as they would if they were to do a search for information on your topic. Don't just think about what people would do to find your site, but what they would do if they didn't know your company existed and were looking for the types of products and services you provide. If you find this a difficult exercise, then ask around. Talk to both people that know about your business and people that don't. Ask what keywords they would use to find a site like yours.

Start by taking your corporate materials, brochures, and other marketing materials and indiscriminately highlighting any words that individuals might search on if they are looking for products or services the company has to offer. Record these words in a text document in your word-processing program.

Next, edit the list by deleting words that either are too generic (for example, "business") or are not appropriate for keyword purposes. Review each word and ask yourself if people would search using that word if they were looking for your products or services.

Always use the plural when forming your keywords. (Adding an "s" forms the plural.) If you list "game" as your keyword and someone uses "games" to do a search, then your site will not be found. If you include the word "games" in your keywords and someone requests information on the word "game," then your site will be found because "game" is part of the word "games." Don't use both versions because you're then running the risk of spamming the search engines, and you want to be able to use other keywords to increase your chances of achieving high rankings. The only time it is appropriate to use both the singular and the plural is if the plural does not include the singular in its entirety; for example, "dairy" and "dairies"—in that case, you should list both the singular and the plural as part of your keyword list. It is also important to note that when most people perform their searches, they will use the plural version. You're more likely to search for "computers" than you are to search for "computer."

Now, reorganize the words in order of importance. By having the most important words first, no matter how many keywords the particular directory will allow, you are ready to submit—simply copy and paste the keywords onto the directory's form.

Now you have a good master keyword list. Different directories allow different numbers of keywords to be submitted. Because you have organized your list with the most important words first, you simply include as many of your keywords as the directory will allow. When a directory will allow multiple submissions for the same URL, you might consider submitting as many times as it takes to include all your keywords. You won't have to change your description or other information every time, just the keywords.

If you plan to submit every page of your site, your master list provides a valuable document. For each page that you are indexing, take a copy of the comprehensive list and delete words that are not appropriate for that particular page. Then reprioritize the remaining keywords based on the content of the page you are indexing. This is then the keyword list for that particular page. Repeat this procedure for every page you will be indexing. This is also a great procedure when you are developing the keyword meta-tag for each page of your site.

There is often the question as to whether to include your competitor's name in your keywords. This follows the premise that if someone searches for them, they will find you as well. My position on this is NO. Due to the fact that several of the search engines read only the first 200 characters for keywords, you would be losing vital space to include keywords that describe or even name a competitor's products or services. In addition, there have been recent legal battles regarding the use of competitors' names within one's keywords.

Keep in Touch with the Trends

There are a number of services available that can help you select the most appropriate keywords for your site. These services base their suggestions on results from actual search queries. WordSpot (*http://www.wordspot.com*) and Wordtracker (*http://www.wordtracker.com*) are two such examples. Wordtracker references a number of sources including Infoseek, Google, Lycos, Yahoo!, and AltaVista for its suggestions and comparisons.

Assign Specific Keywords to Specific Pages

The next step is to allocate specific keywords you have determined are appropriate for your site for search engine purposes to specific pages. You will then populate each page in the appropriate places with the assigned keyword. You do this because you want to ensure that no matter which appropriate keyword or keyword phrase your target market decides to search on, one of the pages on your site is likely to rank in the first couple of pages of search results.

Many sites populate all their pages with the same keywords in the hopes that one of their pages will rank high in the search results. They use the same meta-tags for every page on their site. This is the same as buying 100 tickets on the lottery but selecting the same numbers for every single ticket.

When you have allocated your keywords to the various pages on your site, you will populate or include the keyword assigned in the following places for that particular page:

- Your page title

- The first 200 to 250 characters of your page

- the beginning, middle, and end of your page text

- Between the <NOFRAMES> tags if frames are used on your site

- In "alt" attributes

- In the keywords meta-tag

- In the description meta-tag

- In the comments tag

- In any page <H1>headers</H1> used

- In your domain name

Some search engines rank sites by how early the keyword appears on the site. The earlier a keyword is mentioned on your site, the higher your site may be positioned in search results. And remember the points made earlier: Though you don't want to repeat a keyword hundreds of times (some search engines are on to this), you do want to repeat keywords a number of times on each page of your site.

You can check the effectiveness of your keyword placement and utilization by using Web traffic analysis reports, discussed fully in Chapter 27. You can use Web traffic analysis reports to determine what sites are referring people to you. You can strip down this information further to view only search engine referrals. By looking at this information, you can see exactly what keywords people are using to find you, and you can alter the keywords used based on this information. Refining your keywords is one of the key elements to success—you're letting the search engines tell you what you're doing right and what you could be doing better.

Know Your Competition

Check out your competition. I use the term *competition* very loosely. I mean your industry's leaders (whether or not you compete directly)—people who are selling noncompeting products to your target market, as well as your direct competitors. Search their names and see what they are using for descriptions and keywords. Next, search using some of your keywords and see what sites receive top rankings. This research will illustrate why they have received such a high ranking—and you can incorporate what you've learned into your Web site or doorway page for that search engine or directory.

What does this mean? No one knows exactly how each search engine works, but by searching for your most important keywords and observing what the top-ranking sites are using with respect to their page content, title tags, description meta-tags, keywords meta-tags, and so on, you can formulate a good plan of attack. Remember that if you don't appear in the first two or three pages of search results, it is unlikely that prospective visitors will access your site through the search engine.

Check to see what meta-tags your competitors have. Not only can you learn from the sites that catch your eye, you can also learn from your competitors' mistakes. After you have done a thorough job of this market research, you will be in a good position to develop a description that is catchy and adequately describes your site.

To check your competition's meta-tags in Microsoft Internet Explorer, you simply go to their site, then click on "View" from your menu bar and select "Source" from the drop-down menu. This will bring up the source code for that respective page in whatever your default text browser is. For most people this will be Notepad. Looking for the same information in Netscape is just as easy. From the menu bar, select "View" and then select "Page Source" from the drop-down menu.

Use Descriptive Page Titles

Each of the pages in your Web site should be given a title. The title is inserted between the title tags in the header of an HTML document. Title tag information identifies and describes your pages. Titles can tell readers where the information contained on a page originated. Most Web browsers, such as Netscape, display a document's title in the top line of the screen. When users print a page from your Web site, the title usually appears at the top of the page at the left. When someone bookmarks your site, the title appears as the description in his or her bookmark file. These are all reasons that it is important that a page's title reflects an accurate description of the page.

Go through every page of your Internet site, bookmark each one, and check that your titles represent each page clearly without being lengthy. Longer page titles can dilute the relevancy of your keywords. Keeping your page titles brief (five to ten words or fewer) will increase the potency of your keywords and earn your pages higher search engine rankings. Also, keep in mind that Internet Explorer will bookmark approximately 50 characters, whereas Netscape bookmarks around 40. Your page titles should always identify your company.

Match the keywords you use in your meta-tags with the words you use in your page titles. Search engines check page titles, meta-tags, and page content for keywords. Your pages will be more relevant, and therefore will place higher in the search engines, for certain keywords if these keywords appear in each of these three sections. Position your keywords near the beginning of your page titles to increase your keyword relevancy.

Some of the search engines will retrieve your page, look at your title, and then look at the rest of your page for keywords that match those found in the title. Many search engines use title tags as one of the elements in their algorithm to determine search engine ranking. Among the search engines that use page titles in their ranking criteria are AltaVista, Excite, Google, HotBot, NorthernLight, WebCrawler, and Yahoo!. Pages that have keywords in the title are seen as more relevant than similar pages on the same subject that don't, and may thus be ranked in a higher position by the search engines. However, don't make your title a string of keywords like "cuisine, French cuisine, imported food, ..." because this will likely be considered spam by the search engines and you will end up worse off in the rankings or be removed altogether. Also keep in mind that people will see that title in the search results, and they're more likely to click on a site that has a title that flows and is descriptive—not a list.

Page Text

You want to ensure that the keyword you have assigned to a specific page appears in the first 200 characters on that page as close to the beginning as possible. Keep in mind that the search engine cannot read text that is embedded in an image or graphic. The assigned keyword should appear at the beginning of the text on the page, in the middle, and at the end.

The assigned keyword should be repeated appropriately five times throughout the text on the page. Make sure that this is done so that the document still reads well. It should not be apparent that you are keyword stuffing.

Search Engines' Use of Alt Tags

Some search engines will include information within "Alt tags" when they form the description for your site and in the ranking of your site. Alt tags appear after an image tag and contain a phrase that is associated with the image. Ensure that your Alt tags contain the keywords assigned to the particular page wherever you can. This gives your page a better chance of being ranked higher in the search engines' directories. For example:

> *<image src="logo.gif" alt="Game Nation—Computer Games Logo">*

You do not want your Alt tags to look something like "Game Nation" or "Company Logo" because this does not include any keywords. Be sure you apply proper Alt tags to all images on your site to achieve best results. Keep in mind that users who browse with graphics disabled must be able to navigate your site, and proper use of Alt tags will assist them in doing so.

Guiding the Search Engines with Meta-Information

As we noted earlier in this chapter, a common problem faced by Internet marketers is how to influence search engines to index their site appropriately and how to ensure that their site appears when people use relevant search criteria. The majority of Internet users employ search engines or directories to find Web sites, which they do by typing in a keyword or phrase that represents what they are looking for.

Retaining a certain measure of control over how search engines deal with your Web site is a major concern. Often Web sites do not take advantage of the techniques available to them to influence search engine listings. Most search engines evaluate the "Meta-HTML" tags in conjunction with other variables to decide where to index Web pages based on particular keyword queries.

The Web Developer's Virtual Library defines a Meta-HTML tag as follows:

> *"The META element is used within the <u>HEAD</u> element to embed document meta-information not defined by other*

HTML elements. The META element can be used to identify properties of a document (e.g., author, expiration date, a list of keywords, etc.) and assign values to those properties."

An HTML tag is used in the Head area of a document to specify further information about the document, either for the local server or for a remote browser. The Meta-element is used within the Head element to embed document Meta-information not defined by other HTML elements. Such information can be extracted by servers/clients for use in identifying, indexing, and cataloging specialized document Meta-information. In addition, HTTP servers can read the contents of the document Head to generate response headers corresponding to any elements defining a value for the attribute HTTP-EQUIV. This provides document authors with a mechanism for identifying information that should be included in the response headers of an HTTP request.

To summarize this lengthy definition, meta-information can be used in identifying, indexing, and cataloging. This means you can use these tags to guide the search engines in displaying your site as the result of a query.

Meta and Header Elements

A header without meta-information will look like this:

- <url1><html>

- <url1><head>

- <title>Game Nation—Gaming Software Specialists</title>

- </head>

If you want your site to be displayed properly in search engines, you should create a header as follows:

- <url1><HTML>

- <url1><HEAD>

- <TITLE>Document Title Here</TITLE>

- <url1><META-NAME="keywords" CONTENT="keyword1, keyword2, keyword3">

- <url1><META-NAME="description" CONTENT="200-character site description goes here">

- <url1><META-NAME="robots" CONTENT="index, follow">

- <url1><!—Comments Tag, repeat description here?>

- <url1><HEAD> indicates the beginning of the header, and the ending of the header is marked by </HEAD>

- <url2><TITLE> indicates the title of the page. The end of the title is marked by </TITLE>, which is called the closing tag

<META-NAME="keywords" CONTENT="..."> tells search engines under which keywords to index your site. When a user types one of the words you listed here, your site should be displayed as a result. A space must be used to separate the words. Do not repeat any of the words more than five times. (Many of the bots will not recognize repeated words). And you should list the most important words first, because some bots read only the first 200 characters. You should create a keywords tag for each page of your site listing appropriate keywords for each separate page.

<META-NAME="description" CONTENT="..."> should be added to every page of your site. It is used to provide an accurate description of the page to which it is attached. Keep the description under 200 characters or it may be cut off when displayed by the search engines.

<META-NAME="robots" CONTENT="..."> tells certain bots to follow or not follow hypertext links. The W3 Consortium white paper on spidering (spiders are defined below) offers the following definition and discussion:

- <url1><META-NAME="ROBOTS" CONTENT="ALL | NONE | NOINDEX | NOFOLLOW">

- <url1>default = empty = "ALL" "NONE" = "NOINDEX, NOFOLLOW"

- <url1>The filler is a comma-separated list of terms:

  - <url1>ALL, NONE, INDEX, NOINDEX, FOLLOW, NOFOLLOW

Note: This tag is meant to provide users who cannot control the robots.txt file at their sites. It provides a last chance to keep their content out of search services. It was decided not to add syntax to allow robot-specific permissions within the META-tag. INDEX means that robots are welcome to include this page in search services.

FOLLOW means that robots are welcome to follow links from this page to find other pages. A value of NOFOLLOW allows the page to be indexed, but no links from the page are explored. (This may be useful if the page is a free entry point into pay-per-view content, for example. A value of NONE tells the robot to ignore the page.)

The values of INDEX and FOLLOW should be added to every page unless there is a specific reason that you do not want your page to be indexed. This may be the case if the page is only temporary.

Comments Tag

<!—Comments Tag, repeat description here?—!> is a tag that is read by the Excite and Magellan spiders. A spider is an artificial intelligence agent that reads all of the information on a page and develops a "page description." The comments tag can be used to trick a spider into displaying an accurate description of your pages. The description that a spider creates without this tag often may not be pleasing, and usually doesn't depict what your pages are actually about.

Significance of Your URL

Where possible, apply keywords in your URL. Some search engines give higher rankings to sites that do.

Be sure that you own your own domain name. If your site is listed as a subdirectory on your ISP or Web host's domain, the search engines will not give you as much credibility. You don't want your site to be "*http://www.yourhostsdomain/companies/yourcompany.htm.*" You want to be registered under your own domain, such as "*www.yourcompany.com*" or "*www.keywordorkeywords.com.*" Google prefers domain names that match the keyword being searched for. Try searching for "mp3" on Google. What are the results? The number one result and likely most of the other top results all include mp3 in their domain name. Try a couple of other searches as well—maybe "real," for example. I'll bet Real Networks' home page is the one that comes up first.

Try to use keywords in your subpages where possible. For example, if you sell golf clubs, then you may want to have a subpage named "golf-clubs.htm" or "golf_clubs.htm." (It would appear in your URL as "*http://www.yourdomain/directory/golf_clubs.htm*" instead of a generic subpage named "page1.htm." An important thing to remember here is that some of the search engines can't tell that two keywords exist if you join the words together in your subpage, like "golfclubs.htm." Be sure you separate the keywords with either an underscore (_) or a dash (-). Using these little tips can go a long way in helping you achieve success among the search engines; it certainly helps with Yahoo!.

Site Content Revisited and Other Important Design Factors

To achieve optimum results, I recommend that you design your site content carefully. You want to apply the most important keywords near the beginning of your page because many search engines weigh the content near the start of a site as the most important.

Always have a descriptive paragraph at the top of your Web page. Search engines that do not use meta-tags will use this as their source for a site description and keywords on your site. In addition, search engines will use the content found within the opening paragraph in determining the ranking of your site among search results. Again, be sure to use the most important keywords first, preferably within the first two or three sentences. This is hugely important. Infoseek and AltaVista boost pages that use well-placed keywords near the top of the page content. Make sure that the keywords you use flow naturally within the content of the opening paragraph and relate to the content and purpose of your site. You don't want the search engines to think you're trying to cram in words where they don't fit.

Use your HTML <H1>headers</H1> effectively to indicate the subject and content of a particular page. Most people use them only as a method of creating large fonts. Some search engines, including Google, use the content included within the header text in their relevancy scoring.

As you can tell, textual HTML content is extremely important to the search engines, which brings me to my next point. Never create a page that is excessive in graphical content. For example, don't display information as a graphic file that should be displayed in text. I've seen this done numerous times. A site may have the best opening statement in the world, but the search engines can't use it because the information is presented in the form of a graphic. No matter how great it looks, the search engines can't read your graphics for content.

Do not make your home page excessively lengthy. The longer your page is, the less relevant the information on the page becomes to the search engines. I recommend that you keep your home page short and to the point. Of course, not every technique is going to work all of the time, so you might want to investigate creating doorway pages. AltaVista seems to like pages that are somewhat longer in length.

Little things like how often you update your site can have an effect on how well your site places in search engine results. Spiders can determine how often a page is updated and will revisit your site accordingly. This may lead to higher rankings in some of the major search engines. Remember, you can also resubmit your site manually once you have made changes; however, I don't advise doing so if you already have a high ranking. If the criteria used for ranking a site have changed, you may actually end up worse off.

Before you submit your site, be sure the content on the page you're submitting is completed. Yahoo!, for one, will ignore your submission if you have an "under construction" or similar sign on your page.

Additional Design Techniques

Doorway pages, also known as gateway pages and bridge pages, are pages that lead to your site but are not considered part of your site. Doorway pages are focused pages that lead to your Web site but are tuned to the specific requirements of the search engines. By having different doorway pages with different names (e.g., indexa.html for AltaVista or indexg.html for Google) for each search engine, you can look back and see which page is bringing in the most traffic. Those pages that are not bringing in the traffic can then be edited and resubmitted until you get it right.

Due to the need to be ranked high in search engine results and the enormous competition among sites that are trying to get such high listings, doorway pages increasingly have become more popular. Each search engine is different and has different elements in its ranking criteria. Developing doorway pages allows you to tailor a page specifically for each search engine before submitting to achieve optimal results. Be careful, though; some search engines frown upon the use of doorway pages, so check before creating and submitting one. There are a number of sources online that offer advice for developing dynamite doorway pages. A good place to start is Search Engine Watch, listed in the Resources section of this chapter.

Frames

From a marketing perspective, you should avoid **frames** when developing your Web site. Frames may result in some search engines' being unable to index pages within your site, or they can result in improper pages being indexed. Also, many people simply prefer sites that do not use frames. Frames also cause problems when someone wants to bookmark or add to their favorites a particular page within a framed site. Usually only the home page address is shown.

> **Frames**
> The division of a browser's display area into two or more independent areas.

What I mean by "improper pages being indexed" is that content pages will be indexed, and when the search engines direct users to these content pages, they will likely not be able to navigate your site because the navigation frame probably will not be visible. To prevent this, one technique you can use is a Robots meta-tag in the head section of your HTML that does not allow bots to proceed beyond your home page. As a result, though, you can really submit only your home page, which means you have less of a chance of receiving the high rankings you need on the major search engines. Alternatively, you should include textual links to all major sections within your site to accommodate those users who enter your site on a page other than a home page, and to assist the search engines with indexing your site.

Some search engines can only read information between the <NOFRAMES> tags within your master frame. The master frame identifies the other frames. All too often the individuals who apply frames ignore the <NOFRAMES> tags, which is a BIG no-no. If you do not have any text between the <NOFRAMES> tags, then the search engines that reference your site for information will have nothing to look at. This will result in your site's being listed with little or no information in the indexes, or you will be listed so far down in the rankings that no one will ever find you anyway. To remedy this situation, insert textual information that contains your most important descriptive keywords between the <NOFRAMES> tags. This will give the search engines something they can see, and it also helps those users who are browsing with non–frame-compatible browsers.

Now that the search engines have found you, you still have a problem. They can't go anywhere. Create a link within your <NOFRAMES> tags to allow search engines and users with non-frame-compatible browsers to get into your site. Frames are a headache when designing your site to be search engine friendly. To make your life easier and from a marketing perspective, it's better to avoid them altogether.

Dynamic Pages and Special Characters

CGI (Common Gateway Interface) Programs used to enable Web servers to interact with users.

Don't bother submitting to the search engines those pages that consist of **CGI** content or have question marks (?) in the URL. Search engines simply won't index them. In addition, some search engines such as Lycos will not index sites with the ampersand (&) or percent sign (%) character.

Meta-Refresh

Have you ever visited a site and then been automatically transported to another page within the site? This is the result of a **meta-refresh tag**. This tag is an HTML document that is designed to automatically re-

place itself with another HTML document after a certain
specified period of time, as defined by the document author. Now that I've mentioned this, don't use them. Search
engines generally do not like meta-refresh tags. Infoseek
will not add sites that use a fast meta-refresh. If you do use
a meta-refresh tag to redirect users, then it is suggested that
you set a delay of at least seven seconds and provide a link
on the new page back to the page they were taken from. Some businesses use meta-refresh tags to redirect users from a page that is obso-
lete or is no longer there. Meta-refresh tags also may be used to give an
automated slideshow.

> **Meta-refresh**
> A tag used to
> automatically
> reload or load a
> new page.

Splash Pages and the Use of Rich Media

A splash page is basically an opening page that leads into a site. Often
splash pages consist of a Java or a Macromedia Flash intro that can be
slow to load for some users.

Some Web sites use splash screens that consist of an eye-pleasing
image and an invitation to enter the site. Many splash pages implement
techniques that automatically send you to the home page once you've
seen the splash page, and others will invite you to "Click to enter" in
some form or another. Why do people use splash pages on their sites?
For one, they usually look beautiful. Another reason is to provide the
user with something to look at while images or content for the home
page loads in the background. Individuals also use splash pages as a
means of advertising. Splash pages are usually very attractive in appearance, but they often lack content relevant to search engines.

If you do use a splash page on your site, be sure you include the
proper meta-tags within your HTML header. This is important so that
search engines that use meta-tags can access this information. This ultimately affects your ranking and how your site is displayed to users in
the search results. If possible, include a paragraph or statement on your
splash page that pertains to your site's content. This can help boost
your rankings on some of the major search engines that both do and do
not use meta-tags. Some search engines will review your opening paragraph and use this information when developing a description for your
site that is presented in their search results.

Use of Tables

Tables
Information arranged in columns and rows.

Tables can pose indexing issues with some of the search engines. Tables are a common feature found on many Web sites to display information and position content, but if implemented incorrectly, they can cause the search engines some confusion. Also, by using tables close to the top of a page, you are potentially forcing the content you want search engines to see farther down on your page. Because some search engines look only so far, you might be hurting your chances of receiving a high ranking. If you are using tables, place any important information pertaining to the page content above the table, if possible, to help prevent any potential problems.

Here's an interesting problem some search engines suffer from: Assume you have a Web site, the main color of the background is white, and you have a table on the page with a dark background. If you were to use white in the table, some of the major search engines would pick this up as using same-color text on the same color background and would ignore your site's submission because it will be considered spam to them. Using tables is okay; many people do it—just be careful with your choice of colors.

Spamming

Some Internet marketers try various techniques to trick the search engines into positioning their sites higher in search results. These tricks do not work with every search engine, and if it is discovered that you are trying to dupe the search engines, some may not list you at all. They have been programmed to detect some of these techniques, and you will be penalized in some way if you are discovered. A few of the search engine tricks pertaining to Web site design are as follows:

- Repeating keywords over and over again hidden in your HTML and meta-tags. For example, <!games, games, games, games, games, ...>.

- Repeating keywords over and over again by displaying them at the bottom of your document after a number of line breaks.

- Hiding keywords by displaying them in your document using a very small font.

- Repeating keywords in your document by making the text color the same as the background color.

- Making frequent and regular title changes so that the bots think your site is a new site and they list you again and again.

- Changing the name of your site to have a space, exclamation mark (!), or *A* as the first character so that you come up first in alphabetical lists.

Any time you make significant changes to your site, you should re-submit your site to the search engines. Search engines normally revisit on a regular schedule. However, these search engines are growing smarter every day—some monitor how often the site is updated and adjust their "revisit" schedule accordingly.

Internet Resources for Chapter 6

I have included a few resources for you to check out regarding making your site search engine friendly. For additional resources on a variety of topics, I recommend you visit the Resources section of my Web site at *http://www.susansweeney.com/resources.html*. There you will find additional tips, tools, techniques, and resources.

Bruce Clay—Search Engine Optimization Tools
http://www.bruceclay.com/Web_rank.htm
Free search engine optimization, ranking, Web site promotion, keywords advice, and placement material for designers.

Internet InfoScavenger
http://www.infoscavenger.com/engine.htm
A monthly newsletter publication devoted to helping busy professionals market their products and services on the Web. Invaluable help, techniques, and tips for top search engine placement.

JimTools.com Webmaster's Toolkit Command Center
http://www.jimtools.com
A number of tools are available on this site that you can use for free. There's information on search engines and meta-tags, a link checker, and a link popularity tool.

LinkPopularity.com: The Free Link Popularity Service
http://www.linkpopularity.com
A free service that queries AltaVista, Infoseek, and HotBot to check your link popularity.

Make Your Web Site Search Engine Friendly
http://www.iboost.com/promote/search_engines/positioning/20034.htm
An article with some tips to make your site search engine friendly.

Search Engine Forums
http://searchengineforums.com/bin/Ultimate.cgi
Information pertaining to search engines and Web site promotion presented in the form of a bulletin board.

Search Engine Matrix
http://searchenginematrix.com
Learn about search engines and search engine positioning to achieve greater positioning within any given search engine.

Search Engine Optimization
http://www.searchengineguide.com/optimization.html
A resource filled with links to articles by search engine columnists.

Search-Engine-Secrets.net
http://search-engine-secrets.net
An article detailing the ten steps to search engine placement.

Search Engine Watch
http://www.searchenginewatch.com
A Web site devoted to how search engines work, search engine news, search engine information, tips on using search engines, and more about search engines. More information than you can stand! Be sure to sign up for the Search Engine Report mailing list.

Search Engine World
http://www.searchengineworld.com
A great resource for everything surrounding search engines. Plenty of articles, tips, and information to help you achieve online success. This site also has in-depth information on the various search engine spiders.

Submit It! Search Engine Tips
http://www.submit-it.com/subopt.htm
The purpose of this document is to provide you with background information on search engine technology and some tips on how to get your Web site to appear on the results pages of search engines and directories.

WebReference.com
http://www.Webreference.com/content/search
Search engines and examples, tips, and hints for getting the most out of your search engine, for people who work on the Web.

World of Design—Search Engine Secrets
http://www.globalserve.net/~iwb/search
References to monitor, submit, and improve search engine placements and positions.

KEYWORDS AND META-TAG DEVELOPMENT

A Dictionary of HTML Meta-Tags
http://vancouver-Webpages.com/META
A helpful dictionary of meta-tags to assist you.

How to Use Meta-Tags
http://searchenginewatch.com/Webmasters/meta.html
A tutorial on how to create meta-tags for your Web pages.

Meta-Tag Analyzer
http://www.scrubtheWeb.com/abs/meta-check.html
This will check your meta-tags and your HTML code to help you achieve better placement in search engine results. Let their free Meta-Tag Analyzer program check your meta-tags and help analyze your HTML syntax online.

META-Tag Generator
http://www.submitcorner.com/Tools/Meta
A free meta-tag generator tool to create meta-tags for your Web pages.

Meta-Tags & Search Engines
http://www.Webdigger.com/meta_tags.htm
Need to improve your search engine standings? Here are a few ideas to get you started: meta-tags as well as search engine and Web site design tips.

WordTracker
http://www.wordtracker.com
An online tool for compiling the right combination of keywords. You can run a free trial, but this is a pay service for keyword generation and suggestions.

World of Design
http://www.globalserve.net/~iwb/search_engine/killer.html
A tutorial for writing meta-tags for higher search engine placement and good descriptions.

Note: Resources found in the next chapter on search engine submissions are closely related to the information found in this chapter. I recommend reviewing the resources in the next chapter, as many contain valuable information on designing your site to be search engine friendly.

7

Search Engine and Directory Submissions

There are an estimated billion-plus Web pages on the World Wide Web, so how can you increase your chances of being found? One method is submitting to the many search engines and directories. Once you've optimized your Web site to be search engine friendly, you are ready to face the challenge of submitting to the most important search engines. By "search engines," I'm referring to the combination of search engines, directories, spiders, and crawlers. You need to be within the first two pages of search results to ensure your best possible success online. This is no easy feat, and this chapter will provide you with the knowledge necessary to get on the road to success. This chapter covers:

- Search engines, directories, and their ranking criteria

- An in-depth look at Yahoo!'s submission process

- An in-depth look at AltaVista's submission process

- The submission tools available to you

- Search engine and directory submission pointers

Submission Process

Although people often use the term *search engine* interchangeably for search engines, directories, spiders, and crawlers there is a major differentiation when it comes to submission protocol. The search engines (AltaVista, Lycos, HotBot, Google, etc.) allow you to "Add your URL." Your URL is your uniform resource locator—also known as your Web address, your www.yourcompanyname.com. When you add your URL, it is put in a queue, and when it is your turn the search engine's bot visits your site and includes it in its database. To submit to directories like Yahoo!, you have to go to the directory site and find the appropriate link to their submission form. For the directories, you generally have to complete a detailed form filling in all the blanks of required information. To submit to the spiders and crawlers (WebCrawler, Metacrawler, etc.), you go to the specific crawler and "Add your URL" much the same as you do with the search engines.

A Closer Look at Search Engines and Directories

The previous chapter discussed how search engines and directories differ. Although people use the terms *search engine* and *directory* interchangeably, there are subtle differences. In general, search engines have a much larger index and utilize spiders to add sites to their index. In contrast, directories typically have a smaller index and are maintained by humans. When you're submitting to a site, you can usually tell the difference between a directory and a search engine by the information they request. A search engine typically asks for the URL you wish to submit, and sometimes your e-mail address. A directory will usually ask for much more, including your URL, the category you wish to be added to, the title of your site, a description, and your contact information.

When you do a search on the Internet, in seconds the search engine has digested what you are looking for, searches the millions of pages it knows about, and responds to your request with appropriate sites ranked in order of importance. Amazing! How do they do it?

Search engines use spiders to index your site. Usually a search engine's spider will index or include the pages on your site once you have submitted the request to be added to that database, but sometimes they can't for a number of reasons. They may have problems with frames or image maps on a Web site; they may simply miss a page; and so on. Even though a number of the spiders constantly crawl the Web looking for sites, I suggest you take a proactive approach and submit all appropriate pages on your site to the search engines to guarantee that all your important pages are properly listed. Also, before you submit, check the search engine's submission document to be sure submitting more than one page is permitted, because you don't want your site to be rejected.

A search engine may also have restrictions on the number of pages you can submit in a single day—perhaps only five or ten pages are allowed to be submitted. AltaVista has removed its restriction on the number of pages that can be submitted at a given time, but a kink has been added into the submission process as it pertains to automated-submission software, which is covered in depth later in this chapter.

Some of the search engines share technology. Lycos shares AlltheWeb's database, and as a result some of the search results are the same. In addition, MSN Search uses Inktomi's technology for some of its results. However, all search engines have different ranking criteria to determine who gets top placement, so even though two search engines may use the same database, they will provide different search results. Some search engines determine how often a keyword appears on the Web page. It is assumed that if a keyword is used more frequently on a page, then that page is more relevant than other pages with a lower usage of that keyword. Some search engines look for the keyword in the title of the Web page and assume that if the keyword is in the title, then that page must be more relevant than those that don't have the keyword in their title. Some search engines determine where keywords are used and assume that pages with keywords in the headings and in the first couple of paragraphs are more relevant. Some search engines use the number of links pointing to a particular page as part of their ranking criteria. Some search engines use information contained in meta-tags; others don't look at the meta-tags at all.

To summarize, search engines all have different ranking criteria, and this is why you receive different results when you search on the same keyword with different engines. You should learn as much as you can about each of the major search engines' ranking systems and adjust your submission or your site's content accordingly. One particularly useful site with this information is *http://searchenginewatch.com*.

Some of the more popular search engines are

- AltaVista (Figure 7.1)

Figure 7.1. Alta Vista's home page.

- Excite (Figure 7.2)

- Google (Figure 7.3)

- Lycos (Figure 7.4)

Let's turn our attention to directories now. Because directories are maintained by human administrators, you can expect to wait a longer period of time before seeing your page appear in their index. In general, you can expect to wait between two and eight weeks unless you pay a fee for an expedited review. For example, Yahoo! charges $299 for an expedited review. When you pay the fee, Yahoo! will review your site for inclusion within seven business days. There is no guarantee they will include you—just a guarantee they will review your site and consider including you. It takes longer because the administrators review every page submitted before adding it to their database. Make sure your page is easy

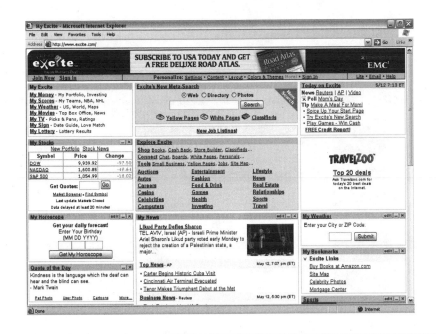

Figure 7.2. Excite's home page.

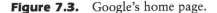

Figure 7.3. Google's home page.

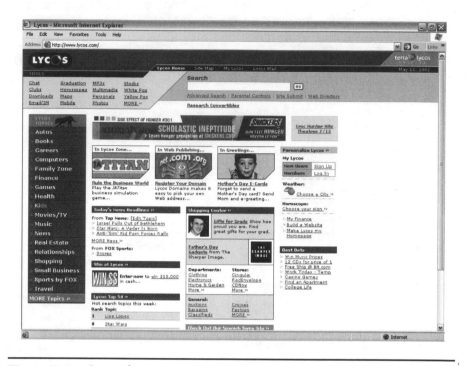

Figure 7.4. Lycos' home page.

to use, visually appealing, and rich in content, because it is the administrators who decide if your page is worthwhile before they include it.

When you submit to a directory, you will also have to take the time to find the best category for your site. Submitting your site to the wrong category could mean a minimal increase in traffic if no one thinks to look for you in the category you submitted to. Also, your site may not be added if you select an inappropriate category. LookSmart's Travel category contains subcategories including Activities, Destinations, Lodging, Transportation, and so on. These categories are often broken down further into other categories within the subcategories. The deeper you go, the more specific the category becomes.

Unlike in a search engine, your site's position in directories depends much less on Web site design and more on the initial submission process itself, which is why it is important to review each directory's submission procedure and submission tips. You will be asked for a lot more information when submitting to a directory. The title, description, and any other information you give them during submission are what will be used to rank your site.

Here are some of the more popular directories

- LookSmart (Figure 7.5)

- Open Directory Project (Figure 7.6)

- Yahoo! (Figure 7.7)

Search engines are known for their enormous databases of indexed Web sites. A couple of the leading search engines have over 500 million Web pages indexed. Google currently claims that it has the largest index, with over 2 billion indexed pages! Open Directory, Yahoo!, and LookSmart are popular directories, and each has approximately 2 million indexed Web pages.

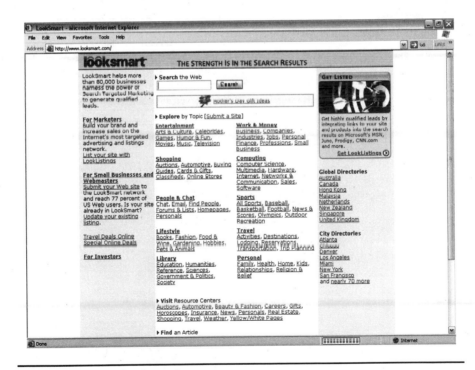

Figure 7.5. Look Smart's home page.

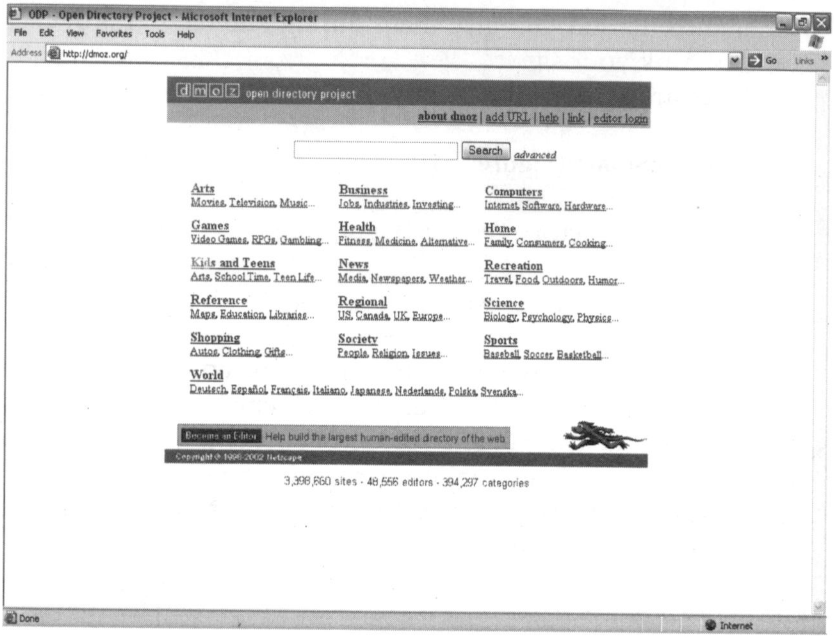

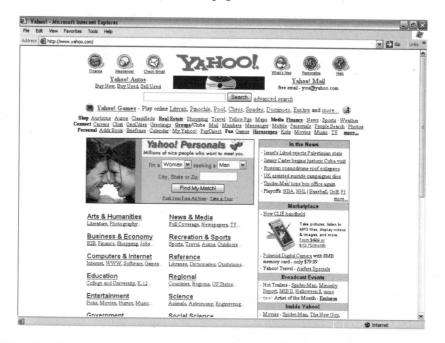

Figure 7.6.   Open Directory's home page.

Figure 7.7.   Yahoo!'s home page.

Maximizing Exposure with Submission Pointers

Submitting to the search engines and directories is a very ti
ing but extremely important task. Don't rush! Take your ti
research, know the ranking strategy employed, and prepai
mission for optimal results. It's very difficult to change youi ᴇɴᴛʀʏ once
it has been submitted, and the last thing you want is a typo. If the time
available for indexing is limited, start by focusing on the most popular
search engines and directories for individual submissions, and use a
multiple-submission site for the less important ones. Remember, 85 percent of all Internet users use search engines and directories to find what
they are looking for.

When submitting to the search engines and directories, take the time
up front to develop the submission material carefully. Organize the information in a logical order in a text file. Then, when you go to submit,
you will be able to copy and paste the content to the appropriate fields
on the submission form. Be sure to spellcheck, check, and recheck everything before you start. Spellcheckers won't pick up misspelled
"works" if that word is also in the dictionary. The information prepared for each page on the site to be indexed should include:

- URL

- Page title

- 10-word, 25-word, 50-word, and 100-word descriptions for the
  page (Different engines allow different lengths of description.)

- List of keywords for each page (See the next section, "Another
  Look at Keywords.")

- Description of the ideal audience for the site

- Categories and subcategories you should be listed under for the
  different directories you plan to submit to

- Contact information:

  - Company name

  - Contact name

- E-mail address

- Company address

- Telephone and fax numbers

Print the submission forms for the various search engines and directories, and examine them to determine that you have all the information required for submission.

When submitting forms to directories, be very careful to fill in every field on the form. Some of the search engines will reject your registration automatically if you have not filled in all the blanks. When you have to choose categories, select them very carefully. It would be a shame to have a great product, great price, and a great site, but be listed in a place where your potential customer would never think about looking for you. Read the FAQs or instructions first to ensure that you understand exactly what information is being requested. Proofread your submission at least twice before you hit the Submit button. It isn't quick or easy to change listings if you make a mistake. Your listing may be wrong for quite a while before it gets corrected.

Another Look at Keywords

It's important to take another look at keywords. Keywords are the words used by your target customers when they do a search for your types of products and services in the search engines or directories. Your keywords will be used in everything you do and are the key determining factor in how you rank in the search results among many of the major search engines.

As a general rule, you should make sure you use keywords where appropriate. Keywords should be applied in your page titles, headers, Alt tags, keyword meta-tags, description meta-tags, hyperlinks, textual content information, and so on. Another rule of thumb is to apply keywords naturally, so that they flow with the information. For example, a description that is just a list of keywords is likely to get you bumped down in search engine results or removed altogether because some search engines consider this spamming. Finally, apply the most important keywords first. Many search engines place greater emphasis on keywords near the beginning of your keywords list, description, and so on.

Be sure to use different keywords and strings of keywords for different pages on your site. Each page is unique, with different content, so by using keywords specific to each page, you're increasing your chances of being found by your target audience. If you have the same keywords on every page, you're limiting yourself to the exact same range of keywords.

Review the keywords section in the previous chapter. It discusses how to develop your master keywords list and how to apply it to the appropriate sections of your site. The keywords you want to use are the ones individuals are likely to use when performing a search.

When applying keywords, the most important places to remember are:

- Your page title

- Your page content—beginning, middle, and end of the page's text

- Your meta-tags—keywords and description

- Between your <NOFRAMES> tag if your site uses frames

- In Alt tags applied to your images

Great Descriptions Make the Difference

It is a good idea to create a number of different descriptions of varying lengths because the different search engines and directories allow different description sizes. Start off creating a description of 10 words, then 25, then 50, and then 100. Make sure that you use the right length description for each search engine, because you don't want it to be truncated when displayed in search results.

Your description should be compelling. When you get your site to appear in the first 20 to 30 top results of a search, the description is what differentiates your site from the rest. It is the description that will entice a prospective visitor to click and visit—or pass and go to a more exciting site.

Always use keywords in your description. Apply the most important keywords first because keywords used farther along in the description are generally given less weight by the major search engines. If possible, use certain keywords in combination with other keywords, but make sure your description flows naturally.

Be sure to use a call to action in your description. It's amazing how many people do what they are told. Perhaps your description could have a line that says, "Visit us now and sign up for our free monthly newsletter."

Get Multiple Listings

One way to get your site listed many times is to submit many times. Because each page on your site is a potential entry point for search engines and each page has a unique URL, you can submit each URL (each page) in the various search engines, directories, and so on. Each page of your site should be indexed to improve your chances of having your site listed in the top ten search engine results. And because every page on your site is different, each page should have a different title, a different description, and different keywords. In doing this, you're increasing your chances of being found by people searching for different criteria and keywords.

It is important to abide by netiquette. In some search sites, the previously discussed practice of submitting multiple times is acceptable and may even be encouraged. In others, it is considered abuse and is discouraged. Use your judgment on this one!

Doorway Pages

Due to the need to be ranked high in search engine results and the enormous competition between sites trying to get listed on search engines, doorway pages have increasingly become more popular. Each search engine is different and has different elements in its ranking criteria. Developing doorway pages allows you to tailor a page specifically for each search engine before submittal to achieve optimal results. Be careful, though; some search engines frown upon doorway pages, so perform a background check before creating and submitting one.

Doorway pages, also known as gateway pages, are pages that lead to your site but are not considered part of your site. Do not include doorway pages on your site's site map! In fact, do not allow any pages within your site to link to the doorway pages you have created. If you do and a search engine spider finds these pages, it will likely consider them spam and you will be removed from their directory, or at a minimum your current ranking will fall.

Doorway pages are focused pages that lead to your Web site but are tuned to the specific requirements of the search engines. By having different doorway pages with different names (e.g., indexa.html for AltaVista or indexg.html for Google) for each search engine, you can look back and see which page is bringing in the most traffic. Those pages that are not bringing in the traffic can then be edited and resubmitted until you get it right. Make sure that the doorway page you create represents the page it leads to.

As one would expect, doorway pages have their drawbacks as well. Doorway pages are often easy to duplicate. Your competition may use your doorway page as a template and tweak or modify it to suit their purposes. If you create a doorway page, be sure not to use a fast meta-refresh tag as discussed in Chapter 6. In addition, if your competition copies and modifies your page to the search engine, it's likely that most of the content will remain very similar. If this is the case, the search engine may think you're trying to spam it by submitting duplicate sites, and you'll both get removed.

A Closer Look at Yahoo!

Yahoo! is the most popular directory among Internet users today. Yahoo! was developed by David Filo and Jerry Yang around April 1994. Today millions of people use Yahoo! every day, and it is definitely a location where you want your site listed.

Yahoo! is not a search engine; it is a directory. Yahoo! has human administrators who review every site submitted. By default, Yahoo! displays information contained within its own directory; however, Yahoo! also allows you to perform searches outside its own database by referencing Inktomi's search technology. To view results returned by Inktomi's engine, click on "Web Pages" at the top or bottom of the page once you have performed your search.

Yahoo!'s directory is broken down into 14 major categories:

- Arts & Humanities

- Business & Economy

- Computers & Internet

- Education

- Entertainment

- Government

- Health

- News & Media

- Recreation & Sports

- Reference

- Regional

- Science

- Social Science

- Society & Culture

Each of Yahoo!'s 14 major categories is broken down into subcategories that also contain sub-subcategories. The deeper you go into the categories, the more content-specific the directories become. When you are looking for categories appropriate for your site, take your time, because you want to be listed in the best location. If you submit to a category that is not appropriate, users may not think to look for you there, or Yahoo! may not even add your site at all. Check out your competitors and perform some searches using keywords you feel people would use when looking for your products or services. Observe the categories that are displayed. The category (or categories) you want to be listed in will likely be included in these. Pick the most relevant categories that apply to your page, but keep in mind that when searches are performed, the categories are displayed in alphabetical order. Once you find a category you wish to submit to, select "Suggest a Site."

Before you go any further, is your site complete? Yahoo! won't add you if you have "Under Construction" signs on your site. Yahoo! likes sites that are complete, contain good and pertinent information, are aesthetically pleasing, and are easy to use. Also, check to see if you're already in their directory. You may not want or need to submit your site if you're where you want to be already. If you are in their directory but want to change the information displayed, then you can fill out a form located at *http://add.yahoo.com/fast/change* that is specifically used for changing information already listed in the directory.

Now that you are ready to submit, take your time to read all of the documentation on submitting. You want to follow their guide to the letter to ensure the best possible chance of being added to their directory. Yahoo! administrators are overwhelmed with submissions and will not take the time to review a site that has not followed their submission directions. Open up your text document where you've saved all of that relevant submission information I mentioned before. It will come in handy here. Fill out the submission form carefully and completely. Before proceeding in the submission process, make sure your information is correct and you have made no errors. You do not want to make mistakes.

Once you have submitted your information, be patient. It takes an average of six to eight weeks for a submission to be reviewed and added to the directory if it's going to be added at all. If you feel you have done everything right, have been waiting for what seems an excessive length of time, and have not been added to the directory, resubmit. If you still aren't added, send a polite e-mail to Yahoo! discussing your situation and request assistance.

Recently Yahoo! changed its submission process for commercial sites. You are now required to pay an annual fee of U.S.$299 for Yahoo!'s express submission service that is guaranteed to get your site reviewed in seven business days. (It is also available to anyone wanting to use the service.) This service does not guarantee that you'll be listed faster or even that you'll be listed at all, however; it just means they'll put a priority on reviewing your Web site.

The following are some other tips to remember when submitting your site to Yahoo!:

- Remember, your submission counts for almost everything here, so do it right. Yahoo! is a directory, not a search engine. Designing your site to be "search engine friendly" means very little here.

- Make sure that what you submit is actually what your site is about. Yahoo!'s administrators will review your site, and if they feel the description you provided does not match up with your site, you will not be added to their directory.

- Keep your description to 25 words or less and use descriptive keywords that flow naturally within the description. Yahoo! reserves the right to modify your description if they see fit. You're the only one who knows what information is important to have included in your description, so you probably do not want Yahoo!'s administrators to modify your description, because you may lose an important part of your description, resulting in less traffic. Also remember that Yahoo! does not like submissions that sound like an advertisement—they like concise, pertinent information.

- Submit a short, relevant title, not something like "The Best Gardening Site on the Web." Also, be sure to use descriptive keywords in your title as well. When searches are performed, your page title will be referenced. In addition, when search results are displayed, they are displayed in alphabetical order. If possible, try to generate a title that starts with a letter near the beginning of the alphabet. If the title you submit is not appropriate, however, Yahoo! may consider your submission spam and your page will be rejected. For example, don't title your site "AAA Gardening Supplies" if that's not the name of your site, just to appear near the top of the rankings. Like the description, make sure your title flows naturally.

- When submitting, develop your page title and descriptions to try to use keywords in combination with others as this can also give you a boost. Check out your competitors to see who's on the top and what they're doing right.

- If you're looking for local traffic, then submitting to a regional category may be appropriate for you.

- Don't fill out the submission form using ALL CAPITALS—they hate that. Use proper grammar and spelling. Before you submit, be sure to check and recheck your submission to be sure all is well.

- If your domain name contains keywords, you will benefit here. Keywords can help you out when a user performs a search on a keyword that is in your domain name.

- Don't forget to fill out Yahoo!'s submission form exactly as requested! Read the help documentation and FAQs, beginning with "How to Suggest Your Site" (see Figure 7.8), which can be found at *http://docs.yahoo.com/info/suggest*.

Figure 7.8. How to suggest a site at Yahoo!.

A Closer Look at AltaVista

Originally launched near the end of 1995, AltaVista is one of the most popular search tools on the Web today. AltaVista is a true search engine whose spider, Scooter, indexes Web pages. Scooter is a "deep-search" spider, meaning it will visit all pages on your Web site as long as it is given the opportunity to. A fast meta-refresh or a dynamic page developed using CGI can cause problems for Scooter. I recommend reading Chapter 6, the search engine friendliness chapter, for more information, because it discusses Web site design and its effects on how your site is indexed by the major search engines. AltaVista also uses LookSmart for some of its results, so be sure to submit your site to LookSmart (*http:// www.looksmart.com*).

Before you submit, make sure your page is complete. AltaVista wants quality pages and does not like to index pages that are incomplete or inappropriate. Every search engine wants to index only quality sites, because if they list a lot of "junk," then users will stop returning.

Submitting to AltaVista (see Figure 7.9) is a simple process. All you have to do is click on "Submit a Site" from the home page. This will take you to the submission page, where you enter your URL into the designated field. AltaVista has recently added a submission code feature to its Web site submission page. For every URL you want to enter, you must enter the submission code. The submission code is generated automatically upon entering the submission section of AltaVista's site. The use of the submission code feature helps to block automated submission software and services, which means that you must add your site manually if you want to add it to AltaVista.

It typically takes 24 to 48 hours before your site is added to AltaVista's index. Scooter will then periodically revisit your site looking to add new and updated pages. If you feel you have done everything right but are not showing up in the index, then send them a polite e-mail asking if there's a problem and if anything can be done. It could be that your site is not optimized for AltaVista and that is why you're not appearing in the results.

AltaVista uses meta-tags to formulate a description of your site, which is then presented to users when they perform a search. In addition, AltaVista uses your keyword meta-tag and your description meta-tag as factors in determining your site's ranking among its results. Keywords applied in your title are also a factor that affects your page's position. If you do not have a description meta-tag, AltaVista will refer-

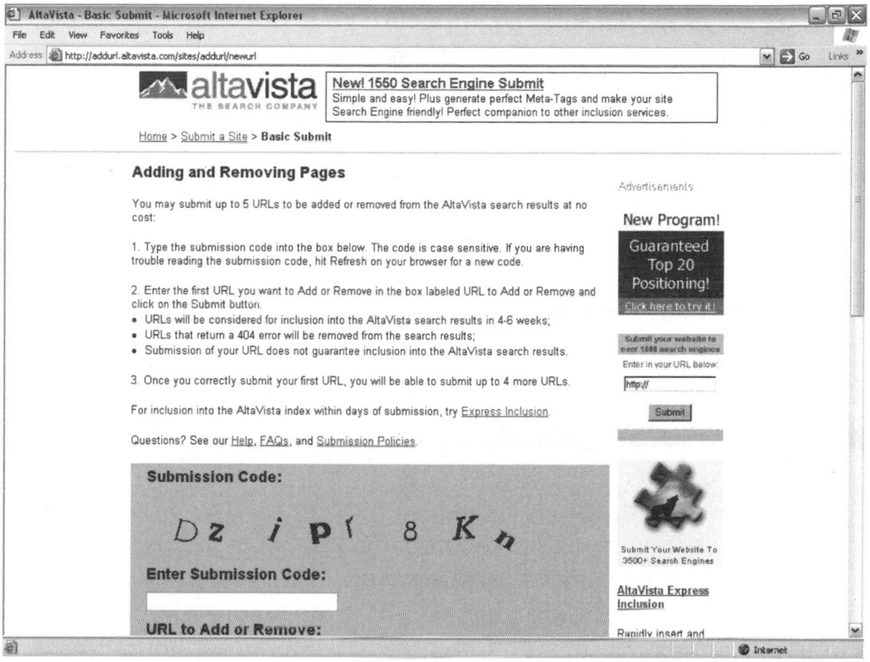

Figure 7.9. Alta Vista's URL submission page.

ence your site's content and formulate its own description based on this. Here are some tips to improve your ranking in AltaVista:

- Your ranking on AltaVista is determined by your site's design, so be sure to make it easily accessible for AltaVista's spider, Scooter.

- Use keywords in your title, meta-tags, Alt tags, and page content. Make sure the most important keywords are used first because more weight is given to the keywords that appear first. Also, try to use some keywords in combination with other keywords because this can boost your ranking.

- AltaVista is a case-sensitive search engine. For any of your keywords that are usually uppercase, you may want to include both the upper- and lowercase versions of the word in your keyword meta-tag.

- Link popularity can influence your position. If possible, increase the number of links pointing toward your site. See Chapter 15 for ways to generate significant links to your site.

- Do not spam AltaVista or your ranking will quickly drop or your site may be removed altogether. For example, AltaVista does not like multiple doorways or pages that repeat the same keyword over and over again (e.g., Gardening, Gardening, Gardening Supplies, Gardening, Gardening).

Effective Use of Submission Tools and Services

There are many search engine submission services available on the Net that will submit your site to varying numbers of indexes, directories, and search engines. They will register your URL, description, and keywords. Use these services only after you have manually submitted to the most important search engines. Check them to see how comprehensive they are before using these services. Here are a couple of sites for you to look at:

Add-Me
http://www.addme.com
This site allows you to submit your page to 18 popular sites for free, using one form. A paid submission service is available for $29.95 to 2,000 search engines, announcement services, and classifieds.

GetSubmitted.com
http://www.getsubmitted.com
This site offers search engine submission and Web site promotion tools.

SiteAnnounce.com
http://www.siteannounce.com
This is a search engine submission service that has been around since 1995.

Submit It!
http://www.submit-it.com
Submit-It! is one of the oldest and most respected submission services, now run by Microsoft.

Although these services save a lot of time, it is essential that you be registered accurately in search engines and directories. For the best results, register individually in as many of the top search engines as you can before you resort to multiple-submission sites. There aren't that many search engines or directories that have long submission forms, so submit manually to ensure the best results. If you have taken the time to do the work described earlier, submit to the major engines yourself. This way you can take full advantage of the legwork you have done targeting the differences between the engines.

To summarize, each search engine is different. Know the unique qualities of each before you submit, and be sure to check out Appendix C of this book, where details are provided on many of the popular search engines and directories.

Complete Your Site before You Submit

Before you submit to any of the search engines and directories, take the time to complete your site. Many of the major search engines and directories are not fond of receiving submissions from people who have pages that are not yet complete. You do not want to spend your time submitting your page only to find out it has not been added because it is "under construction." Also, be sure to validate your HTML before submitting. You want your site to be free of errors to ensure your success with submissions. A few of tools you can use to validate your HTML are:

Dr. Watson, v4.0
http://watson.addy.com

NetMechanic
http://www.netmechanic.com/toolbox/html-code.htm

Search Engine World
http://searchengineworld.com/validator

SiteInspector
http://www.siteinspector.com

WDG HTML Validator
http://www.htmlhelp.com/tools/validator

W3C HTML Validation Service
http://validator.w3.org

Is Your Page Already Indexed?

Before you submit or resubmit to a search engine, check to see if your page is already indexed. Perform a search using the most important keywords you think people will use to find your page. Also, perform a search using your company name. If your page is found and you're happy with the results, you will not need to submit or resubmit. In fact, if you do resubmit, you could end up worse off because you never know when a search engine is going to change its method of determining what pages receive a high ranking. If you are not listed or are not happy with your listing, you can submit your page. If need be, you can edit your page and then resubmit to achieve a higher position. To see if your URL is indexed by AltaVista, enter *url:yourdomain.com/directory/page.html* in the search field of each search engine. Check out the help files for each search engine for more information on how to verify that your URL is included in their index.

Check Out Your Competition

Using the techniques just mentioned, you can check out your competitors' rankings as well. By looking at the top results, you can see what they're doing right to achieve those top placements and learn from them to help you develop a successful submission strategy. You should look at your competition's keyword meta-tag, descriptions meta-tag, page content, page titles, and so on. They may have great keywords you missed. You might want to consider printing some of their pages or information so that you can use it for reference later. Do not copy their information—you just want to use their information for guidance and reference about what has given their site the high ranking. The top results for your keywords and your competitors' can also be analyzed for link popularity, which you can then research to find appropriate links you may able to use to increase your link popularity. This is discussed in the next section.

The Link Popularity Issue

Now that you know who is appearing at the top of the search results, check out the number of links pointing toward their site. Link popularity is becoming more and more important among the major search engines, including AltaVista and Google. Perform a search using your most important keywords on Google to see who is appearing at the top of the results. Chances are the sites near the top contain the most incoming links. Look at the links leading to your competitors because they're likely appropriate links for you as well. If so, ask for a link, ask for a reciprocal link, or add yourself to their links if possible to build up your link popularity. This is a time-consuming task, but it will benefit you in the end. Keep in mind that link popularity is good, but link popularity from quality sites is better. Details on finding appropriate link sites, requesting links, and having your link stand out are all covered in Chapter 15.

It Doesn't Always Come for Free

Some search engines and directories are adopting various pay-for-inclusion or submission policies. There are a couple general variations you should be aware of.

- Pay-per-click

- Paid inclusion

- Paid submission

The basic concept behind a pay-per-click search engine is that you bid for placement based on a specific keyword or keyword phrase. Every time someone clicks on your link and visits your site, you are charged the amount you have bid. If someone in your industry is paying $1.00

for a certain keyword and has the top ranking site, in theory you could bid $1.01 to overtake the number 1 position. Of course, if the second most popular site is paying only 10 cents for that position, it may be more cost-effective for you to target that position depending on your objectives, budget, and the amount of emphasis you want to focus on any given search engine.

Overture is the most well known example of a pay-per-click search engine. An important fact to note here is that search engines often reference other search engines for some of their results. Overture's listings appear in some form on AltaVista, Yahoo!, Go.com, MSN, Metacraweler, and so forth, with others on the horizon.

PayPerClickAnalyst.com provides an overview of information relating to the scope of paid processes used by a number of the leading search tools. I recommend you visit their site at *http://www.payperclickanalyst.com* for more details.

The pay-to-play search engines include:

- Overture

- Ask Jeeves

- 7Search

- Kanoodle

When you choose to participate in the pay-to-play search engines, you need to plan your budget. You have to do your research on what keywords and keyword phrases to buy. Wordtracker is a great tool to help with research. One key point to make is that you don't want to start a bidding war, so be very careful about bidding top dollar. You will want to allocate your budget over several pay-to-play search engines. If your business is cyclical, you may very well want to allocate your budget to participate at specific times of the year as well.

A paid-inclusion search engine or directory does not guarantee you a high-ranking position within a particular search tool; it simply means that your site will be indexed assuming that your site conforms to the search tool's submission guidelines and that you will likely have a greater chance of appearing in the search results. Paid inclusion is used by such search tools as AskJeeves, LookSmart, and Inktomi. Details on their specific programs can be found on their respective sites.

Search tools that offer paid submissions as a service make no guarantees other than that your site will be reviewed for inclusion in that particular directory. Yahoo! offers a business-express submission service to its users. On the site, it clearly states that:

Payment does not guarantee inclusion in the directory, site placement, or site commentary. It only guarantees that Yahoo! will respond to your submission within seven business days.

The key benefit of this type of program is that your site will be reviewed sooner rather than later. It can take months for some search engines and directories to review a site and either index it or reject it.

Purchasing advertising on the most popular search engines and directories will also get you in front of your target audience. Many search tools offer advertising based on targeted keyword buys or sponsorships. Google's new advertising program, called AdWords, shown in Figure 7.10, is one such example.

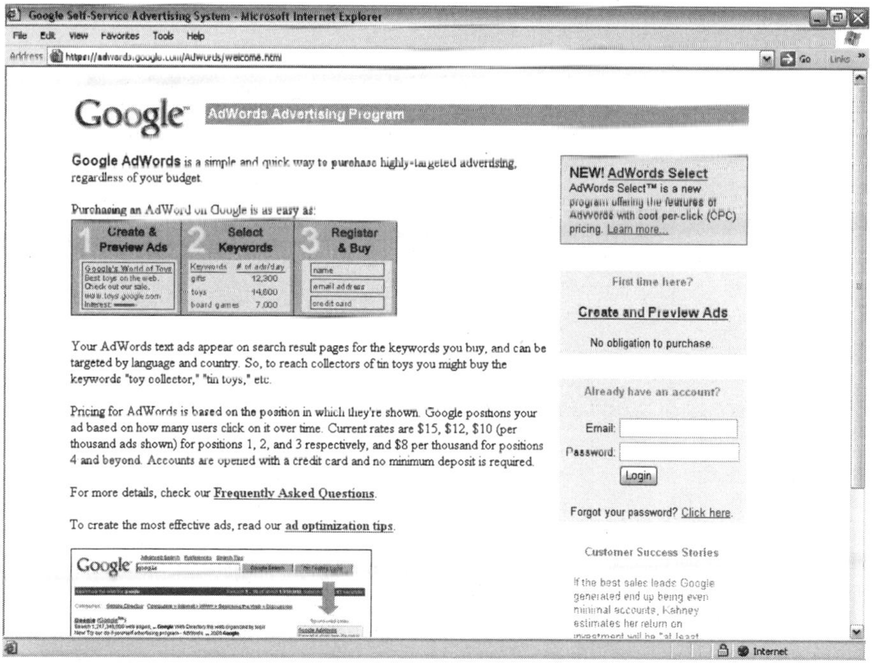

Figure 7.10. Google's AdWords program.

Don't Spam the Search Engines

If you want to achieve high rankings, then you should avoid spamming the search engines. A common name given to spamming the search engines is "Spamdexing." People often use these techniques to try and "cheat" their way to the top of the search engine rankings.

What is considered spam? (See Figure 7.11.)

- Keyword stuffing, which is repeating the same keyword (or keywords) over and over again hidden in your HTML and meta-tags.

- Repeating keywords over and over again by displaying them at the bottom of your document after a number of line breaks.

- Submitting multiple pages from the same domain during the same timeframe is considered spamming by some search engines, so be

Figure 7.11. Alta Vista's spam policy.

sure to do your research and check how many submissions per day they allow from a single domain. Some search engines want you to submit only your home page and allow their spider to do the rest; others say it's okay to submit as much as you want.

- Submitting identical pages but using different page names will also get you removed if it is discovered.

- Hiding keywords, often called tiny text, is also considered spamming. This is when you place keywords on your page by displaying them in your document using a very small font.

- Repeating keywords in your document by making the text color the same as the background color is considered spam.

- Making frequent and regular title changes so that the bots think your site is a new site and they list you again and again.

- Using page redirects or a meta-refresh can result in your site's being eliminated from a search engine's index.

- Using keywords that cannot be found on your page or are unrelated to your page.

- Altering the name of your site to have a space, exclamation mark (!), or A as the first character so that your site is displayed first in alphabetical lists.

Keep a Record

Keep a record of the directories and search engines to which you have submitted. The information recorded should include the following:

1. Date of the submission

2. URL of the page submitted

3. Name of the search engine or directory

4. Description used

5. Keywords used

6. Password used

7. Notes section for any other relevant information

8. Date listed

Some Final Pointers

Here are some important final pointers you should keep in mind. Always, always, always read the submission guidelines before submitting. Search engines and directories will also often provide a number of valuable tips that can help you to achieve better rankings.

Periodically review your rankings in the major search engines and directories. To make this manageable, I suggest you make a list of the search engines and directories to which you have submitted. Divide your list into four groups. Every week check your ranking with each of the search engines and directories in one group. If you have dropped in the ranking or don't appear in the first couple of pages of search results, then you want to resubmit to that particular search engine or directory. The next week you check your ranking with the next group. By doing so you can set a regular schedule for yourself, keep organized, and determine which search engines and directories you need to resubmit to and which you do not. Sometimes your site may be removed from an index because the search engine has flushed its directory, or maybe it is just one of those things no one can explain—either way, you will be on top of things. If you make any significant changes to your site, you also may want to resubmit. You want to ensure that your content is fresh.

You also may want to consider submitting to country-specific search engines and directories. These search engines and directories often will give users the option of searching for sites from a specific country, which may benefit you if you are only looking for an audience in your country. A couple of examples are Canada.com (*http://www.canada.com*—Figure 7.12) and Yahoo! Sweden (*http://se.yahoo.com*—Figure 7.13).

Figure 7.12. Canada.com's home page.

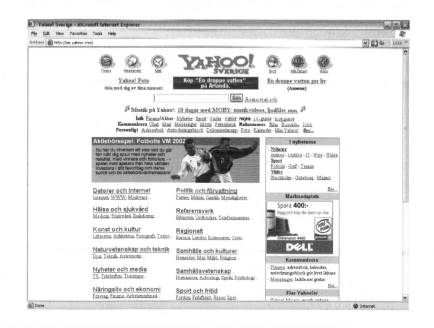

Figure 7.13. Yahoo! Sweden's home page.

Internet Resources for Chapter 7

I have included a few resources for you to check out regarding search engine submission. For additional resources on a variety of topics, I recommend you visit the Resources section of my Web site at *http://www.susansweeney.com/resources.html*. There you will find additional tips, tools, techniques, and resources.

AAA Internet Promotions
http://www.web-ignite.com
One of the first professional Web site promotion services on the Internet, and certainly the most reputable. AAA Internet Promotions manually submits your Web site to search engines and directories.

Browser News
http://www.upsdell.com/BrowserNews/stat_search.htm
A weekly Web-based newsletter that provides a variety of browser news and search engine statistics.

JimTools.com Webmaster's Toolkit Command Center
http://www.jimtools.com
A number of tools are available on this site that you can use for free. There's information on the search engines, meta-tags, link checker, and a link popularity tool.

PayPerClickSearchEngines.com
http://www.payperclicksearchengines.com
A list of pay-per-click search engines.

Position-It
http://www.position-it.com
This site will show you how to use Internet search engines and directories to skyrocket your Web site traffic using search engine secrets for top positioning.

Promotion 101—Web Site Marketing and Promotion Info Center
http://www.promotion101.com
A good resource with a search engine placement guide, free tools, and promotion articles.

Promotion World
http://www.promotionworld.com
Lots of information surrounding online promotion, with some good information on search engine submission and preparing your site to be submitted to the search engines. This site also contains some tools you can use to generate meta-tags and check your position on search engines, and a free search engine submission service.

Search Engine Matrix
http://searchenginematrix.com
Learn about search engines and search engine positioning to achieve greater positioning within any given search engine.

Search Engine Showdown
http://www.notess.com/search
Detailed analysis of Internet search engines and their features, databases, and strategies.

Search Engine Tutorial for Web Designers
http://www.northernwebs.com/set
Lots of valuable information on Web site design, search engine ranking methods, and policies.

Submit-It!
http://www.submit-it.com
A very popular Web site promotion tool. You can use Submit-It! to register your URL with hundreds of search engines and directories.

SubmitWolf Pro
http://www.msw.com.au/swolf
With a database of over 2,500 sites to promote your URL and hundreds of fully automated submission scripts, SubmitWolf can dramatically increase your site traffic. SubmitWolf is loaded with features. It provides detailed submission reports, and it can generate meta-tags to help search engines correctly index your site. It even enables you to add your own engines.

WebReference.com
http://www.webreference.com/content/search

Search engines and examples, tips, and hints for getting the most out of your search engine—for people who work on the Web.

Web Themes Internet Consultants
http://www.Webthemes.com
One of the most active submission and promotion services on the Net. They take a very active role in generating traffic to your site. Web Themes Advertising, Marketing, Promotion and Design (home of The Web Hitman) has been promoting new businesses on the Web since 1995. They have experience and the resources to promote your Web site using a variety of tools to accomplish the task. Their Web page promotion services start with your standard professional submission services and extend to extensive programs for increasing traffic on a daily basis.

SEARCH ENGINE SEARCH FEATURES AND SUBMISSION CHARTS
Search Engine Chart
http://www.advance-training.co.uk/free/chart.htm

Search Engine Features for Webmasters
http://www.searchenginewatch.com/Webmasters/features.html

SUBMISSION TOOLS
AddPro.com
http://www.addpro.com
Free Web site URL submission to 20+ search engines.

MetaCrawlers Top Searches List
http://www.metaspy.com
Ever wonder what the rest of the world is searching for? Catch a glimpse of some of the searches being performed on MetaCrawler at this very moment!

SiteOwner.com
http://www.siteowner.com
Tools to help individuals submit their site to search engines, develop meta-tags, locate dead links, and so on.

SubmitPlus
http://submitplus.bc.ca
SubmitPlus helps you promote your Web site with two very effective Web site announcement programs. They offer free and pay services.

Before you register your site, make sure you check out their "Free Promotion Tools" section for invaluable tips on how to make your Web site ready for the Internet!

The Broadcaster
http://www.broadcaster.co.uk
Broadcaster search engine submission and announcement services cover all aspects of Web site marketing, promotion, and search engine secrets.

Usubmit.com
http://www.usubmit.com
A free service that assists you in submitting your site to 27 of the top search engines.

World Submit
http://www.worldsubmit.com
World Submit will submit your Web site to 1,550 of the world's search engine directories including Yahoo!, what's-new sites, and award sites in 90 categories.

Note: If you haven't already done so, be sure to review the resources for Chapter 6. The information contained in Chapters 6 and 7 is closely correlated, and their resources tie in well together.

8

Utilizing Signature Files to Increase Web Site Traffic

A signature file, or sig.file as it is commonly referred to, is your electronic business card. It takes the form of a short memo and is attached at the end of your e-mail messages. You can use your signature file in a number of clever ways, from just giving out phone numbers and addresses, to offering some substantial information. Sig.files can be used to let people know about a special event or to inform people about an award or honor your company has received. In this chapter, we cover:

- The appropriate size of sig.files

- Content and design of sig.files

- Creating sig.files to add statements to your messages

- The benefits of sig.files

Presenting Your e-Business Card

A signature file is your e-business card. It should be attached at the end of all your e-mails—those that are sent to individuals and especially those that are sent to Usenet newsgroups and mail lists. Most, if not all, e-mail programs allow for the use of a signature file. If yours doesn't, you should consider switching e-mail programs because sig.files can be very effective in drawing traffic to your Web site when used appropriately.

Your sig.file should always include all basic contact information: name, organization, snail address, phone, fax, e-mail, and URL. You should provide every way possible for recipients to reach you; do not provide only the way in which you would like to be contacted. The customer is king and it is the recipients' choice if they would rather call than e-mail you.

Some businesses also have a "click here" on their sig.file, which takes you directly to their Web site. This is a nice idea, but you must also remember to also include your URL so that the recipients will have it. Sometimes people will just print their e-mail to take home that night, and they can't get to your Web site by trying to click on a piece of paper.

You should also include a tag line offering information about your company, its products and services, a current sales promotion, where you will be located at a trade show, a special event you are hosting, an award your company has received, or other marketing-focused information. Sig.files are readily accepted online and, when designed properly, comply with netiquette.

Always remember to place *http://* before Web site URLs and *mailto:* before e-mail addresses to make them hypertext links. This allows the readers to click on the links to take them directly to a Web site or to e-mail you without having to copy and paste the address in their browser or e-mail program.

How to Develop Your Signature File

In preparation for designing and developing your sig.file, you should decide what information you want to include and what you want your e-business card to look like. Depending on the e-mail program you use, you can create your sig.file using Windows Notepad, Microsoft Word, or any other processor and save it as a text file (with a .txt extension), or you can create your sig.file within your e-mail program.

If you are using Microsoft Outlook Express or Netscape Messenger, you would take the following steps to develop your sig.file:

Microsoft Outlook Express 5

1. On the menu bar, click "Tools."

2. On the drop-down box, click on "Options."

3. Click on the "Signatures" tab.

4. Click on "New" to create your sig.file.

5. Type in your sig.file contents.

6. Make sure "Add sig.file to all outgoing messages" is checkmarked under signature settings.

7. Click "Apply."

Netscape Messenger

1. Create your sig.file using any text editor and save it as a .txt file.

2. On the menu bar, click "Edit."

3. Click on "Preferences."

4. In the Preferences dialog box, select the "Mail & Newsgroups" category.

5. Go to the folder named "Identity."

6. In the "Signature File" text box, enter the location and name of the signature file you saved earlier or use the Open dialog box to browse through your folders until you find the location of the file. When you find it, select it and then click "Open," which will return you to the Preferences dialog box. Click "OK" to return to the Messenger window.

If you are using one of the online services, there are different ways to develop your sig.file:

America Online

1. Click on "Mail Center" on the toolbar.

2. Click on "Set Up Mail Signature."

3. Click on "Create," type in the name of the sig.file, and create the sig.file using the different options available.

4. Set the default to "On" so that your sig.file is added to your outgoing mail.

CompuServe

1. Click on "Mail Center" on the toolbar.

2. Click on "Set up Mail Signature."

3. Click on "Create," type in the name of the sig.file, and create the sig.file using the different options available.

4. Set the default to "On" so that your sig.file is added to your outgoing mail.

Prodigy

•   Prodigy uses Microsoft Outlook Express for its e-mail service, so follow the instructions given earlier for Outlook Express.

The Do's and Don'ts of Signature Files

It is a good idea to develop several signature files to use with different groups of recipients. You can use an appropriate sig.file for each different group you are targeting. You should update your sig.file often to reflect current marketing-related information.

Some e-mail programs allow a maximum of 80 characters per line for sig.files. You should design your sig.file to fit well within the limits

```
>>>>>>>>>>>>>>>>>>>>>>>>>>>>>>>>>>>>>>>>>>>>>>>>>>>>>>>>>>>>>>>
John Doe, Director of Marketing              jdoe@gamecorp.com
                                             Tel: (800) 555-0008
 _____                                     Fax: (800) 555-0009
I GAME CORP I                                     290 Young St.
I     ____     I                                  New York, NY
I I           I I        "Free Trial Version @         81010
I_I___IIII___I_I         www.gamecorp.com"
GAME CORP.
>>>>>>>>>>>>>>>>>>>>>>>>>>>>>>>>>>>>>>>>>>>>>>>>>>>>>>>>>>>>>>>
```

of all programs. Use no more than 65 characters per line to be assured that your sig.file will be viewed as you have designed it no matter what reader is being used. As a matter of fact, the fewer characters the better to ensure that what you have on one line appears on one line (and not two) in your viewers' browsers. Sometimes people open and view their e-mail in a small window and not the full screen.

Some people get really innovative in the design of their sig.files. They often include sketches, designs, or logos developed by combining keyboard numbers and punctuation. An example of this is "John Doe" of "Game Corporation," which is in the game software business.

Including graphics in your sig.file is not a good idea. This may look quite nice on your screen, but when you send it to other people who have a different e-mail program or different screen resolutions, it could look quite different on their monitors. You should also stay away from using icons or sketches in your signature files. Check out sig.files attached to messages you receive or those posted to newsgroups to see what you like, what you don't like, and what suits you best. You can always build it, test it on your colleagues, and then decide whether you will use it or not.

The use of sig.files offers a number of benefits to your company. If you use sig.files appropriately, you will be able to promote your company and your online presence in the following ways:

Tag Line
Advertising message, usually included in your signature file attached to an e-mail.

• The use of sig.files will increase your company's online exposure. By merely placing a sig.file at the end of a posting to a newsgroup, you ensure that your company name may be seen by thousands of people. A great **tag line** with a call to action will encourage people to visit your site.

• Like any advertisement, the design and content of your sig.file can be used to position your business and create or complement a corporate image.

- Using your sig.file can enhance the reputation of your company based upon the e-mail that it is attached to. If your postings to newsgroups and mailing lists are helpful and continually appreciated, this will become associated with your company name.

- Using appropriate sig.files, as shown below, will signal to the online community that you are a member that respects proper netiquette.

Sig.file DO's	Sig.file DON'Ts
Do list all appropriate contact information.	Don't list prices of any kind.
Keep it short, say four to eight lines.	Don't use a sales pitch.
Keep it simple.	Don't use too many symbols.
Provide an appropriate and professional tag line.	Don't list the company's products or services.

Sig.files to Bring Traffic to Your Web Site

The major benefit of sig.files is that they can attract visitors to your Web site. Use your signature file as a mini-advertisement for your company and its products and services (called sigvertising). With sigvertising you can go beyond offering the basic contact information. Use your sig.file as a tool to bring traffic to your Web site. Instead of simply listing your company's phone number and URL, give the reader some insight into your company and a reason to visit your site.

One of the most important elements of your signature file from a marketing perspective is the tag line. Your signature file should always include a one-line tag line or catch phrase. A tag line is a small sentence that is used in branding and is often recognizable without even the mention of the company or product name. Does your tag line give the reader a real and compelling desire to visit your Web site?

Do you recognize any of these tag lines?

- "We try harder."

- "It's the real thing."

- "Like a rock."

- "Just do it."

- "Kills bugs dead."

A catch phrase may be something that catches the reader's attention and intrigues her to find out more. You should include a call to action in the catch phrase wherever possible to have your reader take action. I often include the catch phrase "Check out our Web Site Report Card" in my signature file with a hypertext link to my Web site, with very positive results. The recipients often do check out our Web site report card, ask for additional information, and often become clients. It works!

Consider some of the following tag line or catch phrase possibilities to increase the traffic to your Web site:

- Announce a sale or special offer. Briefly mention that your company will be having a sale, or inform people that there is a special offer available on your Web site.

- Offer something for free. Inform readers of free information or samples that they can access if they visit your site.

- Announce an event. If your company is organizing or sponsoring a special event, inform people through your sig.file, and invite them to your site for more information.

- Announce a contest. If your site is holding a contest, tell readers that they can enter by visiting your site.

- Announce an award or honor. If your company or your Web site has received special recognition, tell people about it through your sig.file.

Sig.files are accepted online in e-mail, newsgroups, mail lists, and discussion groups. However, be cautious when developing your sig.files to ensure that they will be well received. Sig.files that are billboards, or sig.files that are longer than most of your text messages, are to be avoided. Sig.files that are blatant advertisements definitely will not be appreciated. The online community reacts unfavorably to hard-sell advertising unless it is done in the proper forum. Here is an example of a sig.file that may offend Internet users:

xxxxxxxxxxxxxxxxxxxxxxxxxxxxxxxxxxxxxxxxxxxxxxxxxxxxxxxxxxxxx
Are you in need of a reliable vehicle?
If you are, come on down to Sunnyvale Volkswagen!
We have the best deals in town and will beat any of our competitors'
prices on new and used cars!
Money-back guarantee!
Great deal on a 1995 Diesel Jetta . . . . $2,995.
Talk to Jane Doe about our new lease incentives!
101 Main Street, Woodstock, New York 10010
Tel: (800) 555-0000
Cell: (800) 555-1010
Fax: (800) 555-1020
www.bug.com
xxxxxxxxxxxxxxxxxxxxxxxxxxxxxxxxxxxxxxxxxxxxxxxxxxxxxxxxxxxxx

Another mistake that people make is that they try to make their sig.files too flashy or eye catching. Using a lot of large symbols may catch people's eye, but the impression it leaves will not be memorable. Here is an example of what not to do:

```
☺☺☺☺☒☺☺☺☒☺☺☺☒☺☺☺☒☺☺☺☒☺☺☺☒☺☺☺☺
 ☺  !Sunnyvale Volkswagen !                              ☺
 ☺  !Jane Doe, Marketing Assistant !                     ☺
 ☺  ! jdoe@bug.com !                                     ☺
 ☺  232 Main Street                    ☎800) 555-0000 ☺
 ☺  Woodstock, New York ▯              ▤ (800) 555-0002 ☺
 ☺  30210 ▭                                              ☺
 ☺          "Test drives @ www.bug.com"                  ☺
 ☺☺☺☺☒☺☺☺☒☺☺☺☒☺☺☺☒☺☺☺☒☺☺☺☒☺☺☺☺
```

Here are some examples of what sig.files should look like:

```
============================================================
Sunnyvale Volkswagen
Jane Doe, Marketing Assistant
mailto:jdoe@bug.com
101 Main Street, Woodstock, New York, 10010
Tel: (800) 555-0000 Fax:(800) 555-0002
        "Our once-a-year sales event is on now @ http://www.bug.com"
============================================================
```

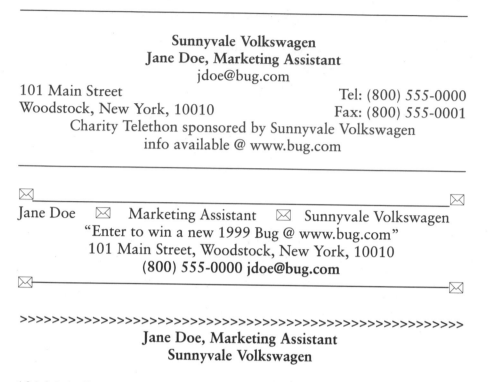

Sunnyvale Volkswagen
Jane Doe, Marketing Assistant
jdoe@bug.com

101 Main Street

Woodstock, New York, 10010

Tel: (800) 555-0000

Fax: (800) 555-0001

Charity Telethon sponsored by Sunnyvale Volkswagen
info available @ www.bug.com

Jane Doe   Marketing Assistant   Sunnyvale Volkswagen
"Enter to win a new 1999 Bug @ www.bug.com"
101 Main Street, Woodstock, New York, 10010
(800) 555-0000 jdoe@bug.com

\>>>

Jane Doe, Marketing Assistant
Sunnyvale Volkswagen

101 Main Street

P.O. Box 101

Woodstock, New York 10010

jdoe@bug.com

Tel: (800) 555-0000

URL: www.bug.com

"1999 Winner of the Best Dealership Award"

\>>>

Internet Resources for Chapter 8

I have included a few resources for you to check out when developing your signature file. For additional resources on a variety of topics, I recommend you visit the Resources section of my Web site at *http:// www.susansweeney.com/resources.html*. There you will find additional tips, tools, techniques, and resources.

123 Promote

http://www.mcn.org/b/sitepromoter/123Exe/123/123PROMO/work-book/email.htm

E-mail guide to e-mail styles, e-mail mail merging, e-mail auto respond-ers, e-mail auto reminders, e-mail netiquette, e-mail headers, signature files, announcements, press releases, business administration, free designs, mailing list announcements, newsgroup announcements, office automation, mass e-mailing, publicity, form letters, form folders, e-mailed databases, programs and software.

Coolsig Signature Files
http://www.coolsig.com
This site contains signature files in a variety of categories.

Esther's Massive Signature File Collection
http://www.contrib.andrew.cmu.edu/~moose/sigs.html
A massive collection of sig.files to review—the good, the bad, and the ugly.

GFOFN Help: How to Make and Maintain a Signature File
http://www.gnofn.org/info/help/ppp/makesig.html
A tutorial on designing and developing your signature file.

Internet Strategist
http://www.techdirect.com/strategy/sigfiles.html
What to do and not to do on sig.files and mailing lists. Learn how to create your personal sig.file and what the different types are used for.

Siglets.com
http://siglets.com
Siglets are short notations, humorous or serious, placed at the bottom of an e-mail, usually in a sig.file. Siglets.com offers you thousands to use for free! As you browse the site, you'll find Siglets for all occasions.

Signature Files
http://www.smithfam.com/news/n8.html
Signature files are an absolutely vital way of promoting your Web site. Learn how to market your product on the Internet from the leading Internet marketing experts, and it is all free.

Webnovice.com
www.Webnovice.com/sig_files.htm
"Everything You Wanted To Know About Signature Files ... But Didn't Know Where To Ask."

Workz.com
http://www.workz.com/content/162.asp
Workz has a great tutorial on developing sig.files properly. Check it out!

9

The E-mail Advantage

E-mail is rapidly becoming one of the most crucial forms of communication you have with your clients, potential customers, suppliers, and colleagues. E-mail is now a widely accessible and generally accepted form of communication. We are seeing a huge increase in commercial e-mail volume. The reason for this significant increase is understandable given that e-mail is a very cost-effective, time-efficient tool that has a high response rate. E-mail is used to build your community online, sell products and provide customer service, reinforce brand awareness, and encourage customer loyalty.

In the online community, e-mail is an extremely efficient way to build and maintain relationships. As a marketing tool, e-mail is one of the most cost-effective ways to maintain an ongoing dialogue with your audience. In this chapter, we cover:

- Strategies for creating effective e-mail messages

- E-mail netiquette

- Customer service and e-mail

- E-mail marketing tips

- Sending HTML versus ASCII (text-based) e-mail messages

Making the Connection

E-mail is a communication medium, and, as with all forms of communication, you do not get a second chance to leave a first impression. E-mail must be used appropriately. People receive large amounts of e-mail each day, and the tips in this chapter will help to ensure that your e-mail is taken seriously.

One of the greatest benefits of e-mail is the speed with which you can communicate. E-mail takes seconds rather than weeks to send a message around the world. The cost of this form of communication is negligible compared to making a long-distance phone call or sending a fax. The economies of scale are significant. One e-mail message can be sent to millions of people across the globe simultaneously. This type of mass mailing is done at a fraction of the cost and a fraction of the time (and internal resources) it would take with **snail mail.**

Snail mail
Slang term for the regular postal service.

All kinds of files can be sent via e-mail, including sound, video, data, graphics, and text. With an **autoresponder,** information can immediately be sent to customers and potential customers 24 hours a day, 7 days a week, 365 days a year in response to their online requests.

E-mail is interactive. Your current and potential customers can immediately respond to you and carry on an ongoing dialogue with you. E-mail is seen much more like a conversation than a text document. It is perceived as being more personal than snail mail and can go quite a long way in building relationships.

Autoresponder
Program that automatically responds to incoming e-mails.

Effective E-mail Messages

Most people who use this medium get tons of e-mail, including their share of junk e-mail. Many use organization tools, filters, and blockers to screen incoming e-mails. The following tips will increase the effectiveness of your e-mail communication to ensure that you have the best opportunity to have your e-mail opened, read, and responded to.

The Importance of Your E-mail Subject Line

When you receive e-mails, what do you use to determine which e-mail to read first, or at all? The subject line, of course! Never send an e-mail message without a subject line. Subject lines should be brief, with the keywords appearing first. The longer the subject line is, the more likely it will not be viewed in its entirety because different people set the viewable subject line space at various widths.

The subject line is equivalent to a headline in a newspaper in terms of attracting reader attention. When you read a newspaper, you don't really read it; generally you skim the headlines and read the articles whose headline grabbed your attention. The same is true with e-mail. Many recipients, especially those who receive a significant number of e-mails daily, skim the subject lines and read only the articles whose subject line grabs their attention. The subject line is the most important part of your e-mail message because this phrase alone will determine whether or not the reader will decide to open your e-mail or delete it.

Effective subject lines will:

- Be brief, yet capture the reader's interest

- Not look like ad copy

- Build business credibility

- Attract attention with action words

- Highlight the most important benefits

- Always be positive

- Put the most important words first

Effective headlines should grab the reader's attention, isolate and qualify your best prospects, and draw your reader into the subheadlines and the text itself. Avoid SHOUTING! Using CAPITALS in your subject line is the same as SHOUTING AT THE READER! DON'T DO IT!! Stay away from ad copy in your subject lines—it is the kiss of death for an e-mail. Most people when they open their e-mail delete all the ads as the first step.

E-mail "To" and "From" Headings Allow You to Personalize

Use personal names in the "To" and "From" headings whenever possible, as this creates a more personal relationship. Most e-mail programs allow you to attach your personal name to your e-mail address.

If you are using Microsoft Outlook Express, the following are the steps to set up your name in the "From" heading:

1. On the menu bar, click "Tools."

2. On the drop-down box, click on "Accounts."

3. Click on the "Mail" tab.

4. Click on your e-mail account, then click "Properties."

5. Click on the "General" tab.

6. Under "User information," type your name and organization in the appropriate boxes. It is the name from this area that will be seen in the "From" field in the user's e-mail program. Then click "Apply," then "OK" and "Close."

For all other e-mail programs, consult the Help file included in the program.

Blind Carbon Copy (BCC)

Have you ever received an e-mail message in which the first screen or first several screens were a string of other people's e-mail addresses to which the message had been sent? Didn't you feel special? Didn't you feel the message was meant just for you? This sort of bulk mailing is

---

BCC
Blind Carbon Copy:
all recipient names
are hidden so that
no one sees who
else has received the
e-mail.

---

very unpersonalized, and most often recipients will delete the message without looking at it.

It is advisable to use the **BCC** feature when sending bulk or group e-mails; otherwise, every person on the list will see that this e-mail was not sent just to him or her. The e-mail recipients will see the list of the other recipients first and not the intended message. They will be required to scroll down past the list of recipients to get to your message. This is not the best way to make friends and influence people. Make sure that you know how to use the blind carbon copy function in your e-mail program.

Even better than blind carbon copy is using a software application that can send personalized messages to each recipient in your database. E-mail applications like this are far more flexible than the BCC method because there is no limitation on the number of messages you can send. The field-merge capabilities enable you to create a more personalized message, and these programs generally have tracking features to know what you've sent to whom.

Before you send any "live" bulk e-mail for the first time using BCC, do a test with a number of your colleagues and friends to make sure you are using the program and features effectively and that all of their addresses appear appropriately in the message.

Effective E-mail Message Formatting

The content of the message should be focused on one topic. If you need to change the subject in the middle of a message, it is better to send a separate e-mail. Alternatively, if you wish to discuss more than one topic, make sure you begin your message with "I have three questions" or "There are four issues I would like to discuss." People are busy; they read their e-mail quickly, and they assume you will cover your main points within the first few sentences of your message.

E-mail is similar to writing a business letter in that the spelling and grammar should be correct. This includes the proper use of upper- and lowercase lettering, which many people seem to ignore when sending e-mail. However, e-mail is unlike a business letter in that the tone is completely different. E-mail correspondence is not as formal as business writing. The tone of e-mail is more similar to a polite conversation than a formal letter, which makes it conducive to relationship building.

In general, you should:

- Keep your paragraphs relatively short—no more than seven lines.

- Make your point in the first paragraph.

- Be clear and concise.

- Use *http://* at the beginning of any Web address to ensure that you make it "live." When you provide the URL starting with the *www,* the reader has to copy and paste the Web address into the address field in the browser if he wants to visit your site. When you place *http://* before the *www,* the link is "live" and the reader just has to click on the address to be taken directly to your site. Make it as easy as possible for your reader to visit your Web site.

- Give your reader a call to action.

- Avoid using fancy formatting such as graphics, different fonts, italics, and bold, because many e-mail programs cannot display those features. Your message that reads: "I *loved* the flowers. **Love 'ya**" could be viewed as "I <I>loved<I> the flowers. <B>Love ya<B>" if the recipient's e-mail software can't handle formatting. Kinda loses the impact!

- If your e-mail package doesn't have a spellcheck feature, you might want to consider composing your message first in your word-processing program. Spellcheck it there and then cut and paste it into your e-mail package.

- Choose your words carefully. E-mail is a permanent record of your thoughts, and it can easily be forwarded to others. Whenever you have the urge to send a nasty response, give yourself an hour or two to reconsider. Those words may come back to haunt you—and they usually do.

If you want to be really careful, test the e-mail in a number of the popular packages to ensure that your message will be received in the intended format.

A Call to Action

When you give your readers a call to action, it's amazing how often people will do as they're told. I'll give you an example of something we did at Connex Network. We ran a series of ten Internet marketing workshops for a large organization. Their staff and selected clients were invited to participate in any, some, or all of the workshops. Their clients could include up to three employees. Since the workshops extended beyond noon, lunch was provided.

Since Connex Network was responsible for organizing and managing the project, we needed to know the approximate number of people who would be attending each of the workshops to organize the luncheons. When we contacted each company's representatives by e-mail looking for participation RSVPs, we conducted an experiment. We sent half the representatives one version of the message and the other half a slightly different version. The only difference between the two messages was that in one, we included a call to action. In that message we asked: "RSVP before Wednesday at noon indicating if you will be attending as we must make arrangements for lunch," and in the other, this same line read: "Please let us know if you are planning to attend as we must make arrangements for lunch."

There was a 95 percent response rate from the group who received the first message. This is because we gave people a call to action and a deadline, and they felt obligated to respond more promptly. Meanwhile, fewer than 50 percent of the people in the second group responded to our message. What does this tell us? To improve your response rate, give your readers a call to action when you send them e-mail. People will respond when told to do something; they act with more urgency when there is a deadline.

Appropriate E-mail Reply Tips

Do not include the entire original message in your replies. This is unnecessary and is aggravating to the original sender of the message. However, use enough of the original message to refresh the recipient's memory. Remember to check the "To" and "CC" before you reply. You would not want an entire mail list to receive your response intended only for the sender. The same applies for selecting "Reply to All" instead of "Reply."

HTML or Text?

Should you send e-mail messages as text or as HTML? HTML messages allow you to basically send a Web page via e-mail. These HTML messages are far prettier and eye-catching than text, and studies have shown that HTML messages deliver significantly higher click-through rates. However, not all e-mail programs support HTML, and therefore any HTML messages sent to users of noncompatible e-mail programs will not be able to be viewed. This issue will only be compounded as more and more people access their e-mail from e-mail enabled cell phones, Palm Pilots, and other devices.

Another thing to keep in mind if you send an HTML e-mail is that any images you use within the e-mail need to be uploaded to a server (usually the server that hosts your Web site) so that when someone views the HTML e-mail, the images load from your server. It is important to keep these images "live" for a period of time as sometimes recipients don't get a chance to view their messages right away. If the HTML e-mail is viewed with broken images (the intended image files do not load), the whole purpose of the HTML e-mail is lost.

In addition, sending HTML e-mails allow you to do some tracking of the number of people who view your message. As mentioned before, each image file is placed on your Web server. It is important to note that each image should have a unique name and should not share the name of any image currently being used on your Web site or in other HTML e-mails. If you send an HTML e-mail, every time someone opens the message a request is sent to your Web server to send the recipient's computer the image files in the e-mail. Each of these requests is logged, and if you have access to these Web server logs or have traffic analysis software set up, you can see how many times a particular image was accessed. Although this method is by no means 100 percent accurate in tracking how many people opened your message, it does give you a basic idea.

Always Use Your Signature Files

As discussed previously, signature files are a great marketing tool. Always attach your signature file to your online communication. (See Chapter 8 for information on signature files.) Also, ensure that the signature files are appropriate for the intended audience.

Discerning Use of Attachments

If you are sending a fairly large volume of data, you may want to send it as an attached file to your e-mail message. However, only include an e-mail attachment if you have the recipient's permission to send an attached file. You would never consider going to someone's home, letting yourself in, finding your way into their living room, and then leaving your brochure on the coffee table. However, people do the online equivalent of this when they send an unsolicited attachment. The attachment is sent across the Internet to the recipient's computer and is downloaded and stored on the computer's hard drive. This is considered quite rude and, in most cases, unwanted.

Also, unless the recipient of your e-mail is aware of the file size and is expecting it, don't send an attachment that is larger than 50K. Although your Internet connection might be a cable modem or a T1 line, and a 3MB file is sent in seconds, the person who is receiving your message and attachment might be using a 14.4 Kbps modem and a slow machine. If you send a 3MB file, it might take the person with the 14.4 Kbps modem two hours to download the file. Needless to say, he or she won't be too pleased.

Another factor to consider when sending an unsolicited attachment is that the attachment you are sending may be incompatible with the operating system or the software on the recipient's system. You may be using a different platform (Mac/PC) or different operating system, and the recipient may not be able to open and read your file. Even PC to PC or Mac to Mac, the recipient may not be able to open and view the attachment if that particular program is not installed on his machine. Someone using a 1994 version of Corel WordPerfect may not be able to read a Microsoft Word 2000 document sent as an attachment. Thus, you will have wasted your time sending the file and the recipient's time downloading the file.

Viruses
Programs that contaminate a user's hard drive, often with unwanted results.

Finally, it is a well-known fact that e-mail attachments can act as carriers for computer **viruses**. You may unknowingly send someone an attachment with a virus, and even if the file you send is virus-free, you may still take the blame if recipients find a virus on their system just because you sent them an attachment. Basically, avoid sending e-mail attachments of any variety unless you have the recipient's permission. Be mindful of the size of the file you intend to send, compatibility with other platforms, and computer viruses. One alternative to sending a large attachment is to post the file on a Web server, and in your e-mail message direct users to a URL from which they can download the file.

Before You Click on "Send"

There are a number of things you should do before you send an important e-mail, especially if it is going to a number of people. Send a test message to yourself or a colleague so that you can check that the word wrap looks good, that the text is formatted properly, and that it displays as you want it to. Check that there are no typos, errors, or omissions.

Expressing Yourself with Emoticons and Shorthand

In verbal communication, you provide details on your mood, meaning, and intention through voice inflections, tone, and volume. You also give clues about your meaning and intention through facial expression and body language. E-mail does not allow for the same expression of feeling. The closest thing we have to this online is the use of emoticons.

Emoticons
Symbols made from punctuation marks and letters that look like facial expressions.

The word *emoticons* is an acronym for "emotions" and "icons." Emoticons are combinations of keyboard characters that give the appearance of a stick figure's emotions. They have to be viewed sideways and are meant to be smiling, frowning, laughing, and so on. Emoticons let you communicate your meaning and intentions to your reader. For example, if your boss gives you an assignment via e-mail and your response is, "Thanks a lot for unloading your dirty work on me," your boss may become upset at your obvious defiance. But if you replied with this: "Thanks a million for unloading your dirty work on me :-)," your boss would understand that you were jokingly accepting the assignment.

Emoticons enable you to add a little personality and life to your text messages. However, their use is not universal and should generally not be used in business correspondence. Some of the more commonly used emoticons include:

:-)	Smiling
:-@	Screaming
:-0 or :-o	Wow!
:-p	Tongue wagging
;-)	Wink
(-:	I'm left-handed
:-V	Shout
:-&	Tongue-tied
:-r	Tongue hanging out
;-(or ;-<	Crying
:-#	My lips are sealed!
:-*	Oops!
:-S	I'm totally confused.
8-0	No way!
:-	Skeptical
:-<	Sad or frown
~~:-(	I just got flamed!
%-0	Bug-eyed
:\	Befuddled
:-D	Laughing, big smile
}:->	Devilish, devious

E-mail shorthand is used in newsgroups and other e-mail to represent commonly used phrases. Some common abbreviations are:

- BTW · By the way

- IMHO   In my humble opinion

- IMO   In my opinion

- IOW   In other words

- JFYI   Just for your information

- NBD   No big deal

- NOYB   None of your business

- TIA   Thanks in advance

- PMFJI   Pardon me for jumping in

- OIC   Oh, I see . . .

- OTL   Out to lunch

- OTOH   On the other hand

- LOL   Laughing out loud

- LMHO   Laughing my head off

- ROFL   Rolling on the floor laughing

- BFN   Bye for now

- CYA   See ya!

- FWIW   For what it's worth

- IAE   In any event

- BBL   Be back later

- BRB   Be right back

- RS   Real soon

- WYSIWYG   What you see is what you get

- <g>   Adding a grin

Since e-mail shorthand is most commonly used in newsgroups and chat rooms, you will be most successful when using these acronyms with others who are familiar with them.

Permission-based E-mail Marketing

Permission and privacy are critical to the success of any e-mail marketing campaign. Although unsolicited snail direct mail may be generally accepted or at least tolerated by many consumers, the rules are completely different online. Unsolicited e-mail runs the risk of damaging your company's reputation, not to mention the very real possibilities of flames, public blacklisting, hack attacks, and even having your Internet services revoked. Online consumers are very quick to let you know when you have crossed the line, and unsolicited e-mail (or spam) definitely crosses the line. Because of this, online marketers are using many techniques to get their customers, potential customers, and site visitors to give them "permission" to send them e-mail on a regular basis.

Permission marketing is really a win–win situation. Recipients receive information that they asked to receive, and the marketer is communicating with an audience that is genuinely interested in what is being marketed; otherwise the recipients would not have given their "permission" to receive the e-mail. Online marketers claim that permission e-mail marketing is one of the best ways to boost customer retention and boost sales. Permission e-mail marketing generally yields response rates ten times that of banner advertising.

So how do you get this coveted permission? Generally you have to provide something of value and of interest to your target market. There are many opportunities on your Web site to ask for permission. The more repeat-traffic generators on your site, the more opportunities you can provide for your Web site visitors to give you the permission. (See Chapter 3 for repeat-traffic generators.) You should leverage repeat-traffic generators with permission marketing and accelerate responses with a call to action. On my Web site I have a call to action that says "Sign up Now" for my biweekly newsletter (see 9.1). Let me provide you with some typical examples:

- Click here to join our mail list and receive our monthly newsletter filled with great tips.

- Click here to be notified when we update our Web site.

- Click here to receive our weekly e-specials via e-mail.

- Click here to be notified when we update our online coupons.

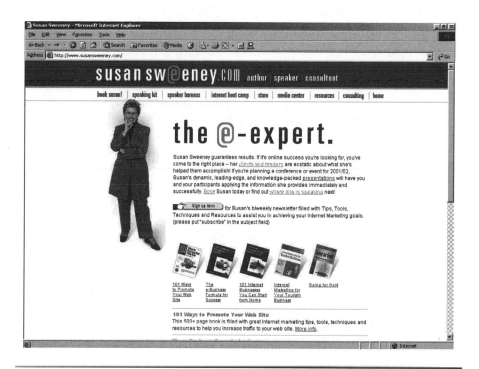

Figure 9.1. Accelerate response with a call to action. See the Sign Up Now! call to action used with my bi-weekly newsletter.

- Click here to be notified when we introduce new products to our catalogue.

- Click here to be notified when we change our monthly free offer.

- Click here to be notified when we change our free sample offer.

- Click here to be notified when we introduce a new contest with great prizes.

- Click here to be notified when we update our What's New page.

- Want to receive our tip of the week via e-mail? Click here.

You get the picture. Almost every page on your Web site provides an opportunity for you to offer permission marketing. Of course, when site visitors click, they are taken to a screen where they add themselves to your mail list. Your mail list program should keep track of the element the visitor gave you permission to send.

Permission marketing enjoys its success because it is personal, relevant, and anticipated. Your messages should be personalized, enhancing the one-to-one relationship marketing element.

Privacy is a very big issue when a Web site visitor is deciding whether to give you an e-mail address or not. It is very important to assure your visitors that you will not pass on their e-mail address to others and you will not use it for anything but the purpose intended. Your privacy policy should clearly be evident on your Web site. The privacy policy can read like a legal document or be short and to the point (see Figure 9.2).

E-mail Marketing Tips

Be prepared. You will receive a number of e-mails requesting information on your company, your products, your locations, and so on, from people who have seen your e-mail address on letterhead, ads, business cards, and sig.files. Don't wait for the first inquiry before you begin to develop your company materials. Here are some tips. Following them will make you more prepared to respond.

Include a Brochure and Personal Note

Have an electronic brochure or corporate information available that you can easily access and send via e-mail. Try to send a personal note in your e-mail along with any material requested.

Gather a Library of Responses

Different people will ask a number of the same questions, and over time you will be able to develop a library of responses to these frequently asked questions. When responding to an e-mail, ask yourself if you are likely to get the question again. If your answer is "yes," then consider developing a document in your word processor called "Frequently Asked

Figure 9.2. Jeff Mowatt (*http://www.jeffmowatt.com*) has his privacy policy clearly stated.

Questions," or "FAQs." In the future when you get a question that you have answered before, simply cut and paste your response from your FAQs file into your e-mail message. Again, always make sure to appropriately edit and personalize your responses.

Have More Than One E-mail Account

By having a number of different e-mail accounts, you can develop databases of all the people who have sent you a message—sorted by their interests. (You will know their interests by which mailbox they choose to send an e-mail to.) For example, you may be able to tell that a person is interested in your virus scanners but not your game software, or interested in your information on making animated **GIFs** but not in your virus archive.

GIF
Graphical
Image File.

The tactic of using separate e-mail accounts and filtering them into different mailboxes can be used for many marketing purposes other than developing e-mail lists. An example would be to place the same advertisement in three different magazines. Associate a different e-mail address with each ad, and determine which ad generates the best response by reviewing the number of responses sent to the different e-mail addresses. You will then know which magazine to use in the future for the best response.

Run an Opt-In E-mail Marketing Campaign

An opt-in e-mail marketing campaign is perhaps the best means to reach your target audience. "Opt-in" refers to the fact that people can willingly subscribe and unsubscribe from your e-mail list. This is important because if people do not want mail from you and you send them unsolicited e-mail, you could be accused of spamming. Spam is the scourge of the Internet and a pet peeve of many people. If it is reported to your ISP that you are sending unsolicited bulk e-mail, you could lose your Internet account.

Send mail only to people who have expressed prior interest in your business, and allow them to unsubscribe themselves from your mailing list if they choose. As mentioned earlier in this chapter, you can use the blind carbon copy method or a specialized e-mail application to conduct an e-mail marketing campaign. Most e-mail marketing software packages will permit you to easily add or delete subscribers from your mailing list. These applications also create more personalized messages than can be achieved using blind carbon copy.

Following Formalities with E-mail Netiquette

When writing e-mails, remember these points:

* Be courteous. Remember your pleases and thank-yous.

* Reply promptly—within 24 hours.

* Be brief.

- Use lowercase characters. Capitals indicate SHOUTING!

- Use emoticons where appropriate.

- Check your grammar and spelling.

- Use attachments sparingly.

- Do not send unsolicited bulk e-mail.

Reply Promptly

People expect an answer the same day or the next day at the latest. E-mail communication is like voice mail. If you do not respond within 24 hours, you send a very clear message to your clients, potential clients, and colleagues: "Your communication is not important to me." Respond within 24 hours even if the message is, "Sorry, I can't get to this immediately. I'll try to have a reply for you by the end of the week." This may be a response you will want to save in a readily available file from which you can copy and paste it into an e-mail message. A prompt reply even if it says you can't respond immediately is better than a delayed full response. The people writing you for information will appreciate the fact that you felt their message was important enough to respond to immediately.

The Heart of Customer Service

Although most customer correspondence via e-mail is very pleasant and businesslike, you will occasionally encounter people who are displeased with the service they have received from you. Very often, a series of courteous, prompt e-mail responses can turn a disgruntled customer into a customer for life. Taking a potentially disagreeable situation and reversing it to a positive one is the heart of customer service. Following is a real example of how a client turned such a situation around. This excerpt was provided to me by Donna Ross of the *Shambhala Sun* magazine at a recent seminar and has been included with the permission of

Donna and the *Shambhala Sun (http://www.shambhalasun.com)*. The name and address of the subscriber have been changed. Customer's first message:

Dear Shambhala Sun Folk:

I sent in a change of address form back a few months ago, but I have not been receiving the latest issues of your magazine at my new address. The last one I received was the January issue at my old address. So let's try again:

Name: Joe Subscriber

Old Address:
100 Some Street
Anaheim, CA 92999

New Address:
49494 Another Street
San Jose, CA 92000

My home phone number is (999) 999-9999.

Thank you for your help and consideration on this matter.

Sincerely,

Joe Subscriber

Shambhala Sun's Response:

Dear Joe:

We do have your new address in our system. Your May issue should be arriving there any minute now. I will send you the missed March issue in this evening's mail. I notice that we have the city for your new address listed as Laguna Hills. In your e-mail, you have it as San Jose. Please let me know which of the two is more accurate. Thanks.

Donna Ross
Shambhala Sun Subscriptions

Customer's second message:

How did you know? The May issue arrived in my mailbox
this very day! As I was just in a fairly bad auto accident and
am laid up, it is most welcome. Thanks for your speedy reply.

Sincerely,

Joe Subscriber

Shambhala Sun's Response:

Actually, it is my job to know. :-) Sorry to hear you are hurt.
Heal well.

Donna Ross
Shambhala Sun Subscriptions

Customer's final message:

Thanks Donna for your concern. It's no surprise that
Shambhala Sun has folks like you working there. Consider me
a subscriber for life.

Sincerely,

Joe Subscriber

P.S.—Although my car was totaled, I am doing fine and
healing quickly.

As has clearly been demonstrated by the example, the value of strong customer relations is immeasurable. If you take great care to respond quickly and courteously to your customers' (even when they're not happy) e-mail messages, you can win them over for life. Nothing exceeds the value of a lifetime customer.

Resources for Chapter 9

...ve included a few resources for you to check out when using e-mail. For ...ditional resources on a variety of topics, I recommend that you visit the ...esources section of my Web site at *http://www.susansweeney.com/resources.html*. There you will find additional tips, tools, techniques, and resources.

123 Promote
http://www.mcn.org/b/sitepromoter/123Exe/123/123PROMO/work-book/email.htm
E-mail guide to e-mail styles, mail merging, autoresponders, autoreminders, netiquette, headers, signature files, announcements, press releases, business administration, free designs, mailing list announcements, newsgroup announcements, office automation, mass e-mailing, publicity, form letters, form folders, e-mailed databases, programs, and software.

A Beginner's Guide to Effective E-mail
http://www.Webfoot.com/advice/email.top.html
Help in writing the e-mail you need. Formats and why you need e-mail are all explained in detail.

Dave Barry's Guide to Emoticons
http://www.randomhouse.com/features/davebarry/emoticon.html
Good resource for emoticons and shorthand. His site has an Emoticon Gallery with lots of examples (10,000 at last count) and an area where you can make your own.

EmailAddresses.com
http://www.emailaddresses.com
A directory of numerous free e-mail services including POP accounts, e-mail forwarding, newsletters, and so on.

E-mail—The Mining Company
http://email.miningco.com/internet/email
Updated weekly, this site consists of articles and links to e-mail resources on many topics: beginning e-mail, finding people, free e-mail, greeting cards, privacy, and much more.

Everything E-mail
http://everythingemail.net
Information and links to make your e-mail account more productive and fun. Resources, guides, and a glossary make things easier for you to understand. This is an extensive Web site dedicated exclusively to e-mail and e-mail services.

I Will Follow.com E-mail Tips
http://www.iwillfollow.com/email.htm
This site offers advice to beginners on all aspects of using e-mail.

Neophyte's Guide to Effective E-mail
http://www.Webnovice.com/email.htm
This site goes through, step by step, the important issues you should keep in mind from start to send.

Smith Family Internet Marketing Support
http://www.smithfam.com/news/ap12.html
"The Secrets of E-mail Marketing Success," an article by Lesley Anne Lowe.

Windweaver
http://www.windweaver.com/emoticon.htm
Recommended emoticons for e-mail communication.

10

Autoresponders

Autoresponders act much like fax-on-demand systems. With fax–on-demand systems you call from your fax machine, dial the specified code, and you'll get back the requested document on your fax machine. The **autoresponder** works much the same way—you send an e-mail to an autoresponder e-mail address and you'll get back the requested information via e-mail. In this chapter, you will learn:

> **Autoresponder**
> An autoresponder is a computer program that automatically returns a prewritten message to anyone who submits e-mail to a particular Internet address.

- What autoresponders are

- Why you should use autoresponders

- What types of information to send via autoresponders

- Autoresponder features

- Tips on successful marketing through autoresponders

What Are Autoresponders?

An autoresponder is a program located on a mail server that is set up to automatically send a pre-programmed reply to the e-mail address that sent mail to it. The reply can be a single message or a series of pre-programmed messages. They can be known by many names such as infobots, responders, mailbots, autobots, automailers or e-mail-on-demand.

Why Use Autoresponders?

One of the major benefits of using an autoresponder is the immediate response—24 hours a day, 7 days a week, 365 days a year, providing immediate gratification for the recipient.

Autoresponders are a real time-saver, eliminating the need for manual responses for many mundane and routine requests. They also enable you to track responses to various offers to assist you in your ongoing marketing efforts.

One big advantage with today's autoresponders is the ability to schedule multiple messages at predetermined intervals. The first response can go immediately, with a second message timed to go two days after the first, a third message to go five days after the second, and so on. Market research tells you that a prospect needs to be exposed to your message multiple times to become a motivated buyer.

Today's autoresponders are getting even more sophisticated in terms of mail list administration. These programs gather the e-mail addresses of people requesting information, which is stored in a database. The program adds the new names to the database and eliminates e-mail addresses that no longer work. Today's autoresponder programs provide reports of site visitors requesting information. This technology is very cost effective when compared to manual responses by a human, not to mention associated telephone and fax costs.

Personalization seems to be a standard feature of today's autoresponder programs. Autoresponders are used to send all kinds of information:

- Price lists

- Welcome letters

- Thank you letters

- Out-of-office advice

- Order confirmations

- Sales letters

- Catalogs

- News releases

- Brochures

- Job lists

- Spec sheets

- Assembly instructions

You can provide a copy of your newsletter so people can read a copy before subscribing... or anything else your target market might be interested in.

Why use an autoresponder when you could just provide the information on your Web site? There are many reasons. With the autoresponder you have the interested party's name and e-mail address; you don't get that from a visitor to your site. The autoresponder also provides you with the opportunity to send multiple messages to your potential customer.

Types of Autoresponders

There are three different types of autoresponders:

- Free

- Web host

- Other autoresponder providers

There are many free or minimal-fee autoresponders available that come with an ad on your responder page. Some Web hosting companies provide autoresponders in their Web hosting packages. There also are many autoresponder service providers that offer packages for a fee if you don't want to have ads placed on your responder page.

The important thing is to get the autoresponder that has the features you are looking for.

Autoresponder Features

When you are looking for an autoresponder, you want to make sure it has all the features to enable you to make the most of this marketing activity. Today's autoresponders keep getting better—new features are being added all the time. Some of the things you want to look for are discussed below.

Personalization

Today's autoresponders capture the requester's name as well as the e-mail address, allowing personalized responses.

Multiple Responses

Studies have shown that a potential customer has to be exposed to your message multiple times before he or she is ready to buy. Many autoresponders allow multiple messages on a scheduled time line.

Size of Message

Some autoresponders have a limit on the size of the message that can be sent. Ensure that your autoresponder can handle any message you would want to send to prospective customers.

Tracking

You must have access to tracking reports that provide you with information to enable you to track the results of your marketing efforts. You need to be able to determine what is working and what is not.

HTML Messaging

Choose an autoresponder that can handle HTML and plain-text e-mails. Studies have shown that HTML marketing e-mails get a higher click-through rate.

Autoresponders are continually being enhanced. Stay current.

Successful Marketing through Autoresponders

The technology is only one piece of this marketing technique. The content of the messages pushed through the autoresponder will be the determining factor in converting recipients of your message to customers. The following tips will help you produce effective messages:

- Personalize. Personalize your messages using the recipient's name throughout the message and in the subject line.

- Tone. Selling is all about relationships. Write your message in a tone that will build that.

- Focus on the reader's needs and how your product or service provides the solution. Focus on the benefits.

- Subject line. Have a catchy subject line, but don't use ad copy. Ad copy in a subject line is a sure way to get your message deleted before it is read.

- Include a call to action. It is amazing how often people do what they are told to do.

- Use correct spelling, upper- and lowercase, grammar, and punctuation. This correspondence is business correspondence and is a reflection of everything related to how you do business.

- Get to the point quickly. Online readers have little patience with verbose messages.

- Write for scanability. Have a maximum of six or seven lines per paragraph.

Internet Resources for Chapter 10

I have included a few resources for you to check out regarding autoresponders. For additional resources on a variety of topics, I recommend that you visit the Resources section of my Web site at *http://www.susansweeney.com/resources.html*. There you will find additional tips, tools, techniques, and resources.

Autoresponder Marketing by iBoost Journal
http://www.iboost.com/promote/marketing/autoresponders
Some interesting articles on autoresponders and how they can assist you in your online marketing.

Care & Feeding of the Press
http://www.netpress.org/careandfeeding.html
Journalists' manifesto for how PR people should work with the media.

FreeAutoBot.com
http://www.freeautobot.com
Another free service which allows you to send automated responses to those asking for more information from a form on your Web site or through an e-mail to you. Allows unlimited follow-up responses that can be sent daily, weekly, monthly, or yearly, and also allows for personalization of your messages.

GetResponse.com
http://www.getresponse.com
An autoresponder system that allows you to send multiple responses without unwanted advertising, and best of all it is free. Also includes the ability to send HTML e-mails.

Responders.com
http://www.responders.com

This site offers free request-form processing, online form builder, and autoresponder e-mails, and allows for easy integration into your Web site. Provides a live demo.

Send Free—The Original Autoresponder Ad Exchange
http://www.sendfree.com
A free service that allows you to have autoresponders running from your Web site but also allows you to advertise your business in the e-mail body of other targeted sites' autoresponders, and vice versa.

SmartAutoResponder.com
http://smartautoresponder.com/index.htm
An autoresponder service that charges a fee of U.S.$15.99 per month. Allows you to customize your autoresponder to your specifications.

11

Effective Promotional Use of Newsgroups

It is estimated that over 10 million people read newsgroups, making newsgroups an ideal marketing vehicle. The number of newsgroups is increasing, with over 100,000 different topics now estimated. People participate in newsgroups by "posting" or e-mailing comments, questions, or answers to other participants' questions, thus taking part in a conversation or thread. Using proper netiquette is important. To do this, read the FAQ files and rules, "lurk" first, and stay on topic. In this chapter, we cover:

- The benefits of using newsgroups in your marketing plan

- Newsgroup netiquette

- Reading the FAQ files, abiding by the rules, and lurking

- How to advertise if advertising is not allowed

- Developing your Usenet marketing strategy

- Identifying your target newsgroups

- Participating in this online community

- How to respond correctly to messages

- How to start your own newsgroup

- Cross-posting and spamming

- Using signature files

Newsgroups—What Are They?

Every day, millions of people from all over the globe enter a virtual community that they share with others who are interested in the same topic. These people are brought together by their common interest in the topic of discussion. While they are in this virtual community, only that specific topic is discussed. There are many communities that are discussing different topics. You can visit and participate in as many of them as you wish.

Newsgroup

A discussion group on the Internet that focuses on a specific subject.

These virtual communities are called Usenet newsgroups. They have their own section of the Internet. There is the World Wide Web part of the Internet where there are many Web sites that you can visit and read, and there is the e-mail part of the Internet where you can send and receive messages, and there is the Usenet newsgroup part of the Internet where discussions are taking place about many different topics.

Usenet newsgroups are hierarchical and are arranged by subject. Each newsgroup is dedicated to a discussion of a particular topic, such as antique cars, home schooling, travel, artificial intelligence, or the latest hot band.

Visitors to these virtual communities, or newsgroups, can "post" messages. These messages may be questions or comments or answers to other participants' questions. Everyone who visits the newsgroup has the opportunity to view these "postings." Often, many visitors participate in these discussions, and every side of the issue is presented.

Usenet has been defined as follows:

Usenet is the Internet's public forum, comprising thousands of newsgroups, each of which is devoted to the public discussion of a narrow, chartered topic such as microbrews, baseball cards, arthritis research, or traveling in Africa.

There are three types of newsgroup visitors:

- People asking questions or advice

- People providing answers or advice

- People who read the discussion without taking part

The Changing Face of Newsgroups

Usenet newsgroups started out as places where academics conducted discussions on research, and they quickly expanded to include newsgroups on every topic imaginable, with participants having wonderful conversations relevant to the topic. Then the commercialization of the Web hit, and today there are many newsgroups that are overrun with advertisements with very little topical discussion taking place. However, there are still many newsgroups that have vibrant discussions with loyal participants that provide a great opportunity for reaching and communicating with your target market.

Every visitor to a newsgroup made an effort to get there. He or she chose the specific newsgroup for a reason, usually an interest in the topic being discussed. If your business's products or services are related to the topic of discussion, you have found a group of your target market (they have prequalified themselves) in one place interested in discussing what you have to offer.

Newsgroups—An Ideal Marketing Vehicle

Usenet facilitates the exchange of an abundance of information on every topic imaginable. Many newsgroups are tight-knit communities with very loyal participants. Each group's readers are interested in the newsgroup topic, so when you find a newsgroup related to your product or service, it is likely that you have found members of your target market.

The number of newsgroups is steadily increasing. Currently it is estimated that more than 100,000 topics are available. Different newsgroups have varying numbers of readers. Some are read by hundreds of thousands of readers a day, and others see very little traffic. The newsgroups you decide to participate in may be read by a relatively small number of people or may have a large number of participants. Large isn't always better. A smaller group may provide you with a better chance of having your message read by your ideal target market; a larger group will provide you with better exposure by sheer volume.

Whether you pick a large group or a small group depends on your objectives and also on your product or service. For example, even though a posting to alt.politics may be seen by 300,000 readers, if what you are trying to sell is reproduction Model T Fords, it will not likely generate more potential business than a posting to a Usenet group such as rec.antiquecars.misc with only 1,000 readers. Not to mention that if your posting to alt.politics is inappropriate for that group, you will have done yourself more harm than good. Newsgroup readers do not appreciate having messages unrelated to their topic posted to their newsgroup, especially if they are advertisements.

If you use an online service, you can still participate in newsgroups because they have similar services. CompuServe has forums or special-interest groups, AOL has forums and clubs, and Prodigy has forums and bulletin boards. The same rules regarding participation, acceptable messages, and marketing activities generally apply. Not only are newsgroups helpful marketing tools, they can also help you identify competitors and trends in your industry, find valuable information from experts in your field, and perform market research activities.

The Benefits of Newsgroups

There are many ways online marketers can benefit from participating in newsgroups:

- Reaching prospective customers. You can immediately reach thousands of your targeted potential customers with a single message.

- Communicating with existing customers. You can provide your loyal customers with valuable information.

- Market research. You can use newsgroups to find out the latest trends, customer needs, what people are looking for, and what they are talking about. These newsgroups can be beehives of information where you can check out your competition and gather invaluable data on your market.

- Reputation building. By answering people's questions and helping to solve their problems, you will build your reputation as an expert in the field.

- Increased traffic. You can direct people to your commercial Web site if you do it in an informative way.

Thousands of Newsgroup Categories

Newsgroups are organized into different types of discussions or categories. Each of the major categories has lots of individual newsgroups in which you can participate. Major newsgroup categories include:

- **alt** = Discussions on alternative topics.

- **biz** = Discussions on business topics. You may find groups that allow advertising here.

- **comp** = Discussions on computer hardware- and software-related topics.

- **humanities** = Discussions on fine arts, literature, and philosophy topics.

- **misc** = Discussions of miscellaneous topics that don't have their own categories such as employment, health, and other issues.

- **news** = Discussions on Usenet news and administration.

- **rec** = Discussions on recreation topics such as games, hobbies, and sports.

- **sci** = Discussions on science.

- **soc** = Discussions on social issues.

- **talk** = Making conversation.

Each of the major categories has a number of subgroups, and each of the subgroups has a number of sub-subgroups. For example, under the rec major group you will find a subgroup rec.sports. Here the discussion revolves around all kinds of sports. Under the subgroup rec.sports you will find sub-subgroups and sub-sub-subgroups, for example:

- rec.sports

- rec.sports.hockey

- rec.sports.hockey.NHL

- rec.sports.hockey.NHL.BostonBruins

As you can see, the longer the name, the narrower is the discussion that is taking place.

Target Appropriate Newsgroups

With the large number of Usenet newsgroups that currently exist and the additional groups that are being introduced every day, it is a formidable task to identify appropriate newsgroups for your company's Internet marketing activities. First, you need to determine which newsgroups your prospective customers frequent.

Look for a close fit between a newsgroup and the product or service you are offering. For example, if your company sells software that aids genealogical work, then one appropriate newsgroup for your business might be soc.genealogy.methods. Try finding newsgroups that your target market may enjoy reading, or ask your clients or customers which newsgroups they participate in or find interesting. Find and make note of appropriate newsgroups that might be of interest to your target customers.

There are many ways to find appropriate Usenet newsgroup listings. You can do a search using the newsgroup functions of the two leading browsers, Netscape Navigator and Microsoft Internet Explorer, and most newsreader programs have a search capability.

Search the newsgroups for keywords that relate to your target market, your product, or your service to identify possible appropriate newsgroups for your marketing effort. A good place to start is Google Groups (*http://groups.google.com*), or you can go to *http://www.google.com* and select "Groups" from the four tabs (Web, Images, Groups, or Directories). Here you can conduct a keyword search of the Usenet newsgroups by typing your keywords into the search box and clicking "Google Search." The search results are displayed in chronological order, with the results at the top being the most recently used. You should choose keywords appropriate for your target customer or client. These methods will identify a fairly large list of potential newsgroups that may be considered for your marketing activities.

If your company specializes in providing exotic vacations to Mexico, you may want to search for keywords like *Mexico, vacation, travel, tropical, resorts, beaches,* and so on, to find potential newsgroups for your marketing effort. A benefit of the Google site is that you can post to the newsgroups directly from the site. You don't have to go through alternative software to do so.

Once you have done your preliminary research and compiled a long list of what you think are the most appropriate newsgroups related to your target market, you are ready to investigate further and qualify your list. The next step is to go to the Usenet Info Center Launch Pad at *http://sunsite.unc.edu/usenet-i/home.html*. There you can look up the newsgroups on your list. From this site you will be able to find out where the FAQ files for each newsgroup are located. The FAQ files will usually provide information on the newsgroup's stance on advertising. Info Center Launch Pad will sometimes provide you with details on the number of people participating in the group.

Read the FAQ Files and Abide by the Rules

Charter
Established
rules and
guidelines.

Read the FAQ files, **charter,** and rules about posting and advertising for each of your target newsgroups. It is very important that you abide by all the rules. If the FAQ files do not mention the group's stance on commercial advertising and announcements, then go back to Google Groups. Conduct a search based on the group's name and charter. This will tell you where the newsgroup stands on commercial activity.

Lurking for Potential Customers

Lurking
Browsing
without
posting.

Once you have narrowed your potential newsgroup list, you will want to visit each and every one to determine if the participants of the newsgroup are, in fact, potential customers. Spend time **lurking.** Monitor the types of messages that are being posted. Is there likely to be an opportunity for you to contribute? Are the participants your target market? Research the newsgroup to ascertain if it will appeal to your customers. The name of the newsgroup may not reveal what the newsgroup is about, so take your time and make sure.

Tips on Posting Messages

After you have become familiar with the rules of your selected newsgroup, have spent some time lurking, and have decided that the newsgroup is one where your target market is participating, you may begin to post messages. Remember to abide by the rules! If the rules do not allow advertising, then do not blatantly post an ad. To take full advantage of the newsgroup, you have to gain the trust of its members. With one wrong message, you could outrage all of the potential customers who participate in the newsgroup.

It is a good idea to run a test before you post a message to a newsgroup. Doing a test will show you how the posting works and will prevent you from making a mistake when it comes to the real thing. For a test mechanism, go to the newsgroup misc.test.

Becoming a respected member in a newsgroup is a way to promote yourself as well as your company. Provide valuable responses—the readers can tell when you are making a valuable contribution and when you are just advertising. In time you may forget that you began reading the newsgroup to promote your business. You will find yourself reading newsgroups in order to participate in stimulating discussions. You will be discussing anything and everything about the newsgroup subject. Only mention your Web site when you find an appropriate opportunity to bring your business knowledge into the conversation.

Newsgroups exist for specific purposes. They can be designed for discussions, news announcements, postings related to particular topics, and even buying and selling goods. They may have hundreds of messages sorted and available for access at any point in time. Newsgroup participants will decide whether to open or pass up your posted message based on the words in the subject area. Make your subject short and catchy so that your message will be read and not be passed over. Try to put the most important words of the subject first. This is a very critical part in posting a message to a newsgroup. Some people adjust the screen to see only the first few words in the subject area. When deciding on the text for the subject area, think about what keywords someone would use to search for information on the content of your message. The worst thing that you can do is post a message to a newsgroup with no subject at all. This will definitely receive no attention and is basically a waste of your time.

Start your message with a short description of how it relates to the group's main topic. People are looking for answers to specific questions, so it is rude to jump into the conversation with a topic that doesn't match the one in the subject line. You should attempt to get your message across right away. You should get to the point of your message in the first sentence. By doing so, you will catch the readers' attention and ensure that they will read the entire message.

Message length should be short, no longer than 24 lines. Short paragraphs of six or seven lines work well. Write for scannability.

When responding to a message in a newsgroup, you have the option of privately responding to the individual who posted the message or responding through the newsgroup. Determine which is more appropriate under the given circumstances. If your message will be of value to the entire group or will appropriately promote your company's capabilities, then post the response to the newsgroup for all to see. If you think that your company has a solution for the individual and would like to provide details to the "target customer," but feel that it would not benefit the other members of the group, then deliver a private response. Often you will choose to do both because once the answer to a question has been received, the original poster may not visit the newsgroup for awhile and you want to make sure he or she has the benefit of your posting. Whichever approach you take, make sure that you respond as quickly as possible so that the first message is still fresh in the mind of the recipient.

Tips to Ensure That Your Messages Will Be Well Received

Here are some basic rules to help you post well-received messages.

Keep to the Newsgroup Topic

Make sure you always stay on the newsgroup topic of discussion. People participate in specific newsgroups because of that subject and don't appreciate off-topic postings.

Stay on the Thread

When responding to a message, use the Reply option to stay on the same thread. When you reply without changing the subject line, your message will appear immediately below the message you are responding to in the newsgroup. This is referred to as "staying on thread." This makes it easy for others to follow the discussion. For an example of this, see Figure 11.1.

Make a Contribution

Informed, quality responses to people's questions will give you credibility with the group and will reflect well upon you and your company. If you post positive and informative information, visitors will return to the newsgroups and look for your posts.

Don't Post Commercials or Advertisements

Advertising is not welcome in most newsgroups, and many charters specifically disallow the posting of ads. Read the FAQ files before posting a message. If the newsgroup does not allow commercial messages or ads, don't post them.

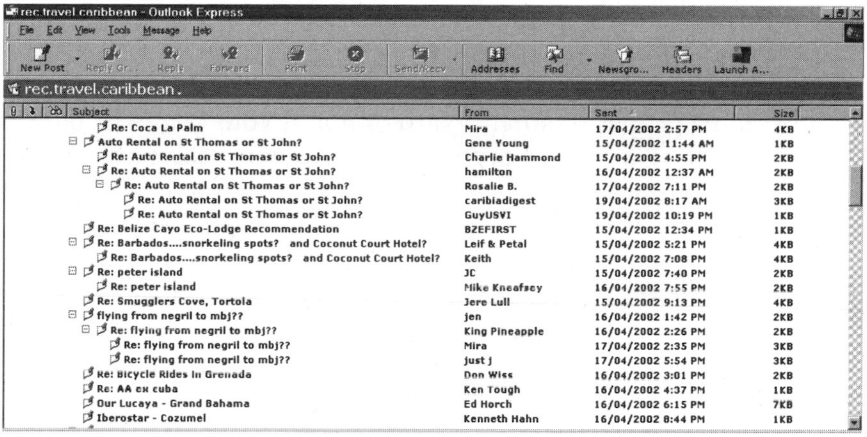

Figure 11.1. It is very important to stay on thread. As you can see in this travel newsgroup, the Auto Rental messages are staying on thread. The message has been replied to, keeping the same subject line.

You Don't Have to Have the Last Word

Don't post gratuitous responses in newsgroups. Never post a message with just a "Thanks" or "I like it" if you have nothing else to contribute. If you feel such a response is warranted or would like to discuss the issue privately, send a private e-mail to the person to convey your appreciation or opinion.

Signature Files as Your e-Business Card

A **signature file,** or sig.file as it is commonly referred to, is your e-business card. It is a short message at the end of an e-mail. Most, if not all, e-mail programs allow for the use of a signature file. Sig.files can be attached at the end of your message when you post to a Usenet newsgroup or a mailing list, even if the group does not allow advertising.

> **Signature File**
> An e-business card usually attached to e-mail.

You can use your sig.file in a number of clever ways. Sig.files can be simple—listing only phone numbers and addresses—or they can be virtual ads for your company. They can be very useful in providing exposure for your company. You can use your sig.file to offer some substantial information, such as letting people know about a special event, informing people about an award or honor your company has received, or promoting a specific product or service your company has to offer.

You can design and use different sig.files for posting to different newsgroups. A particular sig.file may be appropriate for one newsgroup but not for another. Always be sure that the message in your sig.file is appropriate for its audience.

Keep your sig.file short. Usually four to eight lines is a good size. There is nothing more annoying than a sig.file that is longer than the text of the message to which it is attached, or one that resembles a brochure.

Sig.files should include the following:

- Contact name

- Business name

- URL

- Address

- E-mail address

- Telephone number

- Fax number

- A brief company tag line or a company slogan

This is an example of what a sig.file looks like:

Sunnyvale Volkswagen
Jane Doe, Marketing Assistant
jdoe@bug.com

101 Main Street   Toll-Free Tel: (800) 555-1001
Woodstock, NY 10010   Fax: (800) 555-1000
Visit http://www.bug.com to see our latest models

For a complete discussion of sig.files and how to use them, see Chapter 8.

Newsgroup Advertising Hints

Newsgroups have been developed for different audiences and different topics. Some newsgroups are dedicated to posting advertisements. If advertising is appropriate for your company, the following newsgroup types might be included in your Internet marketing strategy. Most of the newsgroups that allow advertising are readily identifiable. The newsgroup name itself might include one of the following:

- biz

- classified

- for sale

- marketplace

Again, read the FAQ files and lurk to determine if the newsgroup is appropriate for your target market before you post. Use a short, catchy subject line with keywords at the beginning—the subject will determine whether your message warrants a read or a pass. Avoid ALL CAPITALS. This is equivalent to shouting on the Internet. Stay away from !!!!, ****, @@@@, and other such symbols.

When you have found a newsgroup whose participants include your target market but the newsgroup does not allow advertising, don't despair. When responding to queries or providing information that is of genuine interest to the newsgroup, you have the opportunity to attach your sig.file. A sig.file can be as effective as an ad if it is designed properly. Your message should offer valuable information pertinent to the discussion. (A thinly veiled excuse to get your sig.file posted will not be appreciated.) If your information is relevant and of value to the participants of the newsgroup, the fact that the tag line in your sig.file is an advertisement will not matter—in fact, it may add credibility to the information you have provided and may enhance your company's reputation.

Cross-Posting and Spamming

Cross-posting is posting identical messages to a number of relevant newsgroups. Doing this is considered to be inappropriate because of the number of common users in associated newsgroups. Spamming is posting identical or nearly identical messages to irrelevant newsgroups without care or regard for the posting guidelines, the newsgroup topic, or the interests of the group. Cross-posting and spamming will annoy the readers of the newsgroup. Doing these things will reflect badly on you and your company and will prevent you from achieving your online marketing objectives.

If you disobey proper newsgroup netiquette, you may quickly learn what a flame is. A flame is a reply that may be posted into a newsgroup, or sent to you by e-mail, that contains extremely negative feedback. In the worst cases, people have been sent e-mails that contain 100 copies of a 16MB file, which could take their computer hours to download or could even crash the server. Although these acts are very immature, you must remember to obey newsgroup netiquette to make sure that this does not happen.

Sometime in your online postings, no matter how careful you are, someone is bound to get upset. Accept this as fact and learn how to handle flames appropriately. Be sensitive to complaints. Learn from them, but do not worry unnecessarily. If someone posts a message that reflects badly on your company, you have three options: Defend your comments in the newsgroup, send the person a private e-mail, or do nothing. Responding to the person via e-mail is the most appropriate response, even though in most cases your message will be ignored.

Earning Respect with Newsgroup Netiquette

Following are ten rules for netiquette. Incorporating them in your newsgroup posting will gain you respect by the other participants.

1. Don't use CAPITALS. They are akin to shouting on the Internet.

2. Don't post ads where they are not welcome.

3. Do provide valuable, on-topic information for the newsgroup.

4. Don't be rude or sarcastic.

5. Don't include the entire message you are replying to in your response. Only quote relevant sections of the original message.

6. Do a thorough review of your message before you post. Check your spelling and grammar. Check your subject; it should be short and catchy with the keywords first.

7. Do provide an appropriate sig.file.

8. Don't post messages that are too lengthy. Online communication tends to be one screen or less.

9. Don't spam or cross-post.

10. Don't post replies that contribute nothing to the discussion (e.g., "I agree" or "Thanks").

Have Your Own Newsgroup

You can start your own newsgroup if you feel it is warranted and appropriate. All group creation requests must follow set guidelines and are first met with discussion. If you need help, you can always find a body of volunteers who are experienced in the newsgroup creation process at group-mcntors@acpub.duke.edu. They assist people with the formation and submission of good newsgroup proposals.

The Discussion

A request for discussion on creating a new newsgroup should be posted to news.announce.newsgroups and news.groups. If desired, the request can also be posted to other groups or mailing lists that are related to the proposed topic. The name and charter of the proposed group and whether it will be moderated or unmoderated should be determined during the discussion period.

The Vote

The Usenet Volunteer Vote Takers (UVT) is a group of neutral third-party vote takers who currently handle vote gathering and counting for all newsgroup proposals. There should be a minimal delay between the end of the discussion period and the issuing of a call for votes. The call for votes should include clear instructions on how to cast a vote. The voting period should last for at least 21 days and no more than 31 days. Only votes that are mailed to the vote taker will be counted.

The Result

At the completion of the voting period, the vote taker must post the vote tally to the applicable groups and mailing lists. The e-mail addresses and names (if available) of the voters are posted along with the tally. There will be a five-day waiting period, beginning when the voting results actually appear. During the waiting period there will be a chance to correct any errors in the voter list or the voting procedure. In order for a proposal to pass, 100 more "YES/create" votes must be received than "NO/do not create" votes. Also, two-thirds of the total number of votes must be in favor of creation. If a proposal fails to achieve two-thirds of the vote, then the matter cannot be brought up for discussion until at least six months has passed from the close of the vote.

The following locations will help you should you wish to create your own newsgroup:

- How to Format and Submit a Newsgroup Proposal: *news. announce.newgroups, news.groups*

- How to Write a Good Newsgroup Proposal: *news.announce. newgroups, news.groups*

- Usenet Newsgroup Creation Companion: *news.announce. newusers, news.answers*

Internet Resources for Chapter 11

I have included a few resources for you to check out regarding newsgroups. For additional resources on a variety of topics, I recommend that you visit the Resources section of my Web site at *http://www.susansweeney.com/resources.html*. There you will find additional tips, tools, techniques, and resources.

Google—The Source for Internet Newsgroups!
http://groups.google.com
The Web site where you can read, search, participate in, and subscribe to more than 50,000 discussion forums, including Usenet newsgroups. Google has recently bought Deja.com, a resource for finding people, getting noticed, and getting answers to all sorts of questions. You can find discussion forums on any topic imaginable.

How to Advertise on Newsgroups
http://www.nsmi.com/noflames.html
How to Advertise on Newsgroups shows step-by-step techniques to follow so you won't get blacklisted. Everything you need to know about how to advertise in newsgroups and mailing lists without getting flamed.

Internet FAQ Archive
http://www.faqs.org
Formerly at the University of Ohio, the Internet FAQ Archive is the place to look for Usenet newsgroup descriptions and Frequently Asked Question (FAQ) lists. They also have quite a bit of general information about Usenet as well.

MG's House of News Knowledge
http://www.duke.edu/~mg/usenet
A great resource filled with information on every aspect of newsgroups, from how to post to how to create your own newsgroup.

Newsgroups
News.newusers.questions
News.announce.newusers
News.newusers
These provide information to new Usenet users on posting, finding appropriate newsgroups, netiquette, and other frequently asked questions new users are faced with.

NIC—Master List
http://www.engl.uvic.ca/OnlineGuide/News/newsGroupsWel.html
See this master list for a description of newsgroups.

Open Newsserver Search
http://www.muenz.com/sdienst/html/sgroup_e.html
English/German search engine that finds open news servers that carry newsgroups matching your search terms.

Tile.net
http://www.tile.net
A service for finding newsgroups and mailing lists as well as their descriptions.

12

Effective Promotion through Publicly Accessible Mailing Lists

Internet mailing lists are quick and easy ways to distribute information to a large number of people. There are thousands of publicly available online lists. You can also create your own Internet mailing lists to keep your clients and prospects informed of company events, product announcements, and press releases. In this chapter, we cover:

- How to identify appropriate publicly accessible mailing lists (discussion lists)

- Subscribing to the mailing list

- Writing messages that will be read

- Mailing list netiquette

- Creating your own mailing list

Connecting with Your Target Audience

Discussion mailing lists are publicly accessible and are focused on a particular subject matter. Participating in a discussion list relevant to your line of business can help you attract new customers. Discussion lists are organized hierarchically by subject matter in a way similar to Usenet newsgroups. Likewise, the membership rate of each discussion mailing list varies. People subscribe to particular lists to participate in that list and to receive all of the postings that are sent to the group, generally because they have an interest in the topic. When you post a message to a mailing list, the message is sent out to everyone who has subscribed to the list by e-mail.

Discussion mailing lists are quick and easy ways to distribute information to a large number of people interested in a particular topic. The difference between discussion mailing lists and newsgroups is that anyone on the Internet can visit newsgroups at any time and read any articles of interest, whereas a discussion list delivers all messages posted directly to the subscribers' e-mail. Only discussion list subscribers can receive these messages. Newsgroups can be viewed by anyone with access to a news server. All they have to do is log onto the news server and enter the name of the newsgroup they wish to peruse, and they can view all postings made to that group. To subscribe to a discussion list, you have to send a subscription message to the list administrator and request permission to join the mailing list. Newsgroup postings can be viewed anonymously, but permission is required to receive and view postings to mailing lists.

Types of Publicly Accessible Mailing Lists

Publicly accessible mailing lists can be one of several types, each with varying degrees of control. Following is a discussion of the two major types of lists.

Moderated Discussion Lists

This type of list is maintained by a "gatekeeper" who filters out unwanted or inappropriate messages. If you try to post an advertisement where it is not permitted, your message will never make it out to the list of subscribers. Similarly, flames (i.e., publicly chastising another list member) are screened out. The gatekeeper will also keep the topic of discussion on track if a few members get off-topic.

Unmoderated Discussion Lists

An unmoderated list is operated without any centralized control or censorship. Many publicly accessible lists are of this type. All messages are automatically forwarded to subscribers. Unmoderated lists tend to have more blatant advertisements and flame wars because there is no gatekeeper to guide the discussion. It is then the responsibility of the list members to police their own actions. If the list participants aren't rigidly abiding by the rules and reprimanding others who stray, the list could end up being a landfill for spammers. When this happens, a lot of members will simply leave the list.

Targeting Appropriate Discussion Mailing Lists

There are four types of mailing lists:

- Publicly accessible mail lists

- Direct mail lists

- Private mail lists

- Bulk mail lists

There are thousands of publicly accessible lists online and a number of sites that provide lists of these mailing lists. Several of the most popular and comprehensive are:

- The List of Publicly Accessible Mailing Lists at *http://www.paml.net* (Figure 12.1)

- Tile.net at *http://tile.net/lists* (Figure 12.2)

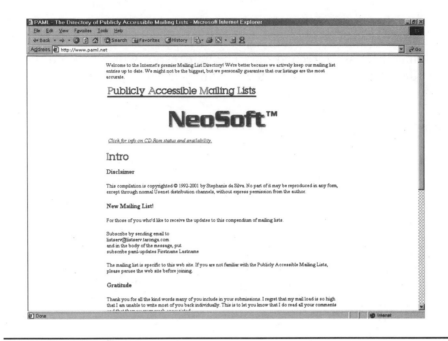

Figure 12.1. The List of Publicly Accessible Mailing Lists.

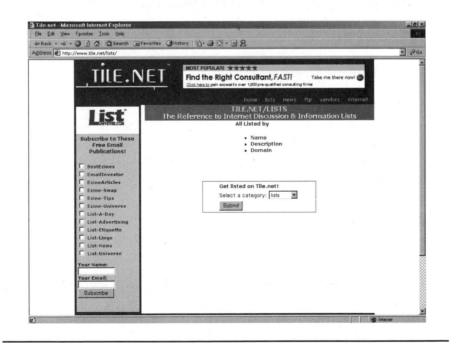

Figure 12.2. Tile.net offers more publicly accessible mailing lists.

- Topica at *http://www.topica.com* (Figure 12.3)

There are also companies online that specialize in providing targeted lists for a fee, much like purchasing a direct-mail list in the offline world. One company that provides this type of list is Post Master Direct Response at *www.postmasterdirect.com*. This company rents e-mail lists of people who have requested information on a particular topic. However, these differ from the discussion mailing lists that we described earlier in this chapter. E-mail lists are simply that—lists of e-mail addresses. If you subscribe to one of these lists, you are not entering into a discussion; you are placing yourself on a mailing list that will receive e-mail advertisements. However, from a marketing perspective, e-mail lists can be useful tools if they are targeted. These direct mail lists are discussed fully in Chapter 14.

Another option is to develop your own private mailing list. This concept is discussed in Chapter 13. Still another option is to purchase bulk e-mail lists. We've all received e-mails that say, "Reach 5 million

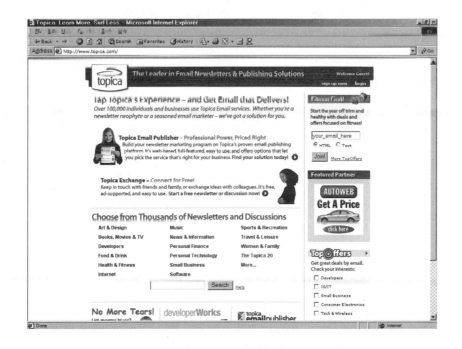

Figure 12.3. Topica provides access to thousands of mailing lists and discussion groups.

================
Spam
Sending the same
message to a large
number of people
who didn't ask for
it. Sending people
annoying mail.
================

with our mailing list available for $29.95." After all, one of the major benefits of the Internet is reaching large numbers of people quickly. This is a questionable practice because it involves **spam.** Bulk e-mail lists are generally sold without the permission of the addressees, much like junk mailing lists. The recipients did not ask to be put on a mailing list. They are not aware of the fact that they are on a list and often do not appreciate being sent unsolicited e-mail. Another drawback is that usually these lists are not targeted. By using bulk e-mail lists, you run the risk of not reaching any of your target market. You also risk annoying those addressees who under other circumstances may have been interested in what you were trying to sell.

The best approach is to choose a list whose subscribers fit your target market as closely as possible. For example, if you are selling geographic information systems to municipalities, a shotgun approach is a waste of both your time and your resources. By using bulk e-mail, you raise the ire of thousands of recipients of your e-mail, destroy your corporate image, and potentially damage your professional credibility. In this case, a targeted list, even though it will likely be much smaller, will get a much higher-quality response rate. Less is sometimes better.

Finding the Right Mailing List

Whether you join a publicly accessible discussion mailing list or choose to purchase an opt-in e-mail list from one of the many online sources, you want to find a mailing list whose members are your target market. You will have to do your homework here, because there are thousands of mail lists to choose from.

There are various meta-indexes of publicly accessible mailing lists where you can search by title or by subject. Some of these sites provide detailed information on the mail lists, such as their content and the commands used to subscribe. We have provided information on a number of these resources in the Internet Resources section at the end of this chapter.

Once you have identified mail lists that have your target market as members, you will subscribe to those lists. To confirm that the list is appropriate for your marketing purposes, lurk a while to monitor the discussion taking place. Once this has been confirmed, you can begin participating in the list by providing valuable content. If advertising is not allowed, abide by the rules. However, signature files are generally allowed, and you can always have that one-line tag line or mini-ad to advertise where advertising isn't allowed.

Subscribing to Your Target Mailing Lists

Liszt (*http://www.liszt.com*), tile.net/lists (*http://tile.net/lists*), Topica (*www.topica.com*), and the List of Publicly Accessible Mailing Lists (*www.paml.net*) are great resources and will provide you with not only a huge list of accessible mailing lists but also specific instructions for joining the particular lists you are interested in. Most lists are subscribed to by sending an e-mail message to the given address with "Subscribe" in the subject line or the body of the message. There are variations on this theme, so you must check the instructions for joining each specific mailing list. After you subscribe, you generally will receive an e-mail response with the rules, FAQs, and instructions on how to use the list.

For the most part, all of the rules for posting to newsgroups apply to mailing lists as well. Read the rules carefully and abide by them. A lurking period should be considered before you post a message. This will help you observe what types of messages are posted and the commonly accepted practices for that particular group.

List Digests

When subscribing to a mail list, quite often you are given the option to subscribe or to subscribe-digest. When you subscribe, you receive each message to the mail list as it is posted. When you subscribe-digest, the messages are accumulated and sent in one e-mail, usually on an overnight basis. The compilation of many individual messages is sent to each subscriber as one bulk message. Many digests contain a table of contents. The good thing about a digest is that you do not receive as many separate e-mail messages and your mailbox doesn't become clogged up. Also, the digest administrator chooses all or only the best postings to include in the list digest. Therefore, blatant advertisements, flames, and postings containing repetitive subject matter are filtered out. In an unmoderated list, you would receive every single message posted to the list. Many of these postings may not be of interest to you and would be deleted anyway. The digest format simplifies things so that you get the information you need without filling your e-mail box.

Composing Effective Messages

As discussed in the previous chapter, your e-mails must be carefully prepared before you post to a mailing list. Remember to make your subject line relevant, keep your messages short and to the point, and always include your sig.file. If you are unsure whether your posting is appropriate for the group, you can send a test message to the moderator asking for advice.

Unlike newsgroups, the members of mailing lists receive all the messages directly into their mailbox every day. Some people prefer to receive the postings in digest form; that is, all the messages for that day are compiled into one e-mail sent to the recipient at the end of the day. At the beginning of the e-mail, the digest provides a listing of all the messages with the "From" and "Subject" identified, followed by the complete messages. Just as individuals who visit a newsgroup don't read all the messages, subscribers to publicly accessible discussion lists do not read every posting. They decide which messages to review based on the subject line. Thus, the content of the "Subject" field is extremely important.

You must never repeat the same or similar messages to a mailing list, as you might do in a newsgroup. Once members of a mailing list have seen your posted message, they will not appreciate seeing it again, whereas a newsgroup has different readers all the time and similar postings are acceptable if they are timed appropriately. The following tips on mailing list postings will assist you in becoming a respected member of their online community:

- Make sure that your messages are "on the subject." List subscribers don't want to receive announcements unrelated to their topic.

- You should be a regular contributor to your list before making any commercial announcement. If your mailing list does not allow advertising (most do not), use your sig.file. Sig.files are generally accepted. Be sure to make effective use of your tag line to get your mini-ad into discussion mailing lists where blatant advertising is not permitted. (See Chapter 8 for advertising when advertising is not allowed.)

- Track and record your responses when you use a new mailing list. You should have a call to action in your posting, encouraging the readers to visit a specific page on your site or to send e-mail to an address designated solely for this purpose. Only by employing an appropriate mechanism to track responses will you know with any certainty which mailing lists are successful and which are not. It's amazing how well calls to action work. For some reason, people tend to do what they're told.

- Set reasonable and achievable goals. As a benchmark, in most e-mail marketing campaigns, a 1 to 3 percent response rate is considered a good response. However, if your mailing list is very targeted and you are offering something of interest or value to a particular group, your response rates should be significantly higher.

Building Your Own Private Mailing Lists

You may want to build your own mailing lists. Generating your own mailing lists is often beneficial because of the many marketing uses the lists have. They can be used to maintain an ongoing dialogue with existing customers regarding updates, support, specials, and so on. They can also be used to communicate with current and prospective customers through distribution of corporate newsletters, price lists, new catalogues, product updates, new product announcements, and upcoming events. A full discussion of private mail lists is provided in Chapter 13.

Starting Your Own Publicly Accessible Mailing List

You can create your own publicly accessible Internet mailing list. This is something you will want to give careful consideration to before you make your final decision. It takes lots of time and effort to do this right, so be sure you're ready and that there will be sufficient return on your investment. First you must give it a name that reflects the discussion that will take place and is enticing for your target market. You will have to draft a FAQ file or charter containing information on what the list is all about. You will have to develop guidelines for participation.

You should create a Web page for your list to provide information about the list as well as its charter and guidelines. You should provide an opportunity to subscribe from the Web site as well. This will add credibility to your mailing list.

Once the list is up and running, you will have to advertise it so that people will actually subscribe. You can promote your list by participating in newsgroups that relate to your mail list topic. Remember not to post blatant ads where advertising is not allowed. Contribute to the newsgroup with your postings and use a tag line in your signature file to promote your mail list. You can also trade e-mail sponsorships with other mailing lists for promotion purposes.

There are a number of places to appropriately announce your list. Get your mail list linked from the many lists of lists on the Internet. We provide some of these in the Internet Resources at the end of this chapter. Make your list worth reading by ensuring that you and others have valuable information on the topic to share. You should make sure you include an opportunity for your subscribers to spread the word or to recommend your mail list to others. You can do this in your mail list messages and also through the companion Web page. In the newsletter or announcement mail lists where messages go only one way, it is easy to encourage your subscribers to send a copy to a friend who they think might be interested. If you encourage viral marketing in this way, you want to make sure you have included the how-to-subscribe information in the messages as well. When encouraging viral marketing through the companion Web page, make sure you include an appropriate call to action. It's amazing how well this works!

Escape the Unsolicited Bulk E-mail Trend

Bulk e-mail is any group of identical messages sent to a large number of addresses at one time. In some cases, bulk e-mail lists have been developed from opt-in lists, and the names are continually filtered through all of the universal "Remove" lists. These lists are often categorized by subject and provide an acceptable marketing vehicle. If you are using opt-in lists and are removing unsubscribe requests from your database, this is considered a legitimate marketing campaign.

However, many bulk lists have been developed by unscrupulous means, and the people on the lists have no interest in or desire to receive unsolicited e-mail. Unsolicited bulk is the single largest form of abuse we have seen to date.

Over the past couple of years, more and more businesses on the Internet focus on services and software products catering to the bulk e-mail market. Software products have been developed that collect e-mail addresses from Usenet newsgroups, online service members' directories and forums, bots that look for "mailto:" codes in HTML documents online, publicly accessible mailing list subscribers, or even your site's visitors. Service companies that collect e-mail addresses and perform bulk mailings abound today on the Internet. Be very careful when considering bulk e-mail for online marketing purposes.

Internet Resources for Chapter 12

I have included a few resources for you to check out regarding publicly accessible mailing lists. For additional resources on a variety of topics, I recommend that you visit the Resources section of my Web site at *http://www.susansweeney.com/resources.html*. There you will find additional tips, tools, techniques, and resources.

AOL, Prodigy, and CompuServe
All have their own areas where you can search for mailing lists.

Campaign E-mail Marketing Software
http://www.arialsoftware.com
This is e-mail marketing software used to conduct legitimate e-mail marketing campaigns. Campaign can import your contact database information and send personalized e-mail messages to all of your contacts.

HTMARCOM
A mailing list that discusses high-tech marketing. To subscribe, send the message "subscribe htmarcom your name" to the e-mail address listserv@usa.net.

Internet Marketing Mailing List
http://www.o-a.com
The Online Advertising Discussion List focuses on professional discussion of online advertising strategies, results, studies, tools, and media coverage. The list also welcomes discussion on the related topics of online promotion and public relations. The list encourages sharing of practical expertise and experiences among those who buy, sell, research, and develop tools for online advertising, as well as those providing online public relations and publicity services. The list also serves as a resource to members of the press who are writing about the subject of online advertising and promotion.

L-Soft's CataList
http://www.lsoft.com/lists/listref.html
CataList, the catalog of listserv lists! From this page, you can browse any of the 56,423 public listserv lists on the Internet, search for mailing lists of interest, and get information about listserv host sites. This information is generated automatically from listserv's lists database and is always up-to-date.

List-Etiquette's Guide to E-mail List Guidelines, Rules and Behavior
http://www.arialsoftware.com
Helpful tips for publishers, subscribers, moderators, and discussion list members regarding good mailing list netiquette.

List of Publicly Accessible Mailing Lists
http://www.paml.net
The List of Publicly Accessible Mailing Lists is posted on this site and once each month to the Usenet newsgroups news.lists.misc and news.answers. The Usenet version is the definitive copy—this Web version is generated from the database and is uploaded several days after the Usenet version is posted. They continually post to Usenet so that the PAML will be archived at rtfm.mit.edu.

Topica
http://www.topica.com
A very big directory of mailing lists and newsletters organized by subject categories. Topica provides details on how to subscribe to each of the mailing lists in its database and provides information on content as well.

13

Establishing Your Private Mailing List

Private mailing lists enable you to create one-way communication to your Web site visitors and are a tremendous vehicle for building relationships and a sense of community with your target market. Generating your own mailing lists is highly recommended because of the many marketing uses a targeted opt-in list has. The list can be used to maintain an ongoing dialogue with both customers and potential customers regarding updates, support, specials, and so on. It can also be used to communicate with current and prospective customers through distribution of corporate newsletters, price lists, new catalogues, product updates, new product announcements, and upcoming events. You have seen how you can join a publicly accessible mailing list, but what if you wanted to establish your own private list? In this chapter, we cover:

- Why have your own mailing list?

- The issue of privacy

- Managing your mail list

- Building your mail list

- Promoting your mail list

Why Have Your Own Mailing List?

There are numerous reasons why it would be appropriate to administer your own list. In fact, some of the same reasons that make it imperative to join someone else's list are also benefits for running a list of your own. Running a private mailing list can be beneficial in other ways, too, including:

- Permission-based marketing

- Establishing yourself or your business as an expert in your field

- Networking

- Conserving contacts

- Building repeat traffic to your Web site (as discussed in Chapter 3)

- Branding

- Promotion of your business's products and services

- Potential source of revenue

You can use a number of methods for soliciting and collecting e-mail addresses, including an online guestbook or other type of registration form to be filled out on your Web site. However, you will have better results if you provide people with an incentive to leave their e-mail address with you.

Place a form with a "Subscribe here" button on your site where visitors can sign up for the mailing list. Calls to action such as "Sign up now to receive our free newsletter" or "Click here to receive our informative newsletter and be included in a drawing for great prizes" might be useful in convincing people to subscribe. Having people register for your mailing list by offering an informative newsletter is a great way to stay in touch with your target market. If you have valuable information that your current and potential customers want, they will gladly give you their e-mail address to obtain your newsletter.

A prime example of this would be my mailing list, which is accessible when you visit my Web site (*http://www.susansweeney.com*) (see

Figure 13.1). Through my private mailing list, I regularly send out valuable Internet marketing tips, tools, techniques, and resources to my subscribers. When visitors come to the site and see that we have a mailing list, they need little encouragement to sign up because they know that they will be receiving valuable information that can help them strengthen their online marketing plan. Other mailing lists provide freebie incentives such as T-shirts, software, or games.

Encourage current and potential customers to subscribe to your private mailing list through traditional marketing techniques including press releases, offline newsletters, advertising, letters, and so on. If you use hardcopy direct mail, you can design a response system that requests the e-mail addresses through a fax-back, business reply card, or 1-800 number, or by asking respondents to go to your Web site or e-mail you directly. You can also ask people to sign up for your mailing list through newsgroup and mailing list postings, an appropriate tag line in your

Figure 13.1. You can sign up for my bi-weekly newsletter at *http://www.susansweeney.com*.

signature files, banner advertising, links from appropriate sites, and other online advertising techniques.

Permission-Based Marketing

There are many opportunities from your Web site to encourage visitors to give you permission to send them e-mail on an ongoing basis. You want visitors to subscribe to your mail list and should exercise every opportunity to accomplish this from your site. The more often you are in front of your target market's eyes through e-mail and site visits, the more they feel a part of your community. Subscribers to your mail list willingly give you their e-mail addresses and are obviously interested in the issues you are discussing. You have acquired their permission to send them e-mail, and you have established yourself as a respected member of the industry. For more information on permission marketing, refer to Chapter 5.

Benefits of Private Mail Lists

The benefits derived from having a private mail list are numerous.

- *Establish Yourself as an Expert.* By operating your own private industry-specific mailing list and offering your advice to members of your list, you will establish yourself as an expert in your field. As a result, you can quickly earn the respect and admiration of your peers and develop new business contacts and clients.

- *Networking.* Having your own private list permits you to network closely with others in your industry and with present and potential clients. Very often, new business relationships and opportunities develop when people with similar interests are brought together. Utilize your mailing list to facilitate the creation of these sorts of relationships. It could be that you find new business partners, establish new clients, or start another business venture.

- *Conserving Contacts.* You develop many great contacts every day in business. Often businesses develop a relationship with a firm, complete a project with the firm, and then lose contact with the client as time goes on. Starting your own private mailing list enables you to stay in constant contact with these individuals. This will help you to maintain the relationships that you have developed with your clients in the long term, and will ultimately result in more business and a stronger reputation for your business.

- *Branding.* Once you have developed your own private mailing lists and have generated a loyal list of subscribers, people will relate the value of your mail list to your company's products or services. Mailing lists are an effective way to brand your business's products and services online. If you send messages to your mail list subscribers on a regular basis, they will be exposed again and again to your business's corporate ID and products and services. This is an effective way to increase the brand awareness for your business.

- *Promotion of Your Business's Products and Services.* It is important to remember that people are subscribing to your mail list to receive valuable information that will help them in some way. It is for this reason that your mail list messages should not be full of blatant advertising; if it is, the retention rate of your subscribers will drop dramatically. However, since launching your own mailing list is such a good branding tool, you should always include a call to action that would encourage a subscriber to click through to your Web site and learn more about your products and services. This is a great way to generate exposure for your products and services.

- *Potential Source of Revenue.* Once your list becomes established and has many subscribers, you may be able to sell advertising to people interested in marketing to your list members. Needless to say, a mailing list becomes an excellent revenue source as its credibility and membership numbers expand. In the end, the time and effort you exert nurturing your list to prominence will pay for itself and more. If you are already a member of a publicly accessible mailing list, take note of the number of advertisements that appear in each posting you receive from the list. Administer your own private mailing list and earn advertising revenue for yourself. However, you have to be ever mindful of the number and type of ads you have in your mail list. The ads should not detract from your message or your credibility.

The Issue of Privacy

Privacy is a growing concern among many online users. You will be able to boost your mailing list's sign-up response rate by guaranteeing that subscribers' e-mail addresses will be kept confidential and will not be sold to anyone else. People are concerned about the privacy of the information they provide you with. If you cannot assure them that your company will use their e-mail address solely for your correspondence with them, they will not feel comfortable giving their e-mail address to you. Provide people with your privacy policy statement. Make them feel comfortable about divulging their e-mail address to your business. To do this, you should place a link to your business's privacy policy in a prominent location on your Web site, especially on your mailing list sign-up page.

You should never add someone's name to your mailing list without his or her permission. People really resent receiving unsolicited mail, even if you give them the option to unsubscribe. However, one method of obtaining more e-mail addresses is to suggest to your subscribers that they recommend your mailing list to a friend (or a few friends). Let your subscribers spread the word about your mailing list. If your list provides useful information, your subscribers will recommend the list to their friends. Some of these people will then subscribe and tell others about your mail list, and so forth. You remember the old commercial: "They told two friends and they told two friends and they told two friends." This viral marketing technique is a quick and cost-effective way to increase the number of people who subscribe to your mailing list. For more information on viral marketing, please refer to Chapter 4.

Managing Your Mail List

There are several ways that you can manage your mail list:

- Use your e-mail program

- Use mail list software

- Outsource your mail list management

Although managing your mail list through your e-mail program may look like a great option in that it doesn't cost you anything and is run from your desktop, giving you ultimate control, there are limitations. Your e-mail program doesn't easily afford you the opportunity to segment your mail list—those that asked to receive your newsletter versus those that asked to receive notification when you update your What's New section, for example. Your e-mail program doesn't generally provide the technology to quickly and easily personalize your communication—that is, insert the recipient's first name in designated areas within the e-mail. E-mail programs do not provide much in the way of tracking information, either. It would be nice to be able to track things like how many people opened your e-mail, how many people sent a copy to a friend, how many people clicked through and visited your Web site. The tracking technology is generally available only through mail list software or from the third party that manages your mail list marketing if you choose to outsource this activity.

Another drawback in using your e-mail program is the administrative headache of manually managing all the "Subscribes" and "Unsubscribes," particularly when you have multiple signup opportunities on your Web site—for example, someone wants to unsubscribe from your e-specials but still wants to receive your newsletter and coupons.

There are a large number of mail list management software programs available to help you better organize your mail list distribution. This software enables you to easily add or remove subscribers to your mail lists. Mail list management software enables you to draft and send properly formatted messages to your subscribers directly from within the software. Mail list software often provides you the opportunity to personalize your e-mails quickly and easily. Many of these programs can be integrated with your Web site so that people can add themselves to your list right from the site. You can also use this software to set up notification mechanisms to reply to subscribers confirming that they have been added to the list. This makes running your mail list less time-consuming, as the software does most of the work for you.

At Connex Network Inc., one of the tools we use is a dynamite mail list management software program called Mailworkz (*http://www.mailworkz.com*) to manage our Internet marketing newsletter. Mailworkz's flagship product, Broadc@st HTML (see Figure 13.2), is a dynamic e-mail marketing solution that enables you to create and send

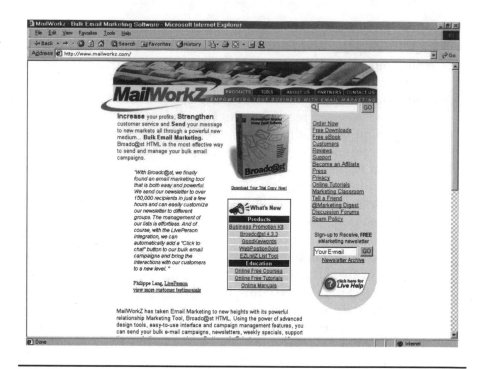

Figure 13.2. Mailworkz (*http://www.mailworkz.com*) offers a dynamite mail list management software program called Broadc@ast HTML.

important e-mail messages—personally and individually to thousands of your mail list subscribers. This tool has been invaluable to us in delivering our mail list to our subscribers on a timely and professional basis. Other recommended mail list software resources can be found in the Internet Resources section at the end of this chapter.

Using your own mail list software means that you have an initial investment in purchasing the program. The cost can run anywhere from an entry-level program at $99 to a robust, full-featured program at $450.

Some of these programs run from your desktop; others have to be run from your server or through your ISP. Most of these programs are sophisticated enough to allow you to segment the e-mail addresses in your database so that you know who has asked to receive what from your Web site.

Most of these programs today have the personalization capability to allow you to insert a recipient's first name throughout the correspondence and in the subject line of the message as well. For this to work, you have to capture the first names for each e-mail address in your database. Keep this in mind when asking people if they'd like to give you permission to send them e-mail for whatever reason—besides their e-mail address, have a mandatory field for their first name.

More and more of these programs are incorporating tracking features into the program so that you can know what's working and what's not. From an administrative perspective, many of these programs do a great job of adding new "Subscribes," deleting "Unsubscribes," and managing undeliverable addresses. This feature alone is worth its weight in gold.

A third option is to outsource your mail list management to a third party. There are companies that specialize in this service with great depth of experience that they bring to all clients. One such company that we have had the pleasure to work with is Inbox360.com (*http://www. inbox360.com*).

When you outsource this activity, of course you have a monthly service fee. The software is run from the outsource company's server or their ISP's server.

Virtually all of the mail list service providers have the latest and greatest features in list management software, allowing you to personalize your messages, segment your lists, and get great tracking reports. Generally, administrative issues like adding the "Subscribes," deleting "Unsubscribes," and managing the undeliverables are handled by the outsource company.

On the down side, you may lose some control—control over content, control over your customer, and control over timing of your message release. It is imperative that you have a clearly laid-out contract with the outsource company, addressing:

- Ownership of e-mail addresses

- Use of e-mail addresses

- Timing of correspondence

- Final approval of content

- Responsibility and timelines for replies to subscribers

It is important that you retain ownership of all e-mail addresses and that the contract clearly states that all subscribers' names and e-mail addresses are the property of your company. I would also have in the contract that you are provided the current list in digital format every month. This way, if you need or want to change service providers, your list goes with you. It takes a lot of effort to build your list, and it is a very valuable asset for your company. Make sure you protect it.

Make sure that your contract clearly states that your e-mail addresses are not to be used by anyone else or provided to anyone else for any purpose whatsoever. People on your list have given you their e-mail addresses in confidence. They trust that you will not abuse the relationship. Make sure it is in your power to live up to that expectation.

Make sure that you have final control over the timing of your communication. It is important that your messages be delivered when you want them delivered. Timing is everything. We discuss timing later in this chapter.

Make sure that your contract has a clause where you have to approve the final content going out to your list. You want to see and approve everything that is going to your list. You want to make sure the formatting is the way you want it; you want to be sure the personalization is working as it should; and you want to make sure there is no problem with graphics or word wrap.

You want to have a clear understanding with the outsource company regarding replies from messages going out to your list. Often the From field, although it looks like it is coming from you, is actually an address that resides with the outsource company. Discuss and agree on what happens when a recipient replies to your communication. Where does it go? When does it go? To receive a batch of replies three weeks after your communication went out is just not acceptable.

There are certain benefits to outsourcing this activity to a third party. The outsource company is an "expert" in mail list marketing. This is their core responsibility. Quite often the outsource company has been involved in many campaigns—they have a lot of experience in what works and what doesn't. Often they can help you tweak your content or your format to assist you in achieving your objectives. Also, outsourcing this activity to a competent third party frees up some of your time and allows you to focus on other priorities.

Building Your Database or Mail List

Once you are committed to private mail list marketing, you want to focus on building your database of e-mail addresses. The more people you can reach in your target market with your marketing message, the better.

There are many ways to grow your list:

- Import from your existing database. You probably already have a customer or prospective customer list that you can import into your mail list. You may have to send a one-time message asking them if they'd like to be on your list. The best way to handle this is with an opt-out message. Tell them what they'll be receiving and how often, and stress the benefits. Tell them that if they'd like to receive it they don't have to do anything—they're already included. Provide instructions for them to unsubscribe if for some reason they don't want to be included.

- Use permission marketing techniques to ask if site visitors would like to be included in your list to receive your newsletter, your e-specials, your coupons, or anything else you want to use to entice them to join your list. See Chapter 5 for more information on permission marketing.

- Collect names and e-mail addresses at your point of contact—registration desk at a hotel, checkout counter in a retail environment, member renewal or registration forms for membership associations or organizations.

- Encourage viral marketing with appropriate communication you have with existing list members. "Send a copy to a friend" works for a number of repeat-traffic generators like coupons, newsletters, e-specials, contest information, special offers, and promotions. Make sure that for every viral marketing communication, you include sign-up information so the recipient can add her name and e-mail address to your list as well. "If you've received a copy of this newsletter… or coupon… or e-special from a friend and would like to be included in our list to receive your own in the future, click here." The link should take them to a sign-up page on your

Web site or open a new message in their e-mail program with "Subscribe" in the subject line and specific details of what exactly they would like to subscribe to in the body of the e-mail message.

- If you use tele-sales, add an element that promotes your mail list and asks if the person would like to join.

Promoting Your Private Mail List

You will promote your private mail list wherever you can reach your target market. You will promote it on your site, online through various online marketing techniques, and offline. You will:

- Encourage your Web site visitors to join your mail list by making sure you have "Join our mail list—click here" calls to action throughout your site. You might enhance this with an incentive "Join our mail list to receive our bi-weekly tips, tools, and techniques and to be included in our drawing for a Palm Pilot—Click here."

- Include a viral marketing element as previously described to encourage your subscribers to recommend your mail list to others.

- Publicize your mailing list in postings to other mailing lists and newsgroups if it is appropriate. There is a moderated mailing list devoted to helping new list owners promote their list. To subscribe, send a message containing the line "Subscribe NEW-LIST firstname lastname" to *listserv@vm1.nodak.edu.*

- Invite your friends, colleagues, current clients, and potential clients to join your list.

- Remember to mention your mailing list in your e-mail signature file. This is an easy way to promote the list.

- If you are looking for a large distribution list, you might even register your mailing list with Topica (*http://www.topica.com*), tile.net (*http://tile.net/lists*), and the Publicly Accessible Mailing Lists index (*http://paml.net*).

Your Communication with Your Mail List

To be successful with private mail list marketing, you have to have a great targeted list and you have to know how to communicate appropriately with your mail list. How often should they receive your messages? When do you start to become an irritant? What time of the day and day of the week are your recipients going to be more receptive to your message? How should your communication be formatted? Should it be text or HTML? These all are important questions to be answered if you want to improve the response to your correspondence.

How often should you communicate? It depends on what you're sending and what they asked to receive. Newsletters should generally be sent out every couple of weeks. Special promotions, coupons, and e-specials generally will be sent out weekly at a consistent time. What's-new updates would generally be sent monthly unless you've got something "hot." Tips of the day should be sent... daily. Tips of the week should be sent... weekly.

When should your communication be delivered? There have been many studies on this topic, and consensus has it:

- For B2B, never send your message late in the day or first thing in the morning

- Not after 2 p.m. on Friday

- Not after 12 noon on Friday in the summer months

- Lunch hour is best for B2B

- Between 6 p.m. and 7 p.m. is best for consumers

When it comes to the formatting of your correspondence, if you communicate in a newsletter, coupons, e-specials, or this type of marketing content, an HTML message has a better chance of grabbing the viewer's attention. If your message is meant to look like a personal one-on-one message, then text-based is better. Your communications should be personalized whenever possible using the recipient's first name appropriately throughout the correspondence and in the subject field.

Your content should always be valuable, fresh, relevant, and succinct. One bad message could result in many "Unsubscribes."

Each paragraph should be written for scannability, containing no more than six or seven lines. Include appropriate calls to action to encourage the reader to take whatever action you want him to take. Always encourage viral marketing—"Send a copy to a friend"—and provide instructions for the friend to subscribe to be included in your list.

Use a personal name in the From field. You want to build a relationship!

Take time with your subject field:

- Avoid ad copy

- Avoid gimmicky slogans

- Build business credibility

- Use action words

- Be positive

- Personalize

Measure, Measure, Measure

You want to improve your effectiveness over time as you learn from experience. This can only happen if you keep track of past performance. You want to track things like delivery rate, how many undeliverables, how many unsubscribes, click-through rates, gross response, and net response. You want to compare response rates within different timings, different types of creativity, different formats, different segments of your list, and different target markets. Once you analyze what is working and what is not, you'll be in a better position to improve you conversion ratios over time.

Where to Go from Here

In this chapter, we discussed reasons you might want to have your own mailing list, how you can set up your mailing list, and other issues you will likely face once your list goes live. Private mailing lists are prime marketing vehicles if you manage them correctly and actively promote them. You can reach out to your target market with a mailing list. This technique of permission, or opt-in, e-mail marketing is the key to your success. If you have something to offer to people in your industry and it is feasible for you to establish and administer a mailing list, give the idea strong consideration.

Internet Resources for Chapter 13

I have included a few resources for you to check out regarding private mail lists. For additional resources on a variety of topics, I recommend that you visit the Resources section of my Web site at *http://www. susansweeney.com/resources.html*. There you will find additional tips, tools, techniques, and resources.

Inbox360.com
http://www.inbox360.com
A dynamite company that offers solutions for your e-mail marketing campaigns. Why not try them out? We did!

LISTSERV
http://www.lsoft.com
LISTSERV e-mail list management software is renowned for its flexibility, scalability, and performance. Start your own Internet mailing discussion list.

Lyris—E-mail List Server
http://www.lyris.com
Lyris is a powerful e-mail list server that automatically delivers your newsletters, announcements, and discussion lists.

Mailman—The GNU Mail List Manager
http://www.list.org

Mailman is software to help manage electronic mail discussion lists, much like Majordomo or SmartMail. Mailman gives each mailing list a unique Web page and allows users to subscribe, unsubscribe, and change their account options over the Web. Even the list manager can administer his or her list entirely via the Web. Mailman has most of the features that people want in a mailing list management system, including built-in archiving, mail-to-news gateways, spam filters, bounce detection, digest delivery, and so on.

MailWorkz
http://www.mailworkz.com
Broadc@st HTML facilitates your online communications campaign; from building quality customer lists through designing and sending your key messages, to handling the responses and requests for more information.

Majordomo
http://www.greatcircle.com/majordomo
Majordomo is a program that automates the management of Internet mailing lists. Commands are sent to Majordomo via electronic mail to handle all aspects of list maintenance. Once a list is set up, virtually all operations can be performed remotely, requiring no intervention from the postmaster of the list site.

NTarget
http://www.ntarget.com
A third-party solution for managing your mail list, with lots of options.

SmartMail
http://www.smartmail.co.nz
SmartMail is an easy–to-use e-mail marketing tool that lets you deliver personalized, branded e-mails right to your customer's inbox.

14

Effective Promotion through Direct Mail Lists

For years marketers have been renting mail lists from reputable companies for direct marketing purposes. These companies take their customers' marketing materials and manage the process of printing labels, affixing the labels to marketing materials, affixing the appropriate postage, and sending it out. The same type of service is available online—the only difference being that the marketing message is sent via e-mail rather than snail mail. In this chapter, we cover:

- How direct mail list companies work

- How to select a company to work with

- How you work with a direct mail list company

- Costs related to direct mail list marketing

- Tips on how to make the most of your direct mail list marketing

How Direct Mail List Companies Work

Online direct mail list companies work on the same premise as offline direct mail list companies. They provide a service to organizations that want to direct-market to a particular demographic or geographic segment of the population. To do this effectively, they develop large databases of individuals that fit specific criteria.

How they generate these databases is what differentiates the good from the bad. The not-so-reputable companies and the bulk mail list companies tend to "grab" e-mail addresses from newsgroups, public mail lists, and a number of other places on the Internet with programs that have been built just for that purpose. Reputable companies, on the other hand, have a number of strategic ways to build their lists of people interested in receiving information on specific topics. They partner with sites that have significant targeted traffic to offer that site's visitors information on a particular topic that would be of interest to that group. They offer the site visitors the opportunity to "opt-in" to receive updates or information on the specified topic.

To "opt-in," there has to be an offer for information on the topic and the visitor has to ask to be put in the list, provide her e-mail address, and quite often also provide her first name. The list company wants the first name so that future correspondence can be personalized.

Some of the more reputable companies require a "double opt-in" to increase the value of their list and to ensure the validity of the names on their list. With a "double opt-in," the site visitor asks to be put on the list to receive updates or information on a particular topic. When the mail list company receives this request, they follow up with an e-mail to the individual notifying him that the request has been received and asking for confirmation of the request by a reply to the e-mail.

These direct mail list companies organize their databases by area of interest. They continually improve their lists by doing a little data mining with their correspondence to the people on their lists. Sometimes they use tracking techniques to hone in on specific areas of interest, sometimes they ask a question or two to access more demographic or psychographic information on the individuals on the list, and sometimes they send a detailed survey-type questionnaire asking for feedback so they can better tailor the information being sent to the individual.

How to Select a Direct Mail Company to Work With

There are a number of factors that you will look at when selecting a direct mail list company to work with. First and foremost, the company will have to be reputable.

The company should have a topic list that meshes with your target market. If you sell tropical fish, the company should have a category that fits. Not all direct mail list companies focus on the same categories. Some have a focus on business topics, others have a focus on individual leisure topics, still others have a focus on technology topics, and some have a combination.

When you have narrowed down the reputable companies with topical lists that relate to your product or service, you will look at costs, tracking, and policies on content. As far as the policies on content go, you want to work with a company that personalizes its correspondence to the individuals on the list. You also want to be able to encourage recipients to visit your Web site, so you don't want to have any restrictions related to hypertext links to your Web site. Some direct mail list companies provide tracking statistics for their customers. It is useful to know how many people read the message, and how many people "clicked through" to your Web site or took the action you wanted them to.

How to Work with a Direct Mail List Company

Once you have selected the direct mail list company or companies you want to work with, you have to:

- Fine-tune the specific list to receive your message

- Provide the message content to the direct mail list company

- Approve the sample message

Then, the mail list company will:

- Compile the specific list

- Develop or format the message you provided to them

- Send you a sample for final approval

- Merge the list with your message so that each person on the list receives a personalized message

- Send out the message to the list

- Track specific actions taken by people on the list once they have received the message

You work with the direct mail list company to have them develop the specific list that meets with your objectives and fits your budget. These direct mail list companies usually can segment their lists to come up with just the right grouping to meet your needs and budget. For example, you might want your message to go out to people interested in white-water rafting. If the direct mail list company's list for outdoor adventure enthusiasts is segmented so they can pull out the white-water rafting segment but that list provides more names than you can afford with the budget you have set, they may be able to segment the list again to only include white-water rafting enthusiasts in specific states.

Costs Related to Direct Mail List Marketing

The costs for direct mail list marketing are always on a per-name basis. Often there is a sliding scale based on volume. The costs per name generally include all the services you need from the direct mail list company, including segmenting and rental of the list, merge and personalization, and delivery of the message. Different companies charge different amounts per name.

Postmaster Direct (*http://www.postmasterdirect.com*) is one of the oldest and most reputable direct mail list companies around (see Figure 14.1). They have over 3,000 topical lists, with over 50 million e-mail addresses. They have the largest database of business-to-business double-opt-in e-mail addresses. One hundred percent of the names on their list are opt-in. They partner with high-traffic reputable sites to generate their lists—sites like About.com, Internet.com, and CNET. Postmaster

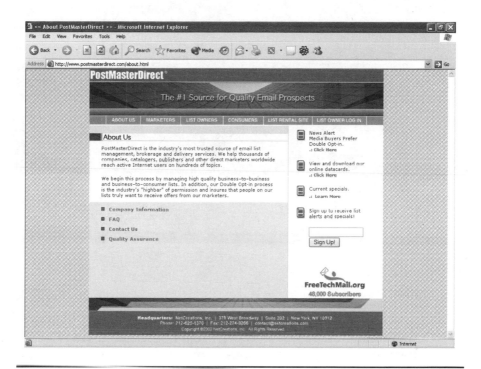

Figure 14.1. Postmaster Direct is one of the oldest and most reputable direct mail list companies around.

Direct costs per name range from 10 cents to 35 cents, including rental, merge, and delivery. They have a minimum order of $1,000.

eDirect.com (*http://www.edirect.com*) is another reputable direct mail list company. They have over 3,000 topical lists, with over 60 million e-mail addresses, both U.S. and international. Their charge is 24 cents and up per e-mail address (see Figure 14.2).

YesMail (*http://www.yesmail.com*) has 14 million e-mail addresses with 750 categories. They charge 25 cents per address (see Figure 14.3).

There are a number of direct mail list companies for you to consider. I have provided a link to many of them from the free Internet Resources section of my Web site (*http://www.susansweeney.com/ resources.html*). Although the pricing information and numbers of topical lists or categories are correct at the time of printing this book, there are always changes, so check the direct mail list company sites yourself before making any decisions.

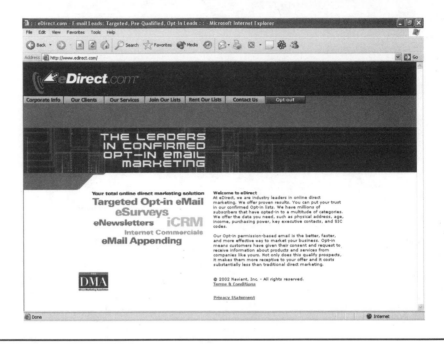

Figure 14.2. eDirect.com is another direct mail list company.

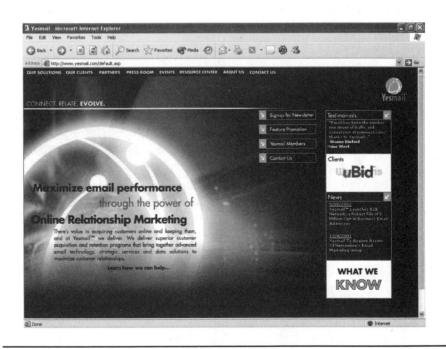

Figure 14.3. YesMail.com has over 750 categories and over 14 million names.

Make the Most of Your Direct Mail List Marketing

Direct mail list marketing is a great way to reach a significant amount of your target market with your marketing message in a short period of time. Ideally, you would like to have each and every one of these names included in your private mail list. If you're smart about the content of the message you have the direct mail list company send out, you can go a long way toward achieving the objective of converting the direct mail list recipients to your private mail list subscribers.

In your direct mail list message, you want to give recipients a compelling reason to visit your Web site. The URL or specific page you provide the hypertext link to in your direct mail message should provide them with not only the content they are expecting, but also a compelling reason why they should join your private mail list and an opportunity to quickly and easily sign up.

To ensure that your message has the best chance of being opened and read, you want to put in the time and effort to have a dynamite subject line. Quite often the subject line is the determining factor in whether the message is opened and read or is one of the many that are deleted before being opened. To help in this regard, you might want to consider including personalization in the subject line. You also want to make sure the subject line copy does not read like an ad. Ads and junk mail are the first to be deleted when individuals open their e-mail.

Write your message for scannability. That's how busy people read their e-mail—they scan it. Grab the reader's attention in the first sentence and the first paragraph. If you don't, she won't read any further.

Of course, you will check to be sure you have used the proper upper- and lowercase, correct grammar, and correct spelling. Just checking—you know yourself how many business e-mails you get that don't take this seriously. Your e-mail is a reflection of the attention to detail you give everything in your business.

Make sure you access and analyze any tracking information available to you from the direct mail list company. Notice what copy works best. Notice what subject lines give a better response rate. Notice the different responses from different direct mail list companies.

Internet Resources for Chapter 14

I have included a few resources for you to check out regarding direct mail list marketing. For additional resources on a variety of topics, I recommend that you visit the Resources section of my Web site at *http://www.susansweeney.com/resources.html*. There you will find additional tips, tools, techniques, and resources.

Act One Lists
http://www.act1lists.com
Act One Lists is a full-service list company specializing in compilation, brokerage, management, data processing, and direct marketing consulting with 26 years of experience.

Direct Mail Library
http://www.amlist.com/Knowledge/articlelist.asp
Lots of articles on everything from how to create your e-mail message to the 12 most common direct mail mistakes.

Direct Marketing Network
http://www.minokc.com/dmnetwork
A searchable database of over 80,000 business listings for direct mail marketing.

DMNews.com
http://www.dmnews.com
An online paper devoted to direct mail marketing.

Dunn & Bradstreet Sales and Marketing Solutions
http://www.zapdata.com
Provider of direct mail list solutions.

GreatLists.com
http://www.greatlists.com
An independent supplier of both domestic USA and international business-to-business and professional marketing lists to clients throughout America and in more than 25 countries around the world.

iList
http://www.ilistinc.com
If you need targeted e-mail lists of consumers and businesses that have expressed an interest in your offer, you've come to the right place. iList provides double opt-in e-mail list services from the top e-mail solution providers in the United States.

Nerd Wide Web Direct Marketing Resources
http://www.nerdworld.com/nw9490.html
Links to lots of companies providing direct mail list solutions.

Tips for Writing your E-mail Message
http://www.htmail.com/article5.html
Tips to keep in mind when writing your e-mail marketing piece.

USAData's Direct Marketing Portal
http://www.usadata.com
USAData's Direct Marketing Portal allows you to easily and quickly launch your own targeted direct mail program.

15

Developing a Dynamite Link Strategy

The more appropriate **links** you have to your site, the better! Expand your horizon by orchestrating links from related Web pages to increase your traffic. In this chapter, we cover:

- Developing a link strategy

Links
Selectable connections from one word, picture, or information object to another.

- How to arrange links

- Getting noticed—providing an icon and tag line hypertext for links to your site

- Link positioning

- Tools to check your competitors' links

- Using links to enhance your image

- Web rings and meta-indexes

- Getting links to your site

- Reciprocal link pages

- Associate programs

- How links can enhance your search engine placements

Links Have an Impact

Developing your link strategy is one of the most crucial elements involved in Internet marketing. It is a very time-consuming task, but it is time very well spent. Links are important for a few reasons.

1. Appropriately placed, they can be a real traffic builder.

2. A number of the frequently used search engines use link popularity as one of their ranking criteria. The more links to your site, the more popular it is; so the number of links you have to your site can significantly impact your placement with the search engines.

3. The more links you have to your site, the more opportunities the search engine spiders have to find you.

Links Have Staying Power

When you post a message to a newsgroup where you promote your Web site through your brilliant contribution and your signature file, you will receive increased traffic while the message is current and is being read by participants in the newsgroup. As time passes, your message appears further and further down the list until it disappears, and then your traffic level returns to normal. The same goes for a promotional effort in a mail list. You can expect increased traffic for a short period of time after your mail list posting, but as soon as everyone has read your posting and has visited your site, traffic levels return to normal.

This is not the same for links. Traffic from links does not go away as easily as other forms of Internet marketing. Links generally stay active for a long period of time. When a link to your site is placed on another

Web site, people hopefully will see it and be enticed to click through to visit your site. As long as the site that hosts your link has new traffic, you will continue to receive traffic through it. The beauty of links is that in three months' time, that link will still be there and people will still be clicking through!

Links are very important because if you have links placed appropriately on a high-traffic Web site, they can turn into traffic builders for your own Web site. They also are important because they can have a major impact on your ranking in some of the major search engines, because some search engines use link popularity in their ranking criteria. Some of these search engines include:

- AltaVista (*www.altavista.com*)

- Excite (*www.excite.com*)

- Google (*www.google.com*)

Once your link strategy is implemented and you begin to see an increase in the number of sites linking to your Web site, you will see your ranking in the previously mentioned search engines improve. For more information on search engines and their ranking criteria, see Chapters 6 and 7.

A Quick Talk about Outbound Links

The more links you have to your site, the better chance you have that someone will be enticed to visit. However, a quid quo pro usually applies, and this means providing reciprocal links, giving people the opportunity to leave your site with the click of a button. To minimize this "flight effect," make sure you place outbound links two or three layers down in your site. Never place outbound links on your home page. You want your visitors to come into your site and see everything you want them to see and do everything you want them to do before they have the opportunity to go elsewhere.

There are two ways you can provide outbound links. The first is by providing a hypertext link from your site to another, where the visitor leaves your site and moves on to the referred site. The second and more preferred method is to have all outbound links open a new browser window when the link is clicked. This way your visitors get to see the referred Web site, but when they are finished and close that browser window, the original browser window with your Web site is still active. The browser window with your site should still be visible on your task bar during your visit to the referred site.

Regularly test all of the links from your site to ensure that they are "live" and are going to the appropriate locations. Dead links reflect poorly on your site even if they are out of your control. There are tools available online that can help you determine whether or not you have dead links. These tools include NetMechanic at *http://www.netmechanic.com* (see Figure 15.1) and Dr. Watson at *http://watson.addy.com*. These tools analyze your page, detecting any dead links that may be on your site. Each of these tools is discussed in more depth in the Internet Resources section at the end of this chapter.

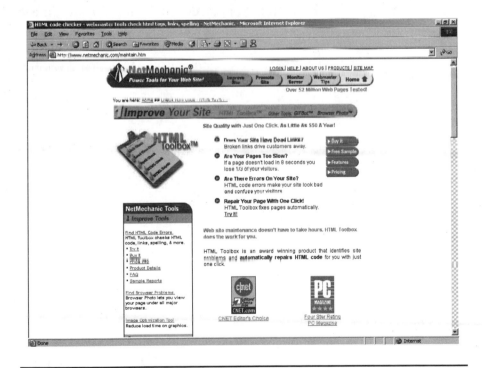

Figure 15.1. The NetMechanic site provides many valuable tools. Its HTML Toolbox can be used to find out if you have dead links on your site or if you have any HTML errors that need correcting.

Strategies for Finding Appropriate Link Sites

Ideally, you should be linked from every high-traffic site that is of interest to your target market. You have to develop a strategy to find all of these sites and arrange links.

The first place to start is with the popular search engines. Most people use search engines and directories to find subjects of interest on the Internet. Most of the people searching never go beyond the first 20 to 30 results that the search engine returns. Thus, these top 20 to 30 sites returned by the search engines must get a lot of traffic. Make sure you search relevant keywords in all the popular search engines and directories, and investigate these top sites for appropriate link sites. Some of these sites will be competitors and may not want to reciprocate links. The best opportunity for links is with noncompeting sites that have the same target market. I suggest you take your most important keywords, do a keyword search in the 20 most popular search engines and directories, and review the top 30 sites in each for potential link sites.

Another strategy to find appropriate link sites is to see where the leaders in your industry and your competitors are linked. I use the term *competitors* very loosely. It would include your direct competitors, your industry leaders, companies selling noncompeting products to your target market, companies selling similar types of products or services to your target market, and companies that compete with you for search engine ranking. See what your competition is doing. Determine where they are linked from, and decide whether these are sites that you should also be linked from. Learn what they are doing well, and also learn from their mistakes. You should be linked everywhere your competition is appropriately linked, and then some.

Explore These URLs

There are many tools on the Internet to help you identify a Web site's links. These tools can be used to see which sites are linking to your Web site. But they can also be used to see what sites are linking to your competition. This is a great way to research where your site could be linked from but isn't—yet! Let me walk you through a step-by-step process to increase the number of links to your Web site.

When determining which sites you should be linked from, you first have to develop a lengthy list of competitors. A competitor can be any business or site that offers the same products or services as you do or anyone targeting the same demographic group as you. Since the Internet creates a level playing field for all businesses, you are also competing against large and small companies from around the globe. Someone using a search engine to find information on services that your company can provide may see results from companies from all across the world in the top ten results.

Once you have developed your extensive list of competitors and have gathered their URLs, you must then find out what sites they are linked from. Tools have been developed to assist you in finding who is linking to your site. In most cases you enter your URL, and then these tools provide you with the list of sites linking to your URL. However, these tools can be used just as easily to determine which sites are linking to your competition and industry leaders by entering their URL instead of your own.

The more organized you are for this exercise, the better. I suggest that you:

1. Gather an extensive list of competitors and their URLs.

2. Choose the tool(s) from the next section that you are going to use for this exercise.

3. Enter the first competitor URL to find the sites linking to it.

4. Copy and paste the results into a Word, Notepad, or other file that you can access later.

5. Enter the next competitor URL to find the sites linking to it.

6. Copy and paste the results into the same Word, Notepad, or other file, adding to your list of potential link sites.

7. Repeat steps 5 and 6 until you have found all the sites linking to your competition. When this is done, you have your potential link sites list.

8. Now develop a link request (see the next section for details) and keep it open on your desktop so that you can copy and

paste it into an e-mail when you find a site you'd like to have a link from.

9. Next, visit every one of the potential link sites to determine whether the site is appropriate for you to be linked from. If the site is appropriate, then send your link request. If the site is not appropriate for whatever reason, delete it from your list. Also delete duplicates. When you get to the bottom of your list, it has changed from a potential links list to a request links list.

10. Follow through and follow up. Follow through and provide an appropriate link to those who have agreed to a reciprocal link. Follow up to make sure that they have provided the link as promised to your site, that the link works, and that it is pointing to the correct page on your site.

11. Submit the Internet address of the page that has provided the link to you to the popular search engines so that they know it's there. This will ensure that your link popularity score increases with that particular search engine.

Tools to Identify Your Competitors' Links

The following tools can be used to obtain a list of locations on the Internet that are linked to your competitors' Web sites:

AltaVista
http://www.altavista.com
To find out where your competitors are linked using AltaVista, simply enter the competitor's URL in the search area like this: link: yourcompetitorsdomain.com. This will return all pages in AltaVista with a link to your competitor's Web site.

Excite and Other Search Engines
Just enter your competitors' URLs and see what comes up. (Be sure to include *http://*.) If anything, the search query will include all indexed Web sites that contain the URL searched.

Google

http://www.google.com

Enter your competitor's URL in the search box like this: link: yourcompetitorsURL. The results will contain all Web sites linking to your competitor's Web site.

Hot Bot

http://www.hotbot.com

Enter your competitor's URL in the search box and change the default from "all the words" to "links to this URL." When you type in the URL, remember to include *http://*. The results will contain all Web sites linking to your competitor's Web site.

Link Popularity (see Figure 15.2)

http://www.linkpopularity.com

Simply type in your competitor's URL and it will give you a list of all the sites linking to that particular site.

Link Popularity Check

http://www.linkpopularitycheck.com

Use this tool to compare your Web site to up to three other competitors' sites using their link popularity check. In addition to a comparison graph of the number of links each site has, it also gives details on exactly where those links are coming from.

WebCrawler

http://www.webcrawler.com/WebCrawler/Links.html

Enter your competitor's URL into the search query box to find out how many links are provided to that page. WebCrawler provides the names of all the referring sites.

Other Potential Link Strategies

Another strategy for finding potential competitors is to visit the many different search engines and do a search on the keywords you feel people would search on if they were looking for your site. The top results can also be considered your competition. You should add them to your list,

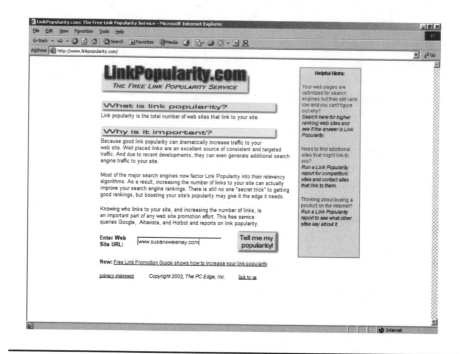

Figure 15.2. Knowing who links to your site, and increasing the number of links, is an important part of any Web site promotion effort. LinkPopularity.com offers a free link popularity check service.

and repeat the procedures discussed earlier to find out where they are linked from and to see if they are appropriate links for your site.

Now you have a starting list of sites you want to link from. Your next activity is to request the link. Remember that although this is a time-consuming exercise, it is also one of the most important activities. Developing a strong link strategy is critical if you want a large volume of traffic to your Web site and if you want high placement in those search engines that give heavy weighting to link popularity.

1. Make a list of your most important keywords for your Web site using your master keyword list and meta-tags (see Chapter 6).

2. Develop a list of the top 30 search engines (check *SearchEngine Watch.com*).

3. Go to each of the 30 search engines and input your most important keyword as identified in step 1.

4. Copy and paste the results into a Word, Notepad, or other file that you can access later.

5. Enter the next keyword and copy and paste the results into the same Word, Notepad, or other file, adding to your list of potential link sites.

6. Repeat step 5 until you have used all the keywords in your list. When this is done, you will have 900 potential sites for each keyword. You now have your potential link sites list.

7. Now develop a link request (see the next section for details) and keep it open on your desktop so that you can copy and paste it into an e-mail when you find a site you'd like to have a link from.

8. Next, visit every one of the potential link sites to determine whether the site is appropriate for you to be linked from. If the site is appropriate, then send your link request. If the site is not appropriate for whatever reason, delete it from your list. Also delete duplicates. When you get to the bottom of your list, it has changed from a potential links list to a request links list.

9. Follow through and follow up. Follow through and provide an appropriate link to those who have agreed to a reciprocal link. Follow up to make sure that they have provided the link as promised to your site, that the link works, and that it is pointing to the correct page on your site.

10. Submit the Internet address of the page that has provided the link to you to the popular search engines so that they know it's there. This will ensure that your link popularity score increases with that particular search engine.

Winning Approval for Potential Links

Now that you have a list of Web sites you would like to be linked from, the next step is to identify the appropriate company contact from whom to request the link. Usually this can be found on the site. Titles such as Webmaster@ or any variation on the theme are usually a pretty safe bet.

If the site does not have an appropriate contact, then try feedback@. You can either send the request there or ask for the e-mail address of the appropriate person.

If you cannot find an e-mail address on a Web site, and you feel that you will benefit a great deal from being linked on that site, you can visit a domain registration service like Network Solutions (*www. networksolutions.com*) to find out contact information for that domain name. Click on the "WHOIS Lookup" link and submit the URL in the WHOIS search to do a search on the domain in question. The results will include the contacts, both technical and administrative, for that Web site. The technical contact most likely will be the person that you are looking for, because that person is the one who most likely looks after the Web site. The administrative contact is usually responsible for the renewal of the domain name, and the billing contact is usually the bill payer for the domain name.

Generally, a short note with the appropriate information in the subject line is most suitable. Your note should be courteous, briefly describe your site's content, and provide the rationale for why you think reciprocating links would result in a win–win situation. It doesn't hurt to compliment some aspect of the site that you think is particularly engaging.

It is a good idea to develop a generic "link request" letter that you can have on hand when you are surfing. You should always keep this letter open on your desktop when surfing the Internet so that you can quickly and easily copy and paste the letter into an e-mail. If you don't have a link request ready and you find a site that you are interested in requesting a link on, you usually jot the site down as a reminder to go back to request a link. Quite often it just doesn't happen. But if you have the request open on your desktop, when you find a site that is appealing from a link perspective, you can simply copy and paste the link request into an e-mail, do a little editing or customizing, and hit the "Send" button.

Here is an example of a link request e-mail:

Dear Web Site Owner,

I have just finished viewing your site and found it quite enjoyable. I found the content to be very valuable, particularly [customize here]. My site visitors would appreciate your content as I think we appeal to the same demographic group.

My site, http://www.mysitename.com, *focuses on [my site content] and would likely be of value to your visitors. I'd like to suggest we trade links.*

Sincerely,

John

When you get a response, it will usually say that they would appreciate the link to their site and will offer to provide a reciprocal link. To facilitate this, you should either have the HTML for the link ready to send or have it available on your site, or both.

Make sure to follow through and follow up. If you said that you would provide a reciprocal link, follow through and do so within 24 hours. Follow up to make sure that your site has been linked from theirs, the link works properly, and it is linked to the appropriate page on your site.

Then remember to send a thank you. Since they are doing you a favor by adding your site to their Web page, you should strive to develop a good relationship with them. This way they may be more generous with the link that they give you. They may place it higher on the page, or even offer you the opportunity of having a small graphic link on their page, which would be dynamite for increasing traffic to your site. These graphic links are explained in more detail later in the chapter.

Another way to get links is to ask for them on your site. In a prominent location on your site, place a link that says something like, "Would you like to provide a link to this site? Click here." Link this message to a separate page that holds several options for links. You can provide viewers with several different sizes of banner ads they could place on their Web site. You can also provide them with a thumbnail icon, the HTML, and your tagline, which they could simply copy and paste into the HTML code on their Web site. Quite often, if you offer viewers these opportunities for links, you will have a better chance of receiving these enhanced link features. If you make it easier for them to add the link, they would be more willing to provide the link, for they can do it at their convenience. Figure 15.3 shows an example of a site that provides the relevant coding and images for people who want to provide a link to the site.

You might want to consider offering an incentive to people who will provide you with a link. It could be something that can be downloaded

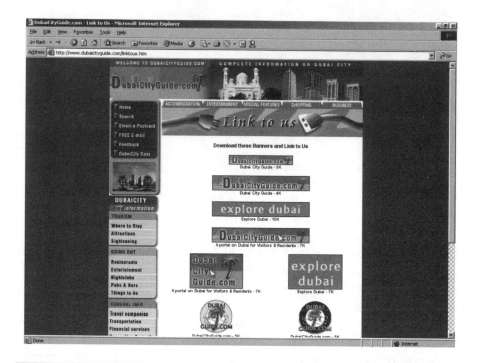

Figure 15.3.   By providing the HTML text and icons on your site, you can make it very easy for viewers to add your link to their site. It is best to supply them with the option of placing a text link, a small button, a large button or a banner advertisement on their Web site.

or a free sample of your product in exchange for a link. This also provides you with another opportunity to market your site because you are giving something away for free, and thus you can be listed on the many Internet sites that identify sites for freebies. Another tactic that you can use is that viewers who provide a link to your site will be included in a drawing for a prize.

You might want to consider running a contest such as "Provide a Link to Us and Win," where you include all those sites linking to you in a drawing once a week or once a month, depending on the size of the prize.

Meta-indexes and **Web rings** are other sources for links. For a complete discussion of meta-indexes and Web rings, see Chapters 17 and 23, respectively.

Web rings
Interlinked
Web sites.

You may need to prompt sites to provide promised links. If you have made an arrangement for a link and, on following up, find that the link is not there, it is appropriate to send an e-mail reminder. When sending the follow-up e-mail, include your icon, HTML, URL, and any other information that may be helpful.

Making Your Link the Place to "Click"

There are links and then there are links. Usually links are your company name hypertext-linked to your home page, and your company's site link is listed with a number of other companies' links. Sometimes, if you are lucky, there is a brief description attached to the link.

You should take a proactive approach with linking arrangements. Explore every opportunity to have your link placed prominently and, if possible, to have it differentiated from the other links on the page. Figure 15.4 demonstrates how having an image associated with your link can make your link stand out among all of the other links.

Once you have an agreement with a site willing to provide a link, you should ask if you could send them an icon and the HTML for the link. The icon (GIF or JPG format) should be visually pleasing and representative of your company. Within the HTML, include a tag line that entices people to click on the link. With the icon or logo, the tag line, and your company's name, your link will stand out from the rest. Since another Web site is going to be generous in providing a link to your site, your image should be only a thumbnail, for you don't want to take up too much space on the host Web site. This image could be your corporate logo or a graphic that is being used in the current promotion for one of your products or services. By having this image and tag line strategically placed on a Web site, the chances that a viewer will click through to visit your Web site are much higher. Here is an example of what it should look like:

Icon
An image that represents an application, a capability, or some other concept.

```
<IMG  SRC="nameofgraphic"><A  HREF="http://www.your
domainname.com"> Catchy tag line here.</a>
```

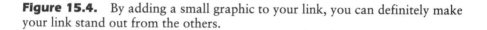

Figure 15.4. By adding a small graphic to your link, you can definitely make your link stand out from the others.

To Add or Not to Add with Free-for-All Links

There are thousands of free-for-all links on the Net. These sites allow you to add your URL to a long list of links, but they provide little in the way of traffic unless you can have your link stand out from the rest. One advantage you can get from being linked from these sites is in search engine ranking in a few of the search engines. As mentioned previously, some search engines use the number of links to your site in their ranking criteria.

Add Value with Affiliate Programs

Another way of benefiting from links to your Web site is by developing an associate program. Associate programs (also called reseller or partnership or affiliate programs) are revenue-sharing arrangements set up by companies selling products and services. When another site agrees to participate in your associate program, it is rewarded for sending customers to your business. These customers are sent to your site through links on your associates' or affiliates' Web sites. By developing and offering this type of program, you generate increased business and increased links to your site and increased link popularity for search engines. Associate programs are explained in more depth in Chapter 16.

Maintaining a Marketing Log

Record all new links to your site in your Internet marketing log. It is important to maintain this log and review it on a regular basis. You must periodically check to make certain that links to your site are operational and are going to the appropriate location. Along with the URL where your site is linked from, you should also keep track of all contact information you may have gathered when communicating with the Web master.

A Word of Caution with Link Trading

You must be aware when trading links that all links are not created equal.

- If you provide a prominent link to another site, make sure you receive a link of equal or greater prominence.

- Be aware, when trading your links with sites that receive substantially less traffic than you do, that you will probably have more people "link out" than "link in" from this trade. Consider trading a banner ad and a link from their site for a link from your site, thus making it more of an equal trade. If their site has more traffic than yours, don't mention it unless they do.

- Never put your outbound links directly on your home page. Have your outbound links located several levels down so that visitors to your site will likely have visited all the pages you want them to visit before they link out from your site.

- When incorporating outbound links on your page, make sure that when the link is clicked, the Web page is opened in a new browser window so that the visitor can easily return to your Web page.

- Sometimes when people update their site, they change the Internet address or delete a page altogether. If you have placed a link on your page to that page, and one of your viewers tries to link out to that page and receives an HTTP 404 error, this reflects badly on your site. You should frequently check your Web site for dead links.

- When you change content on a page within your site, don't create totally new pages; just update the content on your current pages and keep the same file names. There may be links to your pages and if you delete them, anyone trying to click on a link to your site from another site will get an HTTP 404 error. This will result in a dead link on the referring page as well as in any search engine listings you may have.

Internet Resources for Chapter 15

I have included a few resources for you to check out about developing a dynamite link strategy. For additional resources on a variety of topics, I recommend that you visit the Resources section of my Web site at *http:// www.susansweeney.com/resources.html*. There you will find additional tips, tools, techniques, and resources.

TOOLS THAT CHECK FOR DEAD LINKS

NetMechanic
http://www.netmechanic.com
To find out if you have any dead links with NetMechanic, simply enter your URL into the query box and view the results. The site will generate a detailed report, which will outline whether or not you have any dead links—and if so, where.

Dr. Watson
http://Watson.addy.com
Dr. Watson is a free service to analyze your Web page on the Internet. You give it the URL of your page and Watson will get a copy of it directly from the Web server. Watson can also check out many other aspects of your site, including link validity, download speed, search engine compatibility, and link popularity.

Site Owner
http://www.siteowner.com/badlinks.cfm?LID=229
When using Site Owner, you can check your site for various Web site criteria. To check for dead links, you must enter your URL into the query box. The results will outline any dead links that are on your site.

RECIPROCAL LINK INFORMATION

Virtual Promote
http://www.virtualpromote.com/guest6.html
This tutorial covers how to promote traffic to your Web site with reciprocal links. This is a free service for all Web site developers who want to learn more about announcing their Web site and promoting more traffic to the Internet.

FREE-FOR-ALL LINK SITES

FFA Net
http://pages.ffanet.com/links/list.pl
This page has a detailed listing of thousands of free-for-all link pages. It also offers you the opportunity to set up your own free-for-all link pages on the FFA network.

Link-O-Matic
http://www.linkomatic.com/index.cgi?10000
This site allows you to submit your URL to over 450 quality promotional sites with one click, driving traffic to your Web site and saving you loads of time.

Mega Linkage List
http://www.netmegs.com/linkage

An exhaustive listing of over 1,500 directories, classified ad sites, little-known search engines, FFA pages, and more... all compiled for you alphabetically. Although there are some dead or broken links here, a large majority are active, and you will be hard-pressed to visit each one.

Wealth Connection
http://www.wealth-connection.com/ffalist.html
A page listing numerous links to pages offering free-for-all links and various free-for-all link resources.

16

Affiliate Programs

It is a well-known fact that referral business is the easiest and most efficient business to generate. When doing business online, affiliate programs enable you to capitalize on this concept. The concept of setting up a referral business model was first started in 1996 when Amazon.com started paying other Web site owners for referring customers to their Web site. This referral business model caught on, and now many sites are incorporating this model into their everyday business activities. The idea and the corresponding software technology have come a long way since 1996. The software available today makes the process so simple that anyone with basic Web skills can set up an affiliate program.

There are many different affiliate programs available on the Internet. These programs all vary in terms of reliability, quality, and the amount of commissions offered. E-tailers have these programs to develop repeat business and increase sales. A side benefit to having an affiliate program is that every affiliate provides a link to your site, which in turn improves link popularity, which in turn improves search engine ranking in a number of the popular search engines. On the downside, developing and implementing the affiliate program takes time and effort, and you have to be competitive with other affiliate programs to encourage participation. In this chapter, you will learn:

- How to distinguish among the different types of affiliate programs

- How to pick the appropriate affiliate program for your Web site

- Tips to succeed with affiliate programs

- The benefits of affiliate programs

- How to start your own affiliate programs

- Important features for affiliate-tracking software

- Affiliate program resources

Affiliate Programs: Increase Traffic to Your Web Site

To understand the opportunities available, you must first understand the different types of affiliate programs. All pay for referral business, but in different ways. Before you decide to participate in an affiliate program, you must first look at your objectives, your products and services, and your target market, and then decide whether an affiliate program is appropriate for your site. Once this has been affirmed, you then choose the type of program that works for you.

Commission-Based Affiliate Programs

The most common type of affiliate program is the commission-based program. This type of program offers a Web site a chance to make a percentage of sales resulting from the referral. Commissions typically range from 1 to 15 percent. Some programs offer a two-tier commission structure, and some offer an increased amount of commission for those who have higher-traffic sites. A two-tier commission is when an affiliate is paid a commission on each sale (or lead or click-through) they refer and a commission on each sale received by any affiliate they have referred. Some examples of commission-based affiliate programs include:

- Amazon.com (*http://www.amazon.com*)

- One and Only (*http://www.oneandonlynetwork.com*)

- WebPosition *(www.webposition.com*—see Figure 16.1)

Flat-Fee Referral Programs

Flat-fee referral programs will pay a Web site a fixed amount for every new visitor who links from the referring site to the host site and takes certain predefined actions. The required action quite often is making a purchase on the host site. Some flat-fee programs do not require the purchase of an item; the predetermined actions might be downloading a

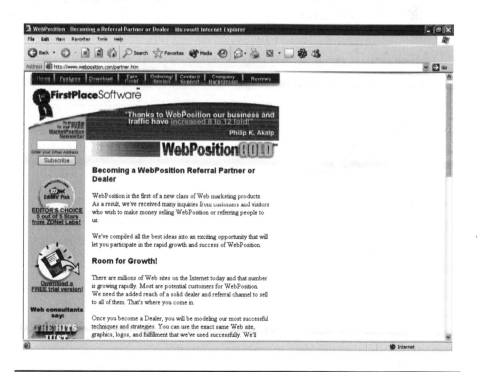

Figure 16.1. WebPosition Gold (*http://www.webposition.com*) has a very popular affiliate program.

free demo, ordering a catalogue, requesting a quote, or taking another action desired by the host site. A good example of this is Ebay (*http://www.ebay.com*), which offers affiliates compensation when visitors to their Web site click through and bid on an item at Ebay (see Figure 16.2).

Click-Through Programs

A click-through program is one in which affiliates receive a fee for every unique visitor who clicks through on the host's banner ad that has been placed on the host Web site. There are many click-through programs available on the Internet. For example, ValueClick (*http://www.valueclick.com*) is a click-through program that eliminates the problems of finding individual advertisers and allows you to place various banner advertisements on your Web site. Whenever a visitor links out from your site through one of these banner ads, you receive a flat fee. Two other popular click-through programs are:

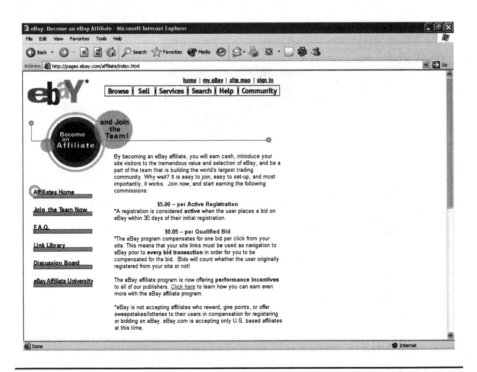

Figure 16.2.   Ebay.com has a flat-fee affiliate program.

- AllClicks (*http://www.allclicks.com*—see Figure 16.3)

- SearchTraffic.com (*http://www.searchtraffic.com*)

Selecting an Affiliate Program That Is Right for You

The first thing that you should do when deciding whether to start an affiliate program is to ask yourself if this fits in with your Web site objectives and if the program is something that would be of interest to your target audience. Click-through programs can serve to increase traffic to your Web site as long as your banner ad is designed with your target market in mind and the banner ad is placed on sites that are of interest to your target market. Commission-based and flat-fee affiliate programs can go further in having the referred visitors do what you want them to

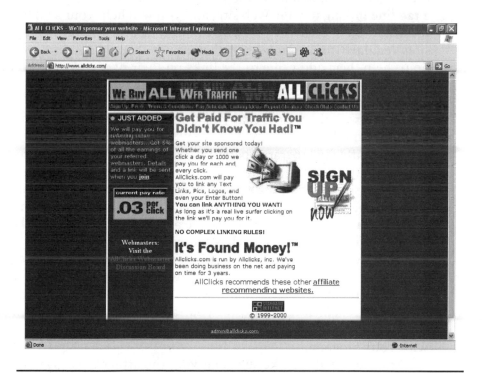

Figure 16.3. AllClicks has one of the top click-through affiliate programs on the Internet.

do when they get to your site. The referring site knows that it receives a commission only when a certain action has been taken by the visitor, whether that action be a purchase, a quote request, or something else. The referring site has a vested interest in having the referred visitor take the desired action and is in a position to suggest or recommend that the visitor take that action.

How to Succeed with Your Affiliate Site

You may have an affiliate program, but are you really doing all that you can to exploit it? There are several things that you can do to be successful with an affiliate program. You should go out of your way to help make the links stand out on your affiliates' sites. Provide different-sized icons that grab visitors' attention and are designed with the target market in mind. Also prepare the proper HTML coding and a tag line linking to your Web site, and you will help your affiliates get the attention of their visitors. You can also inspect your affiliates' Web sites regularly to determine whether or not there is anything you can do to help them add value to the links on their pages. You could offer them advice about where they should locate your links if they are in an obscure place on their Web site. Remember that you don't run their Web sites, so make it clear that you are simply offering advice and not trying to run their site.

Other affiliate program operators offer more advanced tools to their affiliates. For example, a program operator may offer affiliates a generic e-mail newsletter, which the affiliate could easily download, personalize, and send out in its mailing list. This generic newsletter is written in an enticing manner and will encourage the affiliate's mail list subscribers to visit the affiliate Web site and click on the affiliate program link.

The key point is that you should take advantage of as many opportunities as possible to leverage the power of your affiliate program. Through providing your affiliates with these value-added services, you not only strengthen the power of your affiliate program, but you also show your affiliates your commitment to seeing that they are successful with your program.

You should also make sure that you, the affiliate program administrator, do your best to be prompt with reporting and referral payments. People will not want to participate in your program if you are late with payments or don't provide them with detailed reports of their referrals from the previous reporting period. By sticking to the program schedule and doing the best you can for your affiliates, you not only will keep your affiliates happy, you will also advance the interests of your affiliate program.

Benefits of Creating an Affiliate Program

There are many benefits to participating in an affiliate program, especially if you decide to create your own. There are also some not-so-obvious advantages that you can benefit from. By creating your own affiliate program, you may generate a significant increase in traffic to your own Web site. When your affiliates place links on their Web sites linking to your site, you will increase your link popularity. This generates a significant amount of traffic to your site, but also helps to increase your search engine rankings. Some of the major search engines use link popularity in their search engine ranking criteria. Once you have successfully launched your affiliate program and have developed a wide sales force on the Internet, you may be surprised by the amount of new traffic that is coming to your Web site.

Your greatest advantage is the opportunity to expand your sales force to thousands of people. If you run a good affiliate program, your sales force could consist of people all over the world, thus expanding your target market into different cultures that your personal sales force otherwise might not have been able to penetrate.

Another benefit of launching an affiliate program on your Web site is that you will increase the brand awareness for your business. For example, how many times have you seen an Amazon.com logo on a personal or commercial Web site? Over 600,000 people have subscribed to Amazon.com's affiliate program, making it one of the largest programs on the Internet. All of Amazon.com's affiliates place banner ads, buttons, text links, and other promotional tools on their Web site in an effort to encourage their visitors to click through to the Amazon.com Web site and make a purchase. Even though not everybody may click through to the Amazon.com site, their Web site visitors are still exposed to the Amazon.com brand, thus increasing the brand exposure for Amazon.com's products and services. This may ultimately result in those visitors going directly to the Amazon.com Web site in the future to make a purchase, thus bypassing the affiliate's Web site and the need to pay that affiliate a referral for their business.

Starting Your Own Affiliate Program

If you have a product or service that you are trying to sell online, you should consider starting your own affiliate program. It is an easy way to generate a wide sales force for your products or services, while continuing to retain most of the profits. But what is involved in starting your own affiliate program?

First, you must decide which type of program you want to offer to your affiliates. If you expect a high amount of interest in your affiliate program, perhaps click-through and flat-rate programs are not for you. Your program could be very successful in getting visitors to your site, but they may actually never purchase your products or services. With a commission-based program, you don't pay affiliates for referrals that did not produce any sales. Your affiliates have an incentive to recommend specific products to encourage the sale.

The second and most important step in setting up your affiliate program is deciding which type of tracking software you are going to use to monitor your affiliate program. This is important because, like any other part of your Web site, you want it to be as user-friendly as possible. You should make it easy for your affiliates to verify how well they are doing with your program. There are three options for tracking your affiliates' success.

Developing Mirror Sites for Each of Your Affiliates

This is one of the original ways of tracking affiliates. It is a more cost-effective way to track your affiliates, yet it is very time-consuming and has a number of faults. What you actually have to do is set up a mirror site for each of your affiliates. This is a separate page for each of your affiliates to use when directing consumers to your site.

For example, let's say that you are developing your mirror page for your first affiliate. Your site is *http://www.yourdomain.com,* but you can assign your first affiliate the URL of *http://www.yourdomain.com/ index1.html.* Your first affiliate would be indexed as affiliate number one, and all sales that came from that mirror page would be traced to that affiliate. You would repeat this process for the next affiliate, and so on.

The problem that occurs when using mirror sites to track your affiliates is that they are aimed more specifically at people who have only one product to sell. If you have more than one product, you would have to design multiple mirror pages for your affiliates, and this would be very time-consuming. With more pages for each of your affiliates, it may become confusing when tracking sales due to sheer volume. When changes are made to any of the pages (e.g., a graphic is updated), you would have to modify the graphic on each of your affiliates' mirror pages. This too is very time-consuming. If you don't host your site on your own server, you would also have to be concerned with the cost for hosting. With more pages on your ISP's server, you will have to pay more, and if each of these pages is receiving high amounts of traffic (as you hope), you will have to pay for more bandwidth.

Paying an Affiliate Program Service to Track Your Affiliates' Success

Another avenue you can explore when starting your own affiliate program is to pay an affiliate program service to track your affiliates' traffic and their activities. The affiliate program service can provide everything you need to have a good affiliate program. Full-tracking services provide real-time statistics for your affiliates so that they know how they are doing with sales, and the tracking service takes care of the accounting side as well. They calculate the amount due to your affiliates at the end of every reporting period. The affiliate program service providers charge a fee for their services.

Some of the more popular affiliate program services are:

- Affiliate Performance (*http://www.affiliateperformance.com/ap/*)

- My Affiliate Program (*http://www.myaffiliateprogram.com*—see Figure 16.4)

- NetExponent (*http://www.netexponent.com*)

These services take care of everything for you from developing and implementing the program to providing you with activity reports. How-

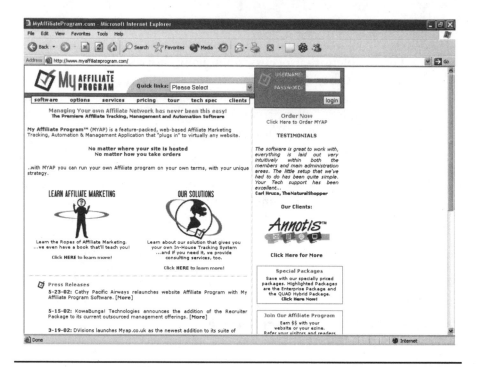

Figure 16.4. My Affiliate Program (*http://www.myaffiliateprogram.com*) is a terrific affiliate tracking software program.

ever, if your objective for starting your affiliate program was to make more money, you might want to do a few calculations to determine the cost. With the affiliate program service, you not only have to pay your affiliates, you also have to pay for the tracking service, which in turn cuts into your profits.

Purchasing Affiliate-Tracking Software

Your third option is to purchase affiliate-tracking software. Companies have developed comprehensive tracking software that allows you to provide maximum service to your affiliates. Depending on what features you would like to provide to your affiliates, the cost of tracking software ranges anywhere from $300 to $15,000.

There are many varieties of affiliate-tracking software. Some software programs are quite unsophisticated and offer very few features, and others offer them all. There are some features that you should watch for when purchasing your software. They can help you to run a very smooth affiliate program and can save you a lot of time. Here are some of the more important features available:

- *Automated Signup.* You should always look for this feature because you want to make it as easy as possible for your affiliates to sign up for your program. It should not take them days to officially sign up; they should be able to do so automatically. You want them to get started as quickly as possible, so as soon as they sign up, they should automatically be sent all information that you feel is necessary for them to quickly incorporate your program on their Web site.

- *Automated Tracking System.* This is one of the most important features that you must look for. You want to make sure that your software is capable of tracking all sales made so that you can reward your affiliates with the appropriate commission. You don't want to have to calculate which Web sites the sales came from at the end of the month. You want to be able to let the software do all of the tracking for you, and at the end of the reporting period provide you with a report outlining payment due to your affiliates.

- *Automatic Contact Systems.* You should be able to contact all of your affiliates whenever you find it necessary. Some software allows you to send messages to all of your affiliates at the click of a button. It compiles their e-mail addresses in a database.

- *Real-Time Statistics.* Real-time statistics allow your affiliates to view their current sales statistics. This will let them know how many people clicked through from their site and how many of those people actually purchased something. This is a very good feature because it is important to keep your affiliates informed about their current sales status in your program.

- *Variable-Payment Option.* Another important feature that you should look for is the variable-payment option. Some forms of affiliate software will only let you work with so many variables, meaning the fixed fee, percentage, or flat rate per click-through that you multiply by the referrals from your affiliates' sites. Some software is only designed for certain types of programs. You might purchase software designed to calculate payments for a click-through program. If you wanted to have a commission-based program that pays a percentage of sales resulting from each click-through, this software would not be good for you. It would not be able to comprehend and manipulate data to calculate the payments, for it is incapable of using the percentage-of-sales variable. You should remember to check this out before you purchase any software.

- *Automatic Check Payment.* Once your affiliate program is up and running, and you have developed an extensive list of affiliates, it can become a hassle to write checks at the end of each payment period. Some software comes equipped with an automatic check payment option that allows your computer to print the checks payable at the end of the payment periods. This can make your affiliate program run very smoothly and can also save you lots of time.

- *Automatic Reporting-Period Statistic Distribution.* Some of the more advanced affiliate-tracking software will automatically e-mail each of your affiliates at the end of the reporting period, which is usually one week. This keeps your affiliates informed as to how much success they are having with your program, and allows them to adjust their marketing strategy to help them to succeed with your program.

Some of the more popular affiliate-tracking software programs available to people wanting to start their own affiliate program are:

AffiliateLink
http://www.affiliatezone.com
AffiliateLink enables you to do everything from signing up affiliates to checking on both administrative and individual affiliate statistics.

Affiliate Shop
http://www.affiliateshop.com

The premier affiliate-tracking system. It provides Webmasters with a powerful and easy-to-use affiliate-management tool. No complicated software to be installed; just cut and paste a few lines of HTML code on your site to get your affiliate program going.

My Affiliate Program
http://www.myaffiliateprogram.com
Kowabunga! Technologies provides affiliate-tracking software that allows you to manage all of your affiliate members and track impressions, click-throughs, and online sales.

The Amazon Example

Amazon.com is a pioneer in the affiliate program game. For this reason, we will now walk through how its affiliate program is set up. The Amazon.com affiliate program model is a good one for you to follow if you intend to establish an affiliate program of your own.

Amazon describes its affiliate program as follows. (The following excerpt is taken directly from *http://www.amazon.com.*)

> *Founded in 1996, Amazon.com Associates is the online affiliate marketing leader. Our program is free and easy to join. Here's how it works: Place links on your site to Amazon.com. Visitors click from your site to Amazon.com and purchase items. You earn up to 15% in referral fees. Link up with the leader! We have the largest and most successful online affiliate program. Over 600,000 Web sites have joined Amazon.com Associates because our program works for you. Why?*

> *You have more ways to earn $. You can earn referral fees on both new and used items at Amazon.com. You work with the best online brand. As an Amazon.com Associate, you send your visitors to the #1 online retailer. Over 30 million satisfied customers have established Amazon.com as the trusted e-commerce leader. You choose from the best product selection. With our Associates program, you gain access to millions of products that can be sold through your site.*

You benefit from easy & helpful resources. <u>Associates Central</u> is your resource-rich Web site designed to help you succeed in our program. We provide you with merchandising tips, an extensive graphics library, and state-of-the-art link building and reporting tools. If you ever have questions, we also have a customer service team dedicated only to your needs.

As Amazon describes it, the affiliate program sounds easy for both the affiliate and Amazon. Upon further inspection, we can see that this truly is the case. Prospective affiliate members can link through to the Amazon affiliate program information page directly from Amazon's home page (see Figure 16.5). You should make your affiliate program this easy to find on your site.

Like Amazon, you will need an information page or section of pages explaining the details of your affiliate program to visitors. The Amazon.com information page (shown in Figure 16.6) is well written

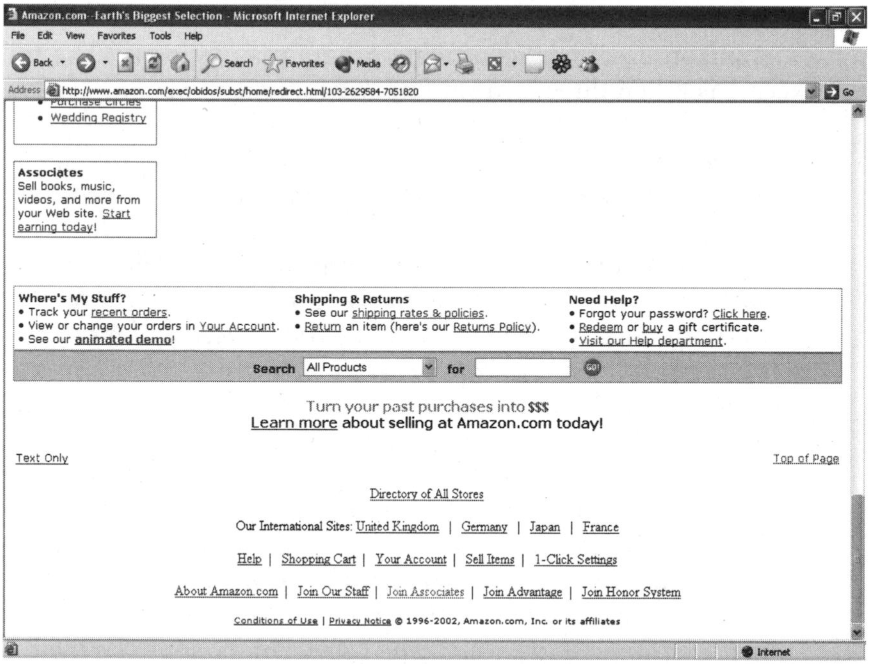

Figure 16.5. Visitors can access the Amazon.com affiliate program directly from Amazon.com's home page by clicking on "Join Associates".

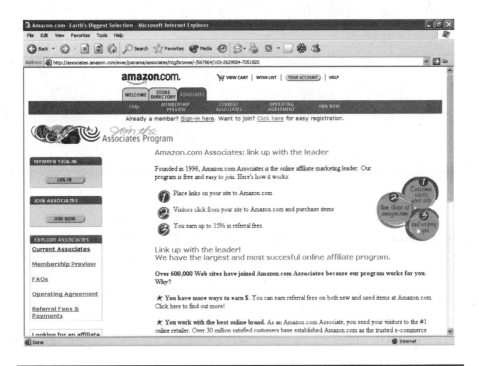

Figure 16.6. Amazon.com provides visitors with detailed information about its affiliate program opportunity.

and walks potential affiliate members through a series of steps that describe the details of the program (what the affiliate program is, the commission rate, how commissions are paid, and so on). Current affiliate program members can also log in to their account from this page and inspect their sales statistics. Be sure that you provide a place on your site for potential affiliate members to log in and find adequate information about your affiliate program so that they understand its potential.

Next you will require a signup form for your affiliate program. Figure 16.7 displays a portion of Amazon's associate program application form. Ask applicants for necessary information only. This will keep the length of your signup form brief and will encourage more new members to join.

Once a person completes and submits the affiliate program application form, Amazon immediately sends the linking code to the new member to include on their site. SusanSweeney.com is a member of the

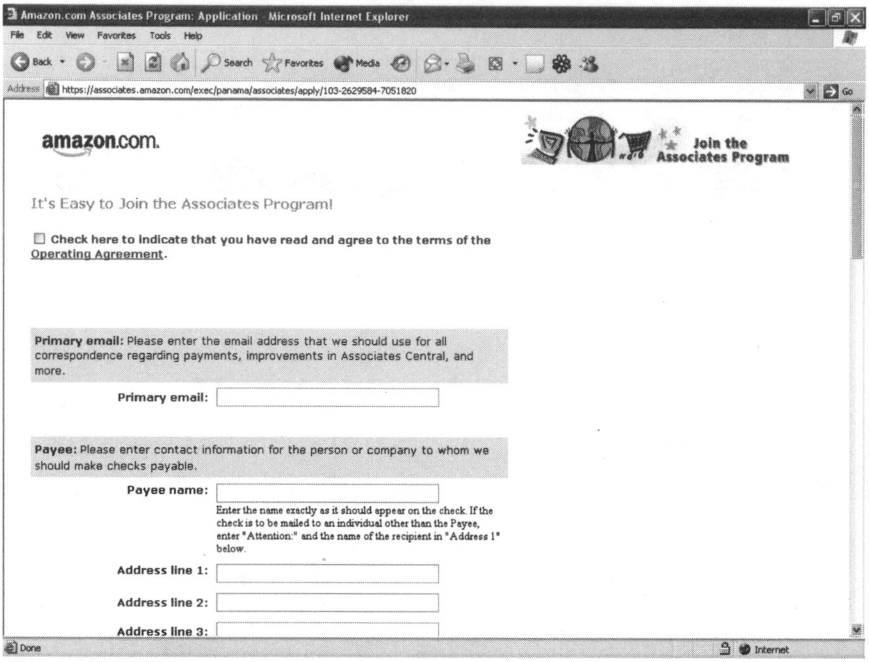

Figure 16.7. Like Amazon.com you should make it easy for new members to join your affiliate program by providing a concise application form on your site.

Amazon affiliate program, and when we joined, we were sent the following code:

```
<url1>
<A HREF="http://www.amazon.com/exec/obidos/ASIN/1885068379/
susansweeney.com">Title of book or image goes here</A>
```

As you can see, the URL to the SusanSweeney.com affiliate page is quite lengthy. However, there is no need to memorize it. The affiliate member (in this case, SusanSweeney.com) simply has to copy and paste this linking text into the HTML code of the pages of his or her site. As described earlier, you should provide affiliate members with tips on where to include and how to present the affiliate link on their site. On the SusanSweeney.com site, we simply link to our Amazon affiliate page by inserting the linking text around a graphic of the book we're selling (see

Figure 16.8). The affiliate link is prominently displayed on our site, so if visitors want to purchase the book, they click on the book graphic and are linked through to Amazon.com, where they can proceed with the transaction (see Figure 16.9).

Thus, Amazon receives the sales request, processes the order, and delivers the book to the customer, and SusanSweeney.com receives a 15 percent commission from the order. Amazon sends SusanSweeney.com a weekly sales report and a check for the commissions earned after our affiliate sales reach a certain level.

Once again, the point of presenting this example of how the Amazon affiliate program operates is to give you some ideas for what you should include in your affiliate program and how you should present the information. With this example and the other details provided in this chapter in mind, you should now be sufficiently informed to initiate an affiliate program of your own.

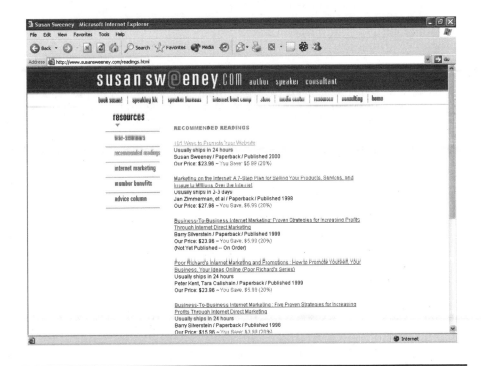

Figure 16.8. Amazon.com can provide listings for one product or an assortment of products, similar to how SusanSweeney.com provides a detailed listing of recommended readings on a section of the SusanSweeney.com site.

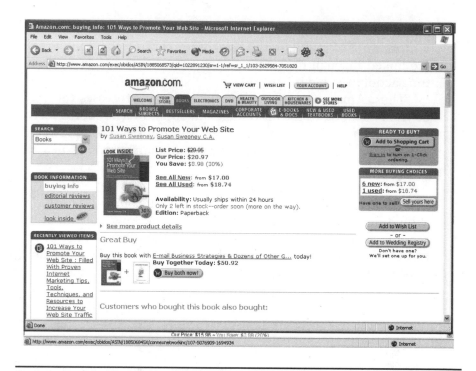

Figure 16.9. Visitors to your affiliate members' sites can link through to your site. The affiliate members receive a commission for each sale they generate. In this image, a visitor had clicked through from the SusanSweeney.com site to the Amazon.com site. SusanSweeny.com will receive a commission if a sale is made.

The SusanSweeney.com Example (Shameless Self-Promotion)

Similar to Amazon.com, but on a much smaller scale, SusanSweeney.com (*http://www.susansweeney.com*) has a successful affiliate program on its Web site that offers affiliates the opportunity to sell a variety of e-business and Internet marketing-related books written by yours truly. Powered by the My Affiliate Program™ affiliate software, the SusanSweeney.com affiliate program is easy to join and is set up in a similar fashion to the Amazon.com affiliate program. The SusanSweeney.com affiliate program can be viewed in Figure 16.10.

SusanSweeney.com describes its affiliate program as follows. (The following excerpt is taken directly from *http://www.susansweeney.com/ affiliate.html*.)

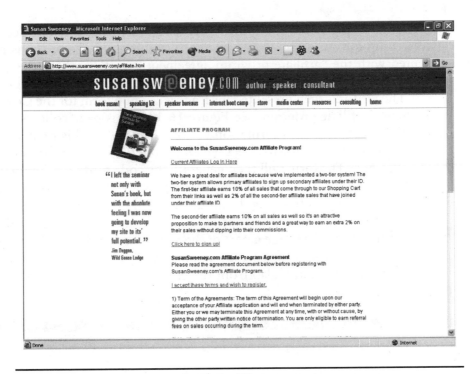

Figure 16.10. SusanSweeney.com's affiliate program.

We have a great deal for affiliates because we've implemented a two tier system!

The two tier system allows primary affiliates to sign up secondary affiliates under their ID. The first tier affiliate earns 10% of all sales that come through to our Shopping Cart from their links as well as 2% of all the second tier affiliate sales that have joined under their affiliate ID.

The second tier affiliate earns 10% on all sales as well so it's an attractive proposition to make to partners and friends and a great way to earn an extra 2% on their sales without dipping into their commissions.

SusanSweeney.com does a dynamite job of outlining the benefits of joining its affiliate program. From this page, visitors can immediately sign up for the affiliate program, and current members are given the opportunity to log in and check their account status. Once a visitor decides to sign up for the SusanSweeney.com affiliate program, he or she is presented with the "affiliate program agreement" which outlines the rules for joining the affiliate program. This can be viewed in Figure 16.11.

The visitor is then presented with a brief signup form for the Connex Network affiliate program (see Figure 16.12). This page collects all of the necessary contact information for the affiliate and his or her Web site, and asks the visitor to select which product(s) will be promoted on the Web site. The form will then generate the code for the individual to place on the site. The signup form also provides the visitor with the option to tell up to five friends about the affiliate program via e-mail, with the incentive that if the visitor's friends sign up for the affiliate program, they will become a part of the visitor's second tier. This means that the visitor would earn a commission on all sales resulting from his or her own efforts, and also from the efforts of those individuals who

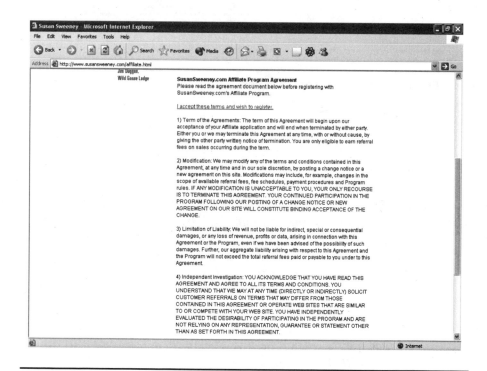

Figure 16.11. When a visitor decides to join the SusanSweeney.com affiliate program, he or she is asked to read and accept the affiliate program operation agreement.

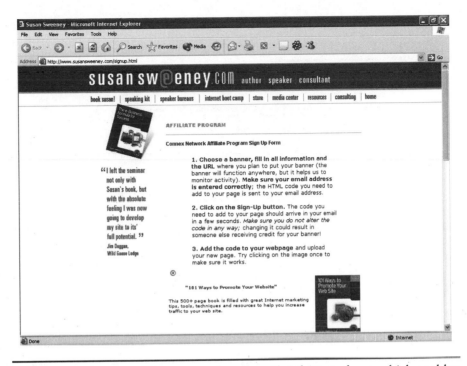

Figure 16.12. SusanSweeney.com has a very brief signup form, which enables visitors to sign up for the affiliate program quickly and with little hassle.

sign up for the affiliate program as a result of this referral. This viral marketing technique is a dynamite way to increase the exposure for the Connex Network affiliate program.

Once people complete the affiliate signup form and submit the application, they are immediately sent the code that they will need to place on the Web site in order to participate in the affiliate program. This can be seen in Figure 16.13.

Similar to how SusanSweeney.com placed links to Amazon.com, Bell's Alaska Travel Guide (*http://www.bellsalaska.com*) is participating in the Connex Network affiliate program (see Figure 16.14). The affiliate link is prominently displayed on this site, so if visitors want to purchase the book, they click on the book graphic and are linked through to the Connex Network Web site, where the transaction takes place. Once the order has been processed, the affiliate is rewarded a commission for his or her efforts.

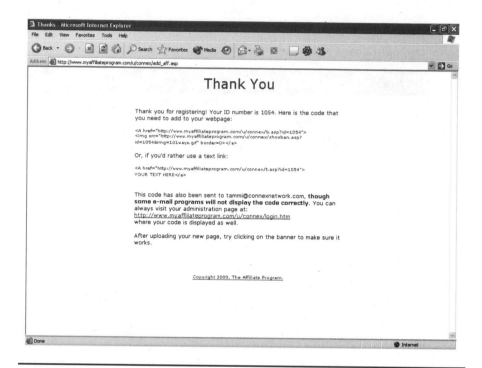

Figure 16.13. Once the affiliates complete the affiliate program application form, they are automatically provided with the code that they need to place on their Web site to link to the SusanSweeney.com affiliate program.

Internet Resources for Chapter 16

I have included a few resources for you to check out regarding affiliate programs. For additional resources on a variety of topics, I recommend that you visit the Resources section of my Web site at *http://www.susansweeney.com/resources.html*. There you will find additional tips, tools, techniques, and resources.

2-Tier.com
http://www.2-tier.com
2-Tier.com offers a directory of over 1,136 different affiliate programs.

Affiliate Handbook
http://www.affiliatehandbook.com

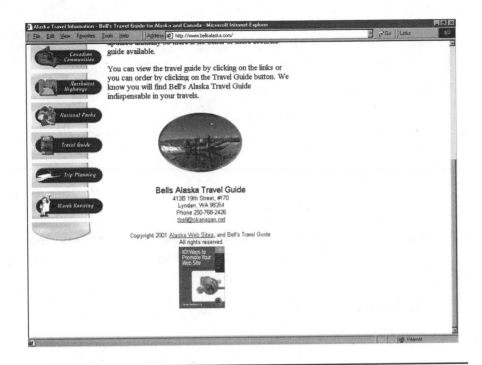

Figure 16.14. Bell's Alaska Travel Guide prominently displays a link to the Connex Network affiliate program directly on its home page.

The definitive resource for affiliate program managers aspiring to develop a best-of-breed affiliate program.

AssociateCash.com
http://www.associatecash.com
AssociateCash.com reviews different associate and affiliate programs and rates them. Learn which affiliate programs earn Webmasters money.

AssociatePrograms.co.uk
http://www.associateprograms.co.uk
A UK guide to affiliate marketing and associate programs. Listings and ratings of many programs by category—Fox Tucker, managing director. Includes headlines, tips, advice, and free weekly news update.

AssociatePrograms.com
http://www.associateprograms.com

The AssociatePrograms.com directory helps you find the best associate programs—also known as referral, partner, revenue-sharing, or affiliate programs—to earn money from your Web site.

CashPile.com
http://www.cashpile.com
Comprehensive directory/search engine for revenue-sharing (affiliate, associate, referral, and bounty) programs.

ClickQuick: Affiliate and Pay-per-Click Program Reviews
http://www.clickquick.com
ClickQuick provides in-depth reviews of Webmaster affiliate, associate, and pay-per-click programs that offer opportunities to make money on the Internet. Also provides reviews of banner ad networks and helpful articles on improving affiliate program performance.

I-Revenue.net
http://www.I-Revenue.net
Claims to be one of the largest affiliate program directories on the Internet.

MakeMoneyNow.com
http://www.makemoneynow.com
A great site filled with resources on affiliate programs, including a directory of programs and tips on starting your own affiliate program.

Refer-it.com
http://www.refer-it.com
Refer-it.com is the authoritative guide to Internet affiliate programs, associate programs, and referral programs. Refer-it is a great resource for merchants with affiliate programs and for Webmasters with affiliate Web sites.

Successful Affiliate Marketing for Merchants
http://www.affiliatemanager.net
Everything you wanted to know about affiliate marketing but were afraid to ask.

MORE POPULAR AFFILIATE PROGRAMS

Amazon.com
http://www.amazon.com

A pioneer in the affiliate program industry, Amazon.com claims to have the earth's biggest selection of products, including free electronic greeting cards, online auctions, and millions of books, CDs, videos, DVDs, toys and games, and electronics.

Barnes and Noble
http://www.barnesandnoble.com
BarnesandNoble.com offers a wide selection of books and has over 120,000 Web sites participating in its affiliate program.

CDNow
http://www.cdnow.com
CDNow is the world's leading online music store.

Chapters Indigo
http://chapters.indigo.ca
Chapters Indigo will give you 5 percent for each purchase made from your Web site.

Reel.com
http://www.reel.com
Reel.com is one of the biggest places online to buy movies.

Priceline.com
http://tickets.priceline.com/affiliates/agreement.asp
Affiliates earn money each time a visitor books hotel, air, or car rental service.

SusanSweeney.com
http://www.susansweeney.com/affiliate.html
Sign up now and start earning money from your site!

***Time* Magazine**
http://affiliate.timeincmags.com/affiliate/time/homepage
Time magazine will give you $6 for every subscription that is generated through your site.

17

Maximizing Promotion with Meta-Indexes

Meta-indexes are intended to be useful resources for people who have a specific interest in a particular topic. Meta-indexes are a large and valuable resource for reaching your target audience and should be utilized to their full potential. In this chapter, we cover:

- What meta-indexes are

- Why meta-indexes are useful

- How to make the links to your site stand out

- How to create your own meta-index

What Are Meta-Indexes?

Meta-indexes are lists of Internet resources pertaining to a specific subject category and are intended as a resource for people who have a specific interest in that topic. These lists, like the one for Internet shopping sites shown in 17.1, consist of a collection of URLs of related Internet resources that are arranged on a Web page by their titles. The owners or creators of meta-indexes put a lot of effort into compiling these lists and are eager to find new sites to add to them. They often will list your site for free because they desire to have the most meta of the meta-indexes— they strive to have the largest of the large indexes, and more sites means a larger index. So if you come across a meta-index that is associated with the topic of your site, feel free to ask for a link.

Some of these meta-indexes have a "Submit" or "Add your site" area; for others, you have to develop an inclusion request e-mail and send it to the owner of the site. In your inclusion request e-mail, you would let the owner know that you had visited the site and feel that your site would be appropriate to be included. Give the reasons you

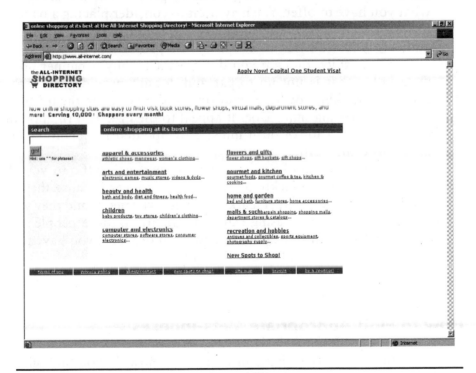

Figure 17.1. All-Internet Shopping Directory–meta-index of malls, stores, products and services on the Web.

think your site appropriate and request the link. You should provide the HTML for the link as well. Review the techniques discussed in Chapter 15 to have your link stand out with the graphical icon, hypertext link, and tag line.

Meta-indexes are directed at a specific topic, such as "Connecticut Country Inns" or "Antique Car Sites." Meta-indexes provide easy access to a number of sites on a specific topic, and they are a great way to draw targeted, interested people to your Web site. In addition, some users may rely on meta-indexes as their only search effort. They may not use a search engine to perform a query on Mexican resorts, for example, if they know a certain meta-index contains 200 sites on Mexican resorts. Where search engine results may show books on Mexican resorts, personal Web pages relating to family vacations at Mexican resorts, etc., experienced Web users know that meta-indexes will only provide links to the Web sites of Mexican resorts. Meta-indexes can increase your chances of being found by people who are interested in what you have to offer. You may want to consider placing a banner ad on one or more of the meta-indexes you find, given that the target audience you want to reach will be the people using these indexes. Choose carefully, though; you don't want to buy a banner ad on a meta-index that is not up to par and doesn't provide you with the traffic are looking for. Take your time and investigate the meta-index before advertising on it. Does it appeal to the eye? Is it of good quality? Are there a lot of dead links? Is it updated frequently? Does it have sufficient traffic?

Meta-indexes can be a great way to increase traffic to your Web site. Word spreads quickly on great meta-indexes because they are a great resource. Your target market will tell two friends and they will tell two friends, thus increasing traffic. In addition, more people will be adding links to your meta-index, and the more links you have to your Web site, the more traffic your site will get.

How to Find Appropriate Meta-Indexes

Now that you know what a meta-index is, how do you find one? You might be browsing on the Web and happen to come across one. A better way to find meta-indexes is through the search engines and directories on the Web.

You need to know how your particular search engine of choice works. Most search engines have advanced search capabilities, so be sure to explore them. When you're looking for meta-indexes, we recommend that you create a more focused search by adding an extra word such as "directory," "list," "index," "table," "resource," "reference," or "guide." By adding one of these words in conjunction with another word—for example, "travel"—you're increasing your chances of finding appropriate meta-indexes. Performing a search on "travel" alone will return far-less-targeted results. Looking for a travel directory alone may not work for you.

Why not? A search for a travel directory on the search engines often means looking for all sites that contain the words "travel" and all sites that contain "directory." You should refine your searches to achieve more accurate results. Some general techniques that use the words "travel" and "directory" as examples you can apply in your search for meta-indexes are:

- Entering *travel directory* generally means: Look for all sites containing the words "travel" or "directory," but try to gather those sites with "travel" and "directory" together.

- Entering *"travel directory"* (with quotation marks) often means: Look for all sites containing the words "travel" and "directory" next to each other.

- Entering *+travel directory* generally means: Find all sites with the word "travel" and preferably the word "directory" as well.

- Entering *+travel+directory* generally means: Find all sites with both words.

Search engines look for information in different ways and allow different techniques to be applied in order to narrow or broaden the search criteria. This information can be obtained by looking at the respective search engines' help page (Figure 17.2).

Many search engines and directories have or give you the option to use an "advanced" search or search "options" page that presents you with the ability to perform more-detailed searches without using the parameters outlined above. Yahoo! (Figure 17.3) and Google (Figure 17.4) are two such sites.

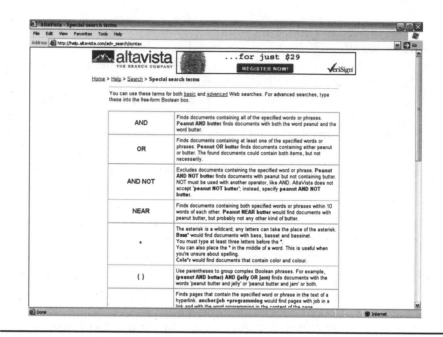

Figure 17.2.   AltaVista's help page and quick-search guide.

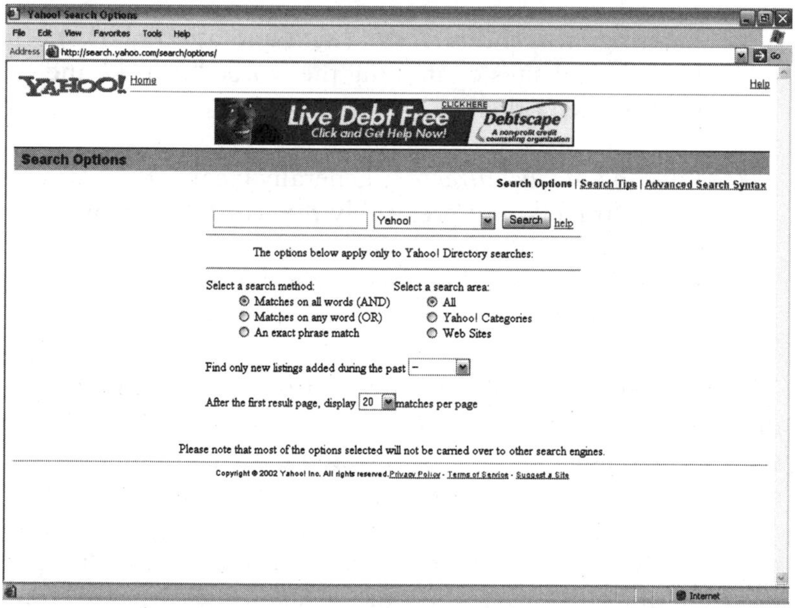

Figure 17.3.   Yahoo!'s advanced search.

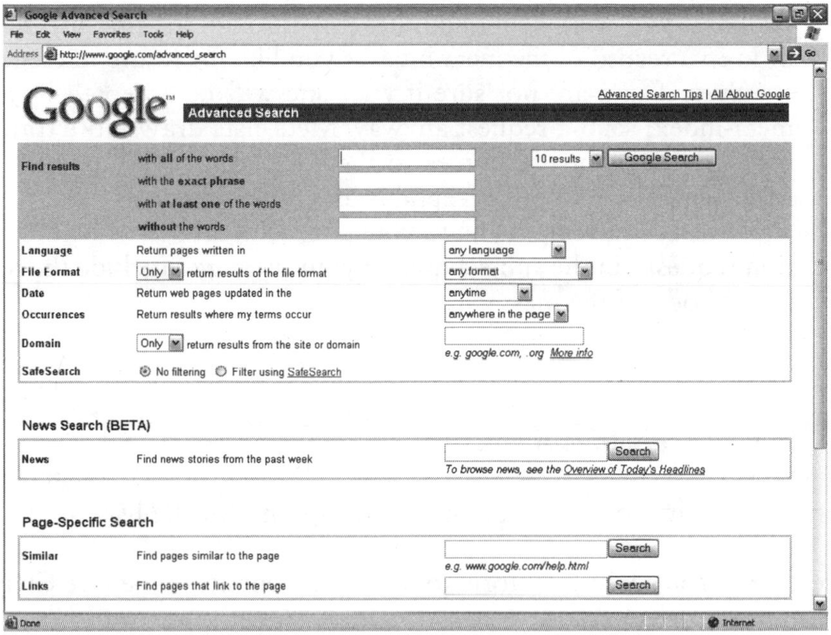

Figure 17.4. Google's search options.

Enlisting Meta-Indexes for Optimal Exposure

To ensure that you are taking full advantage of meta-indexes, search for:

- Appropriate meta-indexes

- Request a link

- Provide the details necessary

- Look at sponsorship or banner advertising opportunities

Meta-indexes can be arranged by subject (sites that provide information on book publishing) or by geography (tourist sites in Alaska). As mentioned before, the major search engines are a good place to start. For example, to find tourist sites in Alaska, conduct a search by entering *+Alaska+tourist+directory*. Once you find a good list and start to check the links, you will likely find other lists through the first list. Bookmark or keep a record of the meta-indexes you like for future reference.

Even if you are not sure if your site will be accepted by a certain meta-index, send a request anyway. Meta-lists draw more traffic when they provide more resources to their readers, so list owners may be fairly lenient on what's acceptable and what's not.

When requesting a link to your site, send an e-mail with "Site addition request" in the subject area of your message. Include the following in the body of the message:

- URL

- Description of your site

- Why you feel your site is appropriate for the list

- Your contact information in your signature file (see Chapter 8)

Once you have identified indexes that appeal to your target market, determine whether additional opportunities might exist for sponsoring or purchasing banner advertising on the site. Meta-indexes that relate to your market are a great place to advertise because they are accessed by your target customers.

Keep in mind that the compilers of meta-indexes are motivated by noncommercial reasons and are under no obligation to add your site to their list or process your request quickly. However, because of the banner advertising revenue potential, more and more meta-index sites have a commercial focus.

To make your link stand out among the many others listed, inquire about adding a prominent link or icon to the meta-index page along with a short tag line, in addition to your company name. If you provide the GIF and the HTML, the meta-index owner may be happy to include it.

A listing on a meta-index may be free, but there may be a fee charged for placing a hypertext link within the listing. However, there also are meta-indexes that charge a fee for the listing. If you are considering paying a fee to be included in a meta-index, consider the volume of traffic the meta-index receives, whether the traffic is targeted, and the cost involved in relation to the return on investment. It may be wise to contact those already listed in the meta-index to see if the listing has been a good investment for them.

Review the Work of Some Meta-Index Giants

Achoo Healthcare Online (Figure 17.5)
http://www.achoo.com

Bed and Breakfast Inns Online (Figure 17.6)
http://www.bbonline.com

Buzzle.com Travel and Tourism Meta-Index (Figure 17.7)
http://www.buzzle.com

GIS Resources on the Web (Figure 17.8)
http://www.gsd.harvard.edu/~pbcote/GIS/web_resources.html

Hotels and Travel on the Net (Figure 17.9)
http://www.hotelstravel.com/homepage.html

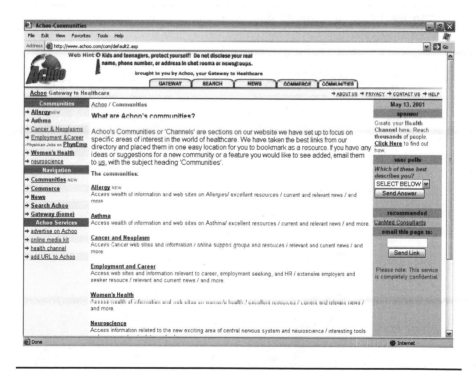

Figure 17.5. Directory of healthcare-related sites.

Figure 17.6.   Bed and Breakfast Inns Online.

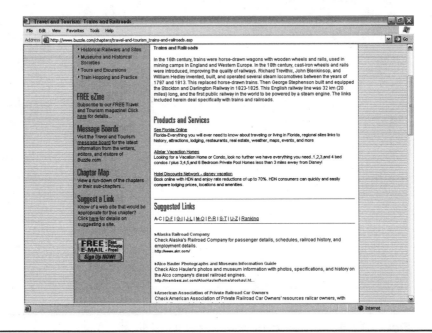

Figure 17.7.   Meta-index of trains and railroads, a subset of Buzzle.com.

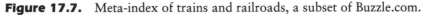

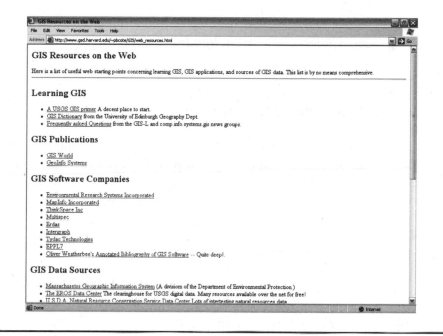

Figure 17.8. GIS Resources on the Web.

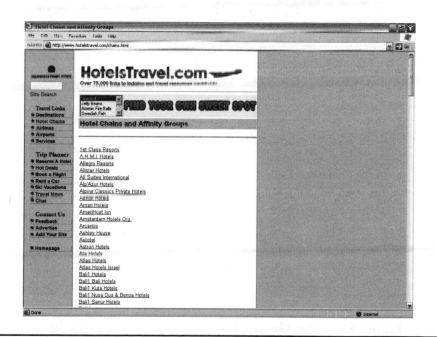

Figure 17.9. A list of links to all kinds of Web sites for hotel chains worldwide.

Jim Gaston's Fountain Pen Sites Meta-Index (Figure 17.10)
http://www.jimgaston.com/sitelink.htm

Internet Resources for Chapter 17

I have included a few resources for you to check out on meta-indexes. For additional resources on a variety of topics, I recommend that you visit the Resources section of my Web site at *http://www.susansweeney.com/resources.html*. There you will find additional tips, tools, techniques, and resources.

Essential Links: Portal to the Internet
http://www.el.com
Essential links to the Internet and the World Wide Web—Essential Links is a portal to the Internet portal sites, news headlines, search engines, Web directories, references, and utilities.

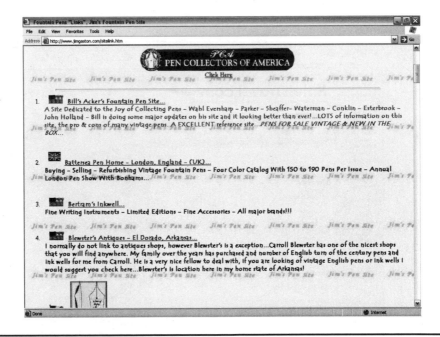

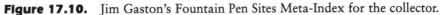

Figure 17.10.   Jim Gaston's Fountain Pen Sites Meta-Index for the collector.

Internet Resources Meta-Index
http://www.ncsa.uiuc.edu/SDG/Software/Mosaic/MetaIndex.html
A meta-index of the various resource directories and indexes available on the Internet.

Metaplus
http://www.metaplus.com
The Webmaster's Ultimate Resource—A meta-index of the directories and essential sites.

Virtual Library
http://vlib.org/Overview.html
The Virtual Library is the oldest catalog of the Web, started by Tim Berners-Lee, the creator of the Web itself. Unlike commercial catalogs, it is run by a loose confederation of volunteers, who compile pages of key links for particular areas in which they are experts. Even though it isn't the biggest index of the Web, the VL pages are widely recognized as being among the highest-quality guides to particular sections of the Web.

WWW Meta-Indexes and Search Tools
http://www.fys.ruu.nl/~kruis/h3.html
A Library of Congress Internet resource page.

18

Winning Awards,
Cool Sites, and More

There are literally hundreds of Cool Sites, Sites of the Day, Hot Sites, and Pick-of-the-Week Sites. Some of these sites require you to submit; others are selected based on such things as:

- Awesome graphics

- Dynamite content that is useful and interesting

- Uniqueness

- Fun features

If you are selected for one of these sites, it can mean a huge increase in the number of visitors to your site. You must be prepared for the increased traffic flow as well as the increased demand for online offerings. In this chapter, we cover:

- Where to submit your site for award consideration

- How to win Site of the Day—tips, tools, and techniques

- Getting listed in What's New

- Posting your awards on your site

- Hosting your own Site of the Day

It's an Honor Just to Be Nominated

There are sites that find and evaluate other sites on the Internet and recognize those that are outstanding by giving them an award. The award sites are generally very discriminating in terms of which sites are selected to be the recipients of their award. They have established criteria defining what is considered "hot" or "cool" and base their award selection on those criteria. Figure 18.1 shows a variety of awards.

What's New Web sites are designed to inform Internet users of new sites and updates to existing sites, and are often selective in which new sites they will promote. The owner of each site also selectively chooses awards for Site of the Day, Week, Month, and Year. As mentioned earlier, some of these sites require you to submit an announcement or site description, and the awards are granted based on criteria such as graphics, dynamic content, uniqueness, and the "fun" quality of your site.

Figure 18.1.   A collage of some of the more popular award sites.

Other sites grant their awards based solely on the personal likes and dislikes of the owner of the site and do not adhere to any criteria at all.

Some awards are taken just as seriously as the Academy Awards. The Webby Awards have a very comprehensive nomination procedure. The following information regarding the Webby is available on that Web site:

THE WEBBY AWARDS

Presented by The International Academy of Digital Arts and Sciences, The Webby Awards is the leading international honor for achievement in technology, creativity and individual achievement.

The Webby Awards honor sites that Internet users visit daily for information, entertainment, community, products and services. Selected by Members of the International Academy of Digital Arts and Sciences, The Webby Awards present honors to Web sites in 30 categories: Activism, Best Practices, Broadband, Commerce, Community, Education, Fashion, Film, Finance, Games, Government & Law, Health, Humor, Kids, Living, Music, NetArt, News, Personal Web Site, Politics, Print & Zines, Radio, Science, Services, Spirituality, Sports, Technical Achievement, Travel, TV, and Weird.

In addition, the Webby Awards in partnership with Nielsen/NetRatings will introduce three new awards, where sites will be awarded based on traffic to sites using Nielsen/NetRatings Internet audience measurement data.

The Webbys strive to combine the rich diversity of perspectives and talent of the online community in order to recognize the finest work by the most skilled people in this dynamic field. The Webby Awards presents two honors in each of the 30 categories: The Webby Award and The People's Voice Award. While members of The International Academy of Digital Arts and Sciences select the nominees for both awards, you, the online community, determines the winners of The People's Voice Awards by voting for the sites that you believe to be the best in each category.

When you win an award, you post the award on your site for all to see. The award icon is usually a link back to the site that bestowed the honor on you.

Choosing Your Awards and Submitting to Win

There are different levels of prestige associated with each of the different award sites. Some are an honor to receive. Some are highly competitive because of the number of submissions they receive.

Some awards are easier to receive than others, such as those from commercial sites that give out awards in an attempt to increase the traffic to their own site. Traffic increases because the award is a graphic link displayed on the winner's site that visitors can follow back to the award giver's site. Other Webmasters give out awards to anybody and everybody who makes a submission. The award is granted with the sole purpose of building traffic.

The bottom line is that awards are valuable assets. The average Web user cannot tell which awards are the prestigious ones and which are given to anyone who submits. So, submit for any awards that you choose to, as long as your site is ready. (A sample submission form is shown in Figure 18.2.)

Where you place these awards is important. If you win a lot of awards, you will want to consider developing an Awards page with a link from your navigation bar to house them.

Something to consider before you submit for an award is whether the huge amount of new traffic will benefit your site. If you sell T-shirts emblazoned with WWW cartoons, then any traffic is good traffic, and awards will benefit your site. On the other hand, if you are a marine biologist specializing in red tides in the Arctic, then the traffic that "Site of the Day" would bring may be more of a hindrance than a help in marketing your services. Always determine if the marketing tools and techniques will increase visitors from your target market before deciding whether to include them in your online marketing strategy.

Getting mentioned on one of the popular Cool Sites lists is probably the single biggest way to draw a tremendous amount of traffic to your site. However, the traffic they send to your site is like a flash flood—fast and furious. Be careful what you wish for—you just might get it! The traffic will be swift and plentiful after you win one of these awards. Be

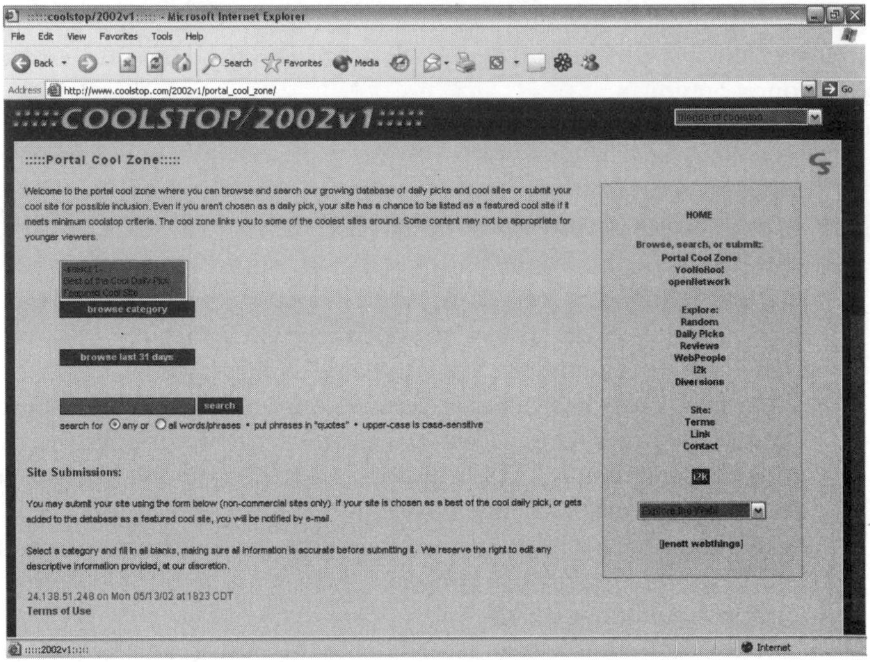

Figure 18.2. Sample award submission form. This one is for Coolstop.

prepared! Have a plan that you can implement on a moment's notice. If you offer something free from your site, be sure that you can access a huge volume of whatever it is and be sure that you have a plan to distribute quickly. If you offer a free download from your site, plan to have a number of alternate **FTP** sites available to your visitors. If you have a "call-in" offer, make sure you have a telephone response system in place and staff to handle the huge volume of calls you may get. You will need a plan to handle the huge volume of e-mails you will get as well.

FTP (File Transfer Protocol)
The simplest way to transfer files between computers on the Internet.

Once you have decided that the type of traffic that comes along with winning the award fits with your marketing strategy, you should make sure your site has the makings of a winner and then submit to as many award sites as you can.

- First, make a list of the URLs of the award sites you are interested in.

- Understand the submission form and guidelines. Review a number of forms to determine the common information requested.

- To save time, develop a document with the answers to the various questions from which you can copy and paste into the different submission forms.

- Submission forms will capture the following types of information:

  – URL

  – Title of your site

  – Contact person (name, e-mail, phone, address)

  – Owner of the site

- Submission guidelines will tell you what types of sites can be submitted. (Some awards do not accept personal pages; others do not include commercial sites.) The submission guidelines will also tell you what meets the definition of "cool" or "new" and what doesn't.

- Some award sites require that you display their award icon on your site. Posting an award on your site can provide a number of positive results—including enhanced credibility.

What's Hot and What's Not in the Name of Cool

Most of the award sites will provide you with their selection criteria. Some award sites look for and base their selection on valuable content; others look for innovative and unique capabilities. Sites vary on what they consider "hot" or "cool," but they are fairly consistent on what doesn't make the grade, as summarized next.

What's Hot	What's Not
Awesome graphics	Single-page sites
Great, original content	Single product promotion
Broad appeal	Offensive language or graphics
Fun features	Lengthy download time

Posting Your Awards on Your Site

If you have managed to collect a few awards for your Web site, you will want to display them somehow. After all, any award is a good award, and the award site that granted you a particular award will expect you to display it in return for the recognition. Posting the awards on your home page might not be the best idea, though. For one thing, the additional graphics that will have to be downloaded will slow the load time for your home page. Second, by posting the awards on your home page, you are placing links leading out of your site on the first page. Thus, you are giving people the opportunity to leave your site before they have even had a chance to explore it. Where should you post your well-deserved awards, then? Simply create an "Awards" section on your Web site. Here, you can list all of your awards without adversely affecting the load time of your home page or losing traffic.

Becoming the Host of Your Own Awards Gala

You can also create your own awards program in order to draw traffic to your site; however, this requires a considerable amount of work to maintain. The benefits of having your own awards program include having links back to your site from the awards placed on winners' sites, which is important for search engine placement because of link popularity, and there are also great opportunities for permission ("Click here to be notified via e-mail when we have a new award winner") and viral marketing ("Tell a friend about this award—click here"). In addition, having your own awards program also provides you with "bragging rights" and the opportunity for press releases to announce your awards, which will gain exposure for your Web site and increase traffic. You will need to work at it on a daily or weekly basis, so you must be committed to it. Be sure there is a benefit from a marketing perspective before you design and develop your own awards program. You must also be prepared to conduct your own searches at the outset to find sites worthy of your award if the quality of sites being submitted to you is not up to your standard.

There are a number of steps involved in getting your awards program up and running:

- You will first have to develop the criteria you will use in your site selection.

- You will have to develop several Web pages related to the award (information on selection criteria, submission forms, today's or this week's award winner, past award recipients page, etc.) in order to promote the award. (Be sure that you stipulate whether you are looking for submissions from commercial sites or personal pages and what criteria will be used in judging the submissions.)

- Your award icon must be developed. Have this icon link back to your site. The award distinguishes the winner; thus, the link will probably be displayed prominently on its site. This is a great traffic builder.

- Finally, you have to announce the award and market, market, market.

Internet Resources for Chapter 18

I have included a few resources for you to check out about winning awards and being designated a cool or hot site. For additional resources on a variety of topics, I recommend that you visit the Resources section of my Web site at *http://www.susansweeney.com/resources.html*. There you will find additional tips, tools, techniques, and resources.

Award Sites
http://www.awardsites.com
Free guide offering... Ratings, Recognition, and Resources. Ideal for promoting, marketing, or just browsing some of the best sites on the

Internet that just happen to offer a diverse range of information, services, or products—including many with excellent Web site award or review programs.

Best of the Planet Awards
http://www.2ask.com
Called the People's Choice Award, where you can decide who's best.

Jayde.com
http://www.jayde.com/goldlnks.html
Awards the Gold Diamond Award to sites with great style, design, and content. Jayde.com also has an award for commercial sites.

Webby Awards
http://www.webbyawards.com
The Webby Awards have been embraced by the online community as the leading creative honors for digital media. The awards recognize the most creative and innovative Web sites of the year and the talented editorial, technical, and design teams behind them.

Hot Sites/Cool Sites

100 Hot Web Sites
http://www.100hot.com
Directory of Web sites based on Web traffic and organized by category.

Cool Site of the Day
http://www.coolsiteoftheday.com
Cool Site of the Day is a wildly popular Internet award site that features interesting, provocative, and irreverent Web sites from around the world.

CoolStop
http://www.coolstop.com
The Best of the Cool Award consistently recognizes truly outstanding sites in terms of design, originality, and content.

JimWorld Way Cool Hot Site Award
http://jimworld.com/hotpg.html
From this site you can visit some of the coolest, most interesting hot sites on the Web. These sites are selected by a blue ribbon panel of one—Jim. The sites here are truly special. Jim receives about 500 sub-

missions every week; that's about 2,000 per month. Out of that he usually finds only one winner. Visit a few of these sites. It's worth the time.

USA Today Hot Sites
http://www.usatoday.com/life/cyber/ch.htm
USA Today scours the Web for sites that are hot, new, and notable. Visit their daily list to find some of the best sites the Web has to offer. They look for sites that may stretch the design envelope and show where the Web is headed—sites that offer something unusual or unexpected, or something just plain useful.

Virtual Reference Meta-Index of Award Sites
http://www.refdesk.com/textcool.html
A listing of different sites that host Site of the Day, Hot Sites, and so on.

Web Pages That Suck
http://www.webpagesthatsuck.com
Keep your site from being nominated to this awards site, and you are probably doing well. However, you can learn a lot from Web Pages That Suck about how to properly design your site from a marketing perspective.

Web Site Awards
http://websiteawards.xe.net
The Web Site Awards Worksheet is a free resource! It helps you apply for Web awards and track your activities. Apply to over 500 award sites around the world!

World Best Websites
http://www.worldbestwebsites.com
World Best Website Awards are granted to exemplary Web sites that are pursuing "best practices" in Web site design and Internet communications.

19

Productive Online Advertising

The world of banner advertising is changing rapidly. Several years ago banner advertising was in vogue, visitors were clicking through, good banner space was hard to find, and prices were rising. What a difference a day makes! The past two years have seen banner advertising prices decline. Quality space is not that difficult to obtain, and click-through rates are on the decline dramatically. Banner advertising is being used primarily to meet branding objectives. Despite all the doom and gloom and bad press, however, banner ads can still be an effective advertising medium if the banner ad is properly developed and it is placed on the appropriate site. We are starting to see a shift toward ads using rich media. Advertising online provides visibility—just as offline advertising does. You must develop a banner advertising strategy that works with your product, your marketing objectives, and your budget. In this chapter, we cover:

- Your online advertising strategy

- Advertising opportunities on the Web

- Banner ad design and impact on click-throughs

- Banner ad sizes and locations

- Placing classifieds

- Tips to creating dynamite banner ads that work

- The cost of advertising online

- Measuring ad effectiveness

- Banner ad exchange networks

- Using an online advertising agency

- Sources of Internet advertising information

Expanding Your Exposure through Internet Advertising

Today, Internet advertising is being recognized in the advertising budgets of businesses around the globe. Banner ads are a way to create awareness of your Web site and increase the traffic to it. Banners are placed on the sites that your target market is likely to frequent, thus encouraging this market to click through and visit you!

The Internet offers many different advertising spaces. Banner ads can be placed on search engines, content sites, advertising sites, and online magazines. The choice of where your ad is displayed is based on the objectives you wish to achieve with your online advertising strategy.

There are a number of advantages to online advertising:

- The response from these ads can easily be measured within one day through Web traffic analysis.

- The amount of information that can be delivered, if your Web site is visited, far surpasses that of a traditional advertising campaign.

- The cost of developing and running an online advertising campaign is much less than using traditional media.

Traditionally, advertising used to be handled by a public relations (PR) firm or advertising company that would come up with your marketing concept. As clients, businesses would review and approve (usually after several attempts) the concepts before they were ever released to the public eye. The PR or advertising firms would be responsible for developing TV, radio, and print ads for the businesses. They would come up with the media buy strategy after reviewing appropriate publications, editorial calendars, pricing, and the discounts that they would receive for multiple placements. The ads were then gradually released over the period of the campaign and finally were viewed by the public. At the end of the campaign, the PR or advertising company would evaluate the success of the marketing campaign. This is very easy if the objective of the campaign was to achieve X number of sales, but it is much more difficult if the goal of your campaign was to generate brand awareness.

Today, online banner ads are developed in much less time and are placed on Web sites very quickly. Web traffic analysis software can tell you the next day if the banner ad is working or not by tracking the number of visitors who clicked through and visited your site through the ad. This provides you with the opportunity to change the site on which you are advertising or to change the banner ad to see if it will attract a greater audience.

Nielsen Net Ratings (*http://www.nielsen-netratings.com*) (Figure 19.1) offers great up-to-date resources to find out who is doing the most online advertising. You can check this resource to find the top ten banners displayed on the Internet each week and the top ten advertisers online.

Maximize Advertising with Your Objectives in Mind

When developing your advertising strategy, you will need to start with the objectives of your advertising campaign. The most common objectives for an online advertising campaign include:

- Building brand awareness

- Increasing Web site traffic

- Generating leads and sales

You have a number of choices to make, such as what type of advertising to use and where to advertise. These choices should be made based on your objectives. If your objective is to increase overall brand recog-

Figure 19.1. Neilsen Net Ratings provides you with continuously updated statistics on who is doing the most advertising on the Internet. The site can also provide you with the top most viewed banner ads on a weekly or monthly basis.

nition, a nicely designed banner ad on one of the high-traffic search engines would be effective. If you would like to develop leads and find new clients, then a more-targeted approach should be taken, such as placing a banner ad on a high-traffic Web site that is frequented by your target market.

When deciding how to proceed with your advertising strategy, consider how many people you want to reach. Do you want a high-quality response from a small number of very targeted people, or do you want to reach a mass audience of grand proportions?

Think about the people you are targeting. If you sell dentistry supplies to dental practices, then you want to target dentists and hygienists. It would not make much sense to put an ad on Yahoo! when you could advertise on a site about new medical discoveries in dentistry.

Always keep your budget in mind when you are devising your online advertising strategy. There are many ways to stretch your advertising dollar. If you have the time, you can find appropriate sites to trade banners. You can also participate in banner exchange programs, which are set up by a third party, and your banner is displayed randomly on other banner exchange participants' pages.

Online Advertising Terminology

Banner Ads

Banner ads are small advertisements that are placed on a Web site. Companies usually develop their banner ads, find appropriate sites for placement, and then either purchase or trade banner space.

Click-Throughs

When a viewer clicks on a banner ad with the mouse and goes to the site advertised, it is called a "click-through." Sometimes banner advertising prices are determined by the number of click-throughs.

Hits

Hits to a site are the number of times that another computer has accessed that site (or a file in a site). This does not mean that if your site has 1,000 hits, 1,000 people have visited it. If your home page has a number of graphic files on it, this number could be very misleading. A hit is counted when the home page main file is accessed, but a hit is also counted for every graphic file that loads along with the home page. So if a person visits six pages on a site and each page has five graphics, at least 30 hits would be generated.

Impressions or Page Views

When a banner ad is viewed, it is called an impression. Banner advertising prices are often calculated by impressions. If a person visits a page six times, this will generate six impressions.

CPM

Cost per thousand, or CPM, is a standard advertising term. CPM is often used to calculate the cost of banner advertising if a site sells advertising based on impressions. If the CPM of banner advertising on the site was U.S.$40 and the number of impressions the ad had was 2,000, then the advertiser would have to pay U.S.$80 for displaying the ad.

Keywords

You can purchase keyword banner advertising on search engines, sites that have sophisticated banner advertising programs, or sites whose banner advertising real estate is maintained by online advertising agencies that have sophisticated banner advertising programs. Your banner ad appears when someone does a search on the keyword that you purchased. This is very good for zooming in on your target market.

Geotargeting

Purchasing geographically targeted banner advertising is one of the latest trends in Internet marketing. This is done by purchasing banner advertising for a range of IP addresses. Every device that connects to the Internet has its own unique IP address. These are assigned centrally by a designated authority for each country. We are now seeing search engines sell IP addresses to help businesses pinpoint their target geographic group. For example, John Doe is building a new home in Utah and is searching for a company selling lumber in his area. Dooley Building Supplies, a lumber company in Utah, happens to be marketing over the Internet, and as part of Dooley's banner advertising campaign they have purchased banner ads by keyword and by IP address. Simply stated, they have said that they only want their banner ad to appear when the keyword "lumber" is searched on by individuals whose IP address is within a certain range (the range being those existing in Utah). When John Doe does his search on the word "lumber," the Dooley Building Supplies banner ad is displayed at the top of the page holding the search results. Someone in Michigan searching for lumber will see a different banner ad.

Jump on the Banner Wagon

Banner advertising is the most common and most recognized form of online advertising. Banner ads are available in various sizes, but the most common banners are displayed at roughly 468 × 60 pixels. (See Figure 19.2 for some of the more popular banner ad sizes.) AdRelevance studies have found that a variety of alternative ad dimensions are emerging as mainstream standards alongside full banner ads. They recently polled 115 high-traffic sites, and the results showed that the standard banner is truly a standard: 95 percent of all sites support the format. About 50 percent of the sites offered a short button (120 × 60 pixels) and about the same percentage offered a micro button (88 × 31 pixels). A new size of banner ad has recently been introduced. These sidebar or "skyscraper" ads are vertical and are 120 × 600 pixels. Because they are two to three times larger than a horizontal banner ad, they cannot be

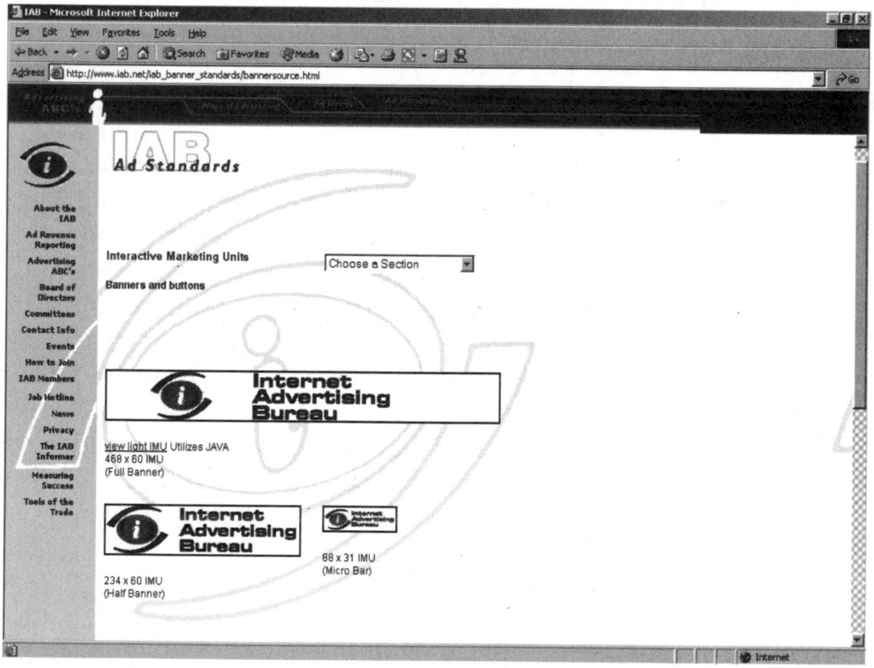

Figure 19.2. There are many different marketing resource Web sites available online that can provide you with the different size possibilities for your banner ads.

scrolled off the screen as quickly and have been reporting a click-through rate of 1 percent.

Banners usually have an enticing message or call to action that coaxes the viewer to click on it. "What is on the other side?" you ask. The advertiser's Web site, of course. Banner ads can also be static, just displaying the advertiser's logo and slogan, or can be animated with graphics and movement.

If you use an advertising or PR company to develop your offline ads, quite often they will provide you with a library of different banner ads that you can use for your online advertising campaign. If you choose not to use an advertising or PR company, you can outsource the banner ad creation activity to another company or create your own.

The banner ad is designed to have a direct impact on the number of click-throughs it will achieve. There are a number of resources online to assist you in developing dynamic banner ads. The Banner Generator at *http://www.coder.com/creations/banner* allows you to create banners online at no charge. The Media Builder at *http://www.3dtextmaker.com* provides you the opportunity to develop animated banner ads directly from its site. Other resources to assist you in designing and building banner ads are identified in the Internet Resources section at the end of this chapter.

As noted previously, there are a wide variety of banner sizes available. You should consult with the owners of the Web sites on which you want to advertise before creating your banner ad or having one created professionally for you.

The objective of your banner ad is to have someone click on it. Do not try to include all of your information in your ad. A banner that is too small and cluttered is difficult to read and is not visually appealing. Many banners simply include a logo and a tag line enticing the user to click on it. Free offers or contest giveaways are also quite effective for click-throughs because they tend to appeal to the user's curiosity.

Exploring Your Banner Ad Options

Static banners are what the name suggests. They remain static on the same Web page until they are removed. Your banner ad will be visible on that particular page until your reader moves to another page.

Animated banners are banners that move on a Web site. Animated banners are usually in **GIF** format and contain a group of images in one file that are presented in a specific order (see Figures 19.3a–c). When using animated banner ads, you can choose to loop the file so that the banner will continue to move between the images in the files, or you have the option to make it stop after a complete cycle.

GIF
Graphics
Interchange
Format.

Rotating banners are banner ads that rotate among different Web pages on the same site. Some rotating banners rotate every 15 or 30 seconds, so a visitor may see several ads while remaining on the page. Other rotating banner ads rotate every time there is a new visitor to the page. Rotating banners are commonly used in high-traffic Web sites.

Figure 19.3a.   This is the first stage in an animated banner ad. It catches visitors' attention and makes them think that the banner is doing a search on popular keywords relating to skiing.

Figure 19.3b.   This is the second stage in an animated banner ad. It acts as though the banner is doing a search on the keywords inputted into the query box.

Figure 19.3c.   This is the final stage in an animated banner ad. It acts as though the search was completed, and now takes its opportunity to promote skiing in Canada. This is great because by the time they are ready to promote Canadian skiing, they have the viewer's full attention.

Scrolling banners are similar to modern billboards. Here the visitor will see a number of billboard ads, scrolled to show a different advertisement every 10 to 30 seconds.

Banner Ad Tips

Follow these tips to ensure that your banner ad will achieve your marketing objectives:

- Make sure that your banner ad is quick to load. If the Web page loads in its entirety before the banner, then the viewer may click away before ever seeing it. Ideally, you should have a very fast banner ad on a relatively slow-loading site. This way your viewers have nothing to do but read your banner ad while they are waiting for the site to load. You should always try to keep your banner ad size under 5K.

- To see how big files are when using any version of Internet Explorer, you can follow these steps:

  - Right-click on the banner ad.

  - Select "Properties."

  - In the Properties window you will see a "Size" line, which will tell you the banner size.

- To see how big files are when using any version of Netscape Navigator, you can follow these steps:

  - Right-click on the banner ad.

  - Select "View Image," and the banner ad will appear on a page of its own.

  - Right-click on the banner and select "View Info." Another page will pop up and give you the information on the banner ad size.

- Keep it simple! If your banner contains too much text or animation, or too many colors and fonts, this will cause viewers to experience information overload. Viewers will not be encouraged to read or click on your banner.

- Make sure your banner ad is legible. Many banners on the Internet are nicely designed but difficult to read. Use an easy-to-read font with the appropriate size. Be careful in your choice of color.

- You should always use Alt tags for those visitors who surf the Internet with their graphics turned off or cannot see your banner ad for whatever reason.

- Make sure your banner ad links to the appropriate page in your site. It is not uncommon to click on an interesting banner only to find an error message waiting for you. This is very annoying to Internet users and counterproductive for your marketing effort. Check your banner ads on a regular basis to verify that the link remains active and is pointing to the appropriate page on your Web site.

- If you are using animated banner ads, you should limit your ads to two to four frames.

- You should always include a call to action such as "Click here." It is amazing how many people will do what they are told. You still have to make your ad interesting and one that grabs their attention. Don't simply say "Click here"—give your audience a compelling reason to do so.

- Test your banner ads with the different browsers, the different versions of these browsers, and at different screen resolutions to make sure that they look the way you want them to.

- If you know absolutely nothing about advertising and graphic design, do not try to create a banner on your own. Go to a professional. If you do design your own banner, get a second opinion and maybe a third.

Interesting Banner Ads

The following are more technologically advanced forms of banner advertising. They are interesting to viewers because they have attributes that are unique or different in some way. These attributes may be more apt to grab viewers' attention and entice them to click on the banner ad.

Expanding Banner Ads. An expanding banner ad (see Figures 19.4a and 19.4b) is one that looks like a normal banner ad but expands when you click on it, keeping you on the same site rather than transporting you to another site on the Internet. Usually these say "Click to Expand," and the viewer then can learn more about what it is that the banner is promoting. Some of the more advanced expanding banner ads have e-commerce capabilities, which allow you to actually order products from the banner, without actually ever going to the Web site.

Figure 19.4a. This expanding advertisement for Investor's Business Daily displays the product, but then prompts the viewer to expand the banner ad.

Figure 19.4b. When the banner expands it explains more about the product, and actually gives the visitor a chance to subscribe directly from the banner ad. This incorporated e-commerce and banner ad technology together.

Animated Banner Ads. Animated banner ads contain a group of images in one file that rotate in a specific order. These banner ads are more likely to receive a higher click-through than a normal banner ad because with moving images on the Web site, your chances of the viewer's reading the banner are increased. These banners also offer you the chance to deliver more information to the viewer than in a normal banner ad because you can show different files, which contain different data. You should limit your banner ads to two to four frames to keep your load time fast and to make sure your viewers read your information before they continue to surf the Internet.

Drop-Down Menu Banner Ads Containing Embedded HTML. Lately we are seeing an increase in banner ads containing embedded HTML (see Figures 19.5 and 19.6). This allows viewers to choose commands from a drop-down menu that relate to the Web site the banner ad is promoting. These banners are great because instead of making viewers click through and then have to navigate through your site, as with a conventional banner, these will direct your viewers to the page of interest on your site. This type of banner ad also is great for co-op advertising programs. Several companies selling noncompeting products or services to the same target market can use this type of banner advertising to get more exposure for their dollar.

Interstitial Ads. These are advertisements that appear in a separate browser window while your visitors wait for a Web page to load. Interstitial ads are more likely to contain large graphics, streaming presentations, and more applets than a conventional banner ad. Studies have found that more users click on interstitial ads than on banner ads. However, some users have complained that interstitial ads slow access to destination pages.

Figure 19.5.   Trips.com advertises using banners with embedded HTML which allow the viewer to choose a specific vacation destination from a pull down menu, and then find out what travel opportunities are available. This is great because the viewer can go directly to the page of interest on the Trip.com site, instead of searching through the entire site.

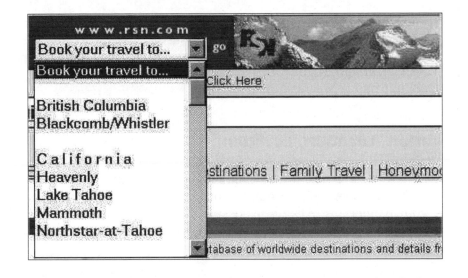

Figure 19.6. Another embedded HTML banner, showing different opportunities for the viewer to choose from.

Java, Flash, and Shockwave Ads. These banner ads allow you to use rich media in your advertisements. By using these technologies, you can incorporate animation and sound into your banner advertisement. Although Java banners are more technologically advanced and offer more features, they also take longer to download and risk not being viewed. Flash was designed to generate faster-loading Web sites, online animation, and advertising. If you want to incorporate rich media into your banners, you may want to go with Flash or Shockwave because you want your visitors to see your banner ads as quickly as possible.

Floating Ads and DHTML. These ads appear when you first view a Web page, and they appear to "fly" or "float" over the page for anywhere from 5 to 30 seconds. They tend to obscure your view of the page, and they often disable mouse input until the ad is finished loading so that you must watch it before being able to access the page content. They have a high click-through rate of 3 percent and are great for branding, although their intrusiveness has been questioned.

Unicast Ads. Although not widely seen on the Internet at the present, their popularity is increasing. A Unicast ad is basically like a television commercial that runs in a pop-up window. It has animation and sound and can last from 10 to 30 seconds. Although they are like television commercials, they go a step further in that a viewer can then click on the ad to obtain further information. They have a 5 percent click-through rate.

Location, Location, Location

As with all types of advertising, the location of the ad is extremely important. There are any number of targeted sites where you can place your banner ads. Always make sure that your banner advertising location is consistent with your objectives.

Search Engines

If your goal is to reach as many different people as possible, high-traffic search engine sites are where you should be. Cost per thousand impressions is usually U.S.$20 to U.S.$50. If you want to be selective with your target market, then a more-targeted buy within the search engine is appropriate. Targeted buys can include tying your banner ad to specific keywords (i.e., every time the keyword is used in a search, your banner ad would appear). Targeted ads generally range in CPM from U.S.$40 to U.S.$90, but quite often they are worth the extra price because of the correlation to the targeted buyer. If you owned a bed and breakfast in Oklahoma and purchased "Oklahoma Bed and Breakfast" as a keyword, whenever someone searched for "Oklahoma Bed and Breakfast," your banner would appear.

Content Sites

If your objectives include bringing interested people from your target market to your site, then advertising on appropriate content sites would be extremely effective. These are sites that concentrate on a specific topic. The CPM of advertising on content sites ranges from U.S.$25 to U.S.$50 depending on the traffic volume they see and the focus of their visitors.

Banner Ad Price Factors

The price of banner ad space varies from site to site. Banner ads often are sold based on the number of impressions or number of click-throughs. As stated earlier, an impression is an ad view, and click-throughs are the actual clicking on the banner ad and being sent to the advertiser's Web site. The price per impression should be less than the price per click-through. Banner ad CPM is between U.S.$10 and U.S.$90 depending on the site you are advertising on—how targeted the audience is and how much traffic the site receives. Search engine banner ad CPMs range between U.S.$20 and U.S.$50. Keyword advertising CPMs range between U.S.$40 and U.S.$90. The cost to run a geotracking campaign can be very costly. Before you sign anything, make sure that you understand what you are paying for.

When site owners charge per impression, there is usually a guarantee that your ad will be seen by a certain number of people. The burden is on the seller to generate traffic to its site. When the charges are per click-through, the responsibility is on you, the advertiser, to design an ad that will encourage visitors to click on it. Sites that charge per impression are more common than those that charge per click-through.

There are obvious advantages to the advertiser when paying per click-through. The advertiser doesn't have to pay a cent for the 10,000 people that saw the banner but did not pursue the link. Sites that do not have a large volume of traffic often charge a flat rate for a specified period of time.

Considerations When Purchasing Your Banner Ad

Before you sign on the dotted line to purchase banner advertising, there are a few things you should consider:

- How closely aligned is the target market of the site you want to advertise on to yours?

- How many sites are there like the one you are considering advertising on? Are there a lot of sites you can use to reach the same audience?

- What banner sizes are allowed? Generally, the larger the banner size, the more it will cost.

- How many ads are on each page? The more ads on a page, the lower the click-through rate for any particular ad on that page. Generally, the more ads on a page, the lower the price per ad.

- What banner rotation system is being used? Is there a comprehensive program that automatically profiles the visitors and provides the appropriate banner? The more targeted the audience, the more expensive the ad; these profiling systems can provide ads to a very targeted audience.

- What are the site's competitors charging?

- Does the site have a sliding-scale ad rate?

Make Sure Visitors Can See Your Banner

A major thing that is often overlooked is the fact that some people still surf the Internet with their graphics turned off. Not a big deal, right? What if you purchased a banner ad? They are not going to see it, so why will they click through? An easy way to make sure that the viewer still knows that your banner is there is to attach an Alt tag to your banner. An Alt tag is a small piece of HTML code that is added to a Web site. It tells the browser what is supposed to be displayed if the graphic cannot be viewed. It is here that you should develop a clever tag line that will still entice the viewer to click through to your Web site. Remember that it is important to include an Alt tag on all of the graphics on your Web site.

Banner Ad Placement: Where Should Your Ad Be?

As it is for an advertisement in a newspaper or in a magazine, the location of your banner ad on a Web site is very important. A past study by graduate students at the University of Michigan has shown us that by placing a banner ad on the lower right-hand corner, next to the scroll bar, you receive a higher click-through rate. This is because when people scroll down the page, their eyes are in the bottom corner, so they see your ad. The study also showed us that placing a banner ad a third of the way down the page received a 77 percent higher click-through rate than those placed at the top. It is very common for the search engines to place their banners a third of the way down the page for prime advertising exposure.

When placing a banner ad, you must always remember your objective, which is to increase the traffic to your site. You should always do research on a Web site before you place an ad on it. You want to find out if it receives high traffic; you don't want to pay for an ad that will not be seen by anyone. You should try to place an ad on a site that is aimed to your target audience. You want to make sure that your banner is as appealing as possible and includes a call to action that will entice visitors to click through.

Making It Easy with Online Advertising Networks

If your objective is to reach a large number of users through a wide variety of sites, Internet ad networks may be appropriate. Ad networks have a wide range of different Web sites that people look at every day. If you are going to join an ad network, you are known as an advertiser. You have to supply your banners to the ad network and determine how you want them to promote you. ValueClick (*http://www.valueclick.com*) is an example of a very popular ad network (see Figure 19.7). ValueClick has 14,300 different Web sites in its network and is emerging as an ad network leader. It can target a specific industry of your choice or advertise your banner to a mass audience. For a more-targeted audience, your CPM will be higher. Even though you have to pay a little more initially, it will save you in the long run.

The benefit of joining an ad network is that the network not only will target your audience, it also will provide you with real-time reports that indicate the success of your banner ads. This allows you to evaluate the success of your current banner ad campaign and offers you the chance to change your marketing strategy if you are not happy with your results. Maybe you want to take a different approach, or maybe a different banner design might work better for you. Whatever it may be, the data that the ad network can provide you with is very beneficial to determining the strength of your banner ad campaign.

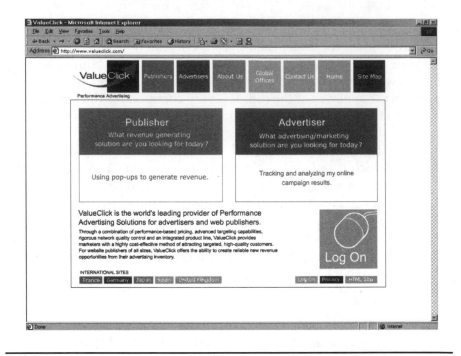

Figure 19.7. ValueClick is one of the world's largest ad networks offering its advertisers the opportunity to target their audience using ValueClick's Web site network.

You can also join an ad network as a publisher. Publishers are the Web sites that banners are placed on. If you have a Web site and would like to make some additional online revenue from your site, you can join an ad network, which will place banner ads on your site and pay you for the usage of this space. Very similar to an affiliate program, or banner exchange, by joining an ad network you can dramatically increase your online revenue. A detailed list of ad networks is listed in the Internet Resources section at the end of this chapter.

Saving Money with Banner Exchange Programs

Banner exchanges work much as you would expect (i.e., your ad is placed on other sites in exchange for someone else's banner ad being placed on your Web site). To register with a banner exchange, you often have to go through a qualifying process. What this means is that your site has to meet certain minimum standards. Once you have passed the test, the banner exchange will provide you with HTML code to insert into pages of your site where the banner ads will appear. Every time this HTML is accessed, a random banner ad appears for the viewer to see.

This process is monitored and tracked. Each banner that is accessed from the exchange and is displayed to a visitor earns you some sort of credit or token. These credits or tokens are used within the banner exchange like a bartering system. The credits you earn are exchanged for having your banner displayed on another site.

Sometimes some of the credits you earn go to the banner exchange itself, as a fee for managing the process. The banner exchange will sell the credits to paying advertisers or use them to promote the exchange. Some banner exchanges will allow you to focus your exposure on your target market.

When determining which banner exchanges to belong to, look for restrictions. When banner exchanges have no restrictions, you never know what could be loading to your pages. Don't join banner exchanges without size specifications for the banners. Your site could be displaying huge 150 × 600 pixel banners that make your visitors wait while they load. Be sure that the load time of every banner displayed on your site will be reasonable.

Here are some of the popular online banner exchange programs. A more complete list can be found through searching on "banner ad network" on your favorite search engine.

- BannerSwap (*http://www.bannerswap.com*)

- Cool Banners Banner Exchange Network (*http://www. coolbanners.com/bp*)

- eBannerx.com (*http://www.e-bannerx.com/bannerx.htm*)

- Neobanners (*http://www.neobanners.com*)

Bartering for Mutual Benefits with Banner Trading

Using this technique requires you to barter with other Web sites to trade banners with their sites. If you are browsing the Internet and find a site that you think appeals to your target market, then ask for a trade. Send the Web master an e-mail outlining your proposition. Include the reason you think it would be mutually beneficial, a description of your site, where you would place that site's banner on your site, and where you think your banner might go on its site.

When you make arrangements like this, be sure to monitor the results. If the other site has low traffic, then more visitors may be leaving your site through their banner than are being attracted. Also, check the other site regularly to make sure that your banners are still being displayed for the duration agreed upon.

Tips for Succeeding with Classified Ads

Classified ads are also displayed on various Web sites. Some sites offer to display classified ads for free; others will charge a small fee. Here are some great tips for creating effective classified ads:

- *Headlines.* The headline of your ad is very important. The subject line determines how many people will read the rest of your ad. Look at the subject lines of other ads and see what attracts your eye.

- *Entice.* Use your classified ad to get people to request more information, not to make immediate reservations. You can then send them a personalized letter outlining all of the information and make a great pitch to attract an order.

- *Be Friendly.* Your classified ad shouldn't be formal and business-like. Make your ad light and friendly.

- *Call for Action.* Do not only offer information about what you are selling. Call the reader for action—for instance, to order now!

- *Do Some Tests.* Run a number of different ads and use a different e-mail address for each one. This way you can determine which ad receives the most responses. You can then run the best ad in a number of different places to find out which place gets the biggest response.

- *Keep a Record.* Keep records of your responses so that you will know which ads were the most successful.

Form Lasting Advertising with Sponsorships

Sponsorships are another form of advertising that usually involve strong, long-lasting relationships between the sponsors and the owners of the sites. Sponsors may donate money, Web development, Web hosting, Web site maintenance, or other products and services to Web site owners in this mutually beneficial relationship. By sponsoring Web sites on the Internet, you can achieve great exposure for your site. People appreciate sponsorships and will look at banner ads that are from a sponsor. The benefits of sponsorships on the Internet are that you can target a specific audience, you usually get first call on banner ad placement, and you show your target market that you care about their interest. Overall, by sponsoring sites on the Internet, you have the opportunity to get directly in the face of your target market.

There are a number of different ways in which you can advertise online through sponsorships. The following is a list of the more common forms of online sponsorship:

- *E-Zines and Newsletters.* An example of this would be Nike sponsoring a Golf Digest e-zine.

- *Content Sites.* An example would be DuPont sponsoring a Nascar racing Web site.

- *Online Chat Sessions.* An example would be CDNow sponsoring a chat on the Ultimate Band List.

- *Events.* An example would be a search engine such as AltaVista or Google sponsoring a seminar on search engine strategy.

Commercial Links

Another form of online advertising is commercial links. A number of targeted sites provide a lengthy list of URLs related to a specific topic. These sites will often provide your listing for free but charge a fee to have a hypertext link activated from their site to yours. There are also Web sites where you can be listed if you don't have a Web site and would prefer to have only your business name and phone number or e-mail address listed. These are great sites, especially because they are targeted toward your demographic group. An example of this would be Franchise Solutions (*http://www.franchisesolutions.com*). This site (Figure 19.8) has a database of franchise and business opportunities targeted toward entrepreneurs wanting to open their own business. If you are a franchiser and are interesting in expanding your business, you would want to have a link on this Web site because your target market will visit a site like this.

Sponsoring a Mailing List

Another online advertising opportunity is presented by mailing lists. Mailing lists provide a very targeted advertising vehicle. Mailing list

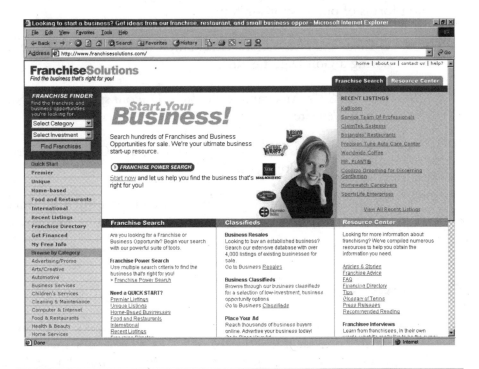

Figure 19.8. Franchise Solutions is a fine example of a commercial Web site that offers companies the opportunity to purchase links on its site. If you are a franchiser, you would want to be on sites like this because they share the same target audience.

subscribers are all interested in the list topic and are therefore potential clients, if you select the mailing list appropriately. The rates for sponsoring lists are quite low. The cost would be determined on a price-per-reader basis and is usually between 1 and 10 cents per reader. Subscribe to the lists that have appeal to your target market and read the FAQ files to determine whether advertising or sponsorship opportunities exist for each mailing list. If the mailing list allows sponsorship, contact the mailing list administrator to inquire about the cost of sponsoring and, if it is reasonable, check availability and sponsors. All of the members of the mailing list have subscribed and want to be on the list; therefore, it is likely that they will read your e-mail. This is an excellent opportunity for you to expose your products and services to these potential consumers. A good example of this would be Trip.com's sponsoring a mailing list about different vacation destinations around the world. Readers are interested in the topic, so they may be encouraged to click through and book a trip.

Online and Offline Promotion

Your advertising strategy shouldn't be limited to online activities. It is important to integrate your offline advertising strategy to include promotion of your Web site. For more information on offline promotion, see Chapter 26.

Internet Resources for Chapter 19

I have included a few resources for you to check out regarding productive online advertising. For additional resources on a variety of topics, I recommend you visit the Resources section of my Web site at *http://www.susansweeney.com/resources.html*. There you will find additional tips, tools, techniques, and resources.

BANNER AD TOOLS

Animated Communications
http://www.animation.com
Another online resource to build your own animated banners in minutes.

Animation Online
http://www.animationonline.com
Create your own animated banner in minutes for free from this site.

The Banner Generator
http://www.coder.com/creations/banner
The Banner Generator is a free service to help you create graphical banners for your Web pages.

Creative Connectivity
http://www.crecon.com/banners.html
Home of the Instant Online Banner Creator.

ONLINE ADVERTISING AGENCIES

Thielen Online
http://www.thielenonline.com/index.htm
Full-service advertising agency, located in Fresno and Sacramento, California, with strategic online marketing and complete Web site development capabilities.

AD NETWORKS

24/7 Media
http://www.247media.com
24/7 Media is a top-reach network of branded sites in a vast variety of categories. This allows advertisers to zone in on their target market and get the results that they want from their online marketing efforts.

B2B Works
http://www.b2bworks.com
B2B Works has well over 70 different industries in its network and is emerging as an ad network leader. It can target a specific industry of your choice or advertise your banner to a mass audience.

DoubleClick
http://www.doubleclick.com
The DoubleClick ad network's goal is to provide solutions to make advertising work for companies on the Internet. Five different types of

services are offered to help advertisers prosper on the Internet. The site will enable you to market globally and locally. It can help you to build brand awareness, or to close the loop on your target market. DoubleClick also offers its clients the opportunity to participate in the e-commerce world by offering online sales technology to advertisers that would like to sell products online.

ValueClick
http://www.valueclick.com
ValueClick is the Internet's largest results-based advertising network. It uses a cost-per-click model, which enables participants to pay only for the viewers who click through to their Web site.

BANNER EXCHANGES

GSAnet
http://bs.gsanet.com
GSAnet Banner Swap is unique in that it offers up to a 1:1 display ratio to members depending on where you locate the banner on your Web page(s). In addition, sites with few visitors see an even greater ratio due to what are called "charity banners."

ONLINE ADVERTISING EDUCATION

Adbility
http://www.adbility.com
A great site about ad networks, brokers, exchanges, pay-per-click and pay-per-sale (commission) ads, counters, trackers, software, and much more.

Advertising Age Magazine
http://adage.com/news_and_features/deadline
This advertising industry publication always has interesting articles on advertising online.

Internet Advertising Bureau—Online Advertising Effectiveness Study
http://www.mbinteractive.com/site/iab/study.html
The IAB Online Advertising Effectiveness Study is the most comprehensive and projectable test of online advertising effectiveness to date. With 12 major Web sites and over 16,000 individual users taking part in the

test, the study ranks as the largest, most rigorous test of advertising effectiveness conducted to date in any medium.

Nielsen Net Ratings
http://www.netratings.com
Nielsen Net Ratings provides you with continuously updated statistics on the top advertisers on the Internet, and which banner advertisements are the most commonly viewed on the Internet. The site also offers a wide range of other Internet-related statistics that may prove important to your marketing needs.

20

The Cybermall Advantage

Cybermalls are Internet shopping centers that contain "stores" related to a specific topic. Some of the more successful malls are those that concentrate on a specific type of product or service category; others focus on a specific geographic area; and still others focus on a specific demographic group. With more and more sites becoming e-commerce enabled, we are seeing a real growth in cybermall participation. These cybermalls bring in targeted, interested people who are looking for a specific type of product or service. The Hall of Malls (*http://www.nsns.com/MouseTracks/HallofMalls.html*) is one site that provides a list of cybermalls you can search to determine if there are any that are appropriate for your company. In this chapter, we cover:

Cybermalls
Internet shopping centers.

- Can your site benefit from being linked in cybermalls?

- Cybermall features

- Types of cybermalls—which is best suited to your business?

- Where to look for cybermalls

- Discounts and coupons to lure customers

- Selecting the appropriate cybermall

- What will it cost?

- Checking visitor statistics

The Advantages of Internet Shopping Centers

Cybermalls are collections of commercial Web sites on the Internet. There are literally thousands of cybermalls, and they are growing in popularity. Cybermalls provide an arena where people can shop online via the Internet. As in traditional malls, cybermall merchants benefit by receiving more traffic due to the promotional power of, and services offered by, the mall owner. These malls are accessed by the consumer through a common Internet address.

Some cybermalls will design, build, and host your Web site, and offer ongoing maintenance of your site for a fee that is comparable to that charged by other Web developers and service providers. Other malls simply provide a link to your site on another server. If you already have a Web site and choose this option, the charges are generally a lot less.

When Are Cybermalls Appropriate?

There are many different reasons that businesses choose the cybermall route. Some businesses choose to participate in a cybermall and also offer their products or services from their own site. Some businesses choose to participate in a number of different cybermalls. Any one of the following may provide sound reasoning for their business decision:

- *You want to increase targeted traffic to your site*. The cybermall has significant traffic from your target market, and by participating in the cybermall you will increase traffic to your site.

- *You don't have a credit card merchant account*. Some financial institutions charge a premium for small-business merchant accounts if the business is going to be selling online, or they may even refuse to provide a merchant account for online vendors. The cybermall may provide merchant accounts or merchant account services to its tenants.

- *You don't know how to work on building traffic to your site or don't have the time to do so.* In a cybermall, the onus is on the mall to perform online and offline marketing activities to increase the traffic to its site. Your site will benefit from the general traffic that comes through the mall doors as long as your product is of interest to the incoming mall visitors.

- *You don't have a secure server.* The fact that a cybermall has a **secure server** may be reason enough to locate your online business there. If you are going to be selling online, you need a secure server, and the volume of business you are going to do may not warrant the purchase price and expertise required to set up your own secure server.

> **Secure server**
> A server that allows secure credit card transactions.

- *You can locate your online storefront in a niche mall that caters to your target market.* If you sell electronic products, being part of an electronics cybermall will be of benefit to you because of the traffic to the other sites in the mall. Likewise, if you sell a children's product, you would also benefit from traffic if you were in a cybermall dedicated to children's products. Think of it in terms of a bricks and mortar mall. If there is a mall for stores offering electronics, then being part of that mall would be beneficial because all that targeted traffic is walking by your store.

- *You don't have credit card validation.* Many malls provide electronic commerce, or e-commerce, solutions for their tenants. Credit card validation online means that once the purchaser provides the credit card number as payment, the transaction is then authorized and approved by the financial institution. The transaction amount is automatically deposited into the bank account of the vendor—minus, of course, the credit card commission and usually the credit card validation charge.

- *You don't have shopping cart capability.* Shopping carts online allow mall visitors to drop items into their shopping cart as they travel through an online store or cybermall with the click of their mouse. When they have finished their shopping, they can review and edit their invoice online. They may decide they wanted two copies of that CD rather than one, and can make the change with one keystroke. Or they may delete a few items when they see that the total of the invoice is more than they were planning to spend. When the online invoice reflects exactly what they want, they complete the transaction by providing their credit card for payment. When a business does not have the technical or financial resources to put shopping carts on its site, a cybermall might provide this valuable service.

Cybermall Categories

Cybermalls can be organized in a number of ways. Some cybermalls are product-specific, some are industry-specific, some are demographic-specific, and still others are geographic-specific.

Product- or Service-Specific Cybermalls

All of the tenants in a product-specific cybermall provide similar types of products. These types of cybermalls are of interest to the same target market. A model airplane cybermall would consist of a number of merchants that all provide products or services related to model airplanes. Other cybermalls that would fit into this category would be computer software cybermalls, electronics cybermalls, environmentally friendly products cybermalls, and vacation malls. Figures 20.1, 20.2, and 20.3 illustrate some of these types of cybermalls.

Industry-Specific Cybermalls

All of the tenants in this situation would be in the same industry. A financial services industry cybermall would provide a wide range of different products and services such as insurance, banking, investment, and accounting services and products.

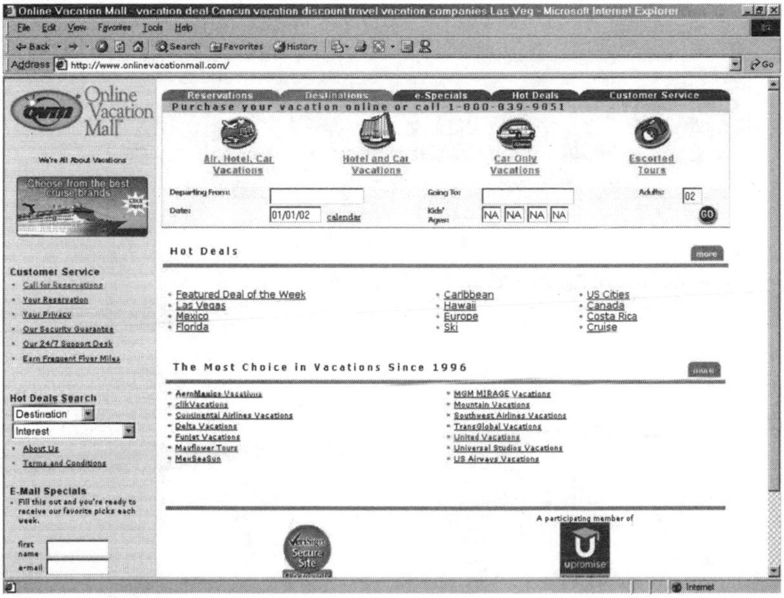

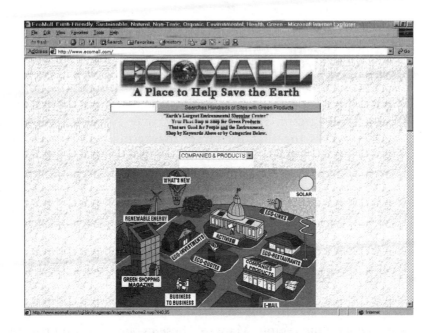

Figure 20.1. Online Vacation Mall allows you to order airline tickets, make hotel reservations, book your car rental, and order attraction tickets from one location.

Figure 20.2. EcoMall provides you with everything green.

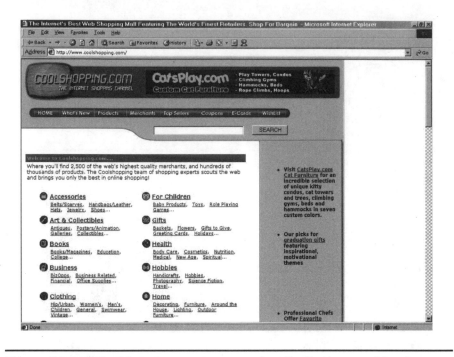

Figure 20.3. *Coolshopping.com* is a general mall offering everything from candy to cars.

Demographic-Specific Cybermalls

There are many cybermalls that target a specific demographic group. These cybermalls provide a variety of products and services that are of interest to a particular group. There should always be some common theme that ties the visitors together for target marketing purposes. A children's cybermall that has vendors providing everything from clothing to books to gifts to toys would be a good example of this type of cybermall. A seniors' cybermall would offer a wide range of very different products and services—from senior travel to insurance to healthcare to estate-planning services—that are of interest to that demographic group.

Geographic-Specific Cybermalls

In geographic-specific cybermalls, all of the tenants are located in the same geographic region. Many of these cybermalls are provided by an

ISP for its clients. In many cases participation in these types of malls is done to provide easy access through a variety of means for the customer, to build name recognition with the local customer base, and as a means of advertising and cross-promotion.

Typical Cybermall Products and Services

Most of the items you would find in your local shopping malls are appropriate for a cybermall. Some businesses that are not typically found in retail shopping centers because of the space requirements, such as car dealerships, are also appropriate for cybermalls. Products and services that are popular in cybermalls today include:

- Software

- Books

- Computers

- Electronics

- Gifts

- Games

- Clothing

- Travel

- Art and collectibles

- Automotive

- Food

- Health and fitness

- Housewares

- Financial products and services

- Professional services

- Sports and recreation

- Specialty shops

Some malls choose to concentrate on a specific niche, such as the one shown in Figure 20.4. The niche can be a type of product or a service category. These malls bring in very targeted, interested people looking for a specific type of product or service. A number of cybermalls focus on niche categories such as new automobiles, used

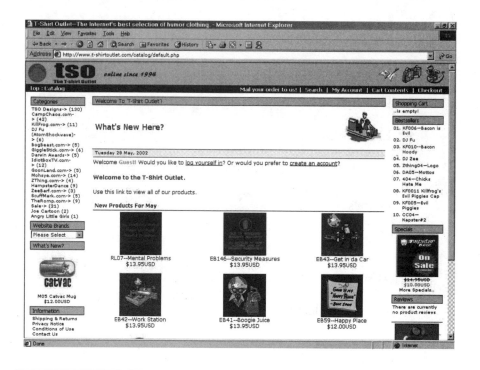

Figure 20.4. The Factory T-shirt Outlet is a storefront that focuses on one product but provides a range of services such as gift wrap, delivery, and a "dressing room" (where shoppers select size and colors).

automobiles, antique or collector automobiles, environmentally friendly products, tourist resorts, electronics, magazines, coins, stamps, and software.

Selecting the Right Cybermall

Before you commit to a cybermall that is going to host your site, you should check out a number of things in your evaluation process. Choosing a successful mall is tricky, but if you use the following guidelines you will be better equipped to make the right decision.

Traffic

Obtain details on mall traffic and the number of unique visitors to the home page of the mall, if possible. Any other count of hits may include hits to the pages of merchants in the mall, which would be misleading. Talk with other merchants residing in the mall about their traffic, as well as their experience with the mall itself (fee increases, hidden costs, server downtime, etc.). Many progressive malls now provide their tenants with access to their Web traffic analysis.

High-Speed Access

The cybermall merchant should have a high-speed connection. If access is slow, the visitors will not wait. This is very similar to traditional retail outlets. If the line at the cash register is too long, customers will not wait and will shop elsewhere.

Home Page and Interface

A good cybermall should have a good-quality, attractive home page with consistent navigation throughout the site. It is great if there is space for specials, coupons, or other advertising that you can participate in.

Domain Name

The mall you choose should have a logical and easy-to-remember domain name.

Hardware

The cybermall's server should be reliable, state-of-the-art, and fast, and have lots of capacity to handle the anticipated volume. There should be technicians available to provide technical support and quickly resolve any problems that occur.

Categories

Before choosing a mall, make sure that your business fits within one of the categories in the mall. Don't join a mall that is targeting a different demographic group from yours.

Online and Offline Promotion

Make sure that the mall you choose is promoted both online and offline. Many of the malls promote online only. The cybermall owner should be able to provide you with details of its Internet marketing strategy to increase the traffic of the targeted market to its site.

Site Maintenance Activities

Successful Web sites must be updated on a continual basis. Ensure that the mall provides software tools to make it easy for you to maintain your own site or, if the mall provides the updates, that the fees regarding changes are not too expensive.

Secure Server

Make sure that the mall has a secure server that allows you to offer secure credit card sales transactions. Most consumers will not purchase online without it.

Credit Card Merchant Account

Merchant accounts for the popular credit cards are usually difficult to obtain for businesses with only a virtual presence. If you don't have a merchant account, you will want to choose a mall that offers this service.

Promotions

Find out what type of promotional efforts the mall is involved in. Many malls indicate that they promote extensively, but be sure they are actually targeting shoppers, not merchants.

Commission Fees

Some malls charge a commission on every sale. Check the details on all commissions, transaction fees, and other charges. If the mall is responsible for all the traffic to your site, it should be compensated for this activity either through your monthly rental charge or by a commission on sales. If you are making an effort to promote your site yourself and the traffic to your site is a result of your marketing efforts, it is unreasonable for the mall to expect to be compensated for each transaction on your site.

Cybermall History and Reputation

Find out how long the mall has been in existence. Talk to existing tenants and past tenants about their experiences.

Tracking

Find out what traffic tracking statistics will be provided to you by the cybermall.

Other Features and Services Provided by the Cybermall

Cybermalls may include a variety of other products and services to their tenants. When comparing cybermalls, make sure you are comparing apples with apples. Some additional features and services provided by cybermalls might include supplying mailing lists and autoresponders, or providing chat rooms and bulletin boards.

Cybermall Features

Cybermalls may provide a number of features to their tenants as well as to the tenants' customers.

Electronic Shopping Carts

Shopping carts like the one shown in Figure 20.5 are commonplace on the Internet. They enable users to click on items they would like to purchase from various mall vendors and put them in their shopping

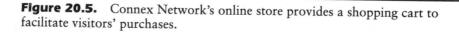

Figure 20.5. Connex Network's online store provides a shopping cart to facilitate visitors' purchases.

cart. At the end of their online shopping trip, they have an opportunity to review the contents of their cart as well as the invoice. Purchases can be edited before an order is placed.

Secure Ordering

Most cybermalls offer a secure server and encrypted transactions for their tenants' online transactions. Technology is advancing rapidly in the area of e-commerce, and the cybermalls are among the first Web sites on the Internet to make use of the latest capabilities. Some malls now offer online charge card authorization and automatic deposit for their tenants.

Search Capabilities

Many cybermalls will provide a site search capability to assist shoppers with finding the items they are looking for.

More Than One Cybermall?

It may be appropriate to join more than one cybermall, especially if you have your own site and are just paying a monthly fee for the link from your storefront in the mall to your site. If you decide that this is appropriate for your business, you should have some mechanism in place to track the traffic to your site to determine which malls are effective. This can be accomplished quite easily these days with all the Web traffic analysis tools that are available. See Chapter 27 for a full discussion of Web traffic analysis.

Cybermall Pricing

Malls charge their tenants in a variety of ways. If you choose a mall that hosts one page as a storefront and a link from that storefront to your site on a different server from the cybermall, the charge is generally a flat fee per month. If your Web site is hosted by the cybermall, you may be charged on a flat-fee basis, your charge may be a basic fee with add-ons, or you may be charged on a commission-on-sales basis. The variable charges are generally either on a commission or a set-fee-per-transaction basis.

Cybermall charges to be linked to their storefront can be anywhere from $25 a month to over $1,000 a month, which includes services and a number of features provided by the host.

Where to Look for Cybermalls

To find cybermalls, you can use the search engines. A number of meta-indexes of cybermalls can be found online. There are cybermall Web rings that can be researched and also cybermalls of cybermalls. There are all kinds of locations and sites listed in the Internet Resources at the end of this chapter to assist you in finding the appropriate cybermall for your business.

Enticing Customers with Coupons and Discounts

To increase the traffic to your cybermall site, you can post coupons either as banner ads or as links from other sites. The sites you choose to host these banner ads or links should be those that appeal to your target market, or you might consider purchasing a keyword from a search engine. See Chapter 19 for advice on appropriate banner advertising.

You can also use online coupons, which can be printed from your site, to increase the traffic to your offline locations. If your customers know they can check your weekly coupons or sales, it will encourage repeat visits from them. You might also consider trading coupons with other online vendors who offer noncompeting products to the same target market.

Internet Resources for Chapter 20

I have included a few resources for you to check out regarding cybermalls. For additional resources on a variety of topics, I recommend that you visit the Resources section of my Web site at *http://*

www.susansweeney.com/resources.html. There you will find additional tips, tools, techniques, and resources.

Access Market Square
http://www.icw.com/mall.html
Access Market Square has an occasion (birthday, anniversary, etc.) reminder service that also provides personalized gift ideas. The site also has a great search engine that allows you to enter names of items, brand names, product types, or store names. They provide a wide variety of products by category, including art, audio/video, automotive, books, clothes, computers, electronics, flowers, food, health, jewelry, music, sports, travel, and others. Access Market Square uses VeriSign for secure ordering capabilities.

American Shopping Mall
http://www.greenearth.com
The American Shopping Mall has been rated among the top most-visited sites on the Internet by *PC Magazine.* It professes to be one of the busiest virtual shopping malls on the World Wide Web, with over 32 million visitors last year and over 50 million visitors since its opening in 1995.

Cosmiverse Marketplace
http://marketplace.cosmiverse.com/market
As the site boasts: "everything under the sun."

The Cybermall.com Directory
http://www.cybermall.com
Evaluation of hundreds of online malls and selection of only what they determine are the very best. Malls cannot purchase a listing on this site (unlike other directories) and are selected exclusively because they provide you with a positive home-shopping experience. You get access to the better shopping malls without fighting through hundreds of them. The categorical listings include brief site reviews to help you find the quality shopping sites you want without all the work.

eMall
http://www.emall.com
This is a great location for organic and natural foods. They have a Complete Health Online Store, a Spice Merchant section with the flavors of Asia, fine teas, and sun-roasted Mexican coffees.

Excite Shopping
http://shopping.excite.com
This is an electronic commerce enabler of small and medium-sized businesses that allows them to cost-effectively engage in electronic commerce through the use of Excite Shopping's proprietary e-commerce tools and services. Excite Shopping offers its electronic commerce services directly to merchants, as well as through partnerships with leading ISPs, Web-hosting firms, and financial service companies with an Internet focus.

The Hall of Malls
http://nsns.com/MouseTracks/HallofMalls.html
The most comprehensive list of all known online malls located on the Net.

Internetmall.com
http://www.internetmall.com
Hundreds of new stores open daily, giving you an exciting array of products and stores to choose from.

Lahego.com
http://www.lahego.com
One-stop shopping at over 1,350 stores.

MallPark
http://www2.mallpark.com
Thousands of online merchants by shopping category! Instant searching. Secure order forms, shopping carts, and merchant accounts to accept credit cards; and merchants can link for free.

Malls.com
http://malls.com
Besides providing a range of products and services from this mall, Malls.com provides a huge meta-index of all the malls on the Net at *http://malls.com/metalist.html*. This list is a great starting point when doing your cybermall research.

Online Stores Mall
http://www.onlinestoresmall.com
Another mall featuring stores in a number of categories.

21

Maximizing Media Relations

Your online media strategy can be extremely effective in building traffic to your site. News release distribution can be done easily. Build the right list of e-mail addresses or make use of one of the online news release distribution services. Most reporters and writers have e-mail addresses. Some do not like to receive e-mailed news releases; others prefer the e-mail versions. When e-mail news releases are sent out, reporters will reply by e-mail; they will expect your response within 24 hours. Develop a media kit that you can e-mail out to editors. In this chapter, we cover:

- Developing your online media strategy

- Public relations versus advertising

- Online public relations versus traditional public relations

- Effective news releases

- News release and distribution services online

- How to distribute news releases online

- Providing an area for media on your site

- How to find reporters online

- How reporters want to receive your information

- Encouraging republication of your article with a direct link to your site or the article

- Providing press kits online

- Electronic newsletters

Managing Effective Public Relations

Media relations are very important to your marketing efforts. The best results are achieved when you integrate both online and offline publicity campaigns. News release distribution can be accomplished easily if you have an established list of reporters and editors, or if you make use of a news distribution service.

Maintaining effective public relations will deliver a number of benefits to your company. Your company and products can be given exposure through news releases, and a positive image for your company will be portrayed. Your relationship with current customers will be reinforced, and new relationships will be formed.

Benefits of Publicity versus Advertising

Media coverage, or publicity, has a major advantage over paid advertisements. Articles written by a reporter carry more weight with the public than ads do because the media and reporters are seen as unbiased third parties. The public gives articles printed in media publications more credibility than they do paid advertisements. Another advantage of distributing news releases is that it is more cost-effective than advertising. You have to pay for advertising space on a Web site or time on the radio, but the costs of writing and distributing news releases are minimal.

One of the disadvantages of news releases compared to advertising is that you don't have control over what is published. If the editor decides to cast your company in a negative light, then there is nothing you can do to stop him or her. If the writer of the piece does not like your company, for whatever reason, this may come across in the article. Basically, after your news release is distributed, you have no control over what will be written about your company.

It is important to note that when generating publicity, you may lose control over the timing of your release as well. For example, you may want an article released the day before your big sale, but the editor may relegate it to a date the following week. There is nothing you can do about this. It is not a good idea to rely exclusively on publicity for important or newsworthy events, because if the release is not reviewed or is not considered newsworthy, you may be stuck with no promotion at all.

What Is a News Release?

Before you begin your media campaign, you should know what news releases are and how to write them. News releases are designed to inform reporters of events concerning your company that the public may consider newsworthy. News releases can get your company free public attention. A news release is a standard form of communication with the media. News releases must contain newsworthy information. Companies that continually send worthless information in a blatant attempt to get their name in the press will not establish a good relationship with the media.

Writing a News Release

Journalists are bombarded with volumes of news releases. To improve the chances of having your story interest the journalist enough to publish it, you must make the journalist's job easier by presenting your news release in an appealing format and style. Your news release should be written as if it was prepared by an unbiased third party. The news release should follow a standard format, which is described in the following paragraphs.

Notice of Release

The first thing the reader sees should be:

FOR IMMEDIATE RELEASE

unless you have sent the information in advance of the time you would like it published. In that case, state it as follows:

FOR RELEASE: Wednesday, April 14, 2003 [using the date you want it released].

Remember that no matter what date you put here, the publication can release the information before or after that date. If the news is really big, it is unlikely that the publication will hold it until the date you have specified.

Header

The header should be in the upper-left corner. It should contain all of the contact information for one or two key people. These contacts should be able to answer any questions regarding the news release. If reporters cannot get in touch with someone to answer their questions, they may print incorrect information or even drop the article altogether.

Contact:
Susan Sweeney
Connex Network Incorporated
(902) 468-2578
susan@susansweeney.com
http://www.susansweeney.com

Headline

Your headline is critically important; if you get it right, it will attract the attention you are looking for. Your headline should be powerful, summarizing your message and making the reader want to continue reading. Keep the headline short—less than ten words.

City and Date

Name the city you are reporting from and the date you wrote the news release.

The Body

Your first sentence within the body of the news release should sum up your headline and immediately inform the reader why this is newsworthy. With the number of news releases reporters receive, if you don't grab their attention immediately they won't read your release. Begin by listing all of the most relevant information first, leaving the supporting information last.

Ask yourself the five W's (who, what, where, when, and why) and answer them up front. Write the news release just as if you were writing a newspaper article for publication. Include some quotes from key individuals in your company and any other relevant outside sources that are credible. If there are any statistics that support your main message, include them as well, providing references.

Your last paragraph should be a short company description.

The Close

If your release is two pages long, center the word "-more-" at the bottom of the first page. To end your release, center the word "end" at the end of your message. A sample news release is shown in Figure 21.1.

Advantages of Interactive News Releases

Online news releases take the same standard format as offline news releases, but the online news release can be interactive, with links to a variety of interesting information that supports your message. When your news release is provided by e-mail and you provide a hypertext link in that e-mail, the journalist is just a click away from accessing all the information he or she needs to complete the story. Appropriate links included in your interactive news releases are:

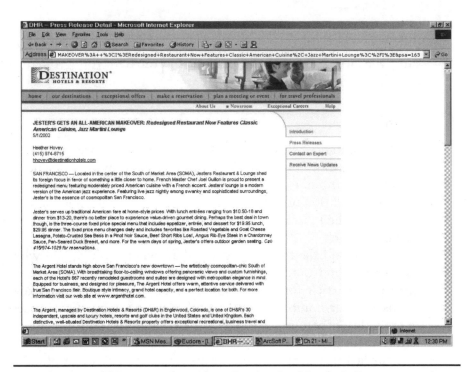

Figure 21.1. This press release from Destination Hotels & Resorts contains several hypertext links, enabling a journalist to quickly access additional information and perform due diligence.

- A link to the e-mail address of the media contact person in your organization so that with the click of the mouse a journalist can ask a question of the contact via e-mail.

- A link to the company Web site so that the journalist can quickly and easily access additional information as part of his or her due diligence or can find required information.

- Links to articles that have been written about the company and related issues, both on the corporate Web site and on other sites.

- Links to graphics and pictures for illustration. If your story relates to a product, have a link to a graphic that can be used.

- Links to key corporate players, their biographies, their photos, and possibly some quotes. Journalists usually include quotes in their stories.

- A link to a FAQ section where you can have frequently asked questions and a few that you wish were frequently asked.

Figures 21.2 through 21.5 are examples of online news releases.

Sending News Releases on Your Own versus Using a Distribution Service

When distributing news releases on your own, you save the money it would cost to have a service do it. You can also be more targeted in

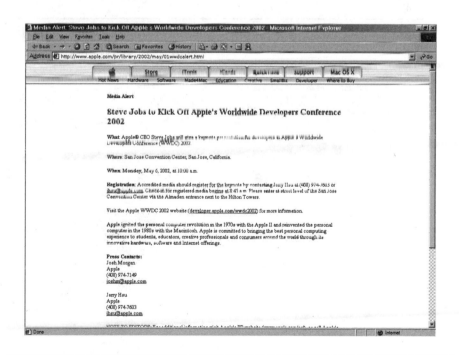

Figure 21.2. This news release from Apple.com contains textual URLs within the release that can easily be used later if the document is printed for later reference.

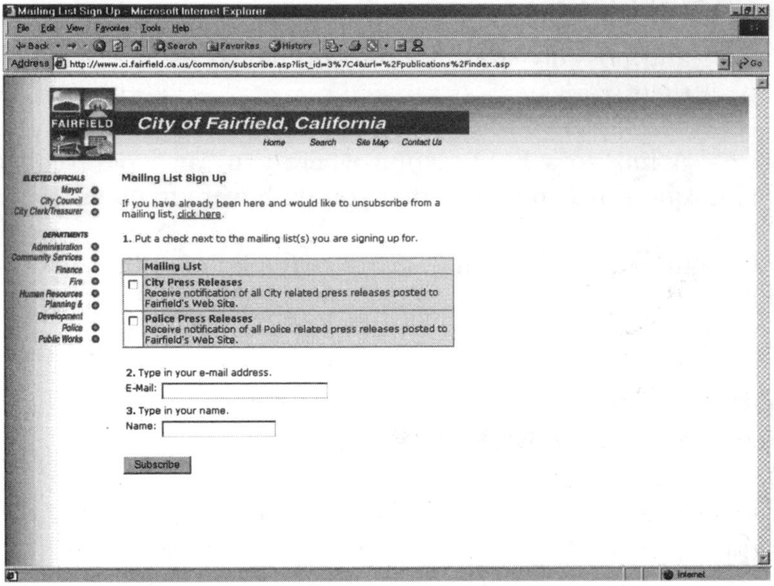

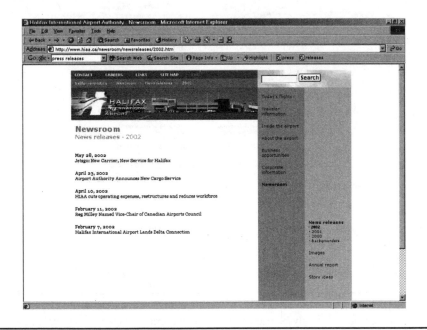

Figure 21.3. The City of Fairfield's site allows you to sign up for notification of all news releases as they are posted to the Web site.

Figure 21.4. Halifax International Airport Authority's Web site shows a chronology of past news releases.

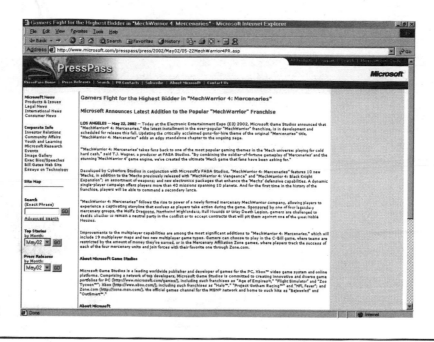

Figure 21.5.   Microsoft's new releases also contain textual hypertext links.

your efforts than a service would be. Some services' lists may be outdated or incomplete. Their lists of reporters and editors may not be comprehensive and may not have been updated. On the other hand, some services may get your news release taken more seriously. A reporter who recognizes the name of the service may be more receptive than if the release were to come from an unknown company. Using a service is bound to save you a lot of time.

If you decide to send your news releases on your own, you will have to build a list of journalists. When reading publications, look for the names of reporters and find out their contact information. If you don't know whom to send a news release to at any publication, you can always call and ask for the name of the appropriate editor. Subscribe to a personalized news service to receive articles about your industry. This is a great way to find the names of journalists who might be interested in what you have to say.

There are a number of online resources to assist you in building your news-distribution list, such as the one shown in Figure 21.6. Mediafinder (*http://www.mediafinder.com*) is a Web site that may be

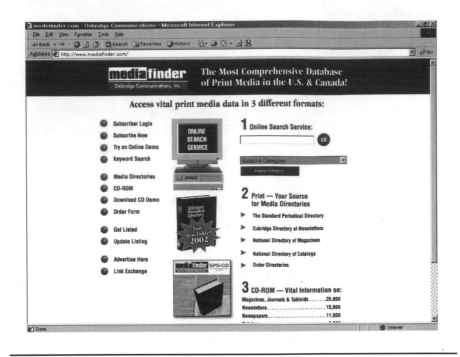

Figure 21.6. Use Mediafinder to locate appropriate magazines, journals, newspapers, newsletters and catalogs.

useful. It provides access to a database of thousands of media outlets including magazines, journals, newspapers, newsletters, and catalogues. Lexis Nexis (*http://www.pressaccess.com/PR/index.htm*) has a large database of journalists and industry analysts (Figure 21.7). Their press access editorial database is available online, 24 hours a day, and contains in-depth information on journalists, publications, calendars, and so on. MediaMap (*http://www.mediamap.com*) is another public relations resource and has detailed profiles on more than 20,000 media contacts, including their phone numbers, fax numbers, e-mail addresses, and work preferences (Figure 21.8). They also have editorial calendars that tell you who will be writing a scheduled story, what the topic of the story is, and when it will be written.

There are a number of news release distribution services online (Figures 21.9 and 21.10). You will find a number of them in the Internet Resources section at the end of this chapter.

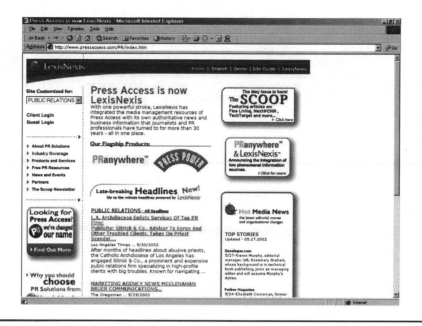

Figure 21.7. Lexis Nexis provides information on editorial calendars, editors, and their preferences.

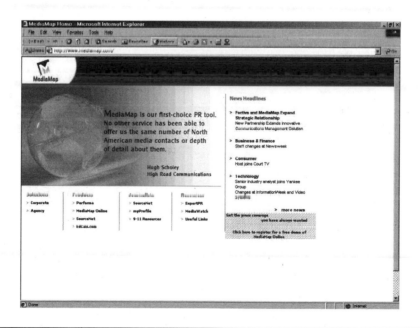

Figure 21.8. MediaMap is a software and media information company.

Figure 21.9. Internet News Bureau is an e-mail news release service company, including the distribution and writing of e-mail news releases.

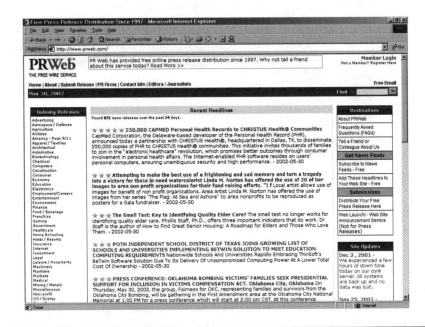

Figure 21.10. You can submit your news release to PRWeb.

Golden Tips for News Release Distribution

When distributing your news releases, don't send them to the news desk unaddressed. Know which editor handles the type of news in your release, and address the news release to that person. Don't send the news release to more than one editor in any organization unless there is more than one angle to the information in the news release. Call ahead, if possible, to discuss and solicit the editor's interest in your news release before sending it. Also, follow up with a phone call a few days later to make sure that it was received and to answer any questions. Be sure to review editorial calendars of publications in your industry to see if there are upcoming articles where your story may make a contribution.

News Release Timing and Deadlines

One of the most important things to remember when sending a news release or advisory is the deadline. Know how far in advance you should send your information for each of the different media. Here are some time guidelines for your news release distribution.

Monthly Magazines

For monthly magazines, you should submit your news releases at least two to three months before the issue you want it to appear in. Magazines are planned far in advance, because it often takes a number of weeks to have the magazine printed and in subscribers' mailboxes.

Daily Newspapers

It is a good idea to have your news release arrive on the editor's desk at least several weeks in advance. If it concerns a special holiday, you should send it even earlier.

TV and Radio

When submitting news releases to TV and radio, remember that you may be asked to appear on a show as a guest. Be prepared for this before you submit the release. TV and radio move very quickly; a story that has been given to the news director in the morning may appear on that evening's news.

Formatting Your E-mail News Release

Your news releases can be e-mailed. Some reporters prefer e-mailed releases; others say they prefer mailed or faxed releases. Check the reporter's preference before you send your news release. If you e-mail your news releases, make sure that your e-mails are formatted properly. Refer to Chapter 9 for guidelines on how to create effective e-mail messages.

Keep your e-mailed news releases to one or two pages with short paragraphs. It is best to insert the news release in the e-mail. Do not send your news release as an attachment. You don't know which platform or word-processing program the reporter is using. You might be using Microsoft Word 2000 on a PC, but the reporter could be using an incompatible program on a Mac and will not be able to open the file. There may also be problems downloading, which may prevent your release from being read. The person on the receiving end of your e-mail may be using an old computer with a slow dialup connection, so what may take you 2 minutes to transfer might take the recipient 20 minutes to download. In addition, you may be using a PC platform but the reporter may be using a MacOS-based computer. Someone who spends 20 minutes downloading your e-mail only to find that it's useless won't be impressed—great start to getting the journalist to do a positive story on you!

Make sure the subject line of your e-mail is compelling. Journalists can easily delete e-mailed releases, unopened, and quite often they do, because journalists receive large volumes of these daily. Make sure your e-mail is clear and concise. Get to the point with the first sentence. If you don't grab the reader's attention at the beginning of the release, the recipient may not keep reading to find out what your news is.

It's very important to be able to send news release information in digital format (as a file rather than hard copy). With a quick copy and paste, the journalist will then have the "first draft" of the story (Figure 21.11). You have made it very easy for him or her to then edit the draft and have a story very quickly. Everybody loves to save time, and a lot of these journalists are under tight deadlines.

What Is Considered Newsworthy

Your news release has to contain newsworthy information for it to be published. One of the main concerns for public relations representa-

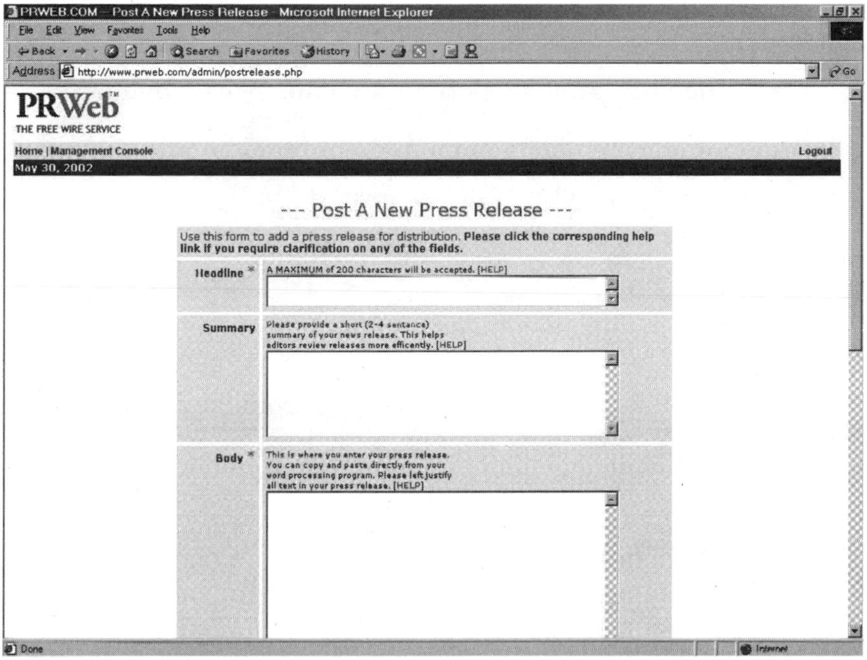

Figure 21.11. When a news release is provided in digital format, it can easily be copied and pasted into another document.

tives is figuring out what is considered newsworthy and what isn't. You have to have a catch, and, if possible, it should appeal to some sort of emotion. Here is a list of newsworthy items:

- A merger or partnership between your company and another

- A free service or resource offered by your company to the general public

- A survey or forum that your company is holding to discuss an already hot news topic

- The appearance of a celebrity at a company event or upcoming online promotions

- Your participation in a trade show

- The findings of a report your company has conducted

- A breakthrough in technology resulting in a significant new consumer product

- The development of new strategic alliances or partnerships

- A charitable contribution by your company

- A milestone anniversary that your company is celebrating

- An award presented by your company

- Holiday/event tie-ins

- Tips, articles, or advice

- Stories with a human interest element

What Isn't Considered Newsworthy

Some things that aren't news to the general public may be news to targeted trade magazines and journals. Use your own judgment when trying to determine if your news release is news or just an excuse to get your company's name in print. If your release focuses on any of the following, it is probably not newsworthy enough to publish.

The launch of a new Web site has not been news for a number of years now. Unless the site is based on a breakthrough in Internet technology or serves the public interest in an innovative way, you won't get a mention in the news. Nor is a new feature or change to your Web site newsworthy information. Even if your site has undergone a major overhaul, this is not news to the general public.

Launching a new product is not newsworthy unless the product represents a significant breakthrough in some area. The upgrade of an old product simply won't cut it.

Preparing Your News Kits/Media Kits

Your press kit is an essential item at news conferences and interviews. This kit can also be sent to reporters when they request more information about a news release you have sent to them. Your press kit should start with a folder displaying your company logo and basic contact information. The folder should have pockets inside so that different sheets of information can be inserted. The following items should be included in your press kit:

- A news release outlining the newsworthy event

- A company history

- Brochures

- Other articles written about your company

- Pictures

- Background information on key players

- FAQs and answers to anticipated questions

- Quotes from key individuals

- Contact information

- Business card

Developing an Online Media Center for Public Relations

If publicity is a significant part of your public relations strategy, you should consider developing an online media center as part of your site (see Figures 21.12 and 21.13). The media center should be easily accessible from your navigation bar. It would include all the components a journalist will need when doing a story on your company. Journalists

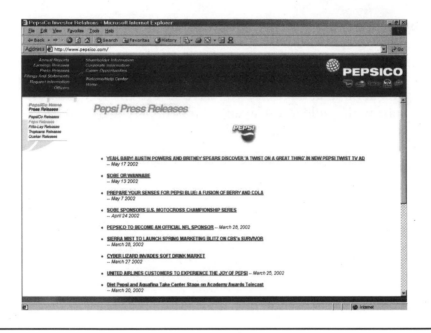

Figure 21.12. Pepsi provides an archive of its news releases online.

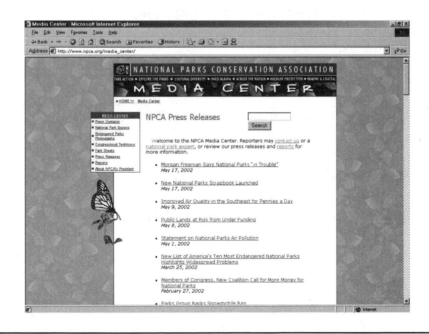

Figure 21.13. The NPCA provides a media center on its site so information is readily available to the press.

should be able to find pictures to include in the story and all the information necessary to do their due diligence. They should be able to send a question to the appropriate media contact within the organization with one click. The media center should include:

- A chronology of news releases distributed by the company.

- The company's history and background information.

- An electronic brochure.

- Links to other articles written about your company.

- Links to story ideas for future articles.

- Links to pictures of a related product or products. Perhaps have a gallery where journalists can choose the pictures they want to include in their story. The TIFF (Tag Image File Format) is preferred by journalists for crispness and clarity and works best for desktop publishing applications. The file will have a .tiff or .tif extension. The .tif format is not supported by Web browsers, so you can make it easy for journalists to acquire the photos by placing thumbnails on your Web site and then having an autoresponder send them the specific photos they request in the appropriate format.

- Background information on key company personnel, along with their pictures, bios, and quotes.

- A link to your company's media contact and contact information.

- FAQs and answers to anticipated questions.

By having a media center on your site, you are sending a clear message to the journalist. You are saying, "You're very important to me! I want to provide you with everything you need to quickly and easily complete your story on our company." With the media center you are providing all the information, in a format journalists can use, to enable them to do the story no matter what time they choose to do it.

You will want to encourage permission marketing by offering visitors the opportunity to be notified to receive your news releases "hot off the press." Place a "Click here to receive notification of our news releases" link on your Web site. In addition, make it easy for visitors to send a copy of your news release to a friend. Sometimes journalists work on stories together, so give the journalist the option to send the news release to a colleague or even to her editor through viral marketing.

Internet Resources for Chapter 21

I have included a few resources for you to check out regarding news releases. For additional resources on a variety of topics, I recommend that you visit the Resources section of my Web site at *http://www. susansweeney.com/resources.html*. There you will find additional tips, tools, techniques, and resources.

NEWS RELEASES

Care & Feeding of the Press
http://www.netpress.org/careandfeeding.html
Journalists' manifesto for how PR people should work with the media.

News Release Tips for PR People
http://marketing.tenagra.com/releases.html
Talks about what a journalist expects to receive and how you should write releases.

Xpress Press—E-mail News Release Information
http://www.xpresspress.com/PRnotes.html
Information on how to write and format a news release to be distributed by e-mail.

WHERE TO SUBMIT YOUR NEWS RELEASES

Businesswire
http://www.businesswire.com
News release distribution service. This site provides a wide range of services and has several showcases.

Click Press Direct
http://www.ideasiteforbusiness.com/clickpressfree.cfm

News release contact list of the nation's top business-related newspapers and magazines. It has a subscription service that allows access to a list of 8,176 publications you can e-mail your press releases to.

Emailwire.com
http://www.emailwire.com
Submit your news releases to over 300,000 business owners, business executives, individual investors, and consumers on Emailwire and to 27,000 journalists, editors, publishers, and syndicators.

Internet Media Fax
http://www.imediafax.com
Custom online news-distribution service that creates targeted media lists "on the fly."

Internet News Bureau Press Release Service
http://www.newsbureau.com
For a fee, you can distribute your news release to thousands of online media outlets here. Also links to a number of good PR resources.

Internet Wire
http://www1.internetwire.com
The Internet Wire offers online news release distribution via e-mail (Figure 21.14).

Partyline
http://www.partylinepublishing.com
The standard media placement newsletter for the public relations trade.

PR Newswire Home Page
http://www.prnewswire.com
A leading source for worldwide corporate media, business, the financial community, and the individual investor.

PR Web
http://www.prweb.com
A dynamite site that distributes news releases but provides an extensive list of PR resources as well.

WebWire.com
http://www.webwire.com

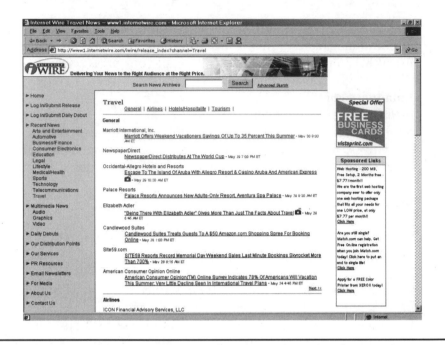

Figure 21.14. Internet Wire is an online news release distribution company.

WebWire is a community of PR professionals, corporate communicators, and individuals who deliver qualified and professional press releases to Web-based emerging and conventional media. Full access to WebWire is provided to the media at no cost, and many aspects of WebWire are free of charge for PR professionals, corporate communicators, and individuals. There is a nominal charge for press release submissions and associated distribution.

Xpress Press News Release Distribution Service
http://www.xpresspress.com
News releases delivered electronically by e-mail to 10,000 journalists and media members in over 73 countries.

News Release Distribution Software

PRWizard
http://www.prwizard.com
PRWizard is a powerful, automated news release submission software that lets you effortlessly broadcast your news release to almost 28,000 targeted media contacts.

22

Increasing Traffic through Online Publications

More than 60 percent of Internet users frequently read online publications, or **e-zines**. You can identify appropriate marketing opportunities by searching for and reading e-zines that are relevant to your business. In this chapter, we cover:

e-zines
Electronic magazines.

- What electronic magazines are

- Finding online sites on which to advertise or arrange links

- How to find appropriate e-zines for marketing purposes

- Submitting articles to appropriate e-zines

- Advertising in appropriate e-zines

- E-zine resources online

Appealing to Magazine Subscribers on the Net

Many Web users frequently read e-zines. This is one of the reasons they are among the most popular marketing tools on the Internet. Five years ago there were a few hundred e-zines in publication. Now there are thousands of e-zines dedicated to a wide variety of topics such as travel, business opportunities, food, childcare—you name it. For any topic you are interested in, there quite likely are several e-zines dedicated to it.

What Exactly Are E-zines?

E-zines, or electronic magazines, are the online version of magazines. They are content-rich and contain information regarding a certain topic in the form of magazine articles and features. Many e-zines display ads as well. Some e-zines are Web site based and others are e-mail based.

Many offline magazines provide a version online as well (Figure 22.1). *Coastal Living, Southern Living, Time, People,* and *Sports Illustrated* are all accessible via the Internet. Some of these provide the full version of their traditional magazine; others are selective about the articles they provide; and still others provide the previous month's edition.

Web-Based E-zines

There are Web-based e-zines that have only an online presence (Figure 22.2). These e-zines are accessed through their Web sites by browsing from page to page. They have the look and feel of a traditional magazine. They include lots of glossy pictures and advertisements. Usually there is no charge to view the Web-based e-zines, but some do charge a subscription fee. These Web-based e-zines tend to be as graphically pleasing as offline magazines.

E-mail E-zines

E-mail e-zines these days come as text or HTML. The text e-zines are not nearly as pretty as the HTML e-mail e-zines or the Web-based e-zines.

Figure 22.1. *Coastal Living* is an example of an offline magazine that has an online version.

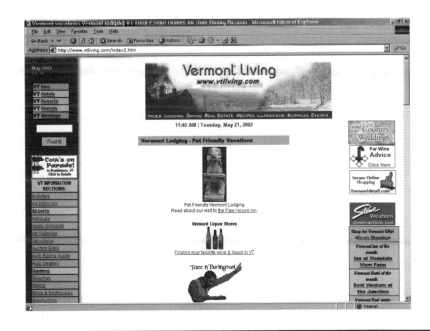

Figure 22.2. *Vermont Living* is a Web-based e-zine.

They tend to be more content-oriented (see Figure 22.3) and, as such, tend to be more of a target-marketing mechanism. E-mail e-zines tend to be several pages in length with several articles and, often, classified advertising. Circulation of these e-zines is often in the thousands. Most of these e-zines run weekly or biweekly editions. Most e-zines are free to subscribers.

Those individuals who are interested in the subject have taken the time to subscribe and ask to receive the information directly in their e-mail box. Once you have found an e-zine that caters to your target market, the e-zine may be a very valuable marketing vehicle.

Every subscriber to an e-mail based e-zine has access to the Internet. These people regularly receive and send e-mail and quite likely surf the Net. If you advertise in this type of medium and place your Internet address in the ad, your prospective customer is not more than a couple of clicks away from your site.

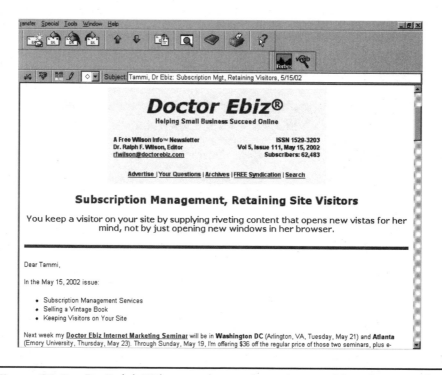

Figure 22.3. Dr. Ralph Wilson produces a dynamite e-mail based e-zine called Dr. Ebiz.

People subscribe because they are interested. Even if they don't read it immediately when it is received, they usually read it eventually. Otherwise, they would not have subscribed. Subscribers will see your URL and product advertisements. For this reason, e-mail e-zines are a great marketing tool.

Using E-zines as Marketing Tools

Online publications are superior marketing tools for a number of reasons. They can be used in a number of different ways to increase the traffic to your Web site. You can:

- Advertise directly

- Be a sponsor

- Submit articles

- Send press releases

- Start your own

Finding Appropriate E-zines for Your Marketing Effort

There are many locations online to find lists and links to both Web-based and e-mail e-zines. A number of these resources are listed in the Internet Resources section at the end of this chapter.

You evaluate the appropriateness of an e-zine's marketing potential by the audience, the reach, and the effectiveness. The most important element of choosing an e-zine is to choose one that reaches your target market. The reason e-zine ads are effective is that there is a high correlation between the target customer and the magazine's subscribers. If you advertise in an e-zine simply because it has the largest subscriber rate, you will probably be disappointed unless your products or services have mass market appeal.

You should review a number of the e-zine-listing sites, such as the one shown in Figure 22.4. Some of these sites have search capabilities on appropriate keywords. Others have their e-zines listed by category. Once you have a list of e-zines you feel fit well with your marketing objectives, you should subscribe and begin receiving and reviewing these e-zines.

The Multiple Advantages of E-zine Advertising

One of the major advantages of e-zine advertising is the lifespan of your ads. E-zines that are delivered to e-mail addresses will be read by the recipient and sometimes be saved for future reference. Many e-zines archive their issues with the ads intact. Advertisers have received responses to ads that are several months old!

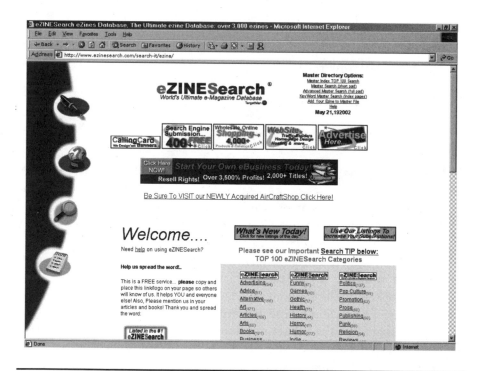

Figure 22.4. eZINE Search (*http://www.ezinesearch.com*) provides a searchable directory of e-zines.

When you place an ad in an e-zine, you will see it in a relatively short period of time, perhaps the next day or the next week depending on how often the e-zine is published. Most traditional magazines close out their ad space months before the issue is available on the newsstand.

Your ad in an e-zine is also much more likely to be noticed because there are so few of them. In a traditional magazine every second page is an ad, whereas e-zines have a much greater focus on content and far fewer ads.

When your ad appears in an e-zine, your customer is just a click away because your ad is usually hypertext-linked to your Web site. This brings your customer that much closer to being able to purchase your products or services.

Another advantage of e-zine advertising is that e-zines are often shared with friends and associates. Most e-zines use viral marketing very effectively, encouraging readers to send a copy to a friend. Your ad may be passed around a number of times after it first enters the mailbox of the subscriber. You are being charged for the ad based on the number of e-mail subscribers. Therefore, the extra viewers of your ad will be at no cost to you.

One of the most tangible advantages of e-zine advertising is the relatively low cost due, in part, to the low overhead for development, production, and delivery. E-zines need to fill all of their available space. If an e-zine advertising section has empty spaces, the publisher often may be willing to negotiate. Some will even barter with you—advertising space at a discounted price in exchange for their e-zine promotion on your Web site.

E-zines provide a very targeted advertising medium. People subscribe to various e-zines because they have a genuine interest in the topics covered. This provides a major advantage over other advertising mediums. E-zine ads have been shown to have very high response rates due to their targeted nature.

Because they are distributed via the Internet, e-zines reach a far wider audience geographically than most traditional magazines. It is not uncommon for an e-zine to have subscribers from all around the world.

There are thousands of e-zines out there related to every topic imaginable. Most e-zines have thousands of subscribers. When you couple the low cost to advertise in these e-zines and the many e-zines that may reach your target market, it is no wonder many companies are allocating more and more of their advertising budgets to online activities.

Guidelines for Your Advertising

Once you have found e-zines that reach your target market, you should consider a number of other factors before you make a final decision on placing your ad.

- Check the ads displayed in the e-zine for repetition. If advertisers have not advertised more than once, then they probably did not see very positive results.

- Respond to some of the ads and ask the advertisers what their experiences were with advertising in that particular e-zine. Be sure to tell them who you are and why you are contacting them. If you are up front, they will probably be receptive to your inquiry.

- Talk to the e-zine publisher and ask questions (e.g., how many subscribers there are). Ask what other advertisers have had to say about their results. Find out what types of ads they accept and if there are any restrictions. Check to see if the publisher has a policy of never running competing ads. Maybe the e-zine has a set of advertising policies that you can receive via e-mail.

- Find out if the publisher provides tracking information and, if so, what specific reports you will have access to.

- Find out if your ad can have a hypertext link to your Web site. If the e-zine allows hypertext links, make sure you link to an appropriate page—one that is a continuation of the advertisement or a page that provides details on the item you were advertising. Provide a link to the order form from this page to assist the transaction.

- In some cases the e-zine will have an editorial calendar available to assist you with the timing of your ad. The editorial calendar will tell you what articles will be included in upcoming issues. If an upcoming issue will have an article relating to your type of product or service, you may choose to advertise in that issue. You might contact the editor regarding a product review or submit an article relevant to the issue topics.

- Make sure that the advertising rates are reasonable based on the number of subscribers, and ask yourself if you can afford it. Find out the "open" rate, or the rate charged for advertising once in the e-zine. Ask what the rate is for multiple placements. If you are not in a position to pay for the advertising now, ask if there are any other arrangements that could be made. For example, the publisher may accept a link on your Web site in exchange for the ad.

- You should develop your ads with your target customer in mind. They should attract your best prospects. Wherever possible, you should link to your site or provide an e-mail link to the appropriate individual within your organization.

- You should develop a mechanism to track advertising responses. You could use different e-mail accounts for different ads to determine which ads are bringing you the responses. You can also use different URLs to point viewers to different pages within your site. If you have a good traffic-analysis package, you will be able to track the increase in visitors as a result of your ad.

- Make sure you are versed in the publication's advertising deadlines and ad format preferences.

Providing Articles and News Releases to E-zines

Besides advertising, a number of other marketing opportunities can be explored with e-zines. Once you have found the e-zines that cater to your target market, these e-zines may be appropriate recipients for your news releases. Refer to Chapter 21 for recommendations on news release development and distribution. The editors may also accept articles of interest to their readership. You might be able to incorporate information on your products and services in an interesting article that would fit the editor's guidelines.

There are many e-zines looking for great content. If you can write articles for them that provide great content for their readers and at the same time provide a little exposure for you, it's a real win–win situation. You'll want to target those e-zines that have the same target market you do and have a broad subscriber base. You'll want to make sure the e-zine includes a resource box at the end of the article crediting you as the author and providing a hypertext link to your Web site or your e-mail address. Having articles published enhances your reputation as an expert, and people like to buy products and services from people who are experts in their field.

Besides sending your articles directly to targeted e-zines, you can also submit them to "article banks" online. Article banks are online resource sites for e-zine publishers. E-zine publishers search through these article banks for appropriate articles for their e-zine and, if they use one, they include the resource box of the author.

Reasons You Might Start Your Own E-zine

You can start your own e-zine. There are lots of resources online regarding e-zine development and administration. Don't make this decision without lots of thought, though, as you can damage your reputation if you don't deliver consistent, valuable content.

There are a multitude of reasons that you should consider developing and distributing your own e-zine. E-zines can be an extremely effective online marketing tool for the following reasons:

- You become established as an "expert." By providing your readers with valuable articles related to your area of expertise, you become, in their eyes, a valued and trusted expert.

- You establish trust. The first time someone visits your Web site, he or she has no idea who you are, how capable you are, or how professional you are. Sure, visitors get an impression from the look and feel and content of your site, but are they ready to do business with you? By providing them with free, valuable content over a period of time, you earn your visitors' trust, and they are more likely to turn to you when they need the type of product or service you provide.

- You generate significant traffic to your Web site. Your e-zine should always reference and provide a hypertext link to something available from your Web site. Once your visitor links through, there should be elements to create stickiness that encourage him to stay awhile and visit a number of pages on your site. The more often people visit your site, the more likely they are to do business with you.

- You build loyalty. Relationship marketing is what it's all about on the Web. You build relationships over time, and your e-zine will help you do just that. Your subscribers receive something free from you every month. Whom are they going to do business with when they have a need for your product or service? People prefer to spend their money with businesses they know and trust.

- You stay current with your customers and potential customers. When you are in front of your subscribers every month, you're not too easy to forget. You can keep them up to date on what's new with your company and your products and services, or what's new in your area of expertise.

Developing Your Own E-zine

If you do start your own e-zine, you should spend sufficient time planning and testing before you publish to ensure that you do it right. You don't get a second chance to make a first impression, and you want your readers to subscribe and tell others about the great e-zine they found. You want them to be excited to read your e-zine every time it is delivered to their e-mail box. The following tips will help you in your e-mail based e-zine planning and preparation:

- Provide great content. This goes without saying. If you have content that people want to read, they will remain subscribers. Don't think that shameless self-promotion is great content; your target audience certainly won't. As a rough guide, make sure your e-zine is 80 percent rich content and no more than 20 percent promotion and ads. Your e-zine should be full of what your target market considers useful information.

- You should keep length a consideration because you want your e-zine to be read and not put aside for later because it is always too long to read quickly. In this case, less is more. Subscribers should be able to read your e-zine in five minutes or less. If you do have a lengthy article, you might give a synopsis in the e-zine with a hypertext link to more detail on your Web site.

- Limit your content to four or five dynamite articles for an e-mail based e-zine. Provide a brief table of contents at the beginning of the e-zine. Keep the copy short and to the point.

- Keep your line length under 60 characters including spaces to avoid word-wrap issues.

- Encourage your readers to send a copy to others they feel might be interested in your great content. Make sure you provide subscribing instructions as well for those who receive these forwarded copies. You should also provide instructions on how to opt out, or unsubscribe (Figure 22.5).

Figure 22.5. Encourage your readers to send a copy to a friend and provide subscribe instructions for those who receive forwarded copies.

- Test your e-zine with different e-mail programs to ensure that your e-zine looks the way you designed it no matter which e-mail program your reader chooses to use. Send test copies to friends with different e-mail readers such as Outlook Express, Netscape Mail, Pegasus Mail, and Eudora. See how it looks, make sure that word-wrap is not an issue, and make sure the hypertext links work.

- Keep your subscriber addresses private and let subscribers know your privacy policy.

As the word about your e-zine spreads, you will have a large community of people who fit your target market reading it.

Once you have your own e-zine, you'll have to:

- Promote it to your target market through newsgroups, mail lists, your Web site, and your e-mail signature file. If you do promote your e-zine in newsgroups and mail lists, be sure it is appropriate to advertise your e-zine in a given newsgroup or mail list before you post. You do not want to be accused of spamming. However, promote your e-zine shamelessly on your site (let people subscribe to the e-zine on your site) and in your signature file.

- Provide an opportunity for subscribers to let others know. In your online e-zine, have a form that allows subscribers to e-mail a copy of the e-zine to their friends and colleagues. Use a call to action statement such as "Do you know someone who might be interested in this e-zine? Click here to send them a copy." This is a great way to pick up additional subscribers because some of the nonsubscribers who read your e-zine might then become subscribers if your content is interesting to them.

- Make it easy for people to subscribe to your e-zine. Provide clear subscription instructions in each e-mail version of your e-zine and on the online version. Have a form handy on your site to collect e-mail addresses from people who wish to subscribe.

- Provide an archive of past issues on your Web site so that visitors can sample your wares before subscribing. Make sure you provide an option for visitors to subscribe from that page as well.

- Don't provide your list of subscribers to anyone. This will protect your subscribers' privacy and keep your list spam-free. Thus, when you mail your e-zine, use the BCC feature or use a specialized e-mail program that hides all the recipients' addresses so the entire list is not compromised. People will not be happy if they start receiving spam as a result of your e-zine.

Internet Resources for Chapter 22

I have included a few resources for you to check out regarding e-zines. For additional resources on a variety of topics, I recommend that you visit the Resources section of my Web site at *http://www.susansweeney.com/ resources.html.* There you will find additional tips, tools, techniques, and resources.

BestEzines
http://www.bestezines.com/ezines/master.shtml
Directory of e-zines organized by category. A great site to find appropriate e-zines to reach your target market.

The Book of Zines
http://www.zinebook.com
Dynamite site with tons of links to e-zines, advice on developing your e-zine, reviews, interviews, how-to section, newly noted, and zine tips.

Ecola Newsstand
http://www.ecola.com
Ecola Newsstand has over 8,400 magazines, newspapers, and publications. There are over 100 categories of magazines to choose from.

Electronic Newsstand
http://www.enews.com
Founded in 1993, this was one of the first content-based sites on the Internet. Since then, the site has grown to become the largest and most diverse magazine-related resource anywhere on the Web.

The Etext Archives
http://www.etext.org/Zines

Complete with a search engine, this site offers places to find all of your online publication resources.

eZINE Search
http://www.ezinesearch.com/search-it/ezine
Billed as the world's ultimate e-magazine database. Searchable by category.

Ezine-Universe
http://ezine-universe.com
Ezine-Universe is a great directory of e-mail based e-zines.

InfoJump
http://www.infojump.com
Browse a huge directory of e-zines by category.

List City's Book of E-zines
http://www.list-city.com/ezines.htm
A list of e-zines organized by category that accept paid advertising as well as all the details and contact information for each e-zine.

The Magazine Rack
http://magazine-rack.com
Provides a searchable directory of online magazines, newspapers, journals, and e-zines.

MediaFinder
http://www.mediafinder.com
A national directory of magazines with details on target audience, publisher, contact, telephone numbers, Web addresses, e-mail addresses, editorial descriptions, issue frequency, and subscription price. In a lot of cases, an information request form is attached should you want further details. Great resource!

23

Web Rings as a Promotion Tool

Web rings provide a different way to organize sites. They are a free service offered to the Internet community. Web rings arrange sites with similar content by linking them together in a circle, or a ring. Each link in the ring is directed to a CGI script on the Web ring's server that sends the viewer on to the next site in the ring. There are literally thousands of rings with subjects such as communications, games, art, real estate, and so on. If there isn't a ring suitable for your site, you can create your own. The types of visitors you will receive from participating in the Web ring will be potential customers who are responsive to the content of your site and curious about your products or services. In this chapter, we cover:

- What are Web rings and how do they work?

- What promotion possibilities are available with Web rings?

- How do I participate and what will it cost?

- Where will I find Web rings that work for my company?

- What Web ring resources are available on the Net?

An Effective Alternative to Search Engines and Directories

Web rings are a fast-growing service on the Internet, providing one of the easiest ways for visitors to navigate the Internet. In each of its tens of thousands of topic-specific rings, member Web sites have linked their sites together, thus permitting more targeted visitors to reach the joined sites quickly and easily.

People increasingly are becoming dissatisfied with search engines and directories as tools to identify specific topic-related sites. Searches on a specific keyword have yielded results that often include totally unrelated sites. For instance, if you were planning a vacation to Mexico and you wanted to search for resorts in Mexico, the search engine results would likely include sites somewhat related but not exactly what you were looking for. The results would include book titles at Amazon.com related to Mexican travel, personal pages with other people's experiences traveling in Mexico complete with pictures from their family vacation, travel agencies, and tour company sites. The Web ring provides an alternative to these tools.

Site owners typically trade links with other Web sites to help advertise each other's sites. The Web ring was developed to enlarge the scope of link trading. A Web ring joins together many sites with a common topic.

Two of the major Web ring sites are:

- WebRing at *http://dir.webring.com/rw*

- RingSurf at *http://www.ringsurf.com*

What Are Web Rings?

A Web ring is made up of a number of topic-specific sites that are grouped together. There are country inn Web rings, Star Trek Web rings, prenatal-care Web rings, BMW Web rings, and remote-sensing Web rings in the huge list of Web rings that exists today. At WebRing there are several major categories:

- Business and Finance

- Computers and Internet

- Cultures and Community

- Entertainment and Arts

- Family and Home

- Games

- Government and Politics

- Health and Wellness

- Hobbies and Crafts

- Music

- Recreation and Sports

- Regional

- Relationships and Romance

- Religion and Beliefs

- Schools and Education

- Science

RingSurf also has many categories:

- Arts and Humanities

- Business and Economy

- Computers

- Entertainment

- Games

- Health

- Hobbies and Crafts

- Internet

- Miscellaneous

- Society and Culture

- Sports and Recreation

Each of these major categories has a number of subcategories, and each of the subcategories has a number of individual rings.

Rings can contain any number of sites. There must be at least five before the ring will be listed in the directories. Generally, the rings will contain somewhere between 20 and 200 sites. Some rings are smaller and some are substantially higher, with close to a thousand sites included.

Each ring was started and is maintained by an individual Web site owner. Through navigation links found most often at the bottom of member pages, visitors can travel to all or any of the sites in a ring. They can move through a ring in either direction, going to the next or previous site, or listing the next five sites in the ring. Visitors can also jump to a random site in the ring or survey all the sites that make up the ring.

An extraordinary system, Web rings are entirely open and free of charge to both visitors and members. As more and more people discover Web rings, we will see phenomenal growth in this as a preferred method to surf the net. At the time this edition was written, RingSurf had 24,523 Web rings with 244,033 member sites.

How Do Web Rings Work?

To surf a ring, all you have to do is use the links at the bottom of the page in the Web ring block. At the bottom of a Web ring participant's pages, you will find the Web ring navigation aid. A common Web ring graphic will include links to the "Next" site in the ring, the "Previous" site in the ring, or a "Random" site in the ring. You also have the option, in many cases, to see a list of the "Next 5" sites in the ring or to view the entire "Index" of the ring's sites. Once you begin surfing a ring, there is no clear beginning or ending, just a circle of related material. The Web ring program compensates for sites that are unreachable because they no longer exist or have server problems. You will always be able to navigate the ring.

When using a search engine, you are provided with a list of resulting sites, only some of which are appropriate. You visit the sites listed and then, depending on which browser you are using, you may use your "Back" button to return to the Results page to make another selection. With a Web ring this backing out is unnecessary. Once you've finished reviewing a site in the ring, you proceed to the next site that is of interest or simply surf through the connected sites one by one.

How to Participate in Web Rings

The first thing to do is find Web rings that are appropriate for your product or service—those that cater to your target market. You can review the directories at the WebRing site *http://dir.webring.com/rw* and also at the RingSurf site *http://www.ringsurf.com.*

Once you have found an appropriate Web ring, you contact the owner to ask permission to join. See Figure 23.1 for an example of this. The owner will review your site to determine your "fit" with the theme. Once you are accepted, the owner will provide you with the required code and accompanying graphics, which you will insert on your page. The ring owner provides all the required material; you slip it into your HTML file, and that's that.

Once the code is on your site, WebRing or RingSurf monitors the traffic and collects the statistics for your site, as they do for all Web ring sites. This is very beneficial to you because you can see how much traffic you are getting through the Web ring.

Any Web site owner who feels no existing ring is suitable can apply to create a new ring. If the application is approved, WebRing or RingSurf will provide all the necessary code and instructions. New Web rings are listed in the directory once they contain at least five sites.

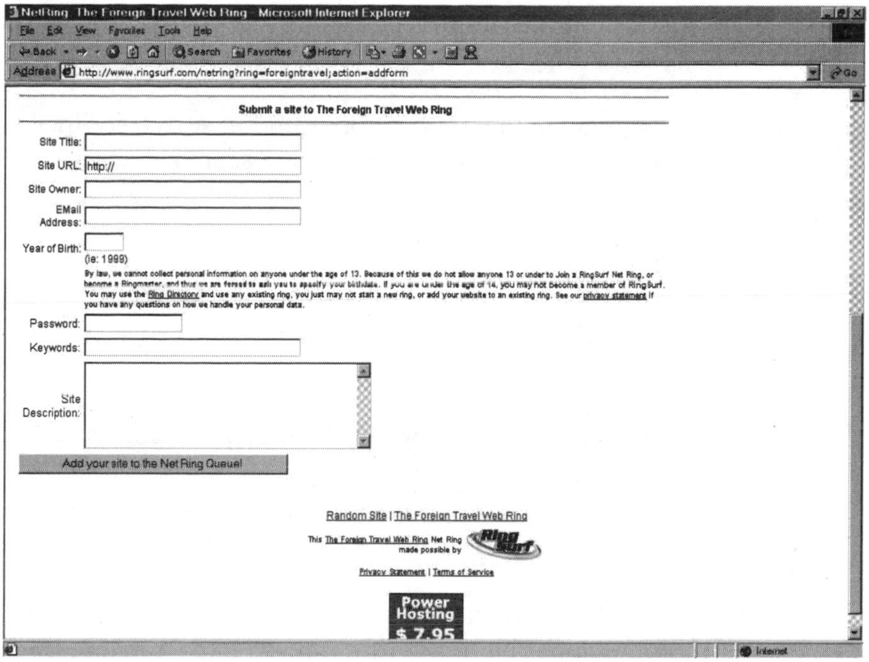

Figure 23.1. This inclusion request was taken from the Foreign Travel Web Ring to show how easy it is to join a Web ring.

Web Ring Participation Costs

The cost to participate in these Web rings is absolutely nil. No application fees, no charge for the approval, no charge for the code to be inserted on your pages, no charge for the increased traffic a Web ring brings.

The Benefits of Web Rings

There are many benefits to both the users of Web rings and the participating Web sites. Benefits to the user include:

- Web rings provide a great navigation tool when looking for more information on a specific topic.

- Web rings are easy to use. They provide one of the most efficient ways to find specific content on the Internet.

- Web rings avoid the duplication found in search engines, where a site may appear several times in one search. Each site is linked only once in each Web ring.

- Web rings speed up search time.

- Web rings eliminate sifting through mounds of search engine results for appropriate sites.

  Benefits to participating Web sites include:

- Web ring participation increases the number of targeted visitors to your Web site.

- The organizers of the Web rings make it easy to monitor how successful your ring is. Traffic reports and "top" rings statistics are made available to participants.

- Web rings drive traffic to your site.

Business Reluctance to Participate in Web Rings

One of the biggest hurdles Web rings face in being adopted by the business sector is that when you join a ring, you are linking to the competition, as shown in Figure 23.2. It is likely that this mentality explains why Web rings have been so popular for personal sites and special-interest groups, but have failed to catch on in today's business community. But, again, small businesses and retail-oriented sites have not shied away from rings. For example, rings and banner programs are hot marketing strategies for stores that sell collectibles. This is particularly true for hard-to-find collectibles. Take the Pez phenomenon: Not being on a Pez Web ring could be a crucial mistake for vendors. After all, if a customer hits a site and it doesn't have a specific Pez, the quest isn't over—it's on to the next site. What better way to get there than via a ring? Your site might just be the next one.

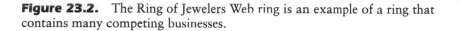

Figure 23.2. The Ring of Jewelers Web ring is an example of a ring that contains many competing businesses.

Lately we have seen a growth in commercial application of Web rings. There are a few reasons for this:

- A number of articles have appeared in Internet marketing magazines related to the high volume of traffic through these Web rings. Businesses have sometimes found that the bulk of the traffic to their site is coming through the Web ring.

- Other articles talk about the benefits of being conveniently located near your competition, bringing more traffic for everyone. Several have likened it to what happens in the real world in the fast-food industry. When a McDonald's opens, you quickly see a Burger King, Wendy's, Pizza Hut, KFC, and Taco Bell all open up close by. This means more business for everyone.

Other Marketing Opportunities Provided by Web Rings

When you have found a Web ring that attracts your target market, you can participate and enjoy the increase in visitors to your site. The Massage and Bodywork Web ring shown in Figure 23.3 is an example of a professional type of Web ring. It is a Web ring devoted to massage schools and educators and other support services for massage professionals. Web rings provide an array of other opportunities as well.

You can search through the list of participants in a Web ring to arrange reciprocal links. You can also search a Web ring for banner-advertising purposes. You can either exchange banners or purchase advertising on these sites. You can find sites that may be appropriate for cooperative advertising purposes. You can exchange coupons with another site you are linked to, which works especially well when you sell noncompeting products to the same target market.

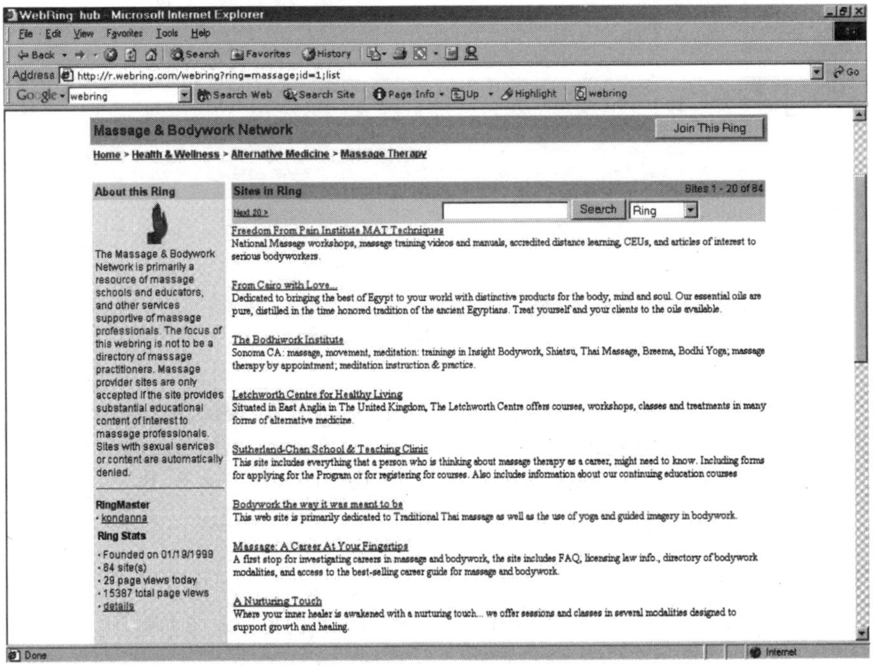

Figure 23.3.   The Massage and Bodywork Web ring is an example of a professional Web ring; it is exclusively for massage schools and educators, and other services supportive of massage professionals.

Internet Resources for Chapter 23

I have included a few resources for you to check out regarding public Web rings. For additional resources on a variety of topics, I recommend that you visit the Resources section of my Web site at *http://www. susansweeney.com/resources.html*. There you will find additional tips, tools, techniques, and resources.

RingSurf
http://www.ringsurf.com
Sites of a particular subject together in a ring. A visitor to any site in the ring can easily move forward or backward through the ring and visit other sites in the ring within that subject area. This drives targeted qualified traffic to all the ring sites. Surfers don't want to deal with mounds of irrelevant search engine results. They want to visit sites on topics they love. It's so simple, and everybody's a winner. RingSurf is a completely free service that lets users quickly, easily, and reliably navigate thousands of related Web sites organized by areas of interest. Joining a Web ring is great way to increase traffic to your site.

WebRing
http://dir.webring.com/rw
Web rings are one of the fastest and most exciting ways to navigate the World Wide Web. In each of its tens of thousands of rings, member Web sites have banded together to form their sites into linked circles. Their purpose is to allow more visitors to reach them quickly and easily.

24

Webcasting and Rich Media

Webcasting is defined by Netlingo (*http://www.netlingo.com*) as: "Using the Internet, and the World Wide Web in particular, to broadcast information. Unlike typical surfing, which relies on a pull method of transferring Web pages, Webcasting uses push technologies."

According to a past study conducted by Arbitron New Media and Northstar Interactive, 70 percent of the Webcast audience clicks for content information, and while listening to or viewing streaming media, nearly 60 percent click through for advertising information. The study also states that approximately half of the Webcast audience buy online-advertised products and 44 percent click online ads. The majority of Webcast users tune in from home (63 percent), followed by at-work users (37 percent percent). In this chapter, we cover:

- Streaming versus nonstreaming media (also known as rich media)

- Advertising with rich media

- Barriers to acceptance of Webcasting

- Uses of Webcasting

- Prominent Webcasters

Streaming versus Nonstreaming Media

Before we explain the marketing implications of Webcasting, or rich media, it is important to explain some of the terms and what the end user requires to view them. Webcasting consists primarily of video and audio. Whatis.com defines rich media as:

> *Rich media is an Internet advertising term for a Web page ad that uses advanced technology such as streaming video, downloaded applets (programs) that interact instantly with the user, and ads that change when the user's mouse passes over it. For example:*

> • *An ad for a Hollywood movie that includes a streaming video sample of a scene from the movie*

> • *A mouse cursor that changes to an image on a particular Web site if the user requests it*

> • *A standard-size banner ad that includes an inquiry form about ISDN installation, capturing the user's filled in personal information and telling the user he or she will be contacted by a company representative—all simply by interacting with an ad on an online publisher's Web page.*

This section talks about streaming and nonstreaming content, with most emphasis placed on streaming because it has the highest promotional potential. What is the difference between streaming and nonstreaming? To put it simply, streaming is presented as it arrives. RealAudio files are an example of streaming media. Meanwhile, nonstreaming requires you to download the entire clip or file before you can listen to it or view it. AVI, MP3, and MOV file formats are nonstreaming file formats.

> • *Video.* This category would include both streaming formats (Real Audio, G2, and Windows Media Player) and nonstreaming video formats (such as AVI and MOV files). Streaming video is often sent from pre-prepared files but is usually distributed as a live broadcast feed. Examples of this include news clips, movie clips, and online movie presentations.

- *Audio*. Audio also includes streaming and nonstreaming formats. RealNetworks is by far the current king, with its RealAudio. Other major leading providers of streaming audio are Macromedia, with its Shockwave, and Microsoft's Windows Media Player.

Obviously, streaming video file formats contain an audio element to them as well. After all, a movie clip is much more interesting when there is sound associated with it.

Other popular Webcasting or push technology formats include:

- ASF (Advanced Streaming Format)—Designed to store synchronized multimedia data and deliver the data over a large variety of networks and protocols.

- CDF (Channel Definition Format)—Permits Web developers to push information to users through the use of channels.

Push technologies involve sending information to your target market across the Internet. Internet users install software on their system that receives content from the Webcaster. For example, they might receive the latest sports scores, the current weather conditions in 20 cities around the world, or current headlines. The information is "pushed" to the client's system. This is different from "pull" marketing, in which the client specifically requests content from a Web site by loading it into the browser.

Technically speaking, e-mail is one of the earliest forms of push technology. Internet marketers send e-mail messages to individuals in their target market without permission to do so from each of the recipients. However, we all know that this is spam. Savvy Internet marketers can still use e-mail to push their message to potential clients, but they must have the potential clients' permission beforehand.

Webcasters can utilize push technologies much like Internet marketers do with e-mail marketing campaigns. RealNetworks (*http://www.real.com*) has been involved in the Webcasting field for several years. Their RealPlayer software is a prime example of how to utilize push technology. The basic version of the player can be downloaded for free from the RealNetworks Web site. Observing Figure 24.1, you can see how active channels have been incorporated into the RealPlayer application. Clicking on one of the active channels in the "Channels" menu automatically connects the user to a streaming audio/video presentation from the site of one of RealNetworks' partners. In this way, RealNetworks assists its partners (ESPN, Fox, ZDNet, etc.) to brand themselves through the RealPlayer Webcasting software, and RealNetworks likely receives a healthy sum of money in exchange for this advertising. The RealPlayer software permits you to subscribe to other channels as well. Thus, RealNetworks gives users a free application, but the company profits from RealPlayer by selling advertising space. RealNetworks is the perfect example of how Webcasting can be used to quickly achieve brand recognition and earn additional revenue.

Aside from RealNetworks, the following companies also provide software to allow for the distribution of channels:

- Apple's QuickTime (*http://www.apple.com/quicktime*)

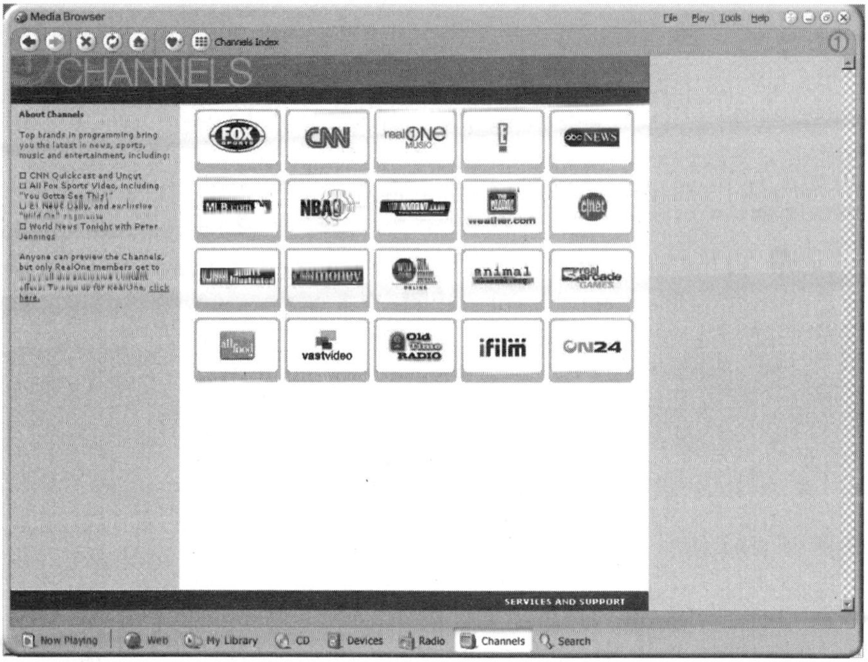

Figure 24.1. RealPlayer receives Internet channels. You can subscribe to new channels or view the channel information of RealNetwork's partners.

- Microsoft Active Channels software (*http://www.microsoft.com*)

- Netscape Communicator's Netcaster (*http://www.netscape.com*)

Advertising with Rich Media

Companies can use rich media by purchasing a "commercial" that precedes an online presentation or audio event, or a company can develop and use rich media on its own Web site to provide a greater sense of interactivity, which will result in more repeat traffic. For an example of this, go to Yahoo! Events (*http://broadcast.yahoo.com*). Yahoo! Events provides current streaming audio and video footage of almost any event you could imagine. For instance, you can listen to the commentary of an entire NBA basketball game. However, just before the game gets under way, you will be greeted by a 25-second audio advertisement. Why is this good advertising?

- Rich media advertising leaves a deeper impression on customers than does a static banner ad.

- Rich media averages higher recall.

- Higher customer recall of rich media makes it easier to brand a company name or product.

- Rich media has higher click-through rates.

- Rich media is more "likeable."

Higher Recall

A recent usage study among consumers who had recently switched from dial-up to high-speed Internet access revealed the following results:

- 93 percent of users download more MP3s than they did when using a dial-up connection.

- 90 percent download more music and videos.

- 89 percent watch more streaming video.

- 86 percent listen to more streaming audio.

- 79 percent transfer a greater number of large files.

- 78 percent share more photos online.

This means that more and more people are likely to remember your company's streaming media presentation than a static banner ad, as they are more apt to view rich media.

Better Branding

It goes without saying that better customer recall leads to better branding. Creating brand awareness with banner ads is difficult because banner ads are not very interactive. The combination of sight and sound possible with rich media advertising makes it much more effective than a static image or looping animated GIF.

More Click-Throughs

A banner ad incorporating Java or Flash Media will have more than twice the number of click-throughs than will a static banner ad. Static banner ads average less than one click-through per hundred impressions. If you have a banner ad that actively engages your customer, you can achieve higher click-through rates and generate more sales leads.

More Likeable

Intel concluded that a nonstreaming interactive banner ad offers a 20 percent potential increase in likeability. People will be more likely to interact with a banner ad that has some sort of game built into it as opposed to a static image. Therefore, an interactive banner ad has the potential to attract a lot of people who are not usually inclined to click on banner ads of any sort. Likewise, a 30-second spot in a streaming multimedia presentation (e.g., watching the Superbowl online) is going to be more acceptable to a user than is a pop-up banner ad.

The bottom line is that if people like you, they will probably buy from you. Both steaming and nonstreaming broadband media advertising increase your chances of making a positive impression on customers.

More Reasons to Use Rich Media Advertising

Given the high recall rates, the cost per branding impression (i.e., the number of times a customer must view the ad before becoming familiar with your brand) decreases. This increases your ROI (return on investment) because you do not have to invest as much in rich media advertising to get your message across as you would with traditional advertising. For instance, to brand your company's name or product using television advertising could require a substantial financial investment. People change the channel during commercial breaks, so it is harder to reach television viewers.

However, when people intentionally subscribe to an Internet channel, they are viewing and listening to information they are interested in. Plus, it is more of an effort to switch channels on the Net than it is to do so watching television. Therefore, the user's tendency to remain "tuned in" is higher.

Also, the Internet is a worldwide network. Television, magazines, and other traditional marketing vehicles are more regionalized. Therefore, a rich media advertisement streaming across the Internet has the potential to reach a much larger audience.

The Barriers of Webcasting (Rich Media) Acceptance

With every new medium, there are bound to be barriers to its public acceptance. Webcasting, both streaming and nonstreaming, is no different. There are six primary obstacles that Webcasting must overcome before it becomes a publicly acceptable advertising medium.

Cost

The possibilities are there, but so are the costs, and you must be aware of this. Although the cost is coming down, the cost of developing streaming media and nonstreaming media still can be considered expensive for some budgets. Moreover, if you're looking to advertise on a site that applies video and audio content, then you must be made aware that most of the sites that apply this technology are high-budget, high-volume, and high-bandwidth sites and will likely ask for quite a fee to advertise.

You must also consider the potential return on investment. We described earlier how rich media advertising has a higher recall rate than standard Web advertising. Also, rich media is more cost-effective and efficient for branding purposes. Therefore, although the initial expense of producing a rich media advertisement may be quite high, it may quickly be recovered by the interest and sales the ad will generate.

Rich Media Advertising Is Not Accepted by All Sites

Although a lot of sites do not have the resources to offer Webcast advertising opportunities, a lot of major sites do. Content sites such as Launch.Yahoo.com and RollingStone.com place ads in front of some of the videos you can view on their site. These streaming media sites offer tremendous exposure opportunities for companies that advertise with them.

There are also sites such as MP3.com (*http://www.mp3.com*) that offer free Webcast advertising. On MP3.com, unsigned music artists can post MP3 versions of their songs for the world to hear. MP3.com is a high-traffic site as a result of the community of artists they have created, and the artists themselves benefit from the increased exposure.

Given the number of Webcast companies and major companies getting involved with Webcasting, companies that do not utilize it may be left behind.

Bandwidth Constraints

Both streaming and nonstreaming media require that users have high connection speeds in order to experience a Webcast as it is intended. To view streaming content, you will need a plug-in or player of some sort. Popular applications used to view or hear streaming content are:

- Windows Media Player

- Quicktime

- RealPlayer

- Macromedia Shockwave Player

It is important to note that the higher the connection speed, the more convenient the use of streaming content will be. If you're still using a 14.4 modem, you're simply not going to get the performance needed to make it worthwhile. This presents an obstacle to people with slower Internet connection rates. Also, some people simply do not wish to download and install the plug-ins necessary to play rich media files. You will not be able to target your Webcasting advertising campaign toward these users.

Irritates User

Does Webcasting annoy users? Sure it does. But this will only be the case for people with low bandwidth or less-robust machines. Also, some people despise advertising in any form, so you probably won't win over any of these individuals either.

Too Complicated

The software to create rich media content exists and, with a little initiative, can be learned by anyone. You first should determine if your target market is likely to be a user of rich media. Here are some software applications you should inspect if you have an interest in creating your own rich media or Webcasting files:

- Streaming Media Creation or Encoding Software

  - RealSlideshowPlus (*http://www.realnetworks.com/products/ media_creation.html*)—This product allows you to create your own streaming media slideshow.

- Emblaze (*http://www.emblaze.com*)—Designed to enable delivery of rich media over any IP network, over any platform, and under any bandwidth.

- Liquid Audio (*http://www.liquidaudio.com*)—Offers solutions for encoding your music and serving it in a streaming media format.

- Stream Anywhere (*http://www.sonicfoundry.com*)—The all-in-one solution for preparing audio and video multimedia for distribution over the Web.

- Quick Time 5.0.2 (*http://www.apple.com/quicktime*)—Create or edit streaming and nonstreaming video and audio files.

- Adobe Premiere 6.0 (*http://www.adobe.com/products/premiere/main.html*)—Adobe's product for media creation.

- Nonstreaming Media Creation or Encoding Software

  - Macromedia Director 8.5 Shockwave Internet Studio and Flash (*http://www.macromedia.com*)—Generate powerful presentations and content for your Web site.

  - AudioCatalyst 2.1 and XingMPEG software (*http://www.xingtech.com*)—Create MP3s and MPEGs from source files.

  - Real JukeBox (*http://www.real.com/jukebox/index.html*)—Create MP3 files from CDs.

Learning to create rich media just requires a little bit of initiative and patience.

The Technology Changes Too Often

Webcasting is a relatively new medium. Of course, new standards are being introduced every few months. The key here is to watch what technologies the major Internet sites are using. If you see some of the major players in the Internet starting to use a particular Webcasting technology, you should investigate it. Generally, the learning curve for new technologies is not very steep since they are based on previous technologies.

Uses of Webcasting

Despite the existence of a few barriers to using Webcasting as a promotional vehicle, you should investigate it if you think your target market may include early adapters to technology. Some important uses of providing rich media content to the general public include:

- Live continuous broadcasts of radio stations and networks

- Broadcasts of cable networks and television stations

- Coverage of sporting events (both streaming and nonstreaming footage)

- Live music including concerts and club performances (both streaming and nonstreaming footage)

- On-demand shows, corporate events, CDs, audiobooks, video titles, and so on

As bandwidth increases and more people have access to higher-end technology, Webcasting will become a regular part of our lives and be more accepted as an advertising medium. The transition to Webcasting has already begun, as is evidenced by the large number of prominent players already entrenched in the field.

Today we are seeing that many major corporations are providing live Webcasts of their corporate annual meetings. This is a great idea for a number of different reasons. If there are company shareholders who are unable to attend the annual meeting in person, they are able to observe the meeting remotely via the Internet and Webcasting. Similarly, potential investors can view your annual meeting online and gain valuable insight into your organization, which might result in the individual's making an investment in your organization. If potential investors or shareholders miss the live Webcast of the annual meeting, they can visit your site and download the event to watch at their convenience. This is just one example of how Webcasting can add value to your Web site, and ultimately your organization.

Many travel and tourism sites are providing Virtual Tours of their locations. A picture is worth a thousand words, and this is certainly the case when it comes to marketing hotels, bed and breakfasts, resorts, golf courses, theme parks, attractions, and other travel destinations.

We are also seeing an increase in the number of professional training organizations providing online training modules, or "virtual seminars," from their Web sites. The increase in online training popularity is a result of the flexibility and cost efficiency offered by these organizations. In order for your clients to attend your seminars in person, they are inconvenienced with scheduling time to go to the seminar. This inconvenience incorporates travel expenses, the seminar fee, and the opportunity costs of being absent from their office. Virtual seminars enable your clients to usually pay a much smaller fee to view the same seminar from the comfort of their desk. Business professionals are also finding online training useful because it allows them to decide when they will view the seminar, as some of the online training sessions can be viewed at their convenience. Others are "live" and available only at a specific time and date.

More-popular online training organizations include:

- The Learning Library (*http://www.learninglibrary.com*)

- Learning.net (*http://www.learning.net*)

- Learn2.com (*http://www.learn2.com*)

- OnlineLearning.net (*http://www.onlinelearning.net*)

- Online-Learning.com (*http://www.online-learning.com*)

Many professional speakers are now offering live Webcasts, downloadable training modules, and streaming video clips from their Web sites in an effort to increase their online bookings. For example, meeting planners and organizers who are looking for speakers for their upcoming conference can visit my Web site, SusanSweeney.com (*http://www.susansweeney.com*), to download streaming video clips of samples of my speaking. This enables visitors to gain a feel for my presentation style and the quality of content that I deliver.

Emerging telecommunication technology allows us to bridge phone lines so that multiple users can speak and listen at the same time. Commonly known as a tele-seminar, this feature provides speakers and trainers with the opportunity to share their expertise over the phone line to an unlimited number of listeners. I regularly hold tele-seminars that people can register for on my SusanSweeney.com Web site. When participants register to participate in my tele-seminar, I provide them with an 800 number to call the day of the seminar and a code that admits them to the call. Prior to the program I provide them with a URL where they can access a streaming video version of my presentation that corresponds with the tele-seminar. This type of "virtual seminar" is becoming extremely popular in the professional speaking and training industry.

Prominent Webcasters

Yahoo!'s Broadcast has Webcast over 36,000 live events including the most recent Super Bowl, the NHL regular season, and the Stanley Cup Playoffs, and even the online premiere of *Casablanca*. Visit *http://enterprise.yahoo.com/broadcast/demo/* to learn more about their advertising opportunities. They offer gateway ads, channel and event sponsorships, multimedia ads, and traditional banner ads. More appropriate to this chapter is the ability to purchase slots and insert Internet-only commercials within Yahoo!'s programming.

Vidnet.com (*http://www.vidnet.com*) places video commercials before allowing you to view a video (Figure 24.2). When selecting to view Nelly Furtado's video, a streaming video commercial for RealPlayer and Intel's partnership was prominently displayed first.

A major use of streaming audio comes in the form of Internet-only radio stations and traditional radio stations that broadcast their signal online. For the radio stations, it's an ideal opportunity to increase market share and increase the number of loyal listeners. Web-Radio.com (*http://www.web-radio.com*) has a large directory of over 5,000 radio stations broadcasting over the Internet (Figure 24.3).

A radio station will benefit from the broader exposure of Webcasting (worldwide as opposed to regional). These online radio stations provide an excellent opportunity for businesses to advertise online. Since online radio listeners broaden the potential audience for a radio station, the station could charge advertisers higher rates. This source of revenue is unquestionably attractive, which is why radio stations are scrambling to establish themselves in the Webcasting world.

Travelago.com's (*http://www.travelago.com*) Web site is an interactive video library of hotels and destinations. Perhaps you own a bed-and-breakfast near a waterfront location. You can use a streaming or nonstreaming video clip to display this scenery, much like when you receive a videotape from a travel agency demonstrating the beauty of a potential vacation destination (Figure 24.4).

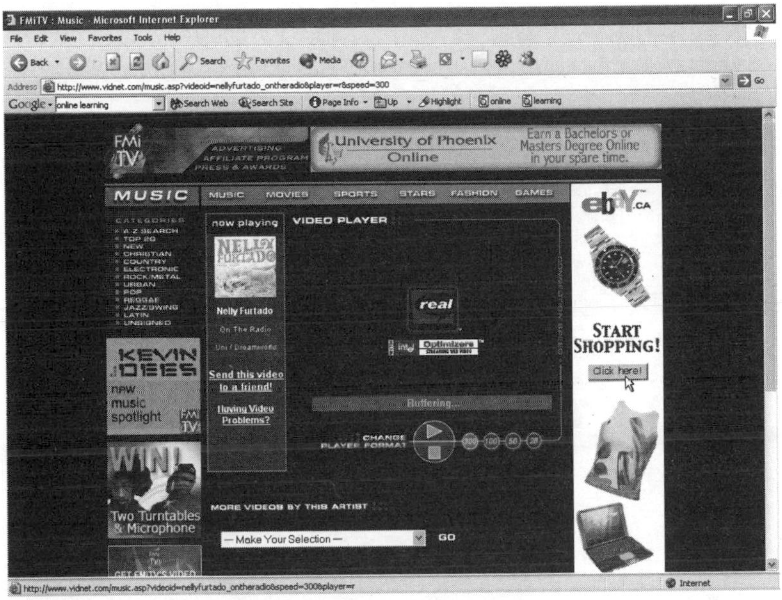

Figure 24.2. Vidnet.com shows us how cross branding can be done with streaming media.

Figure 24.3. Over 5,000 radio stations now stream their programming across the Internet. The existence of Web-radio.com is evidence of the growth in this field.

Figure 24.4.   Travelago provides streaming video of various travel destinations.

Webcasting is a technological phenomenon that offers Internet companies and traditional companies marketing on the Internet a new way to reach their customers. Many Internet giants have already seized the Webcasting reins and now deliver rich media content and advertising to the world. Perhaps you would be wise to investigate Webcasting and do the same.

Internet Resources for Chapter 24

I have included a few resources for you to check out regarding Webcasting and rich media. For additional resources on a variety of topics, I recommend that you visit the Resources section of my Web site at *http://www.susansweeney.com/resources.html.* There you will find additional tips, tools, techniques, and resources.

BeHere Technologies
http://www.behere.com
The only provider of both live and recorded navigable video and image technology... up to 360 degrees in a single frame.

Broadcast.com
http://broadcast.yahoo.com
Yahoo! Broadcast offers a wide variety of on-demand audio and video content, from space shuttle launches to full-length movies.

ChannelSeven.com
http://www.channelseven.com
A large resource for Internet development, marketing, and advertising executives. This site contains information on rich media advertising.

International Webcasting Association
http://www.webcasters.org
The IWA serves as the meeting place for companies active or interested in the delivery of multimedia (audio and video) services to consumers or business customers via the Net and other networks.

Internet Pictures Corp
http://www.ipix.com
This company is known for its 360-degree virtual tours.

The Media CHANNEL
http://www.mediachannel.com
A guide to video on the Internet.

RealNetworks
http://www.real.com
Innovators in the field of streaming media, RealNetworks has several popular Webcasting software applications, including RealPlayer, RealJukebox, and RealSlideshow.

Streaming Media World
http://www.streamingmediaworld.com
Streaming Media World offers media player reviews, news, tools, tutorials, discussion forums, and cool links devoted to streaming video, audio, MP3, multimedia, and GIF animation.

VideoDome.Com Networks Inc.
http://www.videodome.com
Offers a variety of Internet OnDemand video solutions to meet your online video needs.

Virtual Kingdom Interactive Inc.
http://www.virtualkingdom.bc.ca
A company that provides virtual tour technology for your Web site.

VirtualTuner.com
http://www.virtualtuner.com
Directory of live and on-demand radio links for the Internet.

Web-Radio
http://www.web-radio.com
A comprehensive directory of radio stations (broadcasting) on the Web.

WebReference.com
http://www.webreference.com/multimedia/video.html
A directory of multimedia tools including Windows Media Player, Real, Emblaze, and Macromedia.

25

Grand Opening Tips for Your Web Site Virtual Launch

Just as you would have a book or software launch, you can have a Web site launch. In preparation for the Web site launch, you must develop an appropriate launch strategy. In this chapter, we cover:

- Development of your Web site launch strategy

- Web site announcement mailing lists

- Direct e-mail postcards to your customers or prospective clients

Launching and Announcing Your Web Site

A new Web site or your new location in cyberspace can be launched in many of the same ways that you would launch a new physical store location. This may involve both online and offline activities. Just as you would prepare a book launch strategy or a new software product launch strat-

---

Cyberspace
Virtual location where Web sites live.

egy, you can develop an appropriate launch strategy for your new Web site. Sometimes a launch strategy may be more work than the benefit that will be gained. On the other hand, if you are opening the next Amazon, it is imperative.

Your Web Site Virtual Launch

Let's take a look at a traditional retail store grand opening. For the grand opening, which usually lasts for an evening or a day, there will be invitations to the media, press releases distributed, invited guests, opening ceremonies, advertising, and possibly gift giveaways.

A Web site virtual location launch occurs in cyberspace, and the "grand opening" can last for a day, a week, or a month. Many of the activities you would include in your traditional grand opening can also be included in your Internet grand opening. The effectiveness of your launch can be increased with the following tips:

- Media attention can be generated through the distribution of press releases online and offline. (See Chapter 21 for press release distribution information.)

- Guests can be invited to your online opening through postings in newsgroups, newsletters, "What's New" sites, banner advertising, direct e-mail, and signature files, as well as through offline direct mail and advertising.

- Opening ceremonies can be just as exciting online as offline. They can last for a month rather than a day. The opening must be designed to be of interest to the target market.

- You can feature special guests in chat areas for your grand opening or several special guests over the duration. Again, relate your guests and the topics to be discussed to the needs and wants of your target market.

- You can run contests that require visitors to visit various parts of your site to compete for prizes. Perhaps they have to complete a multiple-choice quiz whose answers are found throughout your site. This way you encourage your guests to visit all those pages you want them to. You can also ask if they would like to be notified via e-mail of the winner. This gives you an opportunity to send them e-mail with their permission.

- You can have audio and video greetings from your site.

- You can have press releases regarding your opening available for download by the media. Make your press release interactive. (See Chapter 21 for details on how to do this.)

- Special free gifts can be provided to the first 20 or 50 visitors to your site. You can also provide prizes to the first 100 to link to your site.

- Do some offline advertising for your new URL (see Chapter 26 for innovative offline opportunities), or take advantage of online advertising via Announcement sites.

There are many other innovative "grand opening" attention grabbers that can be brainstormed with appropriate marketing and public relations individuals. Whatever you decide to do, make it memorable, make it appropriate for your target market, and provide reasons for them to return.

Internet Resources for Chapter 25

I have included a few resources for you to check out for your Web site virtual launch. For additional resources on a variety of topics, I recommend that you visit the Resources section of my Web site at *http://www.susansweeney.com/resources.html*. There you will find additional tips, tools, techniques, and resources.

Best-Web-Sites Announcement List
You can join this mailing list by e-mailing the message "sub BESTWEB [your name]" to listserv@vm3090.ege.edu.tr.

Nerd World What's New
http://www.nerdworld.com/whatsnew.html
The newest links added to Nerd World, and a place to show off your site. Not just for nerds.

WhatsNu
http://www.whatsnu.com
The WhatsNu search engine filters Web site listings by date/category and offers the Internet community a free weekly notification of new Web sites launching on the Internet.

26

Effective Offline Promotion

There are many benefits to cross-promoting your Web site using traditional media and print materials. Your Web site can answer a lot of questions and provide more information than you can print in a magazine or newspaper ad. Your site can be kept up-to-date with the latest information available. People can request additional information or order online. In this chapter, we cover:

- Tips for offline promotion of your Web site

- Offline promotion opportunities

Offline Promotion Objectives

Since visitors can be directed from offline promotion to request additional information or order online, you should promote your URL on every piece of promotional material you produce! The more exposure your URL receives, the more likely it is that people will remember it when they go online.

Be creative with your offline promotion campaign. Brainstorm with innovative thinkers to come up with a number of good places to promote your URL; for example, try displaying your URL in your TV and radio commercials, magazine and newspaper ads, and billboards. The more places your URL appears, the more it will get noticed. Some businesses even incorporate their URL into their building and vehicle signage. Answer your telephone "YourCompanyName.com, Good Morning." This is quite effective in letting people know that you want them to visit your Web site and providing them with your URL at the same time. Next time they have a question or want to place an order, they may go directly to the Web site.

Displaying your URL in traditional media encourages people to visit your site for more information about your company. Another benefit is that people usually can order from your Web site. Naturally, your site should be up-to-date, with all of the latest information on products, prices, and sales promotions. If a six-month-old advertisement is seen in a magazine, as long as the URL is displayed in the ad, readers can go to your site and get current information. Your Web site is your most effective advertisement, but it is an advertisement that people have to know about before they can view it.

URL Exposure through Corporate Literature and Material

It is important that your corporate image be consistent in your online and offline promotional campaigns. Businesses should use the same colors, style, fonts, logo, and tag lines on all of their marketing materials. As a rule of thumb, try to place your URL on everything you put your logo on—which means just about every piece of corporate literature. Make sure to include your URL on the following:

- Letterhead

- Business cards

- Corporate brochures

- Envelopes

- Checks

- Fax coversheets

- Report covers

- Flyers

- Advertisements

- Direct-mail pieces

- Newsletters

- Press releases

- Media kits

URL Exposure through Promotional Items

If your company uses promotional items as giveaways at trade shows and events, it is a good idea to incorporate your Web site marketing with these items. Figures 26.1 and 26.2 offer examples of the different promotional products that you can order on the Internet for your business. Promotional items that are used in and around computer workstations are ideal because your URL is visible when people are in a position to actually visit your site. Some examples are:

- Mousepads

- Diskette holders

- Screen cleaning kits

- Software

- Screen savers

- Pens and pencils

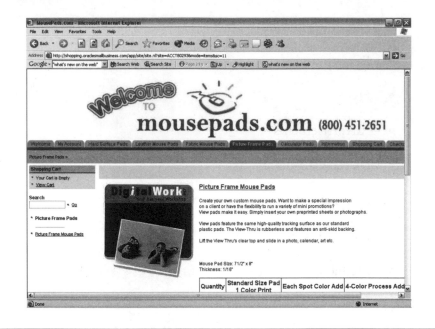

Figure 26.1. Mousepads.com is a site where you can order personalized mouse pads.

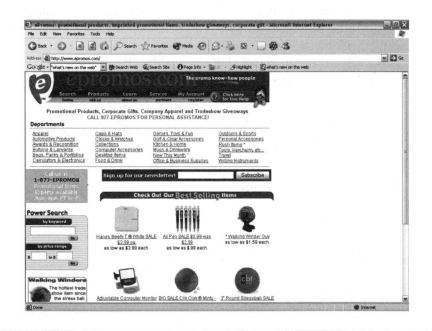

Figure 26.2. At epromos.com you can put your business card on a coffee mug.

- Scratch pads

- Coffee mugs

- Coasters

- Letter openers

- Stress balls

- Calendars

- Sticky notes

URL Exposure through Clothing

Articles of clothing are another great promotional item. When people wear an article of clothing with your URL on it, they become a walking billboard for your site. I personally have a jacket that was provided by Webjacket.com (see Figure 26.3), and the quality is great. Your corporate jacket provides exposure for your company and your Web site. If

Figure 26.3. Webjacket.com allows you to customize your corporate jacket with your logo and your URL right on its site.

you have a corporate uniform, your URL should be displayed. Put your URL and a catchy phrase or tag line on items such as:

- Golf shirts

- T-shirts

- Sweatshirts

- Hats

- Aprons

- Jackets

URL Exposure on Novelty Items

Novelty items can be an effective place to print your URL. If your target market is a younger audience, then put your URL on items that will appeal to them, such as:

- Frisbees

- Balls

- Beach towels

- Sunglasses

- Keychains

- Magnets

- Chocolate bars

- Bumper stickers

Promotion with a Touch of Creativity

Be creative and come up with catchy slogans that have a connection with the promotional item. For example:

- *Clocks:* "Take some time to visit our Web site at ..."

- *Rulers:* "For a measurable difference, visit us at ..."

- *Coffee mugs:* "Take a break and visit our Web site at ..."

- *Tape measures:* "Visit our Web site at *http://www.YourURL.com* and see how our site measures up."

- *Magnifying glasses:* "You don't need one of these to see that our site is the best. Come visit us online at ..."

- *Watches:* "Isn't it about time you visited us at ... ?"

- *Bookmarks:* "Take a break from reading and visit our Web site at ..."

URL Exposure on Your Products

If possible, put your URL on your products themselves. This is an innovative idea that Joe Boxer has implemented. They stitch their URL into the waistband of their underwear.

Internet Resources for Chapter 26

I have included a few resources for you to check out about offline promotion. For additional resources on a variety of topics, I recommend that you visit the Resources section of my Web site at *http://www.susansweeney.com/resources.html*. There you will find additional tips, tools, techniques, and resources.

Advertising Concepts
http://www.bumperstickers.com/ad.htm
"Why Use Promotional Products?" This site gives you good promotional ideas and what these promotional products will do for you.

Bizine
http://www.bizine.com/profit.htm
"Increase Your Profits by Coordinating Online and Traditional Offline Marketing," by Bob Leduc.

Digital-Women.com
http://www.digital-women.com/unique.htm
This includes unique ideas for online and offline promotion.

e-Promos.com
http://www.epromos.com
This site has a huge offering of items appropriate to display your logo.

Free Pint
http://www.freepint.co.uk/issues/040399.htm
"12 Offline Ways of Promoting Your URL," by Nikki Pilkington.

Mousepads.com
http://www.mousepads.com
Mousepads.com allows you to choose from many pre-set styles or will develop a custom one just for you. They also allow you to sign up for their e-specials on their site.

PC Mojo
http://www.pcmojo.com/content/techsuppwebpromoteoffline.htm
Information on why you need to promote your site off the Internet.

Promotional Webstickers
http://www.websticker.com/products.htm
Simple ideas to effectively promote your Web site offline.

Webjacket.com
http://www.webjacket.com
Webjacket.com provides a great quality jacket with your corporate logo and Web address. You design your own right on the site. I have one!

27

Web Traffic Analysis

Today, technology not only allows us to generate interactive Web sites for our viewers, it allows us to learn about our viewers as well. Many Web sites are now using Web traffic analysis software that enables them to analyze not only what page of the Web site their visitors came to first, but also where they came from, how long they were there, and what they did while they stayed. Once you have this information, you can do some calculations to see what is working for you and what is not. In this chapter, you will learn:

- What your Web server's log files can tell you

- How analyzing log files with Web traffic analysis software can benefit your Web site

- How to develop a profile of your visitors

- How to optimize your Web site to accommodate your visitors

- How to get the most for your marketing dollar

- How to generate leads for your business

- How analysis software can help you to manage your online advertising business

- How you can get Web traffic analysis software for your Web site

- The popular brands of Web traffic analysis software

Do You Know Who Is Visiting Your Web Site?

Retailers have always spent endless hours trying to analyze the shoppers who visit their stores. They are constantly trying to collect data about their markets so that they can decide what the best forms of advertising are for their target market, what consumers really want in order to make wiser buying decisions, what services are important to them, what product features their target market is looking for, and so on. The same thing is happening today on the Internet. Companies are constantly collecting data on their target market—their needs, wants, preferences, and desires. Most people are unaware that they are even doing this.

Web traffic analysis software is helping companies to focus on their target market like never before. It is helping them to understand the traffic on their Web site and is enabling them to make the necessary changes that are critical to receive the results that they desire from their Web site. "But how do they do it?" you ask.

Using Log Files to Your Advantage

All Web servers log a list of all the requests for individual files that people have requested from a Web site. These files will include the HTML files and their embedded graphic images and any other associated files that get transmitted through the server. These files can be analyzed by Web traffic analysis tools to generate the following data:

- The number of visitors to your home page

- Where the visitors came from in terms of their IP addresses

- How many times each page on your Web site was requested

- What time, day of the week, and season people access your site

- Which browser your visitor is using

- Which keywords or phrases your visitors are using to find your site using a search engine

- Which advertisements are viewed the most on your Web site

- Detailed information on visitors and demographics

This may not sound like very important information; however, there are some very amazing things you can do with this data. Like any good experiment, you must collect the data first, complete the experiment, and then make the recommendations.

Analyzing Log Files with Web Traffic Analysis Software

By analyzing the data from your log files, you can generate results that could significantly increase the popularity and success of your Web site. By tracking the visitors on your Web site in terms of where they spend their time, how they came to your site, and if they do what you want them to do, you can fine-tune your Web site to fit the specific needs of your target market.

Developing a Profile of Your Visitors

Who is visiting your site? Are most of your visitors from the United States? Canada? Australia? Are your visitors AOL users? University students? Government? Are your visitors primarily Mac or PC users? Which browser are they using? Which version of the browsers are they using?

By analyzing the log files, you can find out a lot about your audience. You can see how the majority of your audience came to your site and what they like to do while they are there—meaning whether they request information or not, if they download products, or if they are interested in free giveaways. You can use this information to find out if your site needs to be changed to accommodate the needs of your visitors. For example, if you find that a lot of your visitors are spending a lot of time on your What's New page, maybe it would be in your best interest to start a monthly mail list to inform your audience of the happenings of your Web site.

The log files can tell you when your audience is entering your site. For example, if the log files indicate that your traffic is mostly at night, you could predict that most people visit your site from home. Since most homes do not have high-speed access, you may want to check your graphic sizes to make sure that it is not taking too long for your site to load. If your analysis tells you that not many people visit your site on Saturday, you may want to select this day as your maintenance day. You don't want to make changes to your site on days when you receive high traffic because it is very displeasing if your visitors receive HTTP 404 errors because your site is temporarily down.

You can also see your visitor's IP address, which the software will translate into his or her geographical location; some of the software is even capable of narrowing the data down to the city (see Figure 27.1). From a marketing perspective, this can benefit you in planning your marketing efforts in other media. If you are planning a television campaign for your business, you may want to start in a city that frequently visits your site, thus increasing the chance of a successful campaign.

It is very common for Web traffic analysis software to indicate which browser your visitors are using when visiting your Web site (see Figure 27.2). Although you want to have a Web site that is designed to be compatible with both older and newer browsers, this data can be used to your advantage. Older browsers that cannot read Java scripting properly and that do not have the proper plug-ins for a Flash introduction may still be in use by your viewers. However, if a majority of your viewers are using the latest browsers, you could incorporate more of the latest technology into your site. Remember that you should always offer a "skip flash" option on your site and the latest Java plug-ins for people with older browsers.

Which Pages Are Popular and Which Pages Are Not?

What pages are most popular with your visitors? Do you see traffic spike when you have new content? Release a newsletter or news re-

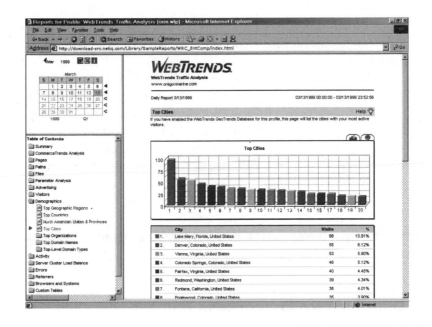

Figure 27.1. WebTrends can tell you what cities are bringing you the most online traffic.

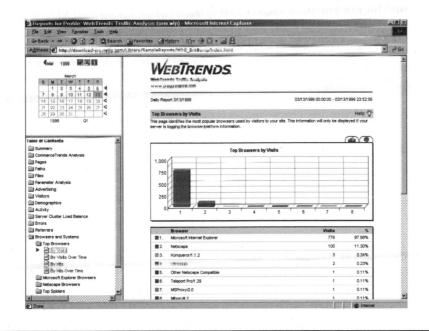

Figure 27.2. This WebTrends report lets you know which versions of each browser your visitors are using.

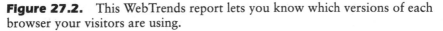

lease? Do you get more traffic on the weekend or during the week? Are your online marketing efforts having an impact? Are people clicking through?

When you look at the log files and see where your audience is spending most of their time on your site, you can also tell where they are not. You can then use this information to determine what the popular pages on your site incorporate that the less popular ones do not. Perhaps the popular pages are similar to the less popular, but are visited by a specific source (i.e., search engines, newsgroups). Maybe there is a content problem on the less-popular pages, or maybe they take longer to load than the other pages and visitors do not want to wait for them to load. Whatever the case may be, you can use this information and attempt to fix those problems that would keep visitors from spending time on all the pages of your site.

Find Out How Each Visitor Found Your Site

By finding out how each visitor came to your site, you can boost your traffic tremendously. You can determine which of your banner ads is producing the best results (see Figure 27.3). You can use this information to help you with the selection of banners you use and also the allocation of your online advertising budget. You can determine how many visitors found your site through the search engines (see Figure 27.4). You can even determine which keyword led to the most visitors through the search engines (see Figure 27.5). If most of your traffic is coming from the Excite search engine (*http://www.excite.com*), you could consider purchasing a banner advertisement on that page. The same theory goes if your traffic is coming from a newsgroup, meta-indexes, and so on.

If you have a number of doorway pages, it would be good to know which ones are drawing the most attention. If the statistics reveal that four out of ten doorway pages are sending most of the traffic to your site, you should analyze the other six doorways to see if you can make them more effective. Maybe the keyword prominence is too low and they are not as effective as you thought when you designed them. If so, you should tweak these pages, then resubmit them to their corresponding search engines.

You can also find out where your visitors go when they leave your Web site. You want your viewers to stay at your site as long as possible. If you notice that the majority of your viewers are not traveling through your entire site and are not viewing important information that you

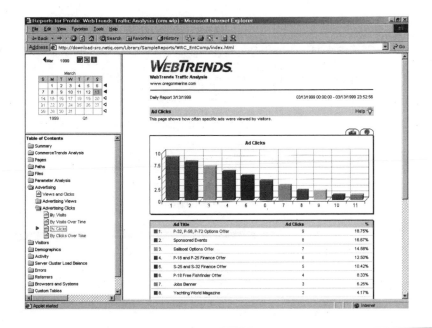

Figure 27.3. This WebTrends report identifies the frequency with which a banner ad is viewed.

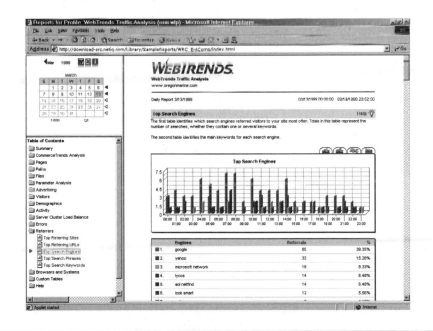

Figure 27.4. This WebTrends report illustrates the first time visitor sessions initiated by searches from each search engine.

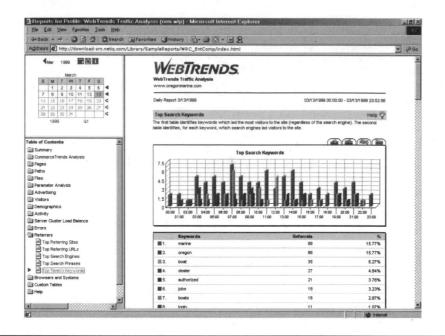

Figure 27.5. This WebTrends report identifies the specific keywords that led the most visitors to the site through the search engines.

want them to see, you may want to manipulate the layout of your Web site to decrease the "flight effect." If you notice that your top exit page is your home page, you may want to try a whole new approach because people seem to be turned off from searching through your site from the beginning.

Single-access pages are pages on your Web site that are accessed through a link or search engine and then are immediately exited. If a high percentage of your Web site traffic is a result of these pages, it is very important that you convey a strong message while you have the visitors' attention. If you have pages like this, you should reevaluate what is on those pages and try to come up with content that will entice your visitor to search through the rest of your site.

Most of the Web traffic analysis software will tell you which keywords and phrases your visitors used to find your site using a search engine. This is extremely valuable information because you can use these keywords to increase your popularity in the search engines. By knowing the most popular keywords your visitors are using to visit your site, you can make sure you use them in your meta-tags, Alt tags, and page titles, and in the text of your page for higher placement in the search engines. Also, by seeing which search engines are being used more by your visitors, you may choose to purchase a banner ad or keywords for that engine to achieve maximum visibility to your visitors.

Another benefit of observing who is viewing your site is that you can see when spiders and crawlers from search engines have crawled to your page. This means that your site most likely will be indexed on their corresponding search engine. This is good to know, not only because it reassures you that you are going to be indexed, but also because by knowing this, you will not resubmit your site to the search engine and risk spamming.

Identifying Your Target Market

After you have collected data from your log files and used the Web traffic analysis software to determine which demographic groups are actually visiting your site, you then must determine whether these are the groups that you want to target. If not, you must then determine how you are going to reach your target market. For example, you may find that you should change your online advertising campaign. Or perhaps you should reevaluate your Internet marketing strategy, taking into consideration the new data that you have collected.

Find Out What Forms of Online Promotion Work for Your Site

When you first launch your Web site, you are going to aggressively implement your Internet marketing strategy by experimenting with all of the different forms of online marketing. However, when you analyze who is actually visiting your site and you find out where the majority of your traffic is coming from, you can then determine where to focus the majority of your marketing efforts. You may find that a link on a particular Web site is resulting in a high amount of traffic to your site; therefore, you may want to consider purchasing a banner advertisement on that site. The same goes for all of the other forms of Internet marketing. If after a short period of time your analysis software tells you that you are receiving low traffic (if any) from a banner ad that you had purchased, you may want to pull it off that site and designate your investment to another site on the Internet. This is a good way to make sure you get the most for your investments in online marketing.

Managing Your Online Business

If you are involved in selling online advertising on your site, Web traffic analysis software can save you a lot of work. When you place your client's banner advertisement on your site, the analysis software can track not only how many people have viewed that specific banner, but also how many people have clicked through. This makes billing your clients very easy, for all you have to do is read the reports generated by your software. If your clients pay per click-through, you simply look up the figure and charge them the appropriate fee. The same goes for paying based on CPM.

How Do You Get Web Traffic Analysis Software for Your Site?

Another option is to use a tracking service like eXTReMe Tracking (*http://www.extreme-dm.com*), where the tracking software resides on the service provider's server. You place the tracker code on your Web site, which provides all the input to the tracking software, and then you have access to all the tracking reports.

You can purchase Web traffic analysis software if you wish, but for it to work it must be installed on the server where you host your Web site. If you host your own Web site, you will definitely have to purchase your own software; however, if you are paying an ISP to host your Web site, the host should already be able to provide some sort of analysis software. Most people don't take advantage of the tremendous marketing opportunities available by analyzing their traffic; therefore, they do not ask their ISP about the software. It should be available to you, for you are paying for their services. If it is not, simply ask them to purchase the Web traffic analysis software of your choice, for they would much rather have you as a client than say no. In some cases they may charge you an additional fee for this service.

Internet Resources for Chapter 27

I have included a few resources for you to check out regarding Web traffic analysis. For additional resources on a variety of topics, I recommend that you visit the Resources section of my Web site at *http://www.susansweeney.com/resources.html.* There you will find additional tips, tools, techniques, and resources.

WEB TRAFFIC ANALYSIS SERVICES

Analog
http://www.analog.cx
"The most popular log file analyzer in the world."

eXTReMe Tracker
http://www.extreme-dm.com/tracking
The eXTReMe Tracker is a completely free service that offers comprehensive real-time reporting with no limit on the amount of traffic that you receive on your Web site. It is capable of tracking your visitors' geographic location, their domain, e-mail address, the browser they are using, and much more.

Funnel Web Analyzer
http://www.quest.com/funnel_web/analyzer
Every person who visits your company's Web site leaves a trail behind. Your Web server logs their every action, and you can use this information to help improve your business. Funnel Web Analyzer provides essential Web site visitor and traffic analysis. It measures everything from server load and referrals to visitor demographics and marketing ROI. Funnel Web Analyzer helps you optimize your Web site by allowing you to analyze how users interact with your site and helps you make informed decisions about what changes you can make to improve their experience.

HitBox
http://www.hitbox.com
HitBox is designed for ad-supported, personal, or e-commerce sites. It's capable of developing user profiles, tracking which sites refer visitors to your site, and how much traffic you receive on a daily, monthly, and annual basis. HitBox can also track how your visitors navigate around your Web site, which can help you in customizing your Web site to your viewers' needs.

The Hitometer
http://websitegarage.netscape.com/turbocharge/hitometer/index.html

The free Hitometer service offers an extensive choice of counters, and reporting of URL statistics, such as how many visitors visit your site per day, month, and year. You can receive your reports online or have them sent to your e-mail.

IBM SurfAid Analytics
http://surfaid.dfw.ibm.com/web/home/index.html
SurfAid customers range from start-ups to Internet giants. Regardless of your traffic volumes, SurfAid processes your data in hours. SurfAid has handled the processing and analysis for some of the world's most heavily trafficked Web sites to date, including the 2000 Sydney Olympic Games.

Personify
http://www.personify.com/products/site_analysis.html
Personify Site Analytics provides comprehensive reporting of your Web site traffic in an easy-to-use, fast, and flexible format. From detailed traffic and navigation reports to high-level summaries, Site Analytics delivers the analysis on your site's page views, sessions, hourly usage, and navigation paths that you are looking for.

Sawmill
http://www.sawmill.net
Sawmill is a powerful, hierarchical log analysis tool that runs on every major platform. It is particularly well suited to Web server logs, but can process almost any log. The reports that Sawmill generates are hierarchical, attractive, and heavily cross-linked for easy navigation. Complete documentation is built directly into the program.

TheCounter.com
http://www.thecounter.com
The Counter provides tracking services to its members. By placing a small image on your Web site, you will get information such as when your visitors came, from where, and by using what browser. If you are just experimenting with Web traffic analysis, you can't go wrong with TheCounter.com

Webalizer
http://www.mrunix.net/webalizer

The Webalizer is a fast, free Web server log file analysis program. It produces highly detailed, easily configurable usage reports in HTML format, for viewing with a standard Web browser.

Web Site Traffic Reports
http://www.websitetrafficreport.com
This free service provides you with a bit of code to insert into your Web page, and then sends you an e-mail daily with your Web traffic report.

Web-Stat Traffic Analysis
http://www.web-stat.com
For $5 per month you can use this service, which provides very detailed Web traffic analysis reports.

WEB TRAFFIC ANALYSIS SOFTWARE

AccessWatch
http://www.accesswatch.com
AccessWatch is open-source shareware. AccessWatch generates browser statistics, referrer, page views, and other Web site traffic statistics.

EasyStat
http://www.easystat.com
EasyStat features real-time tracking and reporting, advanced site traffic and visitor information, search engine placement, and much, much more. All this information is presented within an intuitive and very easy-to-use graphical interface.

LiveStats
http://www.deepmetrix.com/livestats6_corp/features.asp
LiveStats provides a comprehensive suite of customizable reports to analyze trends, profile, segment, forecast, and understand every aspect of your Web site. Reports offer different views, sorting parameters, and date ranges for a nearly limitless number of reports.

Mach5 FastStats Analyzer
http://www.mach5.com/products/analyzer/analyzer.html
A powerful software application that provides detailed analysis of your server's log files.

net.Analysis by net.Genesis

http://netgen.com

net.Genesis offers one of the best log analyzing systems. This is one of the first and one of the best for medium to large sites. Great for intranet access and analysis by non-tech-savvy users. Good integration with IBM Net.Commerce.

NetIQ's WebTrends Enterprise Suite

http://www.netiq.com/products/wrc/Enterprise.asp

The WebTrends Enterprise Suite is one of the most comprehensive Web site analysis software packages available. It provides you with reports on everything from the number of views your banner ads receive on another Web page, to which keyword was used when a visitor found your site using a search engine. You can easily target specific hits and user sessions that include file types and names, entry pages, time and day, user addresses, or any other medium that may have pointed a visitor to your page. WebTrends develops detailed advertising reports, which tell you how often banners on your Web site are viewed and how often people click through. This assists you in selling and billing space to your clients. This is an all-in-one piece of Web traffic analysis software that does more than answer the question of who is actually visiting your site.

NetTracker eBusiness Edition

http://www.sane.com

NetTracker uses an Oracle database engine, which is great for most companies because they don't need a database administrator to use it. The Business Edition can handle really large log files with the speed and agility of an Oracle8 database. The Business Edition also lets you access your data for additional analysis using standard reporting tools such as Crystal Reports and products from Cognos, Information Builders, and more. This product contains 79 standardized summaries, plus you can create and save your own. NetTracker generates usage reports for multiple Web sites, proxy servers, firewalls, and FTP sites.

28

Web Metrics

Over the past few years the Internet has come a long way toward being a sales and distribution channel for most businesses. As with any distribution channel, there are costs involved. Where business costs are involved, the owners want to see a return on their investment. To determine the return on investment, businesses need to measure and analyze a number of things.

Over the past year we have seen more and more companies allocate significantly more of their marketing budget to Internet marketing. Businesses are taking the Internet very seriously these days. Businesses are beginning to measure their Web site's effectiveness from both a marketing and a merchandising perspective. In this chapter, we cover:

- Measuring your online success

- What to measure

- Conversion ratio

- Sales per visitor

- Cost per visitor

- Cost per sale

- Net profit per sale

- Return on investment

- Web metrics tools

Measuring Your Online Success

"E-commerce is a numbers game. The trick is to focus on the right numbers so that you can make accurate decisions about how to improve your Web site, and ultimately, your customer conversion rate. Without e-metrics, the Web continues to be a grand experiment, a government research project that escaped the lab, mutated, and took over the world. But with e-metrics you have the opportunity to approach the Web from an objective, systematic perspective. You can move from trial and error to trial, measure and improve."

Bryan Eisenburg
CIO Future Now Inc.
http://futurenowinc.com

It is becoming imperative that companies track the effectiveness of their online marketing campaigns in real time and make adjustments, if necessary, immediately. It is also imperative that companies track the effectiveness of the elements on their Web site and make adjustments over time.

From a marketing perspective, organizations want to measure and improve advertising effectiveness, click-throughs, cost of customer acquisitions, etc.

From a Web site perspective, organizations want to improve online sales, cross-sells, up-sells, customer retention rates, average order per customer, number of page views per visitor, customer loyalty, newsletters, sign-ups, etc. They want to determine the most popular areas of the site so the content can be improved. They want to identify popular "exit" pages so they can modify and make their site more "sticky."

There are a few basic ways to improve your success online:

- Generate more traffic to your Web site—that's what this book is all about.

- Improve your conversion rate or convert more of your Web site visitors into paying customers.

- Your sales conversion rate is impacted by:

  - How well you have targeted your audience

  - How good your offer is

  - How convincing your copy is

  - How well your audience knows you—loyalty and trust factors

  - Reducing the clicks to buy—the more clicks to the checkout, the more abandoned shopping carts

- Get your customers to buy more. Ways to do this include:

  - Cross-sell

  - Up-sell

  - Improve your sales copy

  - Offer value-added services like gift wrap and expedited shipping

If you don't track, you can't measure. If you don't measure, you don't improve. It is as simple as that.

What to Measure

The digital nature of the Web makes the medium inherently measurable. You need to know what to measure, how to measure it, and how to improve over time. Quite often industry benchmarks are irrelevant. What you are concerned with is measuring your own organization's results and ratios and improving them month after month. As long as you keep getting better at what you're doing and improving your performance and bottom line, does it really matter that there is a benchmark out there that you're not beating? There are too many variables at play that can distort industry-wide or Internet-wide benchmarks.

Some of the key metrics that you want to measure include:

- Conversion ratio

- Sales per visitor

- Cost per visitor

- Net profit per sale

- Return on investment

Conversion Ratio (CR)

A conversion ratio is the number of times a desired action is taken, presented as a percentage of the number of opportunities for the action to be taken.

Although most people look at this ratio as the conversion of a site visitor into a paying customer, there are many other conversion ratios that are relevant. Conversion ratios of site visitors to sign-ups for any permission marketing opportunity (newsletters, coupons, e-specials) is a very important ratio.

By way of example, let's assume you have 300 visitors to your Web site in a day and you have 30 sales in the same time period. The sales conversion ratio would be:

The number of people who purchase divided by the number of people who visit the site: 30/300 = 10%

If you had 3,000 visitors and 30 sales, your conversion ratio would be 1 percent: 30/3,000 = 1%

If you could find a way to increase your conversion ratio from 1 percent to 2 percent, you will have doubled your sales. Obviously the higher the conversion ratio the better.

Sales per Visitor (SPV)

The sales per visitor is calculated by taking the gross sales or total dollar sales amount for a period of time divided by the number of visitors over the same period of time.

If you have $3,000 in sales for the day and 300 visitors, you have a $10 sales per visitor ratio: $3,000 sales/300 visitors = $10 SPV

You want to increase this number over time.

Cost per Visitor (CPV)

Your cost per visitor can be calculated two ways. You can look at your total cost per visitor over all marketing activities, or you can choose to measure your cost per visitor for a specific campaign. The specific-campaign measurement is more relevant because you want to know which Internet marketing activities are most cost-effective and yield a higher return on investment.

To calculate your overall cost per visitor, you simply take all your marketing expenses and divide by the number of unique visitors.

To calculate a campaign-specific cost per visitor, you take the cost of the campaign and divide it by the number of unique visitors provided by that campaign. Let's run an example. Let's say you run a banner advertising campaign that costs you $20 CPM (cost per thousand impressions). And let's further assume you get a 1 percent click-through rate. Your 1 percent click-through yields you ten visitors (1,000 × 1% = 10 visitors). Your cost per visitor for this campaign is $2. You take the campaign cost (in this case, $20) and divide it by the number of visitors (in this case, ten): $20/10 visitors = $2 cost per visitor for this campaign.

Cost per Sale (CPS)

Your cost per sale is calculated as the cost of your campaign divided by the number of sales it produces.

Let's follow through on the previous example. Our campaign cost was $20 for 1,000 banner ad impressions. We had a 1 percent click-through rate, or ten visitors. Let's assume that 10 percent of our visitors bought, so 10 percent is one sale. To calculate our cost per sale, we take our campaign cost and divide it by the number of sales: $20 campaign cost/1 sale = $20 CPS.

Net Profit per Sale (NPPS)

Let's continue with our example. Let's assume that each sale produces at $45 gross profit. Gross profit is calculated by taking the selling price and subtracting the cost of goods sold. Net profit per sale is calculated by taking the net profit and subtracting our cost-per-sale (which is the previous calculation we figured as $20). The net profit per sale for this campaign is: Gross profit per sale – cost per sale: $45 – $20 = $25 NPPS.

Return on Investment (ROI)

The return on investment before non-marketing expenses is calculated by taking the net profit per sale and dividing it by the investment or the cost per sale. In this case, you had a $25 net profit per sale divided by $20 cost per sale: $25/$20 = 125% ROI.

This campaign was profitable. But you need to do these calculations for all of your campaigns so that you can compare them against each other to see where you want to focus your marketing dollars and also to improve your ratios over time on the same types of marketing activities—in other words, get better at the game.

Web Metrics Tools

Now that you have learned how to do all the calculations and your heart is racing thinking about this new full-time job that has just been created, we'll let you in on a few tools that may help.

This aspect is so important, and there has been such a buzz created over the past year that I expect over the next 12 months we will see all kinds of great tools come out of the woodwork to provide the solution.

Some of the tools available include:

- AdMinder (*http://www.adminder.com*). AdMinder can calculate not only the cost per click, but also the cost per sale (or action) and the return on investment for that particular campaign. Allows for easy management of multiple campaigns by displaying ads that are scheduled to run in the near future and ads that are about to expire. Allows for the export of data to Excel or any other spreadsheet software.

- FutureNowInc.com (*http://www.futurenowinc.com/digital salescalculators.htm*—Figure 28.1). The FutureNow Digital Sales Calculator includes 22 metrics.

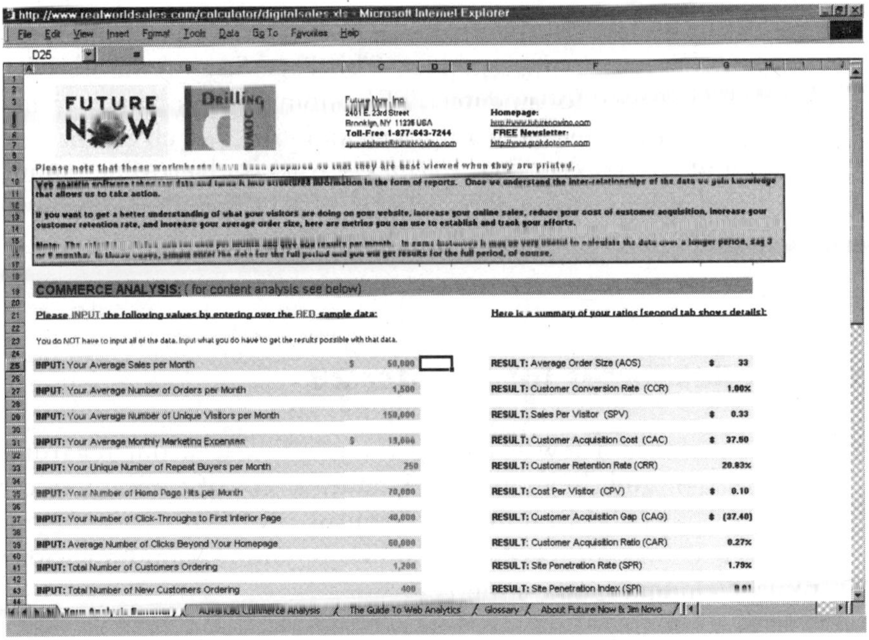

Figure 28.1.   FutureNowInc.com's site offers a downloadable Excel spreadsheet that will assist you in performing calculations.

- NetAuditNow (*http://netauditnow.com*). NetAuditNow is a service that logs onto your Web server, grabs your log files, and then uses them to spit out reports. One of the reports that NetAuditNow generates is the advertising quality and return-on-investment report. This report compares the quantity (total and average number) to quality (time, pages viewed, and purchases) of visitors who came to your site from various ad banners and links. Can report on everything from search engine traffic to total monthly page views and unique visitors.

- Net Quantify (*http://www.netquantify.com*). Online reports reveal which placements generate the most sales, registrations, and any other activity you want to track.

- PromotionStat (*http://www.promotionstat.com*). PromotionStat reports on and separates visitors from different advertising vehicles or sources and tracks their behaviors once they're on your site.

- ROIBot.com (*http://www.roibot.com*). A collection of tools which includes an autoresponder, Web Page Spy (monitors URLs that you specify for updates), FFA Submitter (worthless in my opinion), a Lifeline (server up-time monitor), search engine submitter, and AdTracker. The AdTracker tracks advertising campaign effectiveness and reports referring URLs, browser used, operating system used, and orders placed.

Internet Resources for Chapter 28

I have included a few resources for you to check out regarding Web metrics. For additional resources on a variety of topics, I recommend that you visit the Resources section of my Web site at *http://www. susansweeney.com/resources.html*. There you will find additional tips, tools, techniques, and resources

How to Interpret Web Metrics
http://www.clickz.com/sales/traffic/article.php/992351
An interesting article on how to interpret what all these numbers mean.

Web Metrics and ROI
http://www.stepbystepwebmarketing.com/bottom.php
Another article about Web metrics from the Institute of International Research.

Understanding Web Metrics to Improve Site Performance
http://www.powerhomebiz.com/vol29/metrics.htm
Many online entrepreneurs fail to properly understand and utilize their site's metrics. Here's an in-depth look on how statistics could be used to achieve traffic, marketing, sales, and customer service goals.

About the Author

Susan Sweeney, C.A.

Renowned industry expert and consultant Susan Sweeney, C.A., tailors lively keynote speeches and full- and half-day seminars and workshops for companies, industries, and associations interested in improving their Internet presence and increasing their Web site traffic and sales. Susan is the founder and president of **Connex Network Inc.** (*www.connexnetwork.com*), an international Internet marketing and consulting firm. Susan holds both the Chartered Accountant and Certified General Accountant designations. She is an experienced Internet marketing professional with a background in computers, marketing, and the Internet. Susan is the author of several books on Internet marketing and e-business: *101 Ways To Promote Your Web Site, Internet Marketing for Your Tourism Business, Going for Gold, 101 Internet Businesses You Can Start from Home,* and *The e-Business Formula for Success.* She is also the developer of a two-day intensive Internet Marketing Bootcamp. Susan is a member of the Canadian Association of Professional Speakers, the National Speakers Association, and the International Federation for Professional Speakers.

Connex Network is a marketing firm that provides Internet and international marketing consulting and training services to industry and government. Their clients range in size from single-person start-up operations to multi-million-dollar international firms. Their primary services include Internet marketing workshops, Internet marketing strategies, Web site report cards, Internet marketing consulting, market research, and competitive analysis. During their workshops and training sessions, they ensure that their clients have a complete understanding of the principles involved with developing a strong online presence. The team of Internet marketing analysts at Connex is highly trained in the area of Internet marketing, and all stay up to date with the latest technological advancements and industry trends in the online marketing world. Every person on the team has extensive practical hands-on experience and the necessary skills to use proven tips, tools, and techniques to generate high volumes of traffic to your site.

As a result of technological change and global competitiveness, a strong Internet presence is essential. Susan instructs individuals with her enthusiastic personality combined with her vast hands-on international marketing experience, which keeps her listeners informed and captivated. Let Susan help you increase your traffic and make your business prosper!

Susan Sweeney, C.A.
Connex Network Inc.
75 Brentwood Drive
Bedford, Nova Scotia, Canada B4A 3S2
Phone: 902/468-2578; Fax: 902/468-0380
www.connexnetwork.com
susan@connexnetwork.com

Appendix A: Terminology

404 – File Not Found. This message is returned from a Web server when a requested document cannot be found.

Animated GIF. Special image-editing applications can meld several GIF images into a single image much like slides in a slide show. Each of the images is displayed briefly in turn to create the illusion of motion (similar to cartoon flipbooks).

ASCII text file (American Standard Code for Information Interchange). The worldwide standard format for text files in computers and on the Internet. The code represents all the uppercase and lowercase letters, numbers, punctuation, etc. There are 128 standard ASCII codes in which a seven-digit binary number, 0000000 through 1111111, represents each character.

ASP. Application Service Provider. A company that offers individuals or enterprises access over the Internet to applications and related services that would otherwise have to be located in their own personal or enterprise computers.

Autoresponder. A program that automatically responds to incoming e-mail. It is like an electronic fax-back system for e-mail.

Backbone. Large transmission lines that carry data being transferred from smaller lines. These lines, or paths, connect local or regional networks together for long-distance communication. The connection points are known as network nodes or telecommunication data-switching exchanges (DSEs).

Backend systems. Software systems, usually inventory, accounts receivable, CRM, and others that are internal to a company that are sometimes integrated or that interface with a Web site.

Banner ad. A graphical advertisement on a Web site that links to a particular promotion when the user clicks on it. Banner ads are used to increase product awareness and company and brand identity, and can be a source of revenue (advertising revenue) to the site that hosts the banner ad.

BBS (Bulletin Board System). A computer that can be reached by computer modem dialing (or by Telnet) for the purpose of sharing or exchanging messages or other files. Some BBSs are devoted to specific interests; others offer a more general service. The definitive BBS List says that there are over 40,000 BBSs worldwide.

BCC (**Blind Carbon Copy**). Including e-mail addresses in the BCC field of an e-mail message will hide all the addresses aside from each recipient's address.

Benchmark. A point of reference by which something can be measured or compared. In surveying, a "bench mark" (two words) is a post or other permanent mark used as the basis for measuring the elevation of other topographical points.

Branding. Creating public awareness of a company, product or service so that the company, product, or service is quickly and immediately identified and associated.

Browser. The software used to view the various kinds of Internet resources, or sites.

Bulk e-mail. A group of identical messages e-mailed to a large number of addresses at once. This is a technique commonly employed by spammers, and it results in many very unpersonalized e-mail messages.

Cache. A place to store something more or less temporarily. Web pages you request are stored in your browser's cache (pronounced "cash") directory on your hard disk. When you return to a page you've recently looked at, the browser can get most of the information from the cache rather than the original server. A cache saves you time and saves the network the burden of some additional traffic. You can usually vary the size of your cache, depending on your particular browser.

CGI (**Common Gateway Interface**). Guidelines that define how a Web server communicates with another piece of software on the same machine, and how the other piece of software, the CGI program, talks to the Web server. Any piece of software can be a CGI program if it handles input and output according to the CGI standard.

Cgi-bin. This is the most common name for the directory on a Web server that holds a CGI program. Most programs located in the cgi-bin directory are text files—scripts that are executed by binaries located elsewhere on the same machine.

Chat. Real-time conversation between one or more individuals across a network. IRC and ICQ are common forums for such discussions often held in topic-driven "chatrooms."

Clickstreams. The paths a user takes as he or she navigates a Web page or cyberspace in general. Advertisers and online media providers have developed software that can track users' clickstreams.

Click-through. A hit generated from a banner advertisement when a user clicks on the banner ad.

Click-through rate. This is the percentage of banner ad views that resulted in a user's clicking on it (a click-through).

Cookie. On the Internet, a cookie refers to a piece of information sent by a Web server to a Web browser. The browser software is expected to save the cookie and send the information back to the server whenever an additional request is made. Cookies may contain information such as user preferences, registration or login information, online shopping cart info, etc.

Cost per Click. The rate charged to an advertiser each time a user clicks on their banner ad. This is one method site owners can use to collect advertising revenue from banner ads.

Crawlers. Crawlers quietly comb through Web sites and index the information they find.

CPM (Cost per thousand page views). Banner ad rates are typically measured in cost-per-thousand (page views)—shorthand for the cost of delivering a marketing message to 1,000 people.

CPTM (Cost per thousand targeted ad views). This implies that the audience you have targeted is of a particular demographic group. (See "Demographics.")

CRM. Customer Relationship Management systems. Is an information industry term for methodologies, software, and usually Internet capabilities that help an enterprise manage customer relationships in an organized way.

Cybermall. A collection of online storefronts better known as an Internet shopping mall.

Cybernaut. A person who uses the Internet.

Cyberspace. Used to describe all areas of information resources available through computer networks and the Internet. William Gibson originated the term in his novel *Neuromancer.*

Database marketing. Actively maintaining and updating a database of clients and potential clients (data warehousing), mining the data for specific demographic information (data mining), and focusing your advertising campaign on the target market. For instance, once you determine the people in your database that fit a particular demographic group, you can then send a targeted e-mail marketing message to these people.

Data mining. Obtaining specific information from a data warehouse by running queries. Marketers can determine how many people in a database file fit a certain demographic group and then market to that particular group of individuals.

Data warehouse. A place for storing, retrieving, and managing large amounts of any type of data. Data warehouse software often allows you to conduct fast searches, as well as advanced filtering. Planners and researchers can use this database freely without worrying about slowing down day-to-day operations of the production database.

Demographics. Specific data about the size and characteristics of a population or audience that can be used for marketing purposes.

Domain name. The unique name that identifies an Internet site. A domain name always has two or more parts, separated by a dot. The part on the left is the most specific, and the part on the right is the most general. A given machine may have more than one domain name, but a given domain name points to only one machine. For example, the domain names *connexnetwork.com* and *yahoo.com* can both refer to the same machine.

Download. The transferring of data from one computer to another across the Internet.

DTD (Document Type Declaration). Specifies the organization that issued the language specification and the exact version of the specification. This information is typically found at the beginning of an HTML document or other programming documents. In XML, a DTD specifies the meaning of every tag and tag attribute contained within a set of XML pages.

E-business. Electronic business is the conduct of business on the Internet—not only buying and selling, but also servicing customers and collaborating with business partners.

E-Commerce. The process of buying and selling goods and services on the Internet.

Effective frequency. The optimum regularity with which you execute an e-mail marketing campaign.

E-mail (electronic mail). Mail messages, usually text, sent from one person to another via computer. Messages can also be sent automatically to a large number of addresses on a mailing list.

Emoticons. Symbols made from punctuation marks and letters that look like facial expressions. Commonly used in e-mail and in

Internet chat rooms to convey expressions and additional meaning to written text.

Exposure. How broadly known you or your product is from being on the Internet.

Extranet. A new buzzword that refers to an intranet that is partially accessible to authorized outsiders. Whereas an intranet resides behind a firewall and is accessible only to people who are members of the same company or organization, an extranet provides various levels of accessibility to outsiders. You can access an extranet only if you have a valid username and password, and your identity determines which parts of the extranet you can view.

Ezine, e-zine (electronic magazine). Used to describe an electronic magazine, including those of print magazines such as *National Geographic* and *Newsweek* that have electronic editions. Thus, E-Zine Database includes both electronic-only magazines together with electronic-edition magazines.

FAQs (Frequently Asked Questions). Documents that list and answer the most common questions on a particular subject or problem area. There are hundreds of FAQs on subjects as diverse as car repair and franchise advice.

Firewall. A set of related programs located at a network gateway server to protect the resources of a private network from users of other networks.

Flame, flaming. Flaming usually involves the use of harsh language directed toward a group or an individual for sending unwanted messages (marketing) on a newsgroup or mail list.

Forums. Another name for a newsgroup in which people are formed together in a group to chat and discuss.

FTP (File Transfer Protocol). The common method of moving files between two computers through the Internet medium. FTP is a method for logging onto another computer or Internet site for the purpose of retrieving or sending files.

Hit. A single request from a Web browser for a single item from a Web server; thus, in order for a Web browser to display a page that contains three graphics, four "hits" would occur at the server: one for the HTML page, and one for each of the three graphics. Hits are often used as a rough measure of visits on a server.

Home page, homepage. The main Web page for a business, organization, or person—or simply the main page of a collection of Web pages.

Host. Any computer on a network that can hold files available to other computers on the network. It is quite common to have one host machine provide several services to other machines, such as WWW and Usenet.

HTML, HTM (HyperText Markup Language). The coding language used to create documents for use on the World Wide Web. These documents have a file extension of *html* or *htm*. HTML code looks a lot like old-fashioned typesetting code, where you surround a block of text with codes that indicate how it should appear. HTML or HTM files are meant to be viewed using a World Wide Web client program, such as Netscape or Internet Explorer.

HTTP (HyperText Transport Protocol). The most important protocol used in the World Wide Web for moving hypertext files across the Internet. Requires an HTTP client program on one end and an HTTP server program on the other end.

Hypertext. Clickable text that links to another document; that is, words or phrases in one document that can be clicked on by a reader, causing another document to be retrieved and displayed.

Image map. A single graphic that has multiple hot links to different pages or resources.

Impression. Sometimes used as a synonym for "view," as in ad view. Online publishers offer, and their customers buy, advertising measured in terms of ad views or impressions.

Internet protocol, Internet protocol address. Basically, the set of rules for one network communicating with any other (or occasionally, for broadcast messages, all other networks). Each network must know its own address on the Internet and that of any other networks with which it communicates. To be part of the Internet, an organization needs an Internet network number, which it can request from the Network Information Center (NIC). This unique network number is included in any packet sent out of the network onto the Internet.

Interstitial ad. Meaning "in between"—an advertisement that appears in a separate browser window while you wait for a Web page to load. Interstitials are more likely to contain large graphics, streaming presentations, and applets than conventional banner ads, and some studies have found that more users click on interstitials than on banner ads. Some users, however, have complained that interstitials slow access to destination pages.

Intranet. A private network inside a company or organization that uses the same kinds of software found on the public Internet, but that is only for internal use and cannot be viewed outside the network.

ISDN (Integrated Services Digital Network). A faster way to move more data over existing regular phone lines. Rapidly becoming available around the world, it is priced comparably to standard analog phone circuits. It can provide speeds of roughly 128,000 bits per second over the regular phone lines.

ISP (Internet Service Provider). A provider that allows access to the Internet. Usually there is a cost to the consumer, although there are still some free community networks.

Java. A programming language that is specifically designed for writing programs. It can safely be downloaded to your computer through the Internet and immediately be run without fear of viruses or other harm to your computer. Using small Java programs, called "applets," Web pages can include functions such as animations, calculators, and other fancy tricks that cannot be done by normal HTML.

LAN (Local Area Network). A network limited to the local area, usually the same building or floor of a company.

List server software. An application installed on a publicly accessible server that manages messages sent to and from a mailing list. This software is required if you intend to administer your own publicly accessible mailing list.

Login. The account name used to gain access to a computer system, not a password. Also can mean the act of entering onto a computer system.

Lurking. Reading Usenet newsgroups, consumer online service forums, or Internet mailing lists without posting anything, just reading. A lurker is a person who observes what everyone else is doing within that group.

Mailbot. Software programs that automatically respond to all incoming e-mail. A mailbot, or autoresponder, replies to them by sending the author a file or message.

Mailing list, mail list. A system that allows people to send e-mail to one address, whereupon their message is copied and sent to all other subscribers to the list. This method allows people with different kinds of e-mail to participate in discussions together.

Mailing list manager. A software program that collects and distributes e-mail messages to a mailing list. (See "List server software.")

Meta-Indexes. A listing of Internet resources pertaining to a specific subject category, intended as a resource to those who have an interest in a specific topic. A meta-index is simply a collection of URLs for related Internet resources, all arranged on a Web page by their titles.

Net. The shorthand version for Internet.

Netiquette. Internet etiquette.

Netizen. From the term "citizen," referring to a citizen of the Internet, or someone who uses networked resources.

Netpreneur. An online entrepreneur.

Netscape. Web browser and the name of a company. The Netscape browser was based on the Mosaic program developed at the National Center for Supercomputing Applications (NCSA).

Newbie. A newcomer to the Internet.

Newsgroups. Name given to discussion groups on Usenet.

Opt-in mail list. People are given the choice to take part in a system that allows people to send e-mail to one address, whereupon their message is copied and sent to all other subscribers to the list. This method allows people with different kinds of e-mail to participate in discussions together.

Page view. The number of times a page is viewed.

Password. A code used to gain access to a locked system known only to one person or a specific group of individuals. Good passwords contain letters and non-letters and are not simple combinations such as *john12*.

Permission marketing. Marketing to individuals via the Internet with their permission, either by having the individual opt-in to a mail list or giving permission by other means to receive e-mail and other information.

Portal. A new term, generally synonymous with gateway, for a World Wide Web site that is or proposes to be a major starting site for users when they get connected to the Web or that users tend to visit as an anchor site.

Posting. A message entered into a network communications system, such as a newsgroup submission.

Privacy policy. A policy for protecting the privacy of individually identifiable information. When an organization is engaged in online activities or electronic commerce, it has the responsibility to implement and post a privacy policy.

Registration. You submit personal information to become part of a mail list or newsgroup, in order to receive other information in return.

ROI (Return on Investment). The amount of profit you obtain from your original investment.

Search engine. The most popular way to find resources on the Internet. There are numerous search engines, each with its own unique styles and capabilities.

Secure server. A network-accessible (i.e., the Internet) computer that uses SSL (Secure Socket Layers) for encryption to allow for private online transactions. The encryption protects an online shopper's credit card and personal information from being compromised while conducting an e-commerce transaction.

Server. A computer that stores information and makes these files available to other users on a network or the Internet.

Signature. A block of information used at the end of every message or online document sent by a particular user.

Site. A unique location on the Internet to post your information and get noticed.

SKU. Stock Keeping Unit.

Snail mail. A slang term for the regular postal service.

Spam, spamming. An inappropriate attempt to use a mailing list, Usenet, or other networked communications facility as if it was a broadcast medium by sending the same message to a large number of people who didn't ask for it.

Spider. An automated program that indexes documents, titles, or a portion of each document acquired by traversing the Web.

SQL (Structured Query Language). A specialized programming language for sending queries to databases.

Storefront. A set location on the Web that stores and displays a collection of information about you and your business.

Streaming media. The simultaneous transfer and display of the sound and images on the World Wide Web.

Subject. The subject line in an e-mail message stating the topic of the mail.

Subscribe. Submitting information to an e-zine or mail list in order to receive information.

Superstitial. Non-banner rich media ads that can be any size on the screen and can be authored in most any creative format. Preloaded using a patent-pending "polite" delivery system that eliminates the latency problems often experienced with streaming online advertising solutions, superstitials only play on a user-initiated break in surfing, such as a mouse click.

Telnet. A program that allows people to log on to other computers or bulletin board systems on the Internet and run software remotely from their location.

Thread. A sequence of responses to an initial message posting. This enables you to follow or join an individual discussion in a newsgroup from among the many that may be there.

Thumbnail. A term used by graphic designers and photographers for a small-image representation of a larger image, usually intended to make it easier and faster to look at or manage a group of larger images. For example, software that lets you manage a number of images often provides a miniaturized version of each image so that you don't have to remember the file name of each image. Web sites with many pictures, such as online stores with visual catalogs, often provide thumbnail images instead of larger images to make the page download faster. This allows the user to control which images are seen in full size.

Unsolicited e-mail. Sending e-mail ads to people without their consent.

Upload. The transfer of a file from your computer to a server online.

URL (Uniform Resource Locator). The standard way to give an address of any resource on the Internet that is part of the World Wide Web (WWW). The most common way to use a URL is to enter into a WWW browser program, such as Internet Explorer, Netscape, or Lynx, and type it in the location bar.

Usenet. A system of discussion-groups. Comments are passed among hundreds of thousands of machines, with over 10,000 discussion areas, called newsgroups.

User session. A person with a unique address that enters or reenters a Web site each day (or some other specified period). A user session is sometimes determined by counting only those users that haven't reentered the site within the past 20 minutes or a similar period. User session figures are sometimes used to indicate the number of visitors per day.

Vaporlink. A link within a site on the Internet is supposed to lead to more information (hypertext). A vaporlink is one that has become nonexistent and does not lead anywhere, a dead link.

Viral marketing. Word-of-mouth or friend-to-friend e-mail marketing.

Virtual community. A community of people sharing common interests, ideas, and feelings over the Internet or other collaborative networks.

Virus, viruses. A program (or programs) that, when executed, contaminates a user's hard drive—often with unpleasant results (erases files, sends unauthorized e-mail from your machine, contaminates other documents, etc.).

Visitors. People who have accessed or visited your site.

Web. The shorthand version of World Wide Web.

WWW (World Wide Web). The whole constellation of resources that can be accessed using Gopher, FTP, HTTP, Telnet, Usenet, WAIS, and some other tools. Also referred to as the universe of hypertext servers (HTTP servers), which are the servers that allow graphics, text, sound files, etc., to be mixed together.

Appendix B: Implementation and Maintenance Schedule

To accomplish the best results from your Internet marketing strategy, you should develop an Implementation and Maintenance Schedule.

Schedule

Every Implementation and Maintenance Schedule will be different since every company's Internet marketing strategy will be different. See Table B.1 for a sample schedule. We have provided brief explanations in the following paragraphs to help further clarify the items included in this sample.

- **Domain Name.** Make sure that your domain name is re-registered annually. Your domain name registrar usually sends e-mail notification to you as your anniversary date approaches but including it on your calendar will assist you in making sure you retain your domain name.

- **Search Engine Submissions.** You should take your list of directory and search engine submissions and divide it into four groups. Weekly, you should take one group, go to each of the directories and search engines in that group, and search for your company by name and also by several keywords. If you appear in the first 10 to 20 search rankings and are happy with the description, you don't have to do anything with that search engine or directory.

  However, if your site does not appear or you are not satisfied with the description, you should resubmit all your pages to that directory or search engine. The search engines and directories purge their databases from time to time to ensure that all entries are current. The next week, take the next group and go through the same process. This way you check every directory and search engine at least monthly to ensure that you are still there and are easily accessible.

Name	Weekly	Biweekly	Monthly	Bimonthly	Quarterly	Yearly
Domain name						✓
Search engine submissions			✓			
Press releases				✓		
Banner advertising			✓			
Update/rename titles			✓			
Cool sites			✓			
Check competitors					✓	
Cybermalls					✓	
Newsletter			✓			
Newsgroups	✓					
Guest book	✓					
Signature files			✓			
Mailing lists			✓			
Links		✓				
What's new	✓					
Calendar of events	✓					
Employment opportunities	✓					
Offline promotion					✓	
Tune-ups					✓	
Web browser testing			✓			

Figure B.1. Implementation and Maintenance Schedule.

- **Press Releases.** Schedule press releases at least bimonthly. If you have a major announcement, the press releases may be more frequent.

- **Banner Advertising.** Check banner advertising locations of your ads each month. Determine the effectiveness of these ads and look for new sites for more exposure. Check prices and traffic flow of these new sites to determine how relevant they may be in increasing the traffic to your site. Adjust your banner advertising strategy accordingly.

- **Update/Rename Titles.** Update and retitle your pages monthly unless you add a new section that requires more frequent updates (for example, Tip of the Week). Retitling your pages and updating your site is useful for two main reasons. First, spiders, crawlers, and bots are continuously visiting sites to see if there have been changes (and they update their information accordingly). Second, many of your site visitors use software that lets them know when their bookmarked sites have been updated. They will only revisit your site when they know there have been changes.

- **Cool Sites.** Submit to Cool Sites, Site of the Day, or Top 5%. To better your chances of becoming one, you should check on how often to apply, usually monthly.

- **Check Competitors.** You should review your competitors' sites at least four times a year.

- **Cybermalls.** Cybermalls continually change, as does everything, so do a check each calendar quarter to find new malls or changes to the ones that interest you.

- **Newsletter.** A newsletter should be scheduled monthly so you are getting your name and information in front of clients and potential clients on a regular basis.

- **Newsgroups.** Newsgroups that you participate in should be visited every couple of days, and you should try to post messages.

The more often you post, particularly providing answers to queries or assistance, the more recognized and valued you are (and is your expertise). Make sure you attach your sig.file for maximum marketing effect.

- **Guest Book.**   Your guest book should be checked and monitored so you can see who is visiting and what they have to say. Each week you should copy the new contact list to the appropriate databases (e-mail lists, newsletter, etc.).

- **Signature Files.**   Keep your sig.files current. Review and change them on a regular basis (approximately once a month) with new information or achievements.

- **Mailing Lists.**   New mailing lists appear daily. Review (and update if appropriate) those that you participate in on a monthly basis.

- **Links.**   The more reciprocal links you can get, the better off you are. You should constantly be looking for additional, appropriate sites from which to be linked. At a minimum, you should schedule time biweekly to actively seek appropriate link sites.

- **What's New.**   Your What's New page should be updated regularly, weekly if possible.

- **Calendar of Events.**   If you choose to have a calendar of events on your site, be sure that it is kept current, updated at least weekly.

- **Employment Opportunities.**   This section should be monitored and updated weekly, deleting positions that have been filled and adding new positions as they become available.

- **Offline Promotion.**   Make sure that your offline marketing materials and your online materials are consistent (message, logos, corporate colors, etc.). Also ensure that, where appropriate, you include your URL in your offline promotion materials. This should be checked at least quarterly.

- **Tune-Ups.**   Site tune-ups should be done quarterly unless changes are made to the site. One location to check is Web Site Garage at *http://www.websitegarage.com.* Here you can check spelling, browser compatibility, HTML design, link popularity, loading time, and much more.

- **Web Browser Testing.**   Test your site with the major Web browsers. This should be done whenever there is a new release of Netscape or Internet Explorer. You should check monthly to determine if there have been new releases.

Appendix C: Search Engines

The Most Popular Search Engines

The algorithms the major search engines use to determine your site's ranking and the information reference to index your site change quite often, so what may hold true today may not hold true tomorrow. I recommend visiting the respective search engines before you submit and review any material available in regard to site submissions. Many search engines have information on their submission pages, help pages, and sometimes on a submission tips page. You can also check out various sites on the Internet that offer submission tips and tricks for the major search engines, some of which are included within Chapters 6 and 7 of this book. Two of my favorites are Search Engine Watch (*http:// www.searchenginewatch.com*) and Search Engine World (*http:// www.searchengineworld.com*).

AltaVista
Site address: *http://www.altavista.com*
Submission address: *http://addurl.altavista.com/sites/addurl/newurl* or click on "Submit a Site" from AltaVista's homepage.
AltaVista went live in December 1995. In August 1999, CMGI, Inc. acquired 83 percent of AltaVista's outstanding stock from Compaq. As well, Shopping.com and Zip2 became wholly owned subsidiaries. AltaVista consists of multiple platforms: AltaVista Search, AltaVista Live, AltaVista's Shopping.com, and AltaVista Local Portal Services.
Pages (millions): 550
Meta-tag support: Yes
Index body text: Yes
Frames support: Yes
Image maps: Yes
Alt text: Yes
Link popularity affects position: Yes
Keywords in title important: Yes
Higher rankings for reviewed sites: No
Description: Meta-tag or first text on page

Time to index submissions: 4–6 weeks for basic, also has express option
Type: Spider–(Scooter)
Tips: AltaVista likes keywords that are located near the top of your page, so use descriptive keywords where possible. Keywords used in the title of your page also seem to influence page rankings.

Excite
Site address: *http://search.excite.com/info.xcite*
Submission address: *http://www.overture.com/d/advertisers/p/mbr/* or click on "Submit a Site" from Excite's homepage.
Has been around since 1995. Excite bought out WebCrawler in 1996. These acquisitions are still independently operated.
Pages (millions): 250
Meta-tag support: Just Meta description
Index body text: Yes
Frames support: Yes
Image maps: No
Alt text: No
Link popularity affects position: Yes
Keywords in title important: Yes
Higher rankings for reviewed sites: No
Description: The few most dominant sentences on your page
Time to index submissions: 5 days for free submit, but also paid submissions available
Type: Spider (Architext)
Tips: Make the first hundred characters of your page as descriptive as possible. Excite will try to make the description from the text at the start of your page, but will keep going until it is satisfied that it has enough descriptive sentences. Your sentences must be complete for Excite to use them in forming your description. This does not necessarily mean that uncompleted sentences at the beginning of your page will not be used. Excite would just rather use complete sentences.

Google
Site address: *http://www.google.com*
Submission address: *http://www.google.com/addurl.html* or click on "Add your URL" from Google's About page.
Google was founded in 1998 by Larry Page and Sergey Brin and has quickly become a very popular search tool on the Web.
Pages (millions): 2,073

Meta-tag support: No
Index body text: Yes
Frames support: Yes
Image maps: No
Alt text: Yes
Link popularity affects position: Yes (very important)
Keywords in title important: Yes
Higher rankings for reviewed sites: No
Description: First text found on page, including hypertext links
Type: Spider (Google Bot)
Tips: Keywords in your domain name and link popularity will really help you out with Google. To increase your link popularity, get other sites to link to you. Perhaps you should consider reciprocal links to other sites.

HotBot
Site address: *http://hotbot.lycos.com*
Submission address: *http://hotbot.lycos.com/addurl.asp* or click on "Submit Website" from HotBot's homepage.
HotBot was launched in 1996. HotBot uses Inktomi's search engine technology.
Pages (millions): 110
Meta-tag support: Yes
Index body text: Yes
Frames support: No
Image maps: No
Alt text: No
Link popularity affects position: Yes
Keywords in title important: Yes
Higher rankings for reviewed sites: No
Description: Meta-tag; if none, uses approximately the first 240 to 250 characters in the body of your page
Time to index submissions: 48 hours
Type: HotBot is a part of the Lycos Network
Tips: If you do a search and feel your site is not positioned correctly in the search results, then you can let the people at HotBot know. Send all the relevant information to bugs@hotbot.com.

Lycos
Site address: *http://www.lycos.com*

Submission address: *http://searchservices.lycos.com/searchservices/* or by clicking on "Add Your Site to Lycos" from their homepage.
Lycos went online in 1994. Lycos is a well-recognized spider.
Pages (millions): 625
Meta-tag support: No
Index body text: Yes
Frames support: Yes
Image maps: No
Alt text: Yes
Link popularity affects position: No
Keywords in title important: Yes
Higher rankings for reviewed sites: No
Description: A snippet of the page that has been determined to represent it
Time to index submissions: 2 weeks
Type: T-Rex
Tips: Don't have an image map at the beginning of your page because Lycos will be unable to interpret it.

NorthernLight
Site address: *http://www.northernlight.com*
Submission address: *http://www.northernlight.com/docs/regurl_help.html* or click on "Register URL" from NorthernLight's homepage.
NorthernLight started in September 1995. Their Web results are combined with information from premium material, giving you access to books, magazines, databases, and newswires.
Pages (millions): 350
Meta-tag support: No
Index body text: Yes
Frames support: Yes
Image maps: Yes
Alt text: No
Link popularity affects position: No
Keywords in title important: Yes
Higher rankings for reviewed sites: No
Description: Approximately the first 25 words of the page body
Time to index submissions: 2–4 weeks
Type: Spider–(Gulliver)
Tips: Submit only ONE of your pages to NorthernLight; let their spider find the remaining pages on your site.

WebCrawler
Site address: *http://www.webcrawler.com/info.wbcrwl*
Submission address: *http://www.overture.com/d/advertisers/p/mbr/* or click on "Add your URL" from their homepage.
WebCrawler has been around since 1994 and has since been purchased twice. It is now owned by Excite, but is still operated independently.
Pages (millions): 2
Meta-tag support: Yes
Index body text: Yes
Frames support: No
Image maps: Yes
Alt text: No
Link popularity affects position: Yes
Keywords in title important: Yes
Higher rankings for reviewed sites: Yes
Description: Meta-tag; if none, looks at first textual information body of page
Time to index submissions: 8 weeks
Type: Uses Excite's Spider
Tips: Use of keywords in your page titles, descriptions meta-tag, keywords meta-tag, and in content near the top of your page all influence your ranking with WebCrawler.

Yahoo!
Site address: *http://www.yahoo.com*
Submission address: *http://www.yahoo.com/* and then click on "Suggest a Site."
Established in 1994, Yahoo! is a well-recognized directory. It is the largest of its kind and is the most popular with Internet users. Yahoo! is a directory, but it does not read pages on the net like the other search engines discussed here. To have your site added to Yahoo!, you must fill out a submission form on the site. You must register your site in a category, and your site is checked by employees to verify that it matches the category you have chosen. If your site is commercial in any way, you must register using Yahoo! Express, which is a $299 annual recurring fee.
Pages (millions): Approximately 2
Time to index submissions: 7-day guarantee with Yahoo! Express (does not guarantee a listing, only that your submission will be reviewed)
Tips: Yahoo! gives higher rankings to sites that are reviewed. When submitting pages, submit your base URL (e.g., *http://www.yourdomain.com*),

as this stands a greater chance of being indexed by Yahoo!. Take your time to find the most appropriate subcategories for your site and be sure to fill out their submission form completely and accurately. Yahoo! is very picky about whom they add to their directory.

Other Search Engines and Directories

555-1212.com
Site address: *http://www.555-1212.com*
Submission address: *http://www.infospace.com/info.go555/submit.htm*
In addition to Area Code Lookup, you can shop online, find businesses near you, get your friends' telephone numbers and e-mail addresses, browse classified ads, and much more.

About.com
Site address: *http://www.about.com*
Submission address: N/A

AllTheWeb.com
Site address: *http://www.alltheweb.com*
Submission address: *http://www.alltheweb.com/add_url.php*
Part of the Terra Group Companies, AllTheWeb is fast becoming one of the top search engines.

AOL.com Search
Site address: *http://search.aol.com*
Submission address: *http://search.aol.com/add.adp*
This is AOL's search engine. It once ran off of the Excite engine but now uses the DMOZ.org directory. Submit to DMOZ.org, and AOL will also list your site.

Ask Jeeves!
Site address: *http://www.askjeeves.com*
Submission address: *http://static.wc.ask.com/docs/addjeeves/Submit.html*
Ask Jeeves! accepts fully worded questions and crawls through search directories, engines, and meta-directories until an answer is found.

The Biz
Site address: *http://www.thebiz.co.uk*

Submission address: *http://www.thebiz.co.uk/NewDirUser Subscription/NewDirUserSubscription.asp*
The Business Information Zone has been developed for users seeking UK-relevant business information, products, and services on the Internet, whether users are in the UK or overseas.

BizWeb
Site address: *http://www.bizweb.com*
Submission address: *http://www.bizweb.com/InfoForm*
BizWeb is a Web business guide to 46,290 companies listed in 208 categories.

DMOZ Open Directory Project
Site address: *http://dmoz.org*
Submission address: *http://dmoz.org/add.html*
DMOZ is a directory in which actual humans review your site's content to determine whether or not it meets their standards. Many major search engines including AOL Netfind and AltaVista incorporate the DMOZ directory listings into their own search results.

Dogpile
Site address: *http://www.dogpile.com*
Submission address: N/A
Dogpile obtains its search results from multiple search engines. You cannot submit a site to it directly.

Go.com
Site address: *http://www.go.com*
Submission address: *http://www.overture.com/d/advertisers/p/mbr*

Internet Promotions MegaList
Site address: *http://www.2020tech.com*
Submission address: *http://www.2020tech.com/submit.html*
20/20 Technologies is a one-stop Internet advertising solution. Their services include Web page design, Internet research, and Internet promotions. The submission URL lists dozens of useful search engine submission resources.

Keyword.com
Site address: *http://www.keyword.com*

Submission address: Visit the site and enter a keyword.
This is a free service that allows you to "reserve" a keyword and have searches for a keyword directed immediately to your site. Only one keyword can be reserved per site. **Your Internet keyword will remain active as long it is entered a minimum of six times every 60 days.**

LinkMaster
Site address: *http://www.linkmaster.com*
Submission address: *http:www.linkmaster.com/register.html*

LookSmart
Site address: *http://www.looksmart.com*
Submission address: *http://www.looksmart.com/aboutus/partners/subsite2.html*
LookSmart is a large, selective Internet search directory. Many engines, including MSN Search, currently use it to determine their own search results.

MasterSite
Site address: *http://mastersite.com*
Submission address: *http://mastersite.com/addurl.htm*

Metacrawler
Site address: *http://www.metacrawler.com*
Submission address: N/A
Metacrawler obtains its search results from multiple search engines. You cannot submit a site to it directly.

MSN Search
Site address: *http://search.msn.com*
Submission address: *http://listings.looksmart.com/?synd=zdd&chan=zddresults*
This is Microsoft's entry into the search engine fray. You can submit one URL per day to their engine.

NationalDirectory
Site address: *http://www.nationaldirectory.com*
Submission address: *http://www.nationaldirectory.com/addurl*
Claims to be the "least spammed" search directory on the World Wide Web.

NBCi.com
Site address: *http://nbci.msnbc.com/nbci.asp*
Submission address: N/A
Part of the Infospace network.

Nerd World
Site address: *http://www.nerdworld.com*
Submission address: *http://www.nerdworld.com/nwadd.html*
Nerd World's most prominent feature is its search engine and subject index.

Netscape Search
Site address: *http://search.netscape.com*
Submission address: *http://digitalwork.netscape.com/onlinead/ hypersubmit*
Netscape, maker of one of the world's best-known browsers, also has its own search/portal site.

Overture
Site address: *http://www.overture.com*
Submission address: *http://www.overture.com/d/USm/about/advertisers*
Overture, formerly GoTo.com, is the one of the fastest, easiest, most-relevant search engines on the Web, as well as the small advertiser's best friend. You select the search terms that are relevant to your site. Then you determine how much you are willing to pay on a per-click basis for each of those search terms. The higher your "bid," the higher in the search results your site appears. It's targeted, cost-per-click advertising, and you set the cost per click.

Search.com
Site address: *http://www.search.com*
Submission address: N/A
Search.com obtains its search results from multiple search engines. You cannot submit a site to it directly.

Teoma
Site address: *http://www.teoma.com*
Submission address: *http://static.wc.ask.com/docs/addjeeves/Submit.html*

What-U-Seek
Site address: *http://whatuseek.com*
Submission address: *http://whatuseek.com/addurl.shtml*

Index

Reader Feedback Sheet

Your comments and suggestions are very important in shaping future publications. Please e-mail us at *moreinfo@maxpress.com* or photo-copy this page, jot down your thoughts, and fax it to (850) 934-9981 or mail it to:

Maximum Press
Attn: Jim Hoskins
605 Silverthorn Road
Gulf Breeze, FL 32561

_____

_____

_____

_____

_____

_____

_____

_____

_____

_____

_____

_____

_____

_____

_____

_____

**101 Ways to Promote
Your Web Site,
Fourth Edition**
by Susan Sweeney, C.A.
528 pages
$29.95
ISBN: 1-885068-90-5

**Marketing
With E-Mail,
Third Edition**
by Shannon Kinnard
352 pages
$29.95
ISBN: 1-885068-68-9

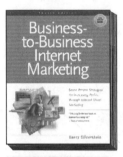

**Business-to-Business
Internet Marketing,
Fourth Edition**
by Barry Silverstein
432 pages
$34.95
ISBN: 1-885068-72-7

**Marketing on
the Internet,
Sixth Edition**
by Jan Zimmerman
488 pages
$34.95
ISBN: 1-885068-80-8

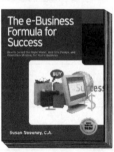

**e-Business Formula
for Success**
by Susan Sweeney, C.A.
360 pages
$34.95
ISBN: 1-885068-60-3

**The Business Guide to
Selling Through
Internet Auctions**
by Nancy Hix
608 pages
$29.95
ISBN: 1-885068-73-5

**101 Internet Businesses
You Can Start
From Home**
by Susan Sweeney, C.A.
520 pages
$29.95
ISBN: 1-885068-59-X

**Internet Marketing for
Less Than $500/Year,
Second Edition**
by Marcia Yudkin
352 pages
$29.95
ISBN: 1-885068-69-7

To purchase a Maximum Press book, visit your local bookstore
or call 1-800-989-6733 (US/Canada) or 1-850-934-4583 (International)
online ordering available at *www.maxpress.com*